ctiveBook included

Paper 3:

The making of modern China, 1860-1997

Larry Auton-Leaf | Nick Shepley
Series editor: Rosemary Rees

ALWAYS LEARNING

PEARSON

Published by Pearson Education Limited, 80 Strand, London, WC2R 0RL

www.pearsonschoolsandfecolleges.co.uk

Copies of official specifications for all Edexcel qualifications may be found on the website: www.edexcel.com

Text © Pearson Education Limited 2017

Designed by Elizabeth Arnoux for Pearson

Typeset and illustrated by Phoenix Photosetting, Chatham, Kent

Produced by Out of House Publishing

Original illustrations © Pearson Education Limited 2017

Cover design by Malena Wilson-Max for Pearson

Cover photo © Bridgeman Art Library/Pictures From History

The rights of Larry Auton-Leaf and Nick Shepley to be identified as authors of this work have been asserted by them in accordance with the Copyright, Designs and Patents Act 1988.

First published 2017

20 19 18 17

10 9 8 7 6 5 4 3 2 1

British Library Cataloguing in Publication Data

A catalogue record for this book is available from the British Library

ISBN 978 1 447 985471

Copyright notice

All rights reserved. No part of this publication may be reproduced in any form or by any means (including photocopying or storing it in any medium by electronic means and whether or not transiently or incidentally to some other use of this publication) without the written permission of the copyright owner, except in accordance with the provisions of the Copyright, Designs and Patents Act 1988 or under the terms of a licence issued by the Copyright Licensing Agency, Barnard's Inn, 86 Fetter Lane, London EC4A 1EN (www.cla.co.uk). Applications for the copyright owner's written permission should be addressed to the publisher.

Printed in the UK by CPI

Websites

Pearson Education Limited is not responsible for the content of any external internet sites. It is essential for tutors to preview each website before using it in class so as to ensure that the URL is still accurate, relevant and appropriate. We suggest that tutors bookmark useful websites and consider enabling students to access them through the school/college intranet.

A note from the publisher

In order to ensure that this resource offers high-quality support for the associated Pearson qualification, it has been through a review process by the awarding body. This process confirms that this resource fully covers the teaching and learning content of the specification or part of a specification at which it is aimed. It also confirms that it demonstrates an appropriate balance between the development of subject skills, knowledge and understanding, in addition to preparation for assessment.

Endorsement does not cover any guidance on assessment activities or processes (e.g. practice questions or advice on how to answer assessment questions) included in the resource, nor does it prescribe any particular approach to the teaching or delivery of a related course.

While the publishers have made every attempt to ensure that advice on the qualification and its assessment is accurate, the official specification and associated assessment guidance materials are the only authoritative source of information and should always be referred to for definitive guidance.

Pearson examiners have not contributed to any sections in this resource relevant to examination papers for which they have responsibility.

Examiners will not use endorsed resources as a source of material for any assessment set by Pearson.

Endorsement of a resource does not mean that the resource is required to achieve this Pearson qualification, nor does it mean that it is the only suitable material available to support the qualification, and any resource lists produced by the awarding body shall include this and other appropriate resources.

Contents

How to use this book

STRUCTURE

This book covers Paper 3, Option 38.2: The making of modern China, 1860–1997, of the Edexcel A Level qualification.

You will also need to study a Paper 1 and a Paper 2 option and produce coursework in order to complete your qualification. All Paper 1/2 options are covered by other textbooks in this series.

EXAM SUPPORT

The examined assessment for Paper 3 requires you to answer questions from three sections. Throughout this book there are exam-style questions in all three section styles for you to practise your examination skills.

Section A contains a compulsory question that will assess your source analysis and evaluation skills.

A Level Exam-Style Question Section A

Study Source 4 before you answer this question.

Assess the value of the source for revealing Chinese attitudes to Japan and the different approaches of the GMD and CCP to repelling the invading Japanese in 1933.

Explain your answer, using the source, the information given about its origin and your own knowledge about the historical context. (20 marks)

Tip

When analysing the usefulness of this source, consider to what extent it was representative of Chinese public opinion.

Section B contains a choice of essay questions that will look at your understanding of the studied period in depth.

A Level Exam-Style Question Section B

To what extent was the Sino-Soviet split in the years 1958–60 caused by ideological differences? (20 marks)

Tip

It is imperative to present a consistent line of argument throughout your essay. For example, if you feel that ideological differences were responsible, when evaluating the personality clash between Mao and Khrushchev you need to justify why it was not as significant as ideologies.

Section C will again give you a choice of essay questions but these will assess your understanding of the period in breadth.

A Level Exam-Style Question Section C

'China's economic development between 1860 and 1997 was mainly motivated by its need to defend itself and to wage war.'

How far do you agree with this opinion? (20 marks)

Tip

A strategy for answering this question would be to acknowledge the importance of war as a motivating factor, but to examine how ideology, the need to raise living standards, and the personal ambitions of leaders played a part.

The Preparing for your exams sections at the end of this book contains sample answers of different standards, with comments on how they could be improved.

FEATURES

Extend your knowledge

These features contain additional information that will help you gain a deeper understanding of the topic. This could be a short biography of an important person, extra background information about an event, an alternative interpretation, or even a research idea that you could follow up. Information in these boxes is not essential to your exam success, but still provides insights of value.

EXTEND YOUR KNOWLEDGE

Tianjin Convention

This convention showed that the era of Chinese domination of Korea was effectively at an end. The Confucian order was again being challenged and China was not strong enough to fulfil the role of older brother. The agreement treated China and Japan as equals. However, the fortunes of China and Japan were shifting; Japan was very much in the ascent while China slumped. The reason for China's approval of the convention was simple: it was not strong enough to repel Japan. Where the Meiji Restoration had given Japan military might, the Self-Strengthening Movement had yet to have a similar effect on China. The Tianjin Convention was, therefore, a Chinese attempt to buy time until it could defeat Japan. In effect, Japan had demonstrated that it had surpassed China in terms of military power

Knowledge check activities

These activities are designed to check that you have understood the material that you have just studied. They might also ask you questions about the sources and extracts in the section to check that you have studied and analysed them thoroughly.

ACTIVITY
KNOWLEDGE CHECK

Western-style economic growth

How significant was T.V. Soong in the development on China's economy? Compare and contrast him with one other key figure discussed in this chapter, and examine both individuals' impact on China's:

- industrialisation
- finance system
- living standards of ordinary people.

Summary activities

At the end of each chapter, you will find summary activities. These are tasks designed to help you think about the key topic you have just studied as a whole. They may involve selecting and organising key information or analysing how things changed over time. You might want to keep your answers to these questions safe – they are handy for revision.

ACTIVITY
SUMMARY

Sino-Soviet relations

1. On an A3 sheet, plot a graph to show the changes in Sino-Soviet relations. On the *x*-axis mark each year 1958-69. On the *y*-axis measure the level of animosity between the PRC and the USSR. Document each key event of this period on your graph.
2. What trends do you notice from your graph?
3. Which events had the greatest effect on the Sino-Soviet relationship? Pick the three events where your graph deviates the most and write a full justification of your choice.
4. Group the events from your graph into themes such as 'ideological', 'personality clash' and 'national security'.
5. Rate each group out of ten, measuring the extent to which it caused the Sino-Soviet split. Write 2-3 sentences for each factor, explaining its overall significance.

Thinking Historically activities

These activities are found throughout the book, and are designed to develop your understanding of history, especially around the key concepts of evidence, interpretations, causation and change. Each activity is designed to challenge a conceptual barrier that might be holding you back. This is linked to a map of conceptual barriers developed by experts. You can look up the map and find out which barrier each activity challenges by downloading the progression map from this website: www.pearsonschools.co.uk/historyprogressionapproach.

progression map reference

Evidence (6b)

The strength of argument

1. Read Extract 8.
   a) What is weak about this claim?
   b) What could be added to it to make it stronger?
2. Read Extract 9.
   a) Is this an argument? If yes, what makes it one?
   b) How might this argument be strengthened?
3. Read Extract 10.
   a) How has the writer expanded their explanation to make their claim stronger?
   b) Can you explain why this is the strongest claim of the three sources?
4. What elements make a historian's claims strong?

Getting the most from your online ActiveBook

This book comes with three years' access to ActiveBook* – an online, digital version of your textbook. Follow the instructions printed on the inside front cover to start using your ActiveBook.

Your ActiveBook is the perfect way to personalise your learning as you progress through your A Level History course. You can:

- access your content online, anytime, anywhere
- use the inbuilt highlighting and annotation tools to personalise the content and make it really relevant to you.

Highlight tool – use this to pick out key terms or topics so you are ready and prepared for revision.

Annotations tool – use this to add your own notes, for example links to your wider reading, such as websites or other files. Or, make a note to remind yourself about work that you need to do.

*For new purchases only. If the access code has already been revealed, it may no longer be valid. If you have bought this textbook secondhand, the code may already have been used by the first owner of the book.

Introduction
A Level History

WHY HISTORY MATTERS

History is about people and people are complex, fascinating, frustrating and a whole lot of other things besides. This is why history is probably the most comprehensive and certainly one of the most intriguing subjects there is. History can also be inspiring and alarming, heartening and disturbing, a story of progress and civilisation and of catastrophe and inhumanity.

History's importance goes beyond the subject's intrinsic interest and appeal. Our beliefs and actions, our cultures, institutions and ways of living, our languages and means of making sense of ourselves are all shaped by the past. If we want to fully understand ourselves now, and to understand our possible futures, we have no alternative but to think about history.

History is a discipline as well as a subject matter. Making sense of the past develops qualities of mind that are valuable to anyone who wants to seek the truth and think clearly and intelligently about the most interesting and challenging intellectual problem of all: other people. Learning history is learning a powerful way of knowing.

WHAT IS HISTORY?

Figure 1 Fragment of a black granite statue possibly portraying the Roman politician Mark Antony.

History is a way of constructing knowledge about the world through research, interpretation, argument and debate.

Building historical knowledge involves identifying the traces of the past that exist in the present – in people's memories, in old documents, photographs and other remains, and in objects and artefacts ranging from bullets and lipsticks, to field systems and cities. Historians interrogate these traces and *ask questions* that transform traces into *sources of evidence* for knowledge claims about the past.

Historians aim to understand what happened in the past by *explaining why* things happened as they did. Explaining why involves trying to understand past people and their beliefs, intentions and actions. It also involves explaining the causes and evaluating the effects of large-scale changes in the past and exploring relationships between what people aimed to do, the contexts that shaped what was possible and the outcomes and consequences of actions.

Historians also aim to *understand change* in the past. People, states of affairs, ideas, movements and civilisations come into being in time, grow, develop, and ultimately decline and disappear. Historians aim to identify and compare change and continuity in the past, to measure the rate at which things change and to identify the types of change that take place. Change can be slow or sudden. It can also be understood as progressive or regressive – leading to the improvement or worsening of a situation or state of affairs. How things change and whether changes are changes for the better are two key issues that historians frequently debate.

Debate is the essence of history. Historians write arguments to support their knowledge claims and historians argue with each other to test and evaluate interpretations of the past. Historical knowledge itself changes and develops. On the one hand, new sources of knowledge and new methods of research cause *historical interpretations* to change. On the other hand, the questions that historians ask change with time and new questions produce new answers. Although the past is dead and gone, the interpretation of the past has a past, present and future.

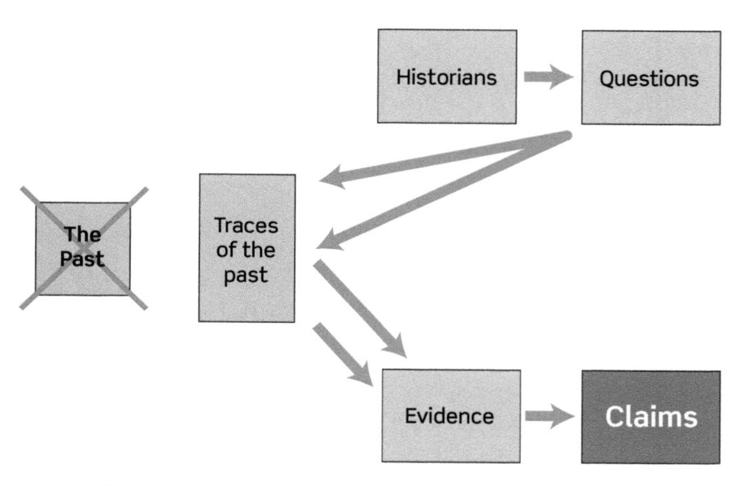

Figure 2 Constructing knowledge about the past.

THE CHALLENGES OF LEARNING HISTORY

Like all other Advanced Level subjects, A Level history is difficult – that is why it is called 'advanced'. Your Advanced Level studies will build on knowledge and understanding of history that you developed at GCSE and at Key Stage 3 – ideas like 'historical sources', 'historical evidence' and 'cause', for example. You will need to do a lot of reading and writing to progress in history. Most importantly, you will need to do a lot of thinking, and thinking about your thinking. This book aims to support you in developing both your knowledge and your understanding.

History is challenging in many ways. On the one hand, it is challenging to build up the range and depth of knowledge that you need to understand the past at an advanced level. Learning about the past involves mastering new and unfamiliar concepts arising from the past itself (such as the Inquisition, Laudianism, *Volksgemeinschaft*) and building up levels of knowledge that are both detailed and well organised. This book covers the key content of the topics that you are studying for your examination and provides a number of features to help you build and organise what you know – for example, diagrams, timelines and definitions of key terms. You will need to help yourself too, of course, adding to your knowledge through further reading, building on the foundations provided by this book.

Another challenge is to develop understandings of the discipline of history. You will have to learn to think historically about evidence, cause, change and interpretations and also to write historically, in a way that develops clear and supported argument.

Historians think with evidence in ways that differ from how we often think in everyday life. In history, as Figure 2 shows, we cannot go and 'see for ourselves' because the past no longer exists. Neither can we normally rely on 'credible witnesses' to tell us 'the truth' about 'what happened'. People in the past did not write down 'the truth' for our benefit. They often had clear agendas when creating the traces that remain and, as often as not, did not themselves know 'the truth' about complex historical events.

A root of the word 'history' is the Latin word *historia*, one of whose meanings is 'enquiry' or 'finding out'. Learning history means learning to ask questions and interrogate traces, and then to reason about what the new knowledge you have gained means. This book draws on historical scholarship for its narrative and contents. It also draws on research on the nature of historical thinking and on the challenges that learning history can present for students. Throughout the book you will find 'Thinking Historically' activities designed to support the development of your thinking.

You will also find – as you would expect given the nature of history – that the book is full of questions. This book aims to help you build your understandings of the content, contexts and concepts that you will need to advance both your historical knowledge and your historical understanding, and to lay strong foundations for the future development of both.

Dr Arthur Chapman
Institute of Education
University College London

QUOTES ABOUT HISTORY

'Historians are dangerous people. They are capable of upsetting everything. They must be directed.'

Nikita Khrushchev

'To be ignorant of what occurred before you were born is to remain forever a child. For what is the worth of human life, unless it is woven into the life of our ancestors by the records of history.'

Marcus Tullius Cicero

The making of modern China, 1860–1997

The history of China 1860–1997 is characterised by a nation trying to find its place in a changing world. Firstly, the period of Western imperialism saw industrialised powers manipulate and exploit China. Then followed the Second World War, when China contributed to its salvation by fighting to victory alongside the Allies (the USA, the USSR, Britain and France). Peace did not last for long and an ideological conflict, the Cold War, soon erupted, in which a US-led capitalist world clashed with its Communist counterpart, led by the USSR. As a newly established Communist republic, China sided with the Soviet Union. However, this relationship was never solid and over time Sino-Soviet relations deteriorated to the extent that, by the late 1970s, China saw the USSR as more of a threat to its interests than the USA. This led to the final period of the book, when China co-operated with the West, adopted its economic models and succeeded in finally establishing itself on an equal basis.

In January 2016, a 36 metre tall statue of Mao Zedong was erected in Henan. Mao was the most significant character in the history of the People's Republic of China (PRC) and one of the most notorious figures of the 20th century. The giant stone and steel edifice was coated in gold paint. It was constructed in Henan province by a wealthy local businessman and was the gaudiest example of the revival in Mao worship. The story was picked up in the Western media and criticism was widespread. Some noted the irony of a statue of Mao being erected in one of the districts that suffered worst in the famine caused by the Great Leap Forward, Mao's wildly misguided and unsuccessful plan to fast-track China's industrialisation. Similarly minded detractors suggested that the funds used to build the statue, approximately £300,000, could have been better spent tackling rural poverty. Others justifiably argued that it did not closely resemble Mao.

SOURCE 1

A Chinese citizen photographing the giant gold-coated statue of Mao Zedong in Tongxu, Henan (2016). Widespread hero worship of Mao has grown more prominent in the People's Republic of China in recent years. In the West, Mao is still seen as a brutal dictator who was responsible for the deaths of millions of his own people. He is seen as a sign of the past and an example of what is wrong with Communism, a megalomaniac whose leadership brought the world closer to nuclear war. In some quarters, he is viewed to this day as a heroic adventurer who stood up to the West.

1860

1860 – Treaty of Tianjin ratified, ending Second Opium War: China opened to the West

1895

1895 – Treaty of Shimonoseki concludes Sino-Japanese War

1911

1911 – Xinhai Revolution overthrows Qing Empire; China becomes a republic

1931

1931 – Japan invades Manchuria

1937

1937 – Second Sino-Japanese War begins as conflict escalates into all-out war

1949

1949 – CCP defeats Guomindang in Chinese Civil War; PRC proclaimed

1958

1958 – Great Leap Forward, China's Second Five-Year Plan begins

1966

1966 – Cultural Revolution begins

1979

1979 – USA gives diplomatic recognition to PRC

1861

1861 - Dowager Empress Cixi assumes control of China

1900

1900 - Anti-foreign Boxer Rebellion defeated by a coalition of Western powers

1919

1919 - May Fourth Movement protests against weakness of Chinese government at the Treaty of Versailles that concludes First World War

1933

1933 - Treaty of Tanggu: China accepts significant land losses to Japan

1941

1941 - Japan bombs US Navy at Pearl Harbor; USA allies with China

1953

1953 - First Five-Year Plan begins industrialisation of Chinese economy

1961

1961 - Sino-Soviet split fully emerges

1978

1978 - Deng Xiaoping becomes 'Paramount Leader' of PRC; China embarks on Four Modernisations, a process of economic modernisation

PRC and Japan sign Treaty of Peace and Friendship

1997

1997 - Hong Kong returns to Chinese rule; last presence of Western imperialism removed from China

What was equally surprising was that a couple of days after the story broke in the West, the statue was demolished. The official announcement was that the statue did not have planning permission. It is more likely that the Chinese Communist Party was trying to save face. However, it is an example of China struggling to deal with the legacy of its modern history. Mao is a controversial figure; a leader who was responsible for great achievements and tragic failures alike. To this day, the ruling Communist Party is unsure how to remember Mao. In excess of 2,000 statues of Mao are dotted throughout the vast country, a massive portrait of Mao continues to be displayed in Tiananmen Square, and his likeness now adorns a huge array of tourist souvenirs. Mao's successor as the leader of the PRC, Deng Xiaoping, summarised Mao's rule as 70 percent good and 30 percent bad. This was no scientific calculation, but a soundbite for Deng to legitimise his own modernisations that shaped China 1978–97. In successfully opening China to Western ideas, trade and investment, Deng integrated China into the global economy. The rule of Deng Xiaoping ends the 1860–1997 period covered by this book. The period covered by this book begins in 1860 with another opening of China to foreign relations in the wake of China's humbling at the hands of the British in the Second Opium War. This heralded a prolonged era of Chinese weakness during which China attempted to learn Western ways but ended up being exploited by stronger nations. Industrialised countries were able to impose unequal treaties on China. The most humiliating of these were the Treaty of Shimonoseki (1895) and the Treaty of Tanggu (1933) signed with Japan, both of which ceded Chinese land to Japanese rule. Japan had traditionally existed in the shadow of China, but it emerged as the most powerful Asian nation.

China laboured under foreign domination until the war it was fighting against Japan became a part of the Second World War in 1941. After the Second World War, the Chinese Communist Party won a bloody civil war over the governing Nationalists and proclaimed the People's Republic of China in 1949.

3.1 The growth of industry

KEY QUESTIONS

- To what extent did China adopt Western technologies in communications and transport in the years 1860–1997?
- To what extent was China successfully industrialised in the years 1860–1997?

INTRODUCTION

Between 1860 and 1997 China's relationship with industrialisation and technology underwent a series of profound transformations. At the start of the period, China's economic and military power was in crisis due to defeats the country had suffered at the hands of Great Britain. The main reason for Britain's victory over China related to the technologies developed during the industrial revolution. Throughout the period 1860–1997, there was tension between traditional Chinese approaches to communication and industry, and the need for more modern approaches, which were required in order to compete with the rest of the rapidly industrialising world and to keep China free from foreign invasion.

The size of China also meant that the Qing Empire and Nationalist and Communist governments required new methods of connecting the outlying provinces to the centres of power in Beijing, Shanghai and Nanjing. Railways, steamships, aircraft and the introduction of the automobile, as well as the building of roads and the growth of Chinese air power were key ways in which this was achieved.

TO WHAT EXTENT DID CHINA ADOPT WESTERN TECHNOLOGIES IN COMMUNICATIONS AND TRANSPORT IN THE YEARS 1860–1997?

Steamships for coastal and river traffic in the later Qing Empire, 1860–1911

Coastal and river communication in 1860

In 1860, China was embroiled in a civil war and had fought two unsuccessful wars against Britain – the Opium Wars (see Chapter 3), between 1839 and 1860. The result was a weakened Qing Empire and British (and later European) control over key **treaty ports** along the Chinese coast. The British were interested in controlling China's waterways and river systems in order to trade deep into the heart of the empire. This would enable them to sell goods, particularly opium, and extract wealth from China, exporting it back to Great Britain.

KEY TERM

Treaty port
A city on China's eastern coast that was opened to European trade and control by the unequal treaties (see Chapter 4) signed by China from 1842 onwards.

1860 – End of Second Opium War

1872 – China Merchants' Steam Navigation Company established

1876 – China's first stretch of railway built by the British at Baoshan

1881 – Fifty miles of track laid between Tianjin and Tangshan

1897 – Work begins on Chinese section of Trans-Siberian Railway

1898 – Boxer Rebellion begins in northern China

1900 – Boxer Rebellion begins in Beijing

1911 – Revolution

1922 – Sun Yat-sen's *The International Development of China* published

1860 1870 1880 1890 1900 1910 1920

Britain was able to control these waterways due to the new technologies of naval steam power. Britain had been able to destroy the Imperial Chinese Navy in the two Opium Wars using iron-hulled steam-powered battleships and modern naval artillery. The effect that British steamships had on China, however, was if anything more devastating than the artillery. By introducing modern mass-produced goods to the interior of China, these ships disrupted the traditional artisan-based economy, where much economic production of goods was done by individuals working in their own homes or in villages.

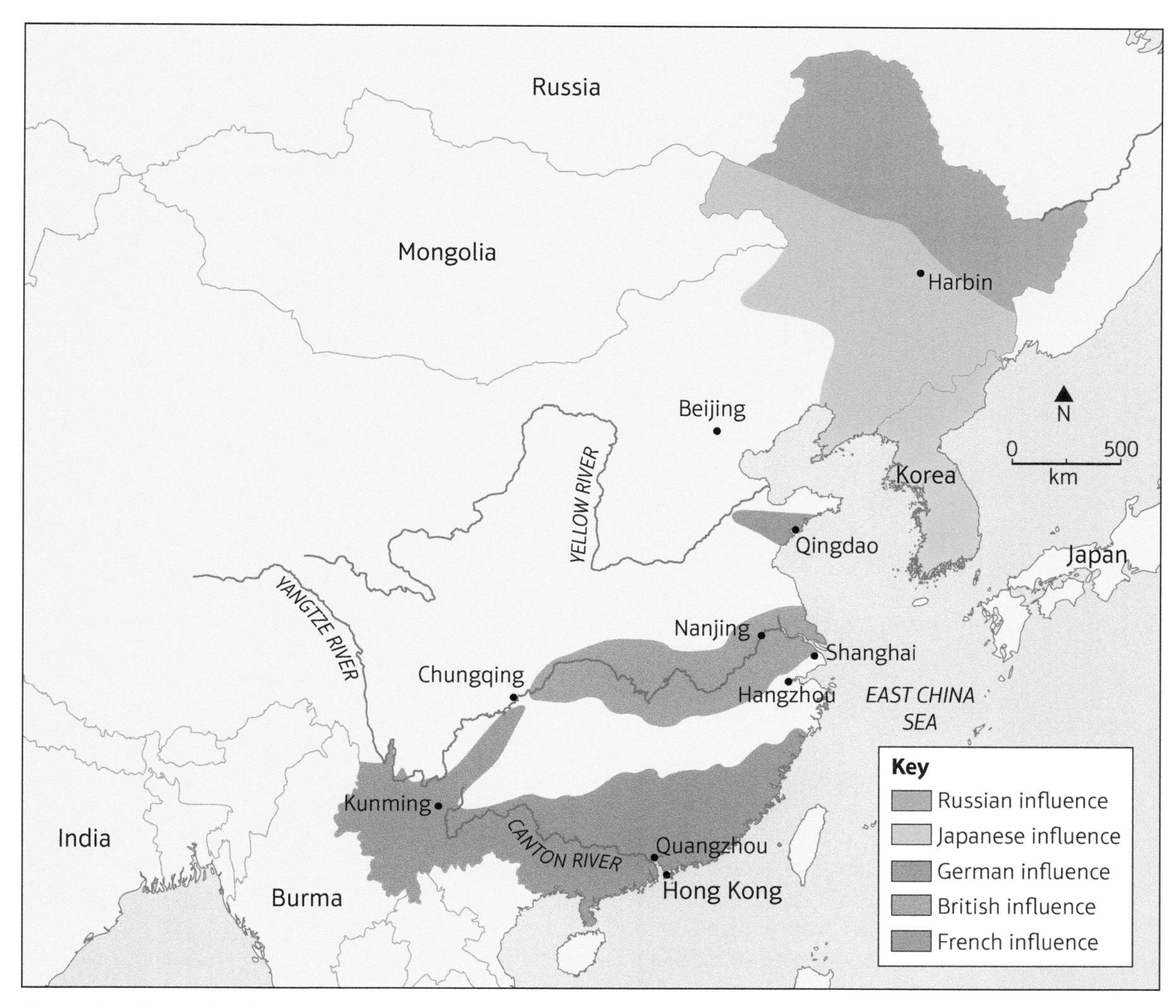

Figure 1.1 China, showing major rivers, cities and areas of foreign influence in 1900.

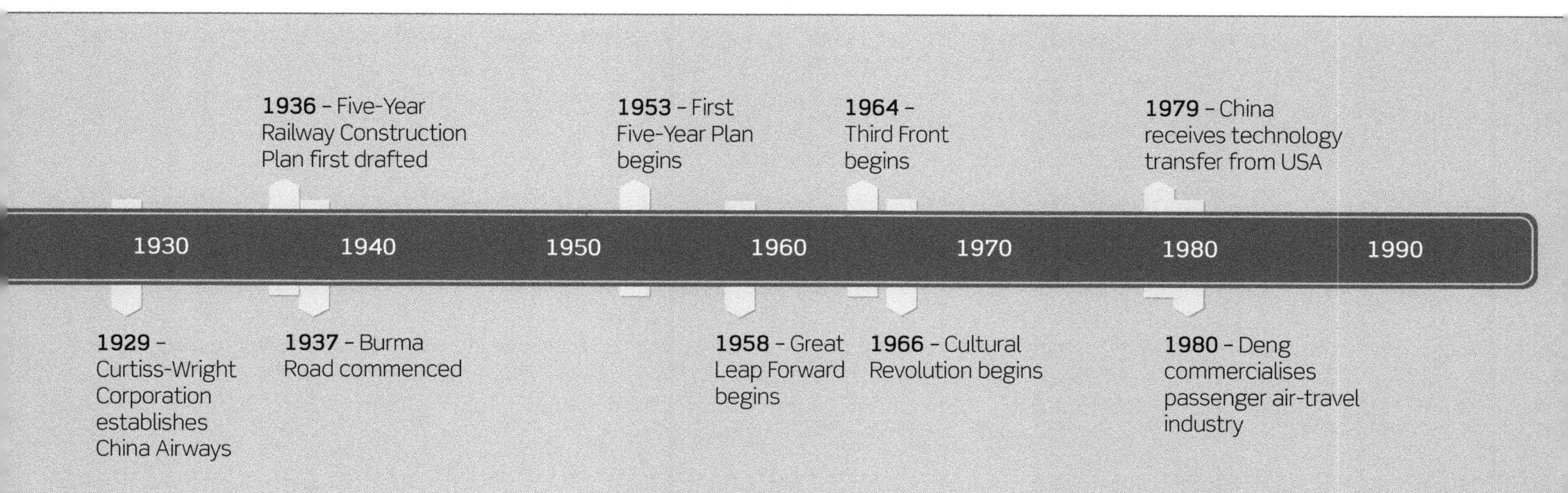

KEY TERMS

Junk
A two-sailed Chinese trading or fishing boat, used on rivers and along the coast.

Sampan
A small fishing boat used by peasants.

British and European penetration of China's rivers

Previously, the only method of navigating China's rivers had been the traditional Chinese **junk** or **sampan**. Countless local and regional economies were plunged into crisis as cheaper and better-made goods flooded markets that had never been accessed by European powers before. Most commerce in China was conducted by Chinese merchants, and used the country's poorly maintained road network. The imperial grand canal that ran from Hangzhou on the east coast to Beijing was the only other major piece of transport infrastructure, but by 1860 sections of it were over 2,000 years old and had fallen into disrepair.

By 1881, there were 50 miles of railway in China, but seven European steamship companies owned dozens of ships that sailed between the treaty ports and the cities along the Canton and Yangtze rivers. The Shanghai Steam Navigation Company, the Yangtze Steamer Company and the Indo-China Steam Company were operated by merchants such as Jardine and Matheson, who had grown wealthy from the Opium Wars fought between China and Britain. This penetration of China by civilian and military steamships brought modern economic and military ideas with it.

The Qing emperors of the period were advised by more forward-looking administrators to pay close attention to how Western powers operated and to emulate their use of steam naval power, but this advice was for the most part ignored. Foreign industrial investment in China began in earnest in the 1890s, so the development of steamships was the first major Western economic advance into China.

China's steamships

The Qing government established the China Merchants' Steam Navigation Company in 1872, but this was operated in a very different way from European businesses involved in the same trade. The company was established by imperial bureaucrats and subsidised with government money, but it was hampered by the control that government officials had over it. The fate of the China Merchants' Steam Navigation Company was linked to that of the officials who founded it: if they fell out of favour with the emperor, so would the company. It was forced not only to make a profit as its Western rivals did, but also to prop up national pride. The company was obliged to sail along routes that Europeans ignored because they were unprofitable, making a loss because profit was not always a key priority. This meant that it had to be heavily subsidised, but the subsidies were also a source of funds for corrupt officials to steal from.

KEY TERM

Extraterritoriality
An arrangement that exempted Westerners in foreign concessions from Chinese laws. These concessions were governed by the laws of the occupying foreign power. It also affected Chinese nationals living in foreign concessions, making them subject to foreign jurisdiction.

Commercial problems for China's steamship industry

Foreign companies that enjoyed **extraterritoriality** were exempt from any Chinese government interference as a result of the treaties signed at the end of the Opium Wars. Foreign captains were hired to pilot Chinese ships, meaning that the industry could not operate without foreign involvement. It was far easier for European steam-navigation companies to establish themselves and grow because they had access to loans from British banks established in the treaty ports, and were able to sell shares to raise finance. Because China's financial system was far less developed, so its steamship industry was mainly dependent on state aid.

This became a growing problem throughout the last quarter of the 19th century as the Qing dynasty's finances dwindled. However, it did not prevent the government from pouring vast sums into the industry, acquiring 33 ships by 1877. Many of these were old and in need of repair, and part of their purchase price had been paid out of loans from European banks. Between 1877 and 1900, the company stagnated. Gradually it made a loss, and 23 ships became too old and run down to remain in service. Corruption, bureaucracy and a lack of modern finance meant that by the time steamships were superseded by railways, Europeans had successfully dominated the market and controlled commerce along China's great rivers.

Foreign gunboats

One foreign power that exerted immense influence along the Yangtze River using armed gunboats was the USA. The first armed US steamers that sailed up the river to expand US trade and protect US merchant shipping set sail to Hankou in 1860. US ships and other European vessels patrolled the river, particularly during periods of anti-Western protest, to make sure that traders and missionaries were safe. By the 1890s, the Yangtze was China's busiest waterway, with steamers, oil tankers, tugboats and mail boats sailing back and forth. This obvious sign of encroaching modernity left many Chinese feeling resentful and fearful of change, as most of the river traffic was foreign. During the

Boxer Rebellion (see page 96), the Boxers identified steamships, along with trains and telegraphs, as being foreign and therefore unwelcome. Royal Navy ships also patrolled the river, and many smaller ships that had been used during the First World War were transferred for use in China in the 1920s.

However, despite periodic outbreaks of anger among China's peasants, there were few threats to British and US steamships in China from Chinese sources. Instead, the power that ultimately destroyed their control of China's waterways was Japan. In 1937, when the Japanese army attacked the city of Nanjing, a US ship, the USS *Panay*, and the British HMS *Bee* were attacked by aerial bombers. Within two years, the invading Japanese had instituted major restrictions on the navigation of China's river network for European and US ships. After the attack on Pearl Harbor, dozens of Western military and commercial ships were attacked and sunk.

Type of loss	Number of ships	Tonnage
Wrecks and accidents	9	6,759
Dismantled or scrapped	9	6,305
Sold	3	2,174
Lost or unaccounted for	2	823

Figure 1.2 Ships lost by the China Merchants' Steam Navigation Company from 1887 to 1893. This represented two-thirds of the company's fleet lost within two decades of their original purchase in 1877. (From Liu, K.C. 'Steamship Enterprise in 19th-century China', *The Journal of Asian Studies*, Vol. 18, No. 4 (August 1959).)

SOURCE 1

The first train leaving Shanghai for Woosung on the 15-mile line in 1876. It was built by the British company Jardine Matheson and paid for by the Qing government, but was dismantled a year later (see page 14).

OPENING OF THE FIRST RAILWAY IN CHINA: THE FIRST TRAIN STARTING FROM SHANGHAI.

EXTRACT 1

Professor Robert Bickers, in the introduction to the book *Treaty Ports in Modern China: Law, Land and Power* (2016), describes how British traders managed to take up residence in Chinese treaty ports during the mid-19th century.

Nineteenth-century European traders... Britons, because the British pioneered the majority of such moves – identify a Chinese port city as geographically well placed, or well positioned within trading networks, and within a regional economy, and so lobby for its opening to foreign residence and trade. They petition their diplomats or politicians at home and in China, directly and indirectly, and make their case through their local and metropolitan press, emphasizing perhaps the imperatives of free trade and the commercial opportunities presented by a new foothold in China.

ACTIVITY
KNOWLEDGE CHECK

British traders in China

1 Study Extract 1. What methods did British traders use in order to increase their influence in China?

2 Study Extract 1 and Source 1. What do they suggest about how Britain was influencing the development of transport in China in the years 1860–76?

3 Summarise the key economic and political changes that happened as a result of the introduction of steamships.

EXTEND YOUR KNOWLEDGE

European colonialism in Asia and China

In the second half of the 19th century, Britain and France colonised much of Asia and the Middle East from Egypt to China. In 1857, Britain took direct control over India, and in 1887 the colony of French Indochina was established (modern Vietnam, Laos and Cambodia). The influence of Britain and other European powers in China, therefore, should be seen within this wider context. Some countries were directly occupied with European military force and administration, but China's experience was different. At no time was China or any part of it (other than Hong Kong) formally added to the British Empire, even though numerous merchants, soldiers and diplomats advocated the formal break-up of the Qing Empire. Instead, it was easier and less costly to impose demands on the existing Chinese government that were favourable to British traders.

Other British colonies such as India, which was formally occupied and directly governed by Britain, existed primarily to benefit British merchants, so Britain's practices in China were in keeping with the rest of the official empire. Britain, France, Germany and other European powers were able to protect their interests in China with military force if necessary, and enjoyed freedom from the rule of Qing law throughout much of the country. This left most Chinese with the impression that their country had been taken over, and that their government was too weak to do anything about it. The period 1860–1911 saw constant unrest for the Qing dynasty as rebels across China channelled the anger of the peasantry and townspeople who demanded an end to foreigners exploiting China's weakness.

The growth of railways

Early rail expansion, 1860–1900

Initially, China's railway network developed faster in northern China than in the south, because the south was connected by steamships through the major river systems. However, the development of rail was hampered by problems similar to those that had held the steamship industry back.

The mid-19th century was the golden age of railway development. Globally, it was an industry pioneered by the British, who used rail to connect raw materials and markets in their empire to ports where commodities such as cotton could be exported and finished goods could be imported.

Having created a railway network in India for this purpose, they began to develop a similar system in China. The first stretch of railway built in China by the British in 1876 was at Baoshan. However, local people protested. They were fearful of the change the railway would bring and expressed their anger at the laying of tracks, saying they ignored the Chinese practice of **feng shui**. To appease the people of Baoshan and prevent further unrest, Qing officials eventually purchased the railway line, dismantled it and sent the steel to Taiwan. This shows that popular concerns about the development of modern and non-Chinese industries and transport played a powerful role in China.

KEY TERM

Feng shui
A Chinese philosophy of physical harmony that relates to the flow of energy in a space or building. It requires the man-made environment to be arranged in line with natural energies.

Photographs of the opening of the railway line show thousands of curious and fascinated Chinese peasants coming to see it. This suggests that despite the superstitious beliefs of some Chinese, others found modern inventions like railways exciting and embraced their development.

In 1881, 50 miles of track were laid between Tianjin and Tangshan as a direct result of the growth in steamships. The director of the China Merchants' Steam Navigation Company, Tong King-Sing, built a coal mine in Tangshan and needed a method of moving coal to the port of Tianjin. He gained permission from the Chinese official Li Hongzhang, known as a moderniser (see page 50), and British engineers constructed the railway using Chinese labour. Imported British locomotives pulled coal wagons and passenger carriages.

Railways presented Qing emperors and administrators with a dilemma: they were a non-Chinese technology that was clearly more advanced than anything China had invented, which undermined traditional Qing ideas about Chinese supremacy. They were suspicious of foreign innovation, but recognised how useful railways were for controlling an often rebellious country. The ability to quickly move troops to different fronts gave the authorities a huge strategic advantage over rebels.

However, rail also helped the Europeans and later the Japanese to penetrate even deeper into China, dominating trade and spreading Christianity through the work of **missionaries**. This penetration was the main cause of rebellions and uprisings after 1860. Along each of the new railway networks that emerged, a 20 mile extraterritorial corridor was established where Chinese law did not apply due to extraterritoriality rules imposed by treaties from European powers. The inability of the Qing government to finance railways left it reliant on foreign investment, resulting in a further weakening of China's position. This weakness was exposed in 1898 when a mass movement erupted in northern China against foreign control of the country. It was known as the Boxer Rebellion (see Chapter 4), and foreign-owned railways became a prime target for rebels.

KEY TERM

Missionary
European Christian evangelist who spread the teachings of the gospel.

EXTRACT

Tim Wright in *Coal Mining and China's Economy and Society* (1984) argues that one main cause of railway expansion was China's growing coal industry.

Most of China's coal deposits were in the north, where water transport [the easiest and cheapest way of moving coal before the advent of steam trains] was less available. Rail transport could reduce costs to under one fifth of the previous level for land transport. Apart from the abortive Wusong [*sic*] railway, the first line in China was built in the 1880s to carry Kaiaking coal to the nearest point of shipment for water transportation. The extension of that line as far as Tianjin and the building of a short railway in Taiwan were the only projects undertaken before 1895.

ACTIVITY
KNOWLEDGE CHECK

Railway development and coal

Read Extract 2 and the section of text called 'Early rail expansion, 1860-1900'. How far is the information in the extract supported by your knowledge? What does the author suggest was a main reason for rail expansion before 1895?

EXTEND YOUR KNOWLEDGE

Dowager Empress Cixi (1835–1908)
Cixi was a concubine to Emperor Xianfeng and became the dowager empress after his death. Her son Zaichun succeeded his father, but Cixi was the real power behind the throne, installing her nephew as emperor in 1875 when her son died. She was a powerful and influential figure who was resistant to most Westernisation but eventually embraced the self-strengthening reforms (see page 40) in the 1890s.

The Trans-Siberian Railway

Throughout the 19th century, the Russian Empire had rapidly expanded across Asia and saw the weakened China as a territory ripe for exploitation. In 1890, the son of Tsar Alexander III of Russia, Nicholas (who would become tsar on his father's death four years later) established the eastern end of the new Trans-Siberian Railway that would link Moscow to the Pacific Ocean and cross through China. Vladivostok had been seized by Russia from China at the end of the Second Opium War in 1860, as Russia swiftly took advantage of China's weakness. The Qing government agreed for the railway to pass through Manchuria and back into Russia, close to the Mongolian border, and work finally began in 1897. The Russian government also built another railway line from the treaty port at Dalian (Port Arthur), which connected with the Trans-Siberian Railway, making it the longest railway line in the world.

The railway network extended Russian power over northern China and Manchuria and resulted in tensions on Chinese soil between Russia and Japan. When the Chinese section of the railway was opened, it was named the Chinese Eastern Railway, and regular traffic from China into Russia began in 1903. The following year, Russia fought a disastrous war with Japan, in large part based around the territorial ambitions of both powers in China and Korea. Russia's rail network in China became a crucial but flawed part of the tsar's war strategy. The railway was unable to supply Russian armies effectively and the subsequent defeat of Russia saw the large sections of the Chinese Eastern Railway in Manchuria and the Liaodong peninsula pass into Japanese hands.

China fought a brief border war over the railway in 1929, and after Japan's 1931 invasion of Manchuria, both the Chinese and the Russians were forced to acknowledge Japanese control of the network. At the end of the Second World War, Nationalist China and the USSR controlled equal sections of the railway, but in 1952 the network was finally handed over to Mao's regime. The Chinese section of the Trans-Siberian Railway was continually fought over by three empires from 1904 to 1945. This shows how strategically important the railway network was in controlling the territory of Manchuria.

Railways and the 'scramble for China'

Historians have called the two decades between the mid-1890s and 1914 the **scramble for China**, as all major European powers began a process of de facto colonisation. During this period, railway building was a central part of expanding European influence. The pace of railway building increased dramatically after 1900, and this coincided with accelerated acquisition of territory in China by European powers. Railways became an important means for colonial powers to extend their control over China.

> **KEY TERM**
>
> **Scramble for China**
> A term used by historians to describe the period from 1890 to 1914 when colonial powers appeared to be attempting to colonise and divide China, similar to their acquisition of African colonies in the 1880s and 1890s.

As mentioned above, Russian railway building across Manchuria gave Russia power in the province, and British railway building in the Yangtze valley gave Great Britain power across a huge swathe of central China. US and Belgian railway builders connected the southernmost Cantonese city of Guangzhou to Beijing, and France connected its empire in Indochina to southern China by building a railway line to Kunming, where France wanted to acquire mineral rights.

Each major act of rail-building by a foreign power was designed to extract wealth, materials or territory from China. The European powers, the USA and Japan were all highly suspicious of each other's rail-building activities in China. They each attempted to use their influence with the Qing government to halt the rail expansion plans of rival powers. Over time this led to a dramatic escalation in the pace of railway building and the demand for concessions from the Qing government as rival European powers, desperate for markets and resources, raced to counter each others' influence. The extent to which railways in China were foreign owned and developed and therefore part of the 'scramble for China' can be seen in the following statistic: in the decade after 1900, China managed to build only a short 120 mile section of track out of a total of 9,000 miles of track in the entire country.

Despite China being an empire based on tradition and a strict adherence to ancient Confucian thought, there was evidence that at every level of society, parts of the population were embracing the new technology of rail travel. Many Chinese felt conflicted that railways were foreign inventions and were mainly built and run by foreigners. Chinese peasants found trains a convenient way of moving livestock and produce to markets that had previously been hours' or days' travel away. The peasants were also able to access towns and cities in a way that had never previously been possible.

During the First World War, when Chinese peasant labour was exported to Europe to dig British and French trenches on the Western Front, the first train journey that peasants from Shandong made was to Shanghai. For first-time peasant train travellers, the experience often led to other questions about the working of the modern world outside the peasant village. Some were keen to know more about the technological, social and political changes that modernisation was bringing to China.

The Rights Recovery Movement and the Railway Protection Movement

In the aftermath of the Boxer Rebellion, the Qing government was acutely aware that foreign control of China's railway system was a huge source of resentment against both the Qing government and foreign powers. It was unable to do much to reduce the ownership of the network by foreign powers. Many of them had loaned the Qing government money in order to pay for the railways, knowing full well that the state of China's finances was so poor that it would be unable to repay the loan.

In 1904, French and Belgian railway lines from southern China (US contractors sold their rights to the Belgians that year) threatened to connect with Russian lines in the north. The Qing government had hoped to be able to control European railway building by dividing it among several European countries and the USA, but a Franco-Russian rail network splitting China in two threatened this policy as the two nations were allies.

Seeing that the Qing government was powerless over the situation, local Chinese gentry and businessmen who lived in the provinces where the railway was meant to be laid tried their best to undermine the project. Some raised money to lay part of the track themselves. Others went to Britain and other European powers to persuade them to complete part of the railway. In Guandong, the local merchants formed the Canton Railway

Company, which only allowed Chinese people to own shares. Chinese people were adopting European railway technologies and the methods of financing and owning them. This development – local elites taking responsibility upon themselves for preserving China's independence in terms of railway technology – is highly significant because it indicates that China's emerging middle class was politically active and focused on solving the country's problems. It also shows that, in the China of the early 20th century, railway technology appeared to offer a chance to retain control over the country.

The organisations that developed were called the Rights Recovery Movement, as they sought to return foreign-owned railway networks to Chinese control. However, this political activism was not purely altruistic. Many rights recovery activists were motivated by financial interests, and owning shares in railways was extremely lucrative. Nationalist politics developed alongside railway reclamation, as Chinese people pledged to buy shares in railways if it meant they would be returned to China. Protesters argued that being a modern Chinese individual and taking an interest in railway ownership and rail technology were synonymous. It was therefore a patriotic act to own shares in the new rail network. However, foreign powers demanded high prices for the sale of railway lines, and the officials and gentry who bought them often had little understanding of railway technology or how to run a commercial rail business, so they re-hired European business and engineering specialists to help them.

By 1904, the government allowed a network of smaller rail lines to develop, financed by the provinces themselves with shares raised from the local population. This gave ordinary Chinese people a sense of ownership over the railway system and drew them into a developing share-owning economy. It was hoped that the establishment of these smaller lines would have a positive effect on the Chinese peasantry, enabling them to take goods and livestock to market. However, very little track was actually laid owing to corruption. So the Qing government intervened, and the government's Boards of Communications and Finance constructed all further railway lines. The government lacked the finance and expertise to do this, and turned to the only source of help available: foreign powers.

The sale of railway rights to Britain, the USA and other powers enabled China to repay debts incurred after the Boxer Rebellion. The decision met with Nationalist outrage and the development of an anti-Qing group called the Railway Protection Movement in 1911. Railways once again became a focal point for popular anger during the **1911 revolution**.

Figure 1.3 The railway lines that had been built in China by c1900.

KEY TERM

The Chinese Revolution of 1911
In 1911, after decades of upheaval and national humiliations at the hands of Europeans and the Japanese, the Qing Dynasty was overthrown. Since the 1890s there had been an organised opposition to the Qing government centred around secret societies, including the nationalist Tongmenghui. In 1911, the decision by significant portions of the Chinese Army to join the revolution doomed the Qing Dynasty and saw general Yuan Shikai seize power as the first president of the Republic of China.

EXTRACT 3

In *The Penguin History of China*, by J. Fenby (2010), the author describes the importance of the Railway Protection Movement to the 1911 revolution.

In May 1911 an imperial decree announced that a permit for the construction of main railway lines would be taken over by the Boards of Communications and Finance. This major centralising move was swiftly followed by an agreement to give work on these projects to a British-American-French-German consortium which was offering the loans the court needed so badly... On 17 June 1911, shareholders in the Szechuan-Hankou Railway Company held a meeting at which policemen sent in to ensure order joined in, shouting, 'We are also men of Szechuan; we love our country.' Protestors marched on government headquarters. A Railroad Protection Female Comrades Association was formed. The railway minister in Beijing made things worse when he branded the protestors as troublesome schoolboys. On the morning of 24 August, a general strike was called in Szechuan. Two weeks later the governor imprisoned nine protest leaders. In a demonstration in Chengdu, soldiers fired on the crowd, killing several people. Militiamen from outlying areas marched into the city to support the railway movement. Though troops repulsed them, more 'comrade armies' formed. Led by the local gentry, the movement took power in several parts of the province.

ACTIVITY
KNOWLEDGE CHECK

Financing railway development

What is the historian in Extract 3 describing in relation to how the building of new railways in 1911 was financed and built? Select the key sentences in this extract that support his view.

EXTRACT 4

This extract describes a meeting between the Prince Regent Zaifeng (Prince Chun) and his vice-minister Sheng Xuanhaui in 1910 about the problems China faced in financing its own railway production. It is taken from *China: How the Empire Fell*, by Joseph W. Esherick and C.X. George Wei (2013).

In his audience with the Prince Regent on being appointed, Sheng Xuanhai reported that 'setting up associations in Hunan and Hubei to resist foreign loans, raise funds and build the railway on their own are only empty promises of no use in solving real problems... They claimed fund-raising figures are unreliable.' If the government lets things develop this way, 'funds will be insufficient and the railway will not be constructed for over thirty years.' Kaifeng was said to be 'greatly moved'. He 'ordered the Ministry of Communication to discuss the matter with the Grand Council, and the ministries of foreign affairs and revenue'. On August 25th [1910] the Ministry of Communications obtained Kaifeng's approval to send officials to Hunan and Hubei to investigate the railway companies and their funds. On October 14, Sheng Xuanhuai reported to Zaifeng that the 'Hunan portion of the Guangzhou-Hankou railway needed around 34 million taels of silver and, by October 1910, the railway company had committed only 1,720,000 taels. The Hubei portion of the Guangzhou-Hankou and Sichuan-Hankou lines needed 67 million silver dollars, of which only 632,400 dollars remained in the Great Qing Bank and Communications Bank in Hankou...' Work has not yet started, and little money has been raised. This shows the extent of the resources of local businessmen.

ACTIVITY
KNOWLEDGE CHECK

Foreign influence in railway building

Examine the previous section and Extract 4 together, then answer the following question: 'China had no choice other than to rely on foreign railway technology and finance.' How valid is this statement?

Sun Yat-sen's railways, 1911–25

The revolutionary Dr Sun Yat-sen, who was the driving force behind the development of the Tongmenhui Party (later the Guomindang, see page 19), had agitated against the Qing dynasty for three decades. He intended to create a modern liberal, nationalist Chinese republic. When he stepped down from the office of president of the republic a year after it had been founded, he was given the role of director of construction of all railways in China. He planned a vast new national network of 70,000 miles of track (scaled back from a more ambitious 1.6 million miles that he had originally planned), in part inspired by the US rail network that had developed in the 19th century.

Sun knew that modern systems of transport were a key factor in binding large and diverse countries into unified nations. Both he and the new president Yuan Shikai believed that China, wracked by chaos and civil war, needed a railway infrastructure to bind it together.

One central problem that Sun faced was financing his new railways. China was virtually bankrupt by 1912 and foreign investors had little appetite for risking more money in a country rapidly sinking into chaos and civil war. The Chinese people had also shown they wanted an end to foreign investment in China's railways during the 1911 revolution.

The fact that the Nationalist father of modern China was forced to look to Europe and the USA once again for the funds to build a modern transport network for China is revealing. It suggests that economic realities made many of the hopes of an autonomous and independent China impossible. Sun Yat-sen's plans included a vision of creating 160,000 miles of track in China at a cost of three billion dollars. His plans were contradictory, as he wanted private foreign businesses to invest in building railways in China, but at the same time he wanted to nationalise the track and rolling stock, something that foreign investors would never have agreed to.

Sun Yat-sen's priority in developing the rail network was political, not economic. He wanted a rail system to politically hold China together, with economic growth as a secondary consideration. His railway plan, for example, did not prioritise the building of lines in areas along the major river systems, as steamboat travel had already connected them with the rest of China. This meant that large inland areas that were heavily populated had no railways planned for them. He created a railway map that he took with him on official trips around China. However, his advisers realised that the planned railway routes he had drawn on the map did not reflect the realities of Chinese geography, and were frequently drawn crossing mountain ranges.

This level of naivety about the enormous physical challenges of connecting China by rail at a time when much of the country was ruled by **warlords**, shows that Sun Yat-sen's idealism was not tempered by pragmatism or reality. The plans he drew up were inherited by the Guomindang government after his death and were later considered by Mao's Communists. One historian of China, Victor Lippit, argued that the map had a huge influence on the Communists' later plans, and while this appears to be true, the main principle of Sun's design – connecting all regional capitals with Nanjing, Shanghai and Beijing – still had not been achieved by 1987.

KEY TERM

Warlord
A general and military ruler who controlled a province of China between 1911 and 1928. The warlords supported the northern Beiyang government.

ACTIVITY
KNOWLEDGE CHECK

Sun Yat-sen's railways

1. Compare Qing attempts to develop the railway network to Sun Yat-sen's efforts. Who had greater success in creating a railway network in China?
2. 'Sun Yat-sen was every bit as dependent on foreign aid to develop railways as the Qing rulers were.' Is this an accurate statement?

KEY TERMS

Diaspora
The movement of people from a nation who are intentionally or unintentionally dispersed to other parts of the world and who often live in close-knit migrant communities.

Tongmenghui
The Nationalist secret society established by Sun Yat-sen. It later became the Guomindang.

Jiang Jieshi's railway development, 1928–49

Even though there were problems with Sun Yat-sen's railway plan, when Jiang Jieshi (see page 109) became president in 1928 his government looked on it as the blueprint for the future. Jiang inherited a railway network based mainly in the north of the country that had 5,237 miles of track (less than Britain had in 1850). The war against China's warlords that raged throughout the 1920s saw much of this network damaged, and traditional modes of transport such as mules and coolies (unskilled Chinese labourers) were widespread. Railway companies that fell under the control of China's warlords were looted for their wealth by the warlords. European and US businesses refused to invest any further in China until a national government was back in control of the entire country. When Jiang either defeated the warlords or reached accommodation with them, along with the Communists (whom he subsequently purged), the growing threat of Japan and the eventual outbreak of war led the railways to be developed not only to unify the nation but also for the needs of national defence.

EXTEND YOUR KNOWLEDGE

Sun Yat-sen and the Tongmenghui

Sun Yat-sen spent much of his life outside China either travelling and studying or in exile. He was born in 1866 in Guangzhou province in southern China and was ethnically from the Hakka people of the region. At the age of ten, he went to live with his older brother in Hawaii, where he was educated in English and lived a comfortable, privileged existence.

Sun grew up overseas and so he was more receptive to Western ideas, culture and politics. As he grew older, he was able to see how modernisation, nationalism and liberal democracy might change China. Living outside China also gave him a new perspective on China's problems. A Chinese **diaspora** had existed across Asia and the Pacific for centuries, and Sun Yat-sen was an integral part of this overseas community, which felt at the same time separate from China but deeply loyal to it and fearful for its future.

He returned to China in 1883 and rejected the superstitious and traditional beliefs of his home village, Cuiheng. Instead, he decided to train as a doctor in Hong Kong, graduating in 1892. His decision to train in Western medicine was significant, as it showed how Sun had embraced a Western type of scientific modernity instead of older Chinese traditions, which were increasingly under threat from Western technology and power. In Hong Kong, he embraced both Christianity and the anti-Qing cause, and he spent time in Britain and the USA campaigning amongst the diaspora, raising funds and conspiring against the Qing dynasty. He was kidnapped by Chinese government officials in London in 1896 and held hostage at the Chinese embassy before British friends raised the alarm and an outcry put pressure on the embassy to release him.

Following this, Sun became a famous international figure and increasingly the face of opposition to the government in China. He formed the **Tongmenghui** in 1905 and established the 'three principles' of society: nationalism (*mínzú zhǔyì*), democracy (*mínquán zhǔyì*) and 'people's welfare' (*mínshēng zhǔyì*)). He believed that the overthrow of the Qing dynasty and the establishment of a modern liberal democratic state similar to Britain or the USA would allow Chinese people to reclaim their national pride by having direct participation in elections and other democratic practices. The huge inequalities of wealth across China and grinding rural poverty would be addressed by a democratic government that was prepared to redistribute wealth and intervene directly to improve the lives of China's poorest. Sun had seen how social reform had been put into practice in European countries to improve the conditions of the poor. He believed that the highest priority was to create a Chinese republic that did not fragment or divide. The periphery of the Chinese Empire was often wild and lawless, and the weakening empire found it increasingly difficult to bind far-away peoples like the Tibetans and Uigurs to the central government in Beijing. Sun thought that modern devices such as roads, railways and the telegraph could do this, but he was also determined to ensure that the Han Chinese were in charge of the new China.

During the revolution in December 1911, Sun was voted president of the Chinese Republic in Nanjing. However, he realised that Prime Minister Yuan Shikai had a monopoly on military power, and Sun handed the presidency over to him in January 1912. Later that year, Sun formed a new party, the Guomindang, which by 1915 was plunged into war with the Qing general Yuan Shikai after Yuan proclaimed himself emperor. In the last decade of his life, Sun Yat-sen saw his new party co-operate with the Communist Party of China, as he believed that this was the only way the government in Beijing could be overthrown and the country finally unified. He also supported the emerging warlords against Yuan Shikai and his successors in Beijing.

Sun Yat-sen died in 1925 at the age of 58.

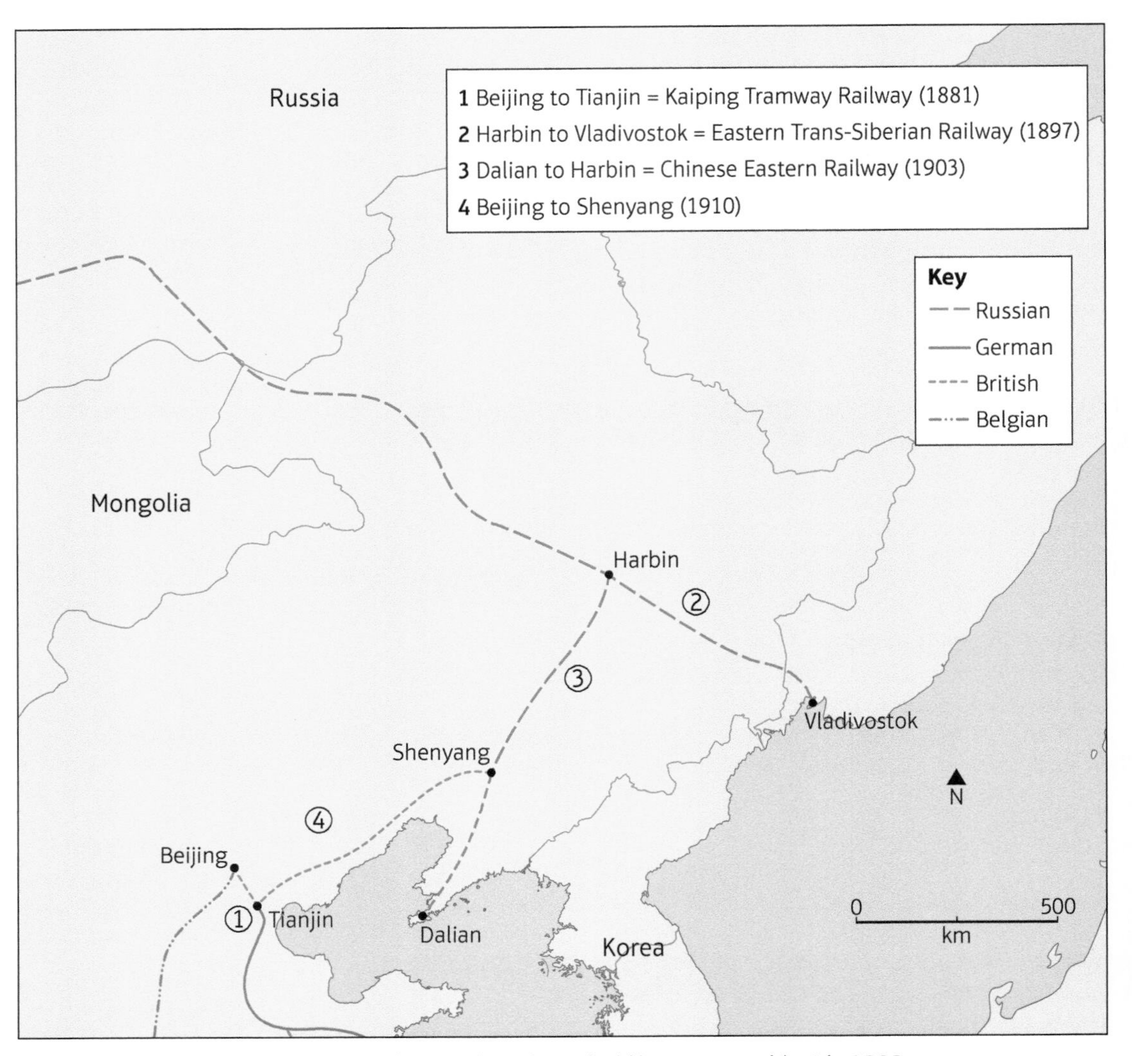

Figure 1.4 China's railway network as it was when Jiang Jieshi became president in 1928.

By 1930, Manchuria was effectively under Japanese control. Through its puppet ruler Zhang Xueliang, Manchuria developed the region's railway network to compete with both Soviet Russian railway networks across the province. Train lines were redirected towards areas of strategic importance and sources of raw materials. The movement of coal was the most important consideration with the new planned railway lines, as coal-powered China's war industries and the efficient organisation of China's resources were key factors in preventing a Japanese victory in China. Instead, Japan was drawn into a long war of attrition that it was unable to win.

The military organisation of the railway system continued after 1945, as China's civil war that had been underway since the 1920s entered its final phase. After the war, the Guomindang launched the Five-Year Railway Construction Plan, first drafted in 1936. This once again set impossible and unrealisable targets for railway expansion. Some 8,317 miles of new track were planned, linking coal mines and agricultural regions to cities and ports, ensuring that the Nationalists, not the Communists, had access to China's mineral wealth and food supplies.

Jiang Jieshi believed that the war against the Communists would last for decades. He thought that by building rail networks that moved resources into Nationalist areas, Mao's forces could slowly be starved. The Five-Year Construction Plan required financial aid from abroad, but also the building of Chinese locomotive factories (something that had not been envisioned previously). Very little of the plan was achieved by the time of the overthrow of the Nationalist regime in 1949. When the Communist regime began to implement its own similar version of the plan, they only built 2,485 miles of track by 1963.

EXTEND YOUR KNOWLEDGE

Mao Zedong and the Communist Party of China

Mao Zedong was born in 1893 in Hunan province in rural China. His father was a former peasant who had escaped poverty by becoming a moneylender and grain merchant, eventually owning over 20 acres of land. Mao was an intelligent boy who was brought up as a Buddhist, but he rejected the religion as a teenager and became politically engaged with the crises that gripped China prior to the 1911 revolution. During the revolution, he witnessed how the landowning classes lost control of the countryside and were victims of mob violence from the peasants. He recounted later in life that he admired this violence and understood how the peasants could be used as instruments of class warfare - something he put into practice against landowners after 1949.

Mao was inspired by the October Revolution in Russia in 1917 and the creation of the world's first Communist workers' state and by 1919 had embraced **anarchism**, but he became a member of the Communist Party of China in Changsha in 1921. Initially the party had support and guidance from Bolshevik Russia, though Lenin did not believe that China was ready for revolution, and urged the Communists to forge alliances with the Guomindang for the foreseeable future. Members of the Communist Party joined the Guomindang in the hope that it would steer the Nationalist party towards the left.

By 1924, Mao sat on the central committee of the Communist Party of China, but he was also part of the Guomindang Central Executive Committee, and the Communists gradually came to control the left wing of the Guomindang party. However, when Sun Yat-sen died, the political climate within the Guomindang changed and the fiercely anti-Communist Jiang Jieshi came to power. Jiang always intended to do something about the Communist influence in the party, but he waited for his moment until the warlords and the northern **Beiyang government** had been dealt with. In 1927, during the joint military operation against the warlords called the '**Northern Expedition**', Jiang purged the Communists, murdering 5,000 in Shanghai alone. By May that year, the Communists had lost over 60 percent of their members.

KEY TERMS

Anarchism
A revolutionary political ideology that argues against the need for a state or powerful institutions controlling the lives of individuals.

Beiyang government
The post-revolutionary 'northern' government in Beijing, established by Yuan Shikai.

Northern Expedition
A military campaign fought by the Nationalists and Communists against China's warlords in order to reunify the country between 1926 and 1928.

Five-Year Plan
The Five-Year Plans were originally a Soviet policy of state-led industrialisation on a massive scale. Industries and government ministries were given demanding targets for production and the development of heavy industry. It was a policy that was directly applied to China by Mao.

Great Leap Forward
This was Mao's Second Five-Year Plan, 1958–62, which was a catastrophic failure. It led to a reduction in economic output and the most devastating famine of the 20th century.

Maoist railway development, 1949–76

Shortly after the People's Republic of China (PRC) was established in 1949, the new Communist government made plans for the railways and published ambitious targets for increasing the total amount of railway track. They roughly hit their target of 700 miles of new track laid each year for the next 15 years. In western China, which was the most industrially underdeveloped part of the country, 40 percent of all the new railway tracks planned for China were to be laid. All businesses in China were nationalised in the decade after 1949, including the railway companies, many of which were at first crippled by exorbitant taxes and the arbitrary arrest of company directors who had not already fled China.

The state-led industrialisation of China that occurred during the First **Five-Year Plan** and Mao's **Great Leap Forward** (see page 57) involved extensive railway-building. Hundreds of thousands of conscripted peasants were used, removing them from food production, which had disastrous consequences. In Yunnan province in 1957 for example, some 500,000 peasants were removed from the land to become industrial workers, and 10,000 of these were committed to building railways in one province. Unskilled labour and poor-quality steel resulted in lines being unable to take trains. They were either closed or they collapsed under the weight of trains.

In addition, the dramatic increase in economic activity was not matched by growth in railway capacity. This meant that the existing system of track was overwhelmed by the number of train journeys it had to accommodate. By 1959, both the rail and the road networks (see page 23) were paralysed as trains and lorries ran out of fuel and there were huge shortages of train wagons. As a result, food requisitioned from the peasants in order to feed the cities rotted in warehouses at stations. In Hunan in 1959, 200,000 tonnes of food sat in warehouses each month, but only 60,000 tonnes could be transported. This was due to an existing rail network that was barely adequate under normal conditions, combined with an economic policy that was hopelessly unrealistic. Mao and the Communist Party had no understanding of the impact that a massive increase in economic activity would have on the rail network.

The biggest expansion of the railway network under Mao began in 1964 in western China, which in 1949 had had only five percent of the nation's railway network. Fears of a Soviet Union threat to the west, and US involvement in Vietnam to the south-west, led Chinese planners to prepare a vast new defence infrastructure in the western provinces, and railways were a key part of this

A Level Exam-Style Question Section C

'China's economic development between 1860 and 1997 was mainly motivated by its need to defend itself and to wage war.'

How far do you agree with this opinion? (20 marks)

Tip

A strategy for answering this question would be to acknowledge the importance of war as a motivating factor, but also to examine how ideology, the need to raise living standards, and the personal ambitions of leaders played a part.

development. The industrialisation of western China was called the '**Third Front**'. Between 1964 and 1980, it consumed 40 percent of China's wealth, and 60 percent of new railways were built in western China. The same labour-intensive methods were employed to build a vast new rail network across the region, and the Communist authorities used ideas that involved mass participation in work schemes, shared sacrifice and the building of socialism in China to shore up morale.

KEY TERM

Third Front
A massive programme of defences in western China to protect the country against the threat of a Soviet invasion.

Most of the building work was across mountainous terrain, and workers' living conditions were poor. Towns and villages were often forced to house workers in barns and stables. Food consisted of rice porridge, and workers grew vegetables near the section of line they worked on to supplement their diet. A working day on the railways was eight hours of hard physical labour, for which the peasants were paid below the average labourer's wage. Of that wage, they actually received only a fifth of their pay in cash, with the rest going to pay for daily expenses. When deadlines approached and sections of track had not been completed, workers were obliged to offer 'voluntary' extra labour. The project, which began with ten new inter-provincial railway lines, involved conscripted peasants and 660,000 members of the Red Army Railway Corps.

Several economists and historians have argued that the Third Front was a mistake and that the resources used to build it could have been better allocated to eastern China, where existing industry could have been improved and China's GDP would have grown faster. It is also doubtful that the railway system would have been much use at the height of Sino-Soviet tensions in the late 1960s and early 1970s, as most lines across western China were incomplete until 1973. However, the new railways connected remote parts of China to the interconnected central and eastern provinces. This reduced travel times, led to a standard industrial measure of time being used uniformly across China, and brought about industrialisation. The Third Front began building a railway into Tibet, allowing China greater scope to colonise the country and to enforce military and police control over most aspects of Tibetan life.

During times of famine, such as between 1958 and 1962, the increased road and rail links made it easier for people to flee their homes to travel to less hard-hit areas. To deter this and to avoid people spreading news of disasters, guards were deployed at border crossings, checkpoints were set up in famine-hit villages, police monitored bus stops, and long-distance buses could only be driven by party members. Stations and railway depots were also manned by members of the railway public security bureau. Anyone who tried to escape was punished and had everything taken from them. There was very little famine-struck peasants could do but wait at home for death.

EXTEND YOUR KNOWLEDGE

Utilising peasant labour
Mao believed that China's advantage over other economies was its vast population. He viewed the Chinese people and particularly the peasants as a natural resource that was under-utilised. Mao believed that when the entire population was set to work it would be a match for the technological prowess of the USA and its allies and the industrial development of the Soviet Union. By collectivising and then communalising all peasant land in China (see page 29), Mao was able to control all peasant labour.

The majority of the workforce could be directed towards massive infrastructure projects such as roads, dams and irrigation. Initially, it appeared as if Mao's predictions about the mass deployment of peasant labour were right. By the Second Five-Year Plan, massive new engineering and infrastructure projects such as the Three Gate Gorge Dam (see page 31) were being completed, but at the cost of thousands of lives. Very little heavy machinery was used and the work of dam- and road-building was done almost entirely by hand.

Daily calorie intake was rarely more than half that required for a human being not undertaking heavy physical labour, and due to organisational chaos, often food would not arrive at mealtimes at all. Peasants were forced to live in improvised tent cities far from home, often in freezing conditions. To meet production targets, they were frequently forced to work all night without breaks, and many simply died of exhaustion. Deaths also occurred as a result of accidents and beatings from soldiers and cadres (see page 46). The levels of sacrifice frequently failed to be matched by the quality of the construction projects once they were completed.

Many roads, bridges and dams were rushed to completion and had serious structural flaws. Some were built in the wrong location or with poor-quality materials, and so within a few years were not fit for purpose. Peasants who died were either buried in unmarked graves or in the foundations of the construction projects that claimed their lives. Mao's projects built with mass labour frequently impressed foreign visitors to China, who marvelled at the apparent dedication and discipline of the workforce, but they actually represent a highly inefficient use of China's workforce. Productivity per peasant was extremely low, and the more important task that the peasantry normally attended to – growing food – was frequently disrupted, resulting in famine.

EXTRACT 5

From *The Penguin History of Modern China* by Jonathan Fenby (2010). Here the author examines the costs of the Third Front.

A vast programme was rolled out in a supposedly safe mountainous region of western China... 380 factories and their labour forces were moved inland from coastal areas. New enterprises were built, operating on a self-contained basis, cut off from towns and villages... As so often with Mao's sudden initiatives, everything had to be done at once, planning was rudimentary and costs soared as a result while projects fell further and further behind schedule and spread severe economic damage. This Third Front almost doubled spending on construction between 1966 and 1970 to 894 million yuan, with expenditure in the south-west leaping to nearly a quarter of the total. The new development ate up huge amounts of coal, power and steel. Pursuing this and 'all out civil war' [the Cultural Revolution] simultaneously, while keeping the general economy running and the country under some form of overall government was beyond the bounds of fantasy.

SOURCE 2 Chinese workers pull engineering equipment on a cart during the Great Leap Forward in 1958 at the height of the crisis in China's rail network.

ACTIVITY
KNOWLEDGE CHECK

Mao's influence on China's railways

1 What problems did rail and transport systems present to the Communist regime in times of famine?

2 Study Source 2. What might it suggest about the functioning of China's railway system?

Railways in the post-Mao era

Mao's successor Deng Xiaoping was acutely aware that railways and prosperity were linked; following the chaos of the **Cultural Revolution**, the rail network had been devastated. Within ten days of taking office, he commissioned a report that showed a 20 percent decline in all freight train journeys between 1965 and 1975. Serious rail accidents were ten times higher in 1975 than they had been a decade earlier, and large numbers of locomotives, carriages and wagons were damaged, with 40 percent fewer new trains being built to replace them than in 1965. Major rail hubs were blocked by track and signal faults, bringing large sections of the rail network to a standstill.

KEY TERM

Cultural Revolution
A period of intense social and economic upheaval in China, beginning in 1966 and ending with Mao's death a decade later. Radicalised student groups known as Red Guards were at the forefront of the revolution. They were fiercely loyal to Mao and attacked most established figures of authority, from party members to teachers and professionals.

In March 1975, following a crucial meeting of the Communist Party secretaries responsible for industry, the central committee of the Communist Party created the 'Decision on Improving the Work of the Railways'. It was drafted by Deng's minister for railways, Wan Li, who imposed directives to end the chaos in the railway system and regulations for punctuality of trains. Deng gave Wan Li far-reaching powers and authority to push through the changes as quickly as possible. This enabled him to mobilise large numbers of workers to rebuild railway infrastructure across the country. Wan Li was helped by the fact that Deng's reforms to industry (see page 60), railways and other parts of China were immensely popular after the chaos and bloodshed of the Cultural Revolution. This meant that workers, engineers and managers worked effectively together to improve the railway network and get the country's transport system moving again.

The development of roads in the 1930s

The building of modern highways in China began in the European treaty ports from the 1860s onwards. By the 1930s, the city of Shanghai closely resembled a European city with its waterfront, the Bund, modelled on Liverpool's docks in Great Britain. Across much of the country, the methods of transportation had not changed in centuries: cart tracks and footpaths connected towns and villages. These often became impassible in poor weather and were not suited to the dramatic increases in usage that occurred throughout the 19th century. The development of rail and steamship travel prevented China's rural routes from collapsing during the period.

Sun Yat-sen's focus had been on the development of China's railways as a means of binding the new republic together, but for Jiang Jieshi, the development of motorways and cars was the ultimate expression of modernity and evidence that China was emerging as an advanced and powerful nation. Throughout the Guomindang era (1928–49), road-building served a second purpose – namely to make it easier to wage war, first against the Communists and then against the Japanese invaders.

Jiang's road-building programme was far more rapid and successful than the Nationalist rail-development efforts. In 1936, there were 10,000 miles of railway and 71,457 miles of road, much of it built after the Japanese invasion of Manchuria in 1931. It was this colonisation of China that spurred road-building as Jiang, with German advice and assistance (see page 29), rapidly began to build a defence industry. Jiang developed thousands of miles of new roads in order to contain and crush the Communists. His encirclement of Mao's forces in Jiangxi saw the construction of 1,500 miles of new roads to keep his forces resupplied. The most strategically important stretch of road built by the Nationalists was the Burma Road, running over 700 miles over mountainous terrain from northern Burma to Kunming. Thousands of Chinese labourers commenced building the road in 1937, and it was used by Britain and the USA until 1942 to supply Jiang's armies with 20,000 tonnes of arms, food and fuel a month.

A huge labour force for road construction was in part a result of the Japanese invasion: large numbers of refugees and displaced people swelled the workforce and were desperate for any kind of employment. Some were not labourers originally, but had been skilled workers or professionals from the cities that were attacked by Japan. By 1939, the road was a stream of trucks moving 24 hours a day, and the drivers became some of the best-paid and most idolised figures in the Chinese workforce, with large amounts of cash to spend.

Embezzlement and corruption were rife in the road-building projects as contractors took large sums of money that was intended to fund construction. The Burma Road was a notorious example of this, and was largely paid for from Chinese-issued war bonds. Jiang's new automobile industry (which was in reality a US industry, producing US vehicles) was also financed in this way.

The development of the telegraph in the 1930s

KEY TERM

Telegraph
A 19th-century electric system of communication using Morse code and a network of cables that spanned the world by the eve of the First World War.

The transport revolution that China underwent in the later part of the 19th century was accompanied by a telecommunications revolution. Both were the result of European powers gaining concessions from China. The introduction of the **telegraph** into China sped up communications within China and between British officials in China and the rest of the British Empire. This meant that decisions about China's future could be taken in London often far more quickly than they could be in Beijing, and could then be transmitted to British officials in China.

The telegraph was the first system for rapidly transmitting information into and within China. It enabled European and US journalists to transmit stories about China back to their own readers, and it was adopted by Chinese journalists as dozens of local and national newspapers, journals and other publications developed. While the Boxers (see page 96) saw the telegraph as a symbol of Western modernity and profoundly anti-Chinese, many other people across the Qing Empire benefited from the telegraph and made good use of it in their daily lives. Urbanisation drew Chinese people away from the land to work in the towns and cities, and the telegraph enabled them to transmit messages and money back to their home villages. British businesses began to establish telegraphy companies in China from 1869 onwards, the first being the China Submarine Telegraph Company, which linked the treaty ports with undersea cables. China was linked to Europe via Singapore and India in 1871.

The Qing government was suspicious of the telegraph system. It saw it as a foreign intrusion into China and was understandably wary of Western motives in creating it. However, many Chinese businessmen, especially those who traded in treaty ports, could see its benefits. The government official Li Hongzhang and the Self-Strengthening Movement (see page 40) also petitioned the Qing government to allow a greater expansion of the telegraph network, but the key difference was that they believed it should be under Chinese control. Li argued for a telegraph network between Tianjin and Shanghai, and for a school to train telegraphers. He said it was both commercially important and also militarily essential: China had lost every war from 1842 to 1937, and poor communications were at the heart of most of these catastrophes. Li knew that as the European, US and Japanese powers became more accustomed to communicating rapidly through the telegraph, it gave them a powerful advantage. By 1887, the Chinese-owned Imperial Telegraph Administration had set up 76 telegraph stations and connected most Chinese cities, and other Chinese companies collaborated with foreign telegraph businesses.

In the 1920s and 1930s, the USA played a significant role in the development of the telegraph in China. The Federal Telegraph Company of California connected China to the USA by telegraph in 1921. This connected Chinese businesses and China's government to the USA, and enabled Chinese families to contact relatives who had emigrated to the USA to find work and start new lives. The company's building of telegraph stations across China meant that people living in cities such as Shanghai, Harbin and Guangzhou were able to access the new trans-Pacific link. This had a significant effect for many Chinese people who were living through a period of intense social and political upheaval. It connected them to new ideas and information from overseas, where friends, family and business contacts could give them information about the wider world.

By 1930, however, the USA had all but pulled out of telegraph provision in China due to pressure from Chinese Nationalists who did not want another vital part of the country's infrastructure falling into foreign hands. In addition, Japanese telegraph companies believed that they had the right to a monopoly over the telegraph network in China.

The decision of the USA to withdraw from China's telegraph network resulted in the closure of stations across China. The provision of telegraphy by the Chinese government (which had nationalised the Imperial Telegraph Administration in 1902–03) was patchy and inefficient. Telegraph wires often fell into disrepair as the government's priority throughout the decade was the defeat of the Communists, which consumed massive resources and saw essential infrastructure like the telegraph being neglected. After 1937 and the invasion of China by Japan, telegraph stations were seen as key objectives to be captured and controlled.

The development of air transport in the later 20th century

After the First World War, air power became the decisive means by which European states and Japan controlled their empires in the 1920s and 1930s. Nearly every government of the period was acutely aware that future wars would be fought from the air and decided by air power. In addition to military aviation, civil aviation rapidly developed throughout the inter-war period and became another part of the transport revolution in China. As with steam trains and steamships, aviation was introduced into China by foreign commercial interests but not, as had previously been the case, by Great Britain. The USA started the first commercial airline in China in 1929 when the Curtiss-Wright Corporation established China Airways. This became the China National Aviation Corporation after merging with the Chinese Air Company in 1937 following Japan's invasion of China. At the end of the **Chinese Civil War** in 1949, civil aviation was not a priority for the new regime, but developing military technology and acquiring fighter-jet technology in the 1950s from the USSR was.

Air travel was considered a bourgeois luxury that China could not afford, and in Mao's opinion it was deeply connected with capitalist consumerism. The Civil Aviation Administration of China (CAAC) passed between a variety of ministries and was eventually made a subsection of the Chinese air force during the Cultural Revolution. The result was chaos. A popular saying among pilots and aviation workers during the period, bitterly describing the collapse of the system was: 'fly a little or a lot, it's all the same; sell many or a few airline tickets, it's all the same; provide good service or bad, it's all the same; consume however much, it's all the same; lose money or make money, it's all the same.'

The costs of the development of the Third Front (see page 22) and the chaos of the Cultural Revolution saw a collapse in air safety standards, with 30 accidents between 1966 and 1976 leading to the loss of 30 planes. The CAAC was removed from air force control in 1979. In 1980, Deng sped up the rapid commercialisation of civil aviation, reducing the power of the bureaucracy and in 1985, the CAAC was made completely independent of state management. It became self-funding and established its own airlines: Air China, Air Southern and Air Eastern. Initially, and despite the reluctance of CAAC managers, the corporation was forced to rent aircraft from overseas. By 1989, there were four times as many Chinese commercial aircraft in use as there were in 1979, an increase from 143 to 722, and passenger travel increased by 436 percent. Nineteen new airports were built in the early 1990s and 29 more were upgraded and enlarged. Small airlines were established after 1984, when the government deregulated the industry and the overall cost of tickets declined dramatically. During the 1990s, competition for ticket sales led to price wars, which saw some tickets sold for less than 50 percent of the advertised price. By 1997, the industry was experiencing serious problems due to excess capacity – there were too many planes and airports for the level of demand for flights, and industry revenues slumped.

Aviation by the end of the 20th century had become an integral part of China's economic development, enabling mass internal migration through air travel for work and education. While unskilled workers poured into the Special Economic Zones from the countryside (see page 33 for more on the SEZs), skilled workers were able to access new jobs at higher rates of pay in distant cities due to the availability of cheap air travel. The increase in mobility of China's workforce had a significant effect on the economy. Skilled workers were not only comparatively rare in the decade after the Cultural Revolution (see page 23 for more on the Cultural Revolution), but they were also part of an immobile labour market. Deng's reforms (see page 48) and the development of travel meant that it was easier for skilled workers to find better-paid work, leading to increased economic growth. However, the low priority that air travel had been given by Mao meant that the aviation industry was still considerably less advanced than that of foreign rivals by 1997.

KEY TERM

The Chinese Civil War
A conflict between communist and nationalist forces that was fought between 1928 and 1949. Both sides were forced to suspend hostilities during the Second World War, but fighting resumed in 1945. In 1949 Mao Zedong and the communists were victorious and established the People's Republic of China. Nationalist armies were forced to retreat to Taiwan, where they established the Republic of China.

A Level Exam-Style Question Section C

'Communications change in China happened largely as a result of foreign intervention throughout the years 1860–1997.'

How far do you agree with this opinion? (20 marks)

Tip

Any question that makes broad statements about major changes over a long period of time is inevitably going to be problematic. The examiner is inviting students to critically evaluate the claim made here.

TO WHAT EXTENT WAS CHINA SUCCESSFULLY INDUSTRIALISED IN THE YEARS 1860–1997?

While China in 1860 was seen by Europe and Japan as the 'sick man of Asia', and was far less advanced than the European powers colonising Asia, it was not a completely un-industrialised country. China's diverse industrial economy in 1860 was primarily domestic, meaning that individual weavers, dyers, carpenters, metalworkers, bakers and brewers made goods to sell in their communities from their own homes. Factory-style manufacturing had yet to emerge in China, though in the European-occupied treaty ports and in Hong Kong, British industrialists were beginning to introduce mass production in industries such as the cotton industry.

The growth of textile production in Shanghai in the later Qing Empire

Prior to 1860, China and India had led the way in the production of cotton for 500 years. Britain's domination of the world cotton industry was comparatively new in the 19th century. However, China had not developed methods of industrial mass spinning and weaving of cotton – most production was done by individual workers. One reason for the lack of industrialisation of the cotton industry in China by 1860 was the status of Chinese women, who married early and left the workforce as a result. This meant that the pool of cheap, un-unionised labour necessary to work in cotton factories was absent. Another factor that meant large-scale manufacturing in China started far later than in Europe related to Chinese peasants, who were living in the countryside in large numbers and had no need to relocate to the cities. This meant that by 1860 there was not a vast army of workers in China's cities, desperate for employment on low wages.

The first major assault on Chinese domestic cotton spinning and weaving came in 1842 at the Treaty of Nanjing following the end of the First Opium War. This gave Britain the right to sell manufactured cotton garments directly into China, destroying the livelihoods of thousands of rural Chinese spinners, weavers and dyers. The result was widespread unrest targeted at foreign cotton imports, and riots in the 1860s in Guangzhou. However, Chinese industrialisation, modelled on the British factory system of production, only finally emerged in the 1890s. Textile factories were set up in the cities of the north and the east of China by nationalist-minded Chinese businessmen and government officials who saw that China's artisans were unable to compete with foreign imports. In the 1870s, woven cloth from British India imported into China was actually cheaper than raw Chinese cotton.

China's cotton workers

The slow start of China's cotton-manufacturing industry meant that, whereas the country had once been the largest cotton grower and manufacturer in the world, by 1900 it was the world's biggest cotton importer. Despite the decline of the domestic cotton industry among the peasants, it still accounted for a large proportion of the Chinese cotton industry and was only overtaken by industrial manufacturing in output in 1936. By the 1930s, Shanghai had become the largest and most industrialised city in China, mainly due to the cotton industry, and the majority of workers in the city's factories were engaged in textile work. The 1920s saw a dramatic increase in textile workers in the city, from 30,000 in 1921 to 131,000 in 1930. This was 50 percent of all workers in Shanghai. Many were women who could no longer work in textiles from home because of the decline in domestic work. They had to work in factories as they were still expected to provide part of the family income.

In the early 1920s, half of all textile workers were men, but strikes in 1921 and 1925 convinced factory owners to employ women, assuming they would be more passive and less militant. The work done by women and children was designated as 'unskilled', and therefore they were paid less than men doing the same work. Labour contractors would supply large numbers of female workers from the countryside and keep whatever pay they received. In return, the workers would receive accommodation and food, but often this was just a sleeping place that they shared with another worker, who slept as they worked, and a meagre diet of rice porridge and some vegetables. Trade union organisation among cotton workers resulted in strikes against these conditions, with 2.2 strikes per 1,000 workers (a tenth of the number of strikes that silk workers engaged in), but each strike averaging 2,800 participants (roughly ten times the size of silk workers' strikes).

SOURCE 3 From Mao Zedong's article 'The Chinese Government and the Foreigners' published in 1923 in the *Hsing Tao* newspaper.

We often say: 'The Chinese Government is the **counting-house** of our foreign masters'. Perhaps there are some who don't believe this. We also say: 'The false show of friendship by foreigners (especially Englishmen and Americans) is merely a pretence of "amity" in order that they may squeeze out more of the fat and blood of the Chinese people'. Perhaps there are some who don't believe this either. Ever since the prohibition against the export of cotton was repealed owing to the opposition of the foreigners, it has been impossible not to believe what we have just said to some extent. Now that the foreigners have put pressure on the government to abolish the cigarette tax in Chekiang and other provinces, it is impossible not to believe it a little more... If our foreign masters want to export cotton, the Council of Ministers thereupon abolishes the prohibition of the export of cotton; if our foreign masters want to bring in cigarettes, the Council of Ministers thereupon 'instructs the several provinces by telegram to stop levying taxes on cigarettes'. Again, I ask my 400 million brethren to ponder a little. Isn't it true that the Chinese Government is the counting-house of our foreign masters?

KEY TERM

Counting house
A treasury or anywhere that money is stored and counted.

SOURCE 4 A Chinese Communist propaganda poster in 1975 showing Mao with China's cotton farmers.

ACTIVITY
KNOWLEDGE CHECK

Mao and China's cotton

1. Study Source 3. What is Mao's view of the relationship between the Qing government and the foreign powers in relation to cotton? List the other ways in which China was disadvantaged in its dealings with Europe, the USA and Japan.
2. 'Mao was able to ensure the wealth of China's cotton was distributed fairly.' How far does Source 4 support this view? How valid is it?

Developments in Manchuria under the Japanese in the 1930s

Japan's interest in Chinese territory was based primarily around economic considerations. Japan had limited resources and a growing population, and had successfully industrialised in the late 19th century. This meant that the country was hungry for new resources and territory to colonise and develop. Some Japanese businessmen and politicians believed that Japanese colonisation of China could have positive outcomes for the Chinese. They believed that Japan could teach China how to become a modern industrialised country. Other voices within Japan's government, however, saw China as a colonial acquisition and nothing more.

KEY TERMS

Washington Conferences
A series of military and diplomatic meetings between the USA, Japan, China and European powers. The second of the two conferences focused on Japan's territorial rights in Asia.

State capitalism
This occurs when governments allow free markets for goods and services, but intervene on behalf of their national industries, subsidising them, nationalising them or providing the infrastructure they need to operate.

Kwantung Army
Japan's army of occupation in Manchuria. It had a great deal of autonomy and often took decisions of vital importance to Japan as a whole without the consent of the government in Tokyo.

At the Paris Peace Conference, the Japanese successfully demanded the Shandong peninsula near Beijing, which was a vital part of the entire Chinese eastern railway network, but they withdrew from these territories in 1922 following the **Washington Conferences**. In 1931, Manchuria was invaded. The whole of Manchuria was seized and renamed Manchukuo (see Chapter 5), and in order to access its vast material resources Japan undertook a huge programme of road and rail expansion, factory- and mine-building. Japan constructed new towns, harbours and telegraph lines, along with military fortifications. Japanese technicians, managers and engineers arrived in Manchukuo from Japan to direct the industrialisation of the region, but the vast majority of manual work was carried out by Chinese peasants and workers who were cheap to employ and used to poor living standards. Iron ore and coal mining were the most important industries developed in Manchukuo, and the resources that were extracted from the region were shipped not only to Japan but to the rest of the Japanese Empire that grew before and during the Second World War.

This infrastructure-building was a form of **state capitalism**. It helped to support Japan's economy which was struggling as a result of the Great Depression, but this was at the expense of Manchukuo. Japan found it was able to export to Manchukuo, and Japanese banks found investment opportunities in the province. Throughout the 1930s, the two economies were gradually merged until they were referred to by the Japanese as the 'Japan Manchukuo bloc economy'. Japan invested nearly 6 billion yen (the equivalent of US$1.5 billion dollars at the time) in Manchukuo industry and the two economies became heavily dependent on one another as a result.

The Japanese occupying military force, the **Kwantung Army**, worked in partnership with Japanese private businesses to exploit the region economically. The expansion of the South Manchuria Railway was the most significant Japanese infrastructure project during the 1930s. The railway line had been in Japanese hands since the Russo-Japanese War (see page 108). The company, also known as Mantetsu, was partly owned by the Japanese government, also built mines, harbours and towns along the railway's route. Manchukuo was so profitable to Mantetsu that it grew in value from 160 million yen to 1 billion yen in 20 years.

This shows that Japan was highly successful not only in economically developing Manchukuo but also in extracting wealth from it. With economic change in the region came social change. In the new towns and cities built by Mantetsu and protected by the Kwantung Army, a generation of Japanese immigrants settled and became the majority. The new towns and cities were built along Japanese lines and the new settlers often felt suspicious of the native Chinese.

Major Japanese conglomerates called Zaibatsu recognised how profitable Manchukuo could be for them. Through their own lobbying organisation, the Japan Industrial Club, they pressed the Japanese government for further expansion. The Zaibatsu were also forced to demand greater expansion by right-wing Japanese nationalists, who had even assassinated Zaibatsu leaders suspected of a lack of patriotism.

EXTEND YOUR KNOWLEDGE

China and Germany (1926–41)
After the 1911 revolution and before the Second World War, the European nation that gave most assistance in China's industrialisation was Germany. Both the Weimar and Nazi regimes helped the creation of a defence industry, roads and factories in China in return for exports of the country's abundant raw materials. It was initially German arms manufacturers who sold weapons into China during the country's civil war in the 1920s, and led the way for other industries.

Germany's army was limited by the Treaty of Versailles (see page 108), meaning that the country's arms industry had to look overseas for new clients. Jiang Jieshi looked to Germany for military and industrial expertise, and he knew that Germany's post-war weakness would prevent it having any colonial ambitions on Chinese territory.

From 1933 onwards and with the advent of the Nazi regime, China was an attractive partner as it had vast material resources that Germany hoped to stockpile for a planned future war. Germany began to invest in Chinese roads and railways in order to help with the export of raw materials. The two countries also developed a three-year plan to create a powerful Chinese defence industry to resist Japan. It meant that vital metals like tungsten for making stainless steel were controlled by the government, and new factories and chemical plants were built with German expertise and finance.

The First Five-Year Plan, 1953–57

In 1953, Mao's government embarked on a rapid expansion of China's industrial base. The First Five-Year Plan for industry began, and central targets were set for the production of iron, steel and coal. Mao received help and support from the Soviet Union, which offered a loan of two billion roubles (Mao had hoped for four billion). China found itself very dependent on the USSR for trade and financial assistance after 1949, as Mao ended economic relations with non-Communist countries. However, in 1952 Stalin announced that the USSR was not able to help China develop to the extent that Mao had envisaged, and demanded precious raw materials such as rubber and rare earth metals in return for Soviet assistance.

The Plan envisioned 694 major industrial developments being built between 1953 and 1957, with Soviet aid for 156 of them. These new projects included 24 power plants, steel mills and oil refineries, and most of them were based away from the coastal provinces (which Mao suspected of having Nationalist sympathies).

Mao had looked to Stalin for advice and guidance on all aspects of policy. Stalin, wary of a nuclear-armed USA, had demanded moderation and restraint in China, particularly with regard to creating a fully socialist economy. However, Stalin's death in 1953 meant that Mao was able to implement whatever policies he saw fit. He believed that he was now the most important figure in world Communism, and that his potential successors in the USSR were nonentities. Mao believed that he needed to create an economic policy even more radical than Stalin's Five-Year Plans in order to demonstrate this. The pace of change that Mao demanded had been questioned by Stalin before he died and also by Mao's own subordinates, Liu Shaoqi and Zhou Enlai. They had been given responsibility for the economy and used a team of economists and managers to plan a gradual transition to socialism, believing that private businesses would still have a significant part to play in China. Mao undermined both men and threatened them with dismissal, announcing that the entire economy, from agriculture to heavy industry, must be transformed into a socialist one in 10–15 years.

Mao had already created a state planning committee in 1952, headed by his close ally Gao Gang, the Communist party boss for Manchuria. Gao's appointment sidelined more cautious economic thinkers and put Mao in full command of economic policy. The majority of Chinese affected by the plan were peasants, whose land was subject to **collectivisation** as a result. In towns and cities, however, the reorganisation of the economy meant that small businesses were forced to join co-operatives and were stripped of their businesses and savings that had accrued over generations.

In total, 800,000 businesses were taken from their owners in 1956. Some of the dispossessed owners were able to continue working in their shops and factories as poorly paid state employees. However, the owners of major enterprises were better able to handle the transition to socialism and develop the connections necessary to get stable jobs with the state. Many were aware of the inevitability of nationalisation and so handed their businesses over without complaint, hoping for protection from

KEY TERM

Collectivisation
The policy of taking land out of the ownership of individual peasants. All land was owned by the village collective and all livestock and tools were shared.

senior members of the regime or from Mao himself. Those who found new jobs with the state were not labelled class enemies and survived until the advent of the Cultural Revolution, when they were denounced, imprisoned and in some instances killed.

At first glance, it appears that China's productivity dramatically increased due to the Five-Year Plan. Between 1953 and 1957, steel production leapt from 1.3 million tonnes a year to 5.2 million tonnes, and coal production almost doubled during the same period. However, grain was requisitioned from the countryside to pay the Soviet Union for its investment and expertise, and to feed the cities. This created rural hunger and partly caused the 1958–62 Great Famine, which killed an estimated 40 million people. The perceived successes of the First Five-Year Plan convinced Mao and his allies in the party that further plans would yield even greater successes and that they must be pursued with vigour.

EXTEND YOUR KNOWLEDGE

The role of Soviet advisers in China

All of Mao's most fundamental economic and industrial policies had previously been put into practice in the USSR. The Five-Year Plans and collectivisation had both been key parts of Russia's economic development in the 1930s, and Mao believed they could be applied directly to China. After Mao visited Stalin in Moscow in 1949, the USSR became China's biggest economic partner. Thousands of Russian economists, engineers, agronomists and management specialists crossed into China at Mao's request to help bring Stalinist industrialisation to China.

A shortage of Chinese specialists meant that Mao's regime became dependent on Soviet expertise, and Sino-Soviet companies that were founded as joint partnerships were run almost entirely by Soviet staff. As relations between the two powers deteriorated, Mao became increasingly resentful of the presence of Soviet advisers in China. By the mid-1950s, the number of Soviet advisers had decreased dramatically as Chinese specialists were trained in Soviet-style management and planning principles.

Approximately 7,000 Chinese managers and engineers had been trained in Russia during China's First Five-Year Plan. One steelworks at An Shan sent 700 staff to the USSR. During this period, the USSR helped China by transferring technology, following the signing of the Sino-Soviet Scientific and Technical Co-operation Agreement in 1954.

The USSR gave China the blueprints for 600 types of factory, 1,700 kinds of industrial machines and information on production processes. In a second agreement in 1956, the USSR gave advice on hydroelectricity, irrigation and civil aviation. The Soviet Union hoped to see an industrialised China that could be a strong trading partner, which would benefit the economies of both countries.

Electrification

In 1949, there were 33 small hydroelectric power plants across China, providing a fraction of the electricity that the country needed. Mao's policy of electrification brought the biggest and most immediate benefits to rural China, which in 1949 consumed 0.5 percent of the country's electricity. From 1949 to 1999, nearly a billion more Chinese people had access to electricity, and in 2015 the numbers without power were under 100 million. Considering the rapid growth in the population, this was a significant accomplishment.

In 1949, there was little money or expertise available to rapidly expand the electricity grid, and its development was centrally planned until 1977. However, hydroelectricity was developed in China at an enormous human and environmental cost. By January 1958, one-sixth of the entire Chinese population was engaged in digging dams and other irrigation projects. This massive transfer of labour from food production to manual labouring caused crops to go unplanted and unharvested, and was a major contributing factor in the famine that followed (see page 47).

Due to a lack of heavy machinery, nearly all dam-building was done by hand, but for each project thousands of lives were lost due to overwork. Some dams, such as the Ming Tombs Dam near Beijing, never generated any electricity or preserved any water because they were built in the wrong locations and therefore dried up after a few years.

In 1958, the Communist Party experimented with the electrification of 100 villages in five separate counties, and three years later the government began to devolve the responsibility for managing the electricity system in rural villages to county administrations. This was the start of a trend that ended up with two separate electricity systems, one for local and regional areas and the other which was national and supplied heavy industry and China's cities.

The electrification of China's villages brought important advantages to the Communist Party. It enabled public-address loudspeakers to be installed in villages (previously these had been run from generators), which allowed Maoist propaganda to be heard across rural China. It also demonstrated to China's peasants that the regime was able to make significant changes in their lives. By the end of the 1970s, China had access to more electricity than at any time in the country's history, but it still suffered from significant energy shortages.

After 1977 and the end of Maoism, the management and development of the electricity grid were handed over to local governments. During the First Five-Year Plan (see page 29), electrification technology imported from the USSR had been used to create hydroelectric plants which powered heavy industry, but rural China saw little if any improvement in the provision of electricity.

A survey in 1979 revealed that 40 percent of the rural population had been short of energy for cooking for more than three months. The market reforms introduced by Deng Xiaoping after 1978 (see page 48) resulted in an increase in rural electrification during the 1980s. This was mainly because counties and provinces had been given control over investment in electrification, and it was no longer a centralised, state-led process. The growth of small business in special economic zones called Township and Village Areas (TVAs) required greater electrification and generated the wealth to reinvest in the electricity grid. Local areas with suitable water resources were encouraged to establish their own hydroelectric dams from 1983 onwards, and China began the biggest project of dam-building in history.

In the 14 years from 1983 to 1997, the Chinese government used hydroelectric power to electrify every village in 650 counties, but the building of coal-fired power stations had a greater effect on the rest of the country. Coal was seen by the Chinese government as being a far more reliable source of power, but by the end of the 20th century China was suffering from appalling air pollution problems as a result.

EXTEND YOUR KNOWLEDGE

The Three Gate Gorge Dam

One of Mao's ambitions during the Second Five-Year Plan (more commonly referred to as the Great Leap Forward), was to build a dam on the Yellow River, one of China's largest waterways. For centuries, the river had continually flooded, devastating low-lying farmland and killing large numbers of peasants.

Mao believed that if he could dam the river and prevent it flooding, he would be remembered as a saviour of China. He also believed that water could be used to irrigate barren lands in the north and dams could be created to control floods in the south. If water was directed throughout China the way Mao demanded, he believed it would lead to massive increases in grain production. This would power China into industrialisation, giving the country a food surplus to sell overseas and pay for new industrial infrastructure. It would also ensure that workers in the cities could be fed cheaply. In much of Mao's writing on industrialisation, he believed that nature was a force that had to be tamed and a 'war' needed to be waged against it.

From 1952, he had begun to visit the Yellow River flood plains near the city of Kaifeng, and indicated that something must be done about the river. With help from Soviet surveyors, a site for a dam was located at Three Gate Gorge in Henan. It was estimated that a million peasants would have to leave the villages where they and their families had lived for centuries.

Even when the project began in 1957, some engineers suggested that it could have fundamental flaws. The Yellow River was full of silt (it was named because of its colour), and it transported 1.6 billion tonnes of sediment each year. Several engineers pointed out that this silt would undermine the dam if it was allowed to build up behind it. Mao angrily rejected these claims and denounced the engineers in the *People's Daily* newspaper.

Tens of thousands of workers and peasants blocked the river by 1958 and the dam was built a year later. It included hydroelectric turbines which began to generate electricity. The sediment raised water levels up-river and caused the flooding of Xi'an, which meant that the dam had to be redesigned to allow the silt to flow through. Not only did Mao's pledge to make the 'Yellow River run clear' fail to materialise as the silt deposits flowed freely again, but the water level also fell, ensuring that the hydroelectric turbines stopped working. The dam was initially heralded as an achievement of Mao's ideas, but by 1961 it was so silted up that it ceased to be a showcase for foreign visitors.

THINKING HISTORICALLY Change (7a)

Convergence and divergence

Changing communications 1860–1964

1860	1868	1881	1922	1964
British defeat China for a second time	First Chinese steamships set sail	First section of railway laid between Tianjin and Tangshan	Sun Yat-sen's Railway Plan announced	Mao's Third Front in western China begins

Industrial development 1860–1964

1860	1915	1930	1949	1953
Cotton riots in Guangzhou against foreign imports	Twenty-One Demands give Japan far-reaching controls over Chinese industry	Shanghai becomes the biggest industrial cotton producer in China	The start of a decade of nationalisation of Chinese industry	First Five-Year Plan commenced, coinciding with Stalin's death

1 Draw a timeline across the middle of a landscape piece of A3 paper. Cut out ten small rectangular cards and write the above changes on them. Then place them on the timeline with communications events above the line and industrial events below. Make sure there is a lot of space between the changes and the line.

2 Draw a line and write a link between each change within each strand, so that you have four links that join up the changes in the communication part of the timeline and four that join the industrial changes. You will then have two strands of change: *communication* and *industrial*.

3 Now make as many links as possible across the timeline between political change and religious change. Think about how they are affected by one another and think about how things can link across long periods of time.

You should end up with something like this:

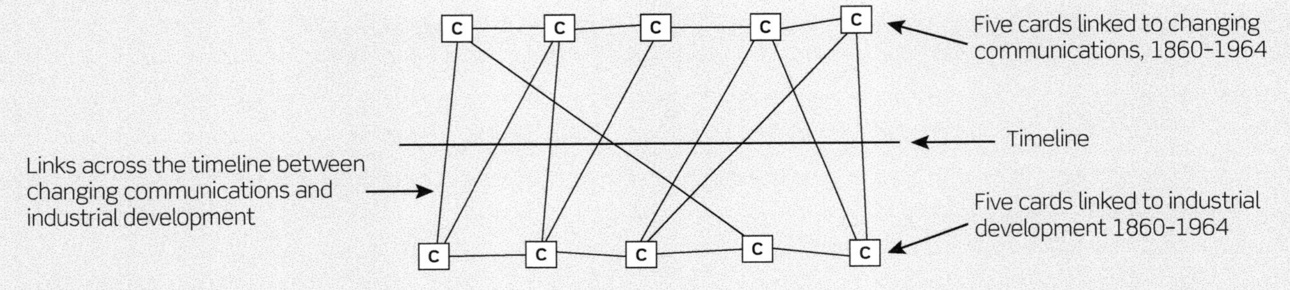

4 How far do different strands of history interact with one another? Illustrate your answer with two well-explained examples.

5 At what point do the two strands of development converge (i.e. when do the changes have the biggest impact on one another)?

6 How useful are the strands in understanding the impact of changing communications and industry on China's independence between 1860 and 1964?

Technological innovation in the digital age

The Sino-Soviet split saw a dramatic change in the way China accessed scientific and technological information. Between 1949 and 1961, Chinese academics and scientists translated engineering, physics and chemistry textbooks and papers from the USSR (80 percent of all books imported into China in the 1960s were science and technology based). However, by the 1970s the fear that the Soviet Union posed a major strategic threat to China caused a shift towards the USA as a source of technological knowledge. In the last decade of his life, Mao Zedong was acutely aware of the problems China faced due to poor scientific and technological knowledge.

The Cultural Revolution and ongoing 'thought reform' from the 1950s onwards had devastated China's universities and schools, weakening scientific research and innovation. Mao was divided in his attitude towards the West. He believed that the stalemate achieved in the Korean War (see page 163) showed that superior Western technology had not outmatched Chinese revolutionary zeal, and he also resented the idea that the answers to China's problems lay overseas.

However, at the same time he recognised that China had to learn from the West and he was keen to adopt Western technology, particularly in the field of computing. When US President Richard Nixon visited China in March 1972, he and Mao agreed that as part of the thaw in relations between the two countries, China would receive a technology transfer. However, this did not formally occur until 1979. When Deng Xiaoping visited the USA, both countries signed 25 protocols for co-operation in scientific and technological projects, and Chinese technicians visited US laboratories, factories and production lines.

SOURCE 5 Deng Xiaoping applauding US President Jimmy Carter in 1979 in a state visit to the USA. Deng visited the USA to see how it had become wealthy from using modern technology, and to arrange technology transfers to China.

In the 1980s and 1990s, Special Economic Zones (SEZs) such as Shenzhen in China opened, where international high-technology manufacturers exploited a low-wage workforce to create components for computers, mobile phones and microchips. Much of the technology itself was designed overseas and Chinese businesses manufactured or assembled it. To the Chinese Communist Party (CCP), the USA and Europe represented available investment and sources of technology that could be transplanted to the enterprise zones, and they were also markets for finished products.

By 1985, exports reached US$25 billion (though not all from high-tech manufacturing) compared to US$10 billion in 1978. Businesses found investing in the SEZs attractive because of tax breaks and subsidies, and the products they made were not sold into China, so did not threaten domestic Chinese businesses. In 1992, Deng ensured that the reforms he had begun in 1978 would continue. At the party congress that year, he promoted younger party members to key positions within the government, excluding many of his contemporaries who had come to power in 1949.

These younger **technocrats** had grown up with Deng's reforms since 1978 and accepted them unconditionally as the correct path for China. They prevented conservatives (who were critical of Deng in the aftermath of student protests that ended in the Tiananmen Square massacre) from demanding an end to the reforms.

KEY TERM

Technocrat
Someone skilled or knowledgeable about science or technology, who has influence with the ruling power.

Deng's beliefs about 'thought reform'

During the Cultural Revolution, large numbers of academics, scientists, intellectuals and teachers had been sent to work as peasant labour in the countryside on large communes. The ideological purpose behind this was to re-educate supposed 'bourgeois' class enemies in the revolutionary values of the peasantry. Mao believed that if they were reduced to peasant living standards and forced to work with their hands and experience the same back-breaking labour as the peasants, then they would become better revolutionary citizens. Deng viewed this as an enormous waste of resources. He did not think that academics and intellectuals were in any way improved by experiencing poverty and stated that 'poverty is not socialism'. He argued that the time and resources that had gone into training an expert were wasted by sending them to work in unskilled labour roles for years on end. Deng rehabilitated many academics who had survived the Cultural Revolution and returned them to roles in education.

EXTEND YOUR KNOWLEDGE

Hong Kong and Chinese trade

Both the Guomindang and Communist governments viewed Hong Kong before 1997 as sovereign Chinese territory, and Mao saw the island colony as an outpost of imperialism and a threat to his regime. During periods of high tension, such as the Korean War and the Cultural Revolution, Hong Kong was spared the threat of invasion, even though there was little that Britain could have done if Mao had decided to seize the colony. Mao managed to continue trading with the capitalist world through Hong Kong during the embargo placed on China as a result of the Korean War.

Despite his determination to eradicate capitalism in China, Mao still saw the strategic value of a capitalist outpost on China's border. However, after 1979, this policy of unofficial toleration towards Hong Kong changed. Deng recognised that Hong Kong, while a separate state, was an integral part of China's economic success and was a gateway for international trade and finance to access cheap labour and resources in China. Hong Kong Chinese businessmen and women invested in China and international businesses that wished to do business in the new SEZs established their headquarters in Hong Kong. However, Deng was aware that the colony was also a democratic society, and the first elections to Hong Kong's legislative council were held in 1985.

He did not wish to see Hong Kong's democratic practices transferred to China to 'contaminate' the mainland. In the ten years after 1979, Hong Kong contributed 59 percent of all foreign direct investment into China. It was China's largest trading partner, with 48 percent of all Chinese exports going to Hong Kong (normally commodities like rice, with 83 percent being resold across the rest of Asia). Only 29 percent of imports into China from Hong Kong throughout the 1980s were manufactured in Hong Kong, the rest came from overseas. These statistics show that Hong Kong had a special role as a gateway into China, making importing and exporting easier.

SOURCE

From a speech entitled 'The reform of the system for managing science and technology is designed to liberate the productive forces', given by Deng Xiaoping on 7 March 1985 at the National Conference on Work in Science and Technology.

I am very pleased that nowadays even the peasants in mountainous areas know that science and technology are part of the productive forces. They may not have read my speech, but through their own practice they have come to realise that scientific and technological advances can help them expand production and become prosperous. Peasants regard scientists and engineers as brothers who help them shake off poverty; they refer to them as the 'gods of wealth'. That term was invented not by me but by the peasants. But it means the same thing I was trying to say in my speech at the conference on science.

I am also happy that comrades in scientific and technological circles have done so much work over the past few years. Our country's economic development is sound, and the prospects are getting better year by year. The people are pleased about that, and the whole world has recognised it. This includes your contribution. The Central Committee of the Party has called for the work in science and technology to be geared to the needs of economic development. You comrades have worked hard and scored many achievements. In addition, regarding yourselves as the masters of the country, you have put forward many good ideas for it. Whenever our scientists, professors and engineers visit a factory or a local area, they are warmly received and invited to offer advice on the country's strategies, prospects and programmes. In our thousands of years of history it is unprecedented for scientists and engineers to take part in making decisions on economic and social policy. This shows that they enjoy much higher political and social status than ever before. The better you do your work and the more achievements you have to your credit, the better the people throughout the country will understand the value of knowledge and the more they will be encouraged to respect and acquire it. It is by your work that people judge the role of science and technology in the modernisation programme and the importance of scientists and engineers.

ACTIVITY
KNOWLEDGE CHECK

Industry and foreign policy under Deng Xiaoping

Study Sources 5 and 6. What do they indicate about Deng's technology and foreign policies? How did industrial and foreign policy relate to one another?

SOURCE

From Mao's speech, 'On the correct handling of contradictions among the people', 27 February 1957, at the end of the First Five-Year Plan.

Under the rule of imperialism, feudalism and bureaucrat-capitalism, the productive forces of the old China grew very slowly. For more than fifty years before liberation, China produced only a few tens of thousands of tons of steel a year, not counting the output of the north-eastern provinces. If these provinces are included, the peak annual steel output only amounted to a little over 900,000 tons. In 1949, the national steel output was a little over 100,000 tons. Yet now, a mere seven years after the liberation of our country, steel output already exceeds 4,000,000 tons. In the old China, there was hardly any machine-building industry, to say nothing of the automobile and aircraft industries; now we have all three. When the people overthrew the rule of imperialism, feudalism and bureaucrat-capitalism, many were not clear as to which way China should head - towards capitalism or towards socialism. Facts have now provided the answer: Only socialism can save China. The socialist system has promoted the rapid development of the productive forces of our country, a fact even our enemies abroad have had to acknowledge.

EXTRACT

In *Mao: The Unknown Story* (2005), Jung Chang and Jon Halliday claimed that the First Five-Year Plan was devised by Mao to build up China's military power, making the country a super power and Mao a world leader.

Mao was in a rush for his arsenal. In September 1952, when Chou [Zhou] Enlai gave Stalin Beijing's shopping list for its First Five Year Plan, Stalin's reaction was: 'This is a very unbalanced ratio [of military production to civilian production]. Even during wartime we didn't have such high military expenses.'... According to official statistics, spending during this period on the military, plus arms-related industries, took up 61 per cent of the budget - although in reality the percentage was higher, and would rise as the years progressed.... The Chinese people were told, vaguely, that the equipment from the USSR used in China's industrialisation was 'Soviet aid', implying that the 'aid' was a gift. But it was not. Everything had to be paid for - and that meant mainly with food, a fact that was strictly concealed from the Chinese people and still largely is. China in those days had little else to sell. Trade with Russia, Chou told a small circle, 'boils down to us selling agricultural products to buy machines'. Throughout the 1950s, 'the main exports were rice, soya beans, vegetable oil, pigs' bristles, sausage skins, raw silk, pork, cashmere, tea and eggs', according to official statistics. What China was exporting to Russia, and its satellites, consisted overwhelmingly of items that were basic essentials for its own people, and included all the main products for which China's population depended for protein.

EXTRACT

From *Mao's China and After* by Maurice Meisner (1977).

Between 1952 and 1957 Chinese industry grew at an even more rapid pace than the ambitious 14.7 percent yearly increase set in the Plan. The actual per annum increase was 18 percent, according to official statistics and 16 percent according to more conservative Western estimates. Total Chinese industrial output more than doubled, and growth rates in key heavy industries were even greater. Rolled steel production, for example, increased from 1.31 million metric tons in 1952 to 4.48 million in 1957; cement from 2.86 million to 6.68 million; pig iron from 1.9 million to 5.9 million; coal from 66 million to 130 million; and electric power from 7.26 billion kilowatt hours to 19.34 billion. In addition, China was now for the first time producing small but significant numbers of trucks, tractors, jet planes and merchant ships. In all... the Chinese industrial production between 1952 and 1957 grew more rapidly than Russian industry during the first Soviet Five Year Plan in 1928–32.

Evidence (6c)

Comparing and evaluating historians' arguments

In the period studied in this chapter, China was ruled by several different types of regime, from imperial to Nationalist and then Communist. In Source 7, Mao compares the industrial achievements of the previous regimes to that of the ruling Communist Party.

Inevitably, Mao made claims about the success of Communist Party industrial policy in comparison to the achievements of other eras. It is the job of historians to critically evaluate how accurate these claims are. We cannot simply dismiss them or assume they are accurate, but must compare them to other available data and examine the views of other historians.

Extracts 6 and 7 are two historians' verdicts on Mao's First Five-Year Plan.

1. Are there any areas of agreement between Extracts 6 and 7 at all? Create two columns showing where they differ. Is it possible for both perspectives to be valid?
2. How strong are the assertions in Extracts 6 and 7? Do the historians sound confident in their views? How are they using language to show this?
3. Which historian's views are most similar to Mao's pronouncements in Source 7? Are there issues that one or both of the historians raise that are not addressed by Mao's speech?
4. Are both historical accounts equally credible, or are there reasons to prefer one over the other?

Conclusion

By 1997, China had successfully become a major manufacturing and industrial power with a strong network of rail, road, water and air transport. However, throughout the period 1860–1997 the efforts of numerous Chinese leaders had both positive and negative impacts on this process of development. In addition to this, China did not develop in isolation; European, Japanese and US businesses and governments had a key role to play in China's economic transition. Economic change also happened within the context of a revolutionary century for China. Two dramatic changes of government occurred in 1911 and 1949 and China also experienced invasion and war, which saw the loss of large parts of the industrial economy, but also the development of economic output to defeat Japan.

The development of transport in China appears to have been integral to binding the country together during periods of civil war and revolutionary upheaval. Railways, roads, steamships and telegraph technologies did more than simply allow Chinese people to traverse the vast distances across the country, they helped to develop China as a nation state. The idea that one might cross the entire country by rail or that people at the periphery of China might be connected to the centre in Beijing fostered in many Chinese people a stronger sense of nationhood, which is why Nationalists like Sun Yat-sen sought to build railways. After 1949, Mao saw railways and industry as key to China's defence. He strongly suspected that China would face external enemies seeking to overthrow the Communist revolution, and he believed that rapid industrialisation was the way to prevent this.

Following Mao's death, China underwent another phase in radical economic development, but one that was based far more in pragmatism than in ideology. Deng Xiaoping, like Li Hongzhang, sought to use relationships with foreign powers to transform China's economy and transport infrastructure. Despite the introduction of SEZs and Deng's visit to the USA to arrange a transfer of technology, the Communist Party maintained control of power. In this regard, there are similarities to the Qing government before 1911: both rulers wanted the economic benefits that improved transport, communications and industry could bring, but neither was willing to allow any political change to occur as a result, even though dramatic social changes occurred. Between 1860 and 1997, the Chinese population reacted to changes in transport and industry in a variety of ways. Some welcomed steam trains, ships and aircraft, while others were more apprehensive about the pace of technological development. Throughout the Qing, Nationalist and Communist regimes, China's industrial workforce gradually grew and often experienced hard living and working conditions. Industrial development often failed to be matched by improved living standards. This suggests that throughout the period, while industrial and transportation development was a priority for governments, improving living standards often was not.

ACTIVITY
SUMMARY

Bringing about industrial change

1. What do you think was the most significant industrial or communications change in China throughout the period 1860–1997? Find evidence within the chapter to support your argument.
2. To what extent had China industrially modernised by 1997? Present evidence to support your argument.
3. 'Mao Zedong's industrialisation of China was largely a failure.' How valid is this statement? Present evidence to support your view and contrast Mao's policies with those of Sun Yat-sen and Jiang Jieshi.
4. How far do you agree with the view that industrialisation in China between 1860 and 1997 was the result of European intervention?

WIDER READING

Bickers, R. *The Scramble for China: Foreign Devils in the Qing Empire, 1832–1914* (second edition), Penguin UK (2016)

Caryl, C. *Strange Rebels: 1979 and the Making of the 21st Century*, Basic Books (2013)

Dikötter, F. *The Tragedy of Liberation: A History of the Chinese Revolution 1945–1957*, A&C Black (2013)

Fenby, J. *The Penguin History of Modern China*, Penguin (2010)

3.2 Ideologies and individuals behind economic growth

KEY QUESTIONS

- To what extent was economic growth driven by ideas and ideologies in the years 1860–1997?
- How far were key individuals responsible for bringing about economic growth in the years 1860–1997?

INTRODUCTION

An ideology, put simply, is a system of ideas or beliefs that human beings create to understand or change the world. In China in the 19th and 20th centuries, they have exerted enormous power and brought about immense change, and this chapter explores how ideologies have influenced economic growth. In addition to the power of ideas, key individuals have also played a part in transforming China from a declining empire at the mercy of Europe and Japan, to an economic powerhouse by the end of the 20th century.

Historians are frequently divided over the question of the role of 'great men' in history. From the 1960s onwards, the belief that famous individuals were mainly responsible for shaping events became less accepted and a 'history from below' approach was more widely adopted. This suggested that change happened because of the collective actions of large numbers of unknown men and women who made up social classes and groups. In recent years, however, the focus on leaders and their ideas has become significant again, and this chapter examines not only the actions of important individuals, but also their thoughts and values and the way these were communicated to the Chinese people.

TO WHAT EXTENT WAS ECONOMIC GROWTH DRIVEN BY IDEAS AND IDEOLOGIES IN THE YEARS 1860–1997?

Ideas and ideologies as factors promoting change, 1860–1997

Chinese ideas about economic growth before the defeat in the Opium Wars were based on inflexible concepts of Chinese superiority. For centuries, the successive dynasties that had occupied the imperial throne had viewed China as the centre of world civilisation and knowledge. They saw everything beyond their borders as barbaric and backward. This unchanging view of China was in part based on a long history of innovation and scientific knowledge. However, by the 19th century Europe had undergone an industrial revolution and China's technological advantages had long since been lost.

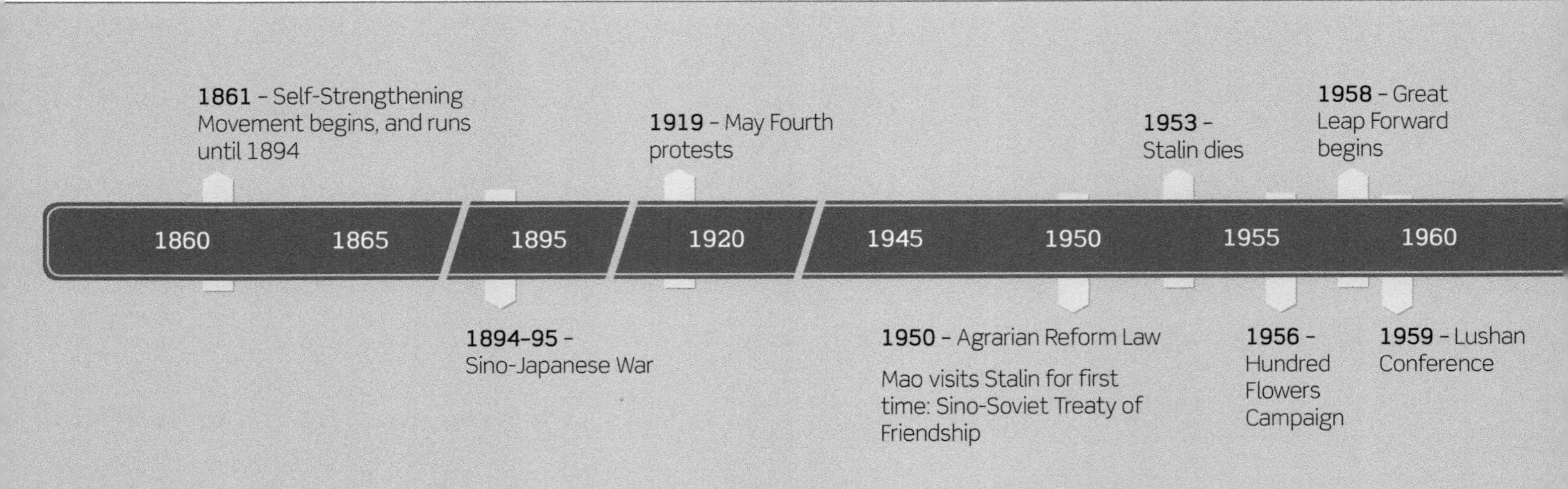

One major obstacle to change was the imperial throne itself. Each emperor was supposed to represent harmony between heaven and earth, and dramatic economic change was interpreted as a threat to this balance. A second factor likely to stifle economic change was the stratified nature of Chinese society. Each emperor governed the vast and diverse empire with a huge bureaucracy. Throughout rural China, notable figures in towns and villages had authority as a consequence of the rank that was bestowed on them. This vast structure of governance was made up of thousands of magistrates and administrators with a vested interest in maintaining the status quo, so new ideas were rarely adopted if they challenged traditional **Confucian beliefs**.

Despite these obstacles, by 1860 new economic ideas and ideologies had emerged in China. A belief began to spread that **industrialisation**, trade and commerce, and a new system of banking and finance were needed to help modernise China. Some of these concepts were introduced by European traders, missionaries and imperialists, and others were adopted by outward-looking Chinese merchants and **mandarins**. Before Europeans had started to dominate China's waterways (see page 10), rivers such as the Yangtze were used for trade, with junks and sampans carrying goods between China's major cities. Banking had also developed in China before 1860, and not all banks were the product of European treaty ports – Chinese merchants had lent money to each other and to the peasants for centuries.

The key difference between trade and finance in Europe and in China was the fact that China had not had an industrial revolution. This lack of industrialisation was largely due to the ideas and beliefs that dominated China. Moneylending did not initially support the building of factories or railways, and the imperial government did not favour this type of economic activity. Instead, the dominant economic beliefs in China supported continuity, not change. This meant that the dynamism of 19th-century capitalism that created industrial revolutions and provided the modern means for waging war in Britain and the rest of Europe was alien to China by 1860. The result, was decades of crisis as China struggled to catch up with Europe and prevent further losses of sovereignty.

KEY TERMS

Confucian belief
Confucius was a 6th-century BCE Chinese philosopher whose ideas dominated Chinese culture throughout imperial times. His teachings centred on traditional values and respect for authority and the established order. In China, this meant support for the emperor, and China being the dominant country in South Asia.

Industrialisation
The development of an economy based on mass production of goods in factories with a large industrial workforce.

Mandarin
One of the Qing Empire's senior administrators and bureaucrats. The mandarins exercised immense power in the running of China.

Free trade
The principle that goods should be traded internationally without any taxes, tariffs or other obstacles.

EXTEND YOUR KNOWLEDGE

Western economic ideas and China

Since the mid-18th century, Great Britain and other European powers had become wealthy and powerful around the world, due in part to the commercial ideas they adopted. From the 1830s onwards, Britain was able to introduce new commercial and industrial ideas into China (see Chapter 3). The British believed in, and demanded, **free trade** and were willing to go to war when this principle was threatened. By 1860, free trade had been effectively imposed on China by Britain following the Opium Wars. It led to an influx of cheap manufactured British and European goods into China which Chinese hand-made goods could not compete with in terms of price or quality.

Chinese officials like Li Hongzhang believed that it would be impossible to prevent trade with the rest of the world on these terms, and instead China needed to industrialise. Industrialisation was also a Western economic idea that had developed throughout the 19th century and had given Europe key advantages over China. In the period 1860–1997, China became one of the most industrialised countries in the world, and by the end of the 20th century it had become a net exporter of manufactured goods.

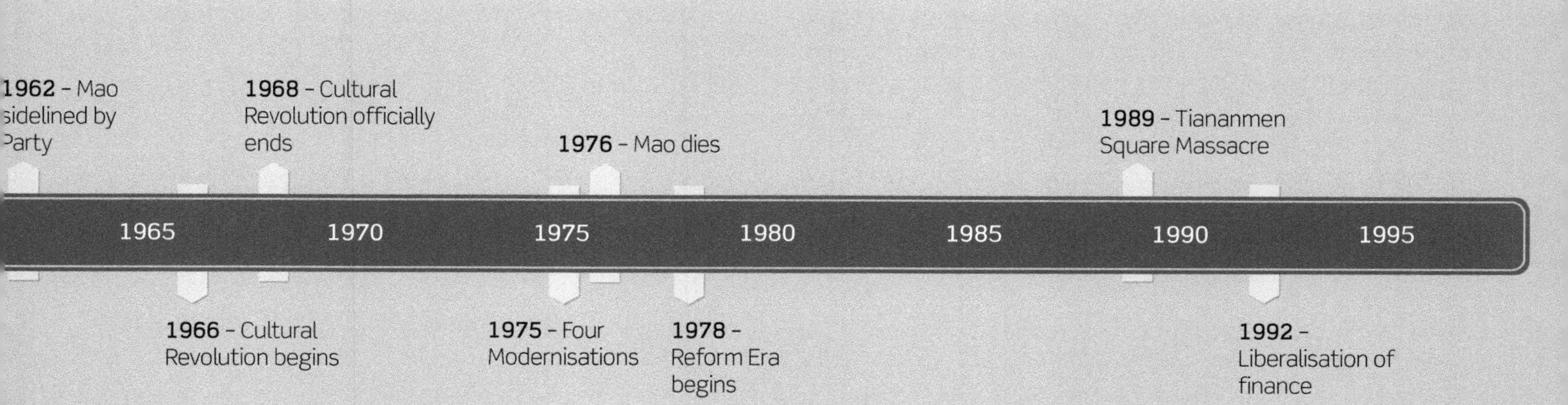

The Self-Strengthening Movement, 1861–95

In the aftermath of China's second defeat by the British in 1860, the mandarin Li Hongzhang (see page 50), instituted the start of three decades of economic reform. This process became known as the Self-Strengthening Movement, and the ideas at its heart were relatively straightforward.

- Li argued that in order to force foreign armies from Chinese soil, China must first be economically powerful. The nation must be patient and bide its time, building up the country's industrial base and not risk war with a European power too soon.
- While the economy should be transformed, the imperial government should remain unchanged, as changes to the Qing dynasty might trigger a political or social revolution.

The regent to the Tongzhi and Guangxu emperors, Prince Gong, and his closest royal confidants were enthusiastic about economic change along Western lines. Gong was receptive to Li's suggestions when he realised that China's military strength would be improved. Many veterans of the Opium Wars and the Taiping Rebellion became enthusiastic supporters of the movement, initially seeing it as a means of equipping China with a modern arsenal to repel foreign invaders.

The idea of a self-strengthening movement was first suggested by the Chinese intellectual Feng Guifen in 1861. He approached the Qing administrator and former general Zeng Guofan that year with a series of essays explaining the changes that needed to take place in China. He believed that Confucian ideas should remain the basis of Chinese society, and that Western scientific ideas should simply be employed as a practical way to solve the country's problems.

The first phase of self-strengthening ran between 1861 and 1872, and focused on the development of military power and the acquisition of scientific ideas. The government purchased European iron-hulled battleships and established shipyards and munitions factories. Officers were sent to be trained in Germany, Britain and the USA. Scientific texts were translated into Chinese, and the Qing government hired British and European engineers and experts to help transform China's munitions industry.

Paradoxically, the devastating defeats that Britain inflicted on China created opportunities for skilled British workers who were prized as experts to run Chinese armaments factories, even if they lacked manufacturing experience. Li Hongzhang and many of the administrators who worked under him were businessmen in their own right and established dozens of their own factories, schools, mines, printing presses and shipyards. There was often widespread corruption as officials authorised projects that would directly benefit them and diverted government money into their own pockets. The royal court was divided between pro-modernisers in the guise of the two emperors, and a conservative anti-industrial group led by the Dowager Empress Cixi (see page 15). She grew in power throughout the 1870s and 1880s, and was one of the foremost anti-European members of the royal family, rejecting the idea that Europeans had anything to teach China.

During the 1870s, there was a change of emphasis in the Self-Strengthening Movement. Li Hongzhang became convinced that until economic self-sufficiency was achieved, military modernisation would have little effect. He knew that Europeans were able to beat China through the use of modern technology, but also through vibrant and productive economies. The development of new industries such as coal, cotton and steamship navigation companies (see Chapter 1) by the Qing government was a key feature of the second stage of the movement. In Britain, the prevailing ideology of **economic liberalism** meant that the government stayed out of the running of business as far as possible, believing that business free from government interference was always preferable and more profitable.

KEY TERM

Economic liberalism
The belief that the state should play as small a part in the functioning of the economy as possible. Businesses and consumers should be free to buy and sell goods and services with minimal regulation or taxation.

In heavily bureaucratic China, it was a given that officials were the only class who were able to successfully administer major projects like the development of new industries. New industries were run by businessmen and industrialists and were designed to generate profits. However, they were ultimately controlled by the government, and other priorities could easily be imposed on them.

Some industries, particularly the steamship industry along China's rivers (see Chapter 1), could be used to bolster national pride by sailing along unprofitable routes, but this had a damaging effect on efficiency and profitability. Corruption and the tendency of new state-backed industries to form official and unofficial monopolies led to a weakening of business in many sectors of the economy. This shows that one of the core beliefs of the Self-Strengthening Movement, that central government administration was essential, actually undermined China's growth. The power of local and national administrators was so deeply embedded in China and pivotal in holding the empire together, that it was inconceivable that they would not have a key role in managing and benefitting from industrialisation.

A backlash against the ideas of the Self-Strengthening Movement was the key feature of its third phase from 1885 to 1895. The movement had always been suspect in the eyes of traditionalists in Beijing. New industries were developed in a piecemeal fashion in China's provinces. They were not centrally directed or controlled from Beijing, and this was a key weakness in the movement. Mandarins were unable to impose self-strengthening ideas on local administrators who were loyal to traditional Confucian ideas. Between the mid-1880s and the mid-1890s, the pace of change gradually slowed. It was only a further military crisis that renewed demand among China's educated middle class, students and forward-looking government officials for government-led modernisation.

EXTRACT 1

Historian J. Fenby explains the shortcomings of the Self-Strengthening Movement in the *Penguin History of Modern China* (2010).

The self-strengtheners operated on the basis of loyalty to a system which was not designed to accommodate, let alone encourage, change. The necessary legal and administrative underpinnings were missing. Traditional remittance banks could not offer sufficient long-term capital, and attempts to set up a modern financial institution came to nothing. Though some young men were being sent abroad to study, especially to Japan, China had few experienced managers and lacked the entrepreneurial spirit that powered the industrial revolution in the West. Companies such as those set up by Li had lax controls, particularly when the founders were diverted into another of their myriad activities.

SOURCE 1

A statue to Li Hongzhang in a modern Chinese steel factory. Since the reforms of Deng Xiaoping (see pages 47–49), statues to Li have been erected across China.

ACTIVITY
KNOWLEDGE CHECK

Ideology and the Self-Strengthening Movement

1. What impression of China's traditional ideas that opposed the Self-Strengthening Movement does the author in Extract 1 give?
2. What view of the significance of Li Hongzhang's ideas is presented in Source 1?
3. How far is the view that 'Li Hongzhang's ideas were essential for the development of China' supported in Source 1 and Extract 1?

The impact of war with Japan on modernisation and industrialisation

Between 1894 and 1895, China fought a war with Japan over territorial rights in Korea (see Chapter 4), and suffered a series of crippling defeats within months of the outbreak of hostilities. One of the direct effects of this crisis was the dramatic increase in popular demands for modernisation. The first period of self-strengthening had been argued for mainly by China's outward-looking elites. However, following the defeat by Japan, modernisation merged with popular patriotic nationalism and resulted in widespread protests for change. Students, the urban gentry and even China's peasants demanded that the country adopt the same methods that Japan had embraced in order to defend itself against foreign aggression. Cixi and the conservatives who surrounded her became increasingly unpopular and other traditions, such as the complex and increasingly irrelevant imperial civil service examinations (see page 76), were openly criticised.

Practices such as foot-binding for women became the subject of open debate and criticism in the dozens of newspapers that had opened in the 1880s and 1890s (see page 24), and students protested against the peace treaty with Japan that had been signed. More than this, however, they also called for a modern army, banking system, constitutional government, railway network, agricultural reform and industrialisation. There were calls for a new education system, help for the poorest parts of China, and for the wealthy and modern Chinese living in Malaya, Singapore, the USA and Indonesia to be invited back to China to participate in this great change.

More prominent public figures who had always backed modernisation were encouraged by this grassroots support and were able to speak openly about it as a result. Two political ideas were beginning to merge in the 1890s: industrial modernisation and political liberalisation. It became clear to reformers that unless a modern elected government that was accountable to the people and free from corruption was established, the economic reforms necessary to defend China would fail. Within three years of 1895, 103 study societies, 183 new schools and 62 publishing houses were all established in China's major cities with the express purpose of supporting modernisation. Collectively, these new institutions became known as the Young China Movement.

Many 'self-strengtheners' were motivated by the fear that China would be colonised by Europe or Japan. Some scholars and journalists drew direct comparisons with India, which had been colonised by the British. They also looked to the example of Japan, which had recently defeated China in war.

Japan was almost unique in Asia for having resisted being either partially or completely colonised by European powers. In the eyes of Chinese modernisers, this came down to Japan's decision to embrace modern European and US economic, military and political reforms; this was the key to national survival in an era of European imperialism.

The May Fourth Movement, 1915–24

Between 1915 and 1924, a new interest in Western science and technology developed among Chinese students, intellectuals and business people. The enthusiasm for modern technology was matched by a rejection of traditional Chinese values such as Confucianism and the belief that the answers to China's problems lay in the past.

One reason for the rejection of Chinese values was the failure of the 1911 revolution (see page 17) to create a modern republic in China. The chaos that ensued after 1911 convinced many Chinese people that the revolution was not yet complete. It needed to be not only a political revolution, but also an intellectual, scientific and cultural revolution, sweeping away old and backward ideas. This new outlook stressed the importance of Western economic and scientific innovation in China. Only by abandoning tradition could China copy the success of Japan, which had adopted Western economic, scientific and military reforms in the late 19th century to become a rising world power at the start of the 20th. The name of the movement came from demonstrations in 1919 against the outcome of the **Paris Peace Conference**.

KEY TERM

Paris Peace Conference
A meeting of over 50 nations from December 1918 to May 1919, led by Britain, France and the USA. Among other issues, China and Japan's competing claims to the Shandong peninsula were debated. Japan was eventually awarded the territory under American pressure as a concession to entice Japan to join the new League of Nations.

China had limited involvement in the First World War, sending labourers to the Western front to dig British and French trenches. The Beiyang government (see page 21) hoped that at the end of the war a new popular mood of anti-imperialism in Europe and the USA might see an end to European and Japanese exploitation of China. When Chinese demands for self-determination were ignored at the Paris Peace Conference, mass protests erupted and China's weakness on the international stage was once again a topic of immense concern and anger. This led many key thinkers to again blame the country's technological backwardness, comparing it unfavourably to Japan. Many thinkers within this new wave of radicalism drew inspiration from the Self-Strengthening Movement and argued that China could only have a say in international affairs if it scientifically and industrially modernised itself.

EXTEND YOUR KNOWLEDGE

The protests on 4 May
The end of the First World War in China was greeted with celebrations in Beijing, Shanghai, Nanking and other major cities. No Chinese soldiers had fought in the war, and the Chinese cheered what they believed was the birth of national self-determination, an end to empires and secret treaties. However, when it became clear that the British, French and Americans at the Paris Peace Conference had chosen to support Japan's claims to Chinese territory, there was an explosion of anger. On 3 May 1918, students from across Beijing began to organise and gather at Beijing University, preparing to lead a mass demonstration of nationalist anger at Tiananmen Square the following day.

By the early morning of 4 May, 3,000 protesters had gathered on the square, and by the afternoon the crowd had swelled to tens of thousands. Angry protesters marched on the international legation and ransacked the Japanese embassy. Over the next few days, violence spread throughout China, with protests in other main cities. The demographic makeup of the protesters began to change: instead of only idealistic students who had time for politics, peasants, manual workers and clerks all became involved.

The southern revolutionary government accused the north of treachery, and the northern government looked to the Japanese for support, which Japan was willing to give. The students, radicals, intellectuals and nationalists who had cheered the end of the war now vented their fury against the hypocritical West. The young Chinese who protested on 4 May suddenly saw Western promises as hollow and bankrupt, particularly the Wilsonian 14 Points. These were US President Woodrow Wilson's criteria for a post-war world. The clause that excited the most passion in China was clause five, which said that all nations had the right to self-determination.

The New Culture Movement

Even before the crisis of 4 May, anti-traditional thinking had been developing, largely as a delayed consequence of the 1911 revolution. Intellectuals from 1916 onwards had focused on questioning and challenging traditional ideas and increasingly identified them as the source of China's weakness. Chen Duxiu, one of the co-founders of the Chinese Communist Party, began to publish a magazine of new ideas in 1915 called *New Youth*. In it, he wrote: 'Our task today can be said to be the intense combat between the old and the modern currents of thought.' This suggests that many intellectuals in the period 1916–24 (when the May Fourth period is generally thought to have ended) saw a war of ideas being waged in China.

The previous period of modernisation, the Self-Strengthening Movement, saw traditional ideas only partially displaced. After 1911, there were more writers and thinkers engaging with larger audiences and demanding a complete break with the past. One thinker similar to Chen was the writer Zhang Shizhao, who was impressed with Japan's strength and believed that China should copy its Western-style reforms. Another key figure was Cai Yuanpei, the president of Beijing University, who encouraged his students to travel to Europe in order to absorb modern scientific and economic ideas. The generation of radicals who were mobilised by the May Fourth Movement focused on the perceived source of Chinese weakness: traditional Confucian thinking. Alongside the May Fourth Movement, another strand of thinking emerged: the **New Culture Movement**. Both operated outside Chinese law, and members were able to write and publish their ideas freely in Western treaty ports, beyond the jurisdiction of the Chinese government.

KEY TERM

New Culture Movement
Pioneered by a generation of intellectuals and writers between 1910 and the mid-1920s, the New Culture Movement pre-dated the May Fourth Movement and in part inspired it. By the time of the Paris Peace Conference, many Chinese thinkers believed that old Confucian ways needed to be abandoned and new beliefs embraced in order to save China from its enemies.

The merchants and the workers

The Chinese middle class who lived in the treaty ports felt they were economically disadvantaged. The ports were run by committees of European and Japanese businessmen (normally dominated by the British), and election to the committees was normally determined by a **property qualification**. Well-to-do Chinese in ports like Shanghai demanded a place on the committees, partly as a matter of national pride but also to ensure that their commercial trading rights were protected and promoted. They also demanded an end to the practice of extraterritoriality (see page 12). Chinese merchants in the spring of 1919 had been very active in protesting against extraterritoriality, and they saw an opportunity to extend their own commercial interests in the treaty ports. They protested for a restoration of China's rights, but in reality they wanted an improvement in their own economic circumstances.

KEY TERM

Property qualification
The right to vote being based on the value of property a person owns.

In Shanghai, Chinese businessmen allied themselves with workers and trade unions and created the Shanghai Commercial Association, which was to be the political organisation to represent Chinese business in the city. Merchants and unions of factory workers organised a boycott of Japanese goods, street vendors refused to sell them, rickshaw drivers refused to take Japanese customers and dock workers refused to offload cargo from Japanese ships because of Japan's occupation of Chinese territory. The use of economic power to achieve political goals and the widespread participation in the protests across all social classes meant that the movement was viewed as a revolutionary event in modern Chinese history.

The movement began to splinter by 1922 as it drifted in two directions. On one hand, some Chinese revolutionaries discovered **Marxism**. They had no trust in **Western liberalism** but viewed China as backward and in need of foreign ideas to save it. Individuals such as Lu Xun formed the Chinese Communist Party. Other revolutionaries embraced **pragmatism**, a belief proposed by the US philosopher John Dewey and translated into Chinese in 1915. Pragmatists argued that fixating on one ideology was a mistake, and that selecting ideas and beliefs based on whether they would practically work was the most realistic approach. In this manner, it was hoped, the greatest number of Chinese people would benefit. These ideas were more readily embraced by the **Guomindang** (GMD).

KEY TERMS

Marxism
The ideas and philosophy of the German revolutionary thinker Karl Marx. At the heart of his beliefs was the idea that all history was the history of class struggle and in the current, bourgeois phase of history, the working classes (proletariat) and the middle classes (bourgeoisie) were competing. The proletariat provided the labour that the bourgeosie profited from. Marx argued that a proletarian revolution would follow and socialism would be the resulting final phase of history, ending with the establishment of true classlessness with Communism.

Western liberalism
A belief in parliamentary democracy, written constitutions, civil liberties, limits on the power of the state and free markets.

Pragmatism
The belief that it is preferable to avoid rigid ideologies and instead deal with things in a way that is based on practical considerations.

Guomindang (GMD)
A Chinese nationalist party that became the Chinese government in 1928.

Marxism and the Soviet-inspired cult of heavy industry

In the half decade following the end of the Chinese Civil War (see page 25) and Mao Zedong's seizure of power in 1949, the USSR exerted an immense ideological power over the new Chinese regime. The Soviet dictator Stalin was both admired and resented by Mao, but the economic policies he had introduced during the 1930s were in Mao's view unquestionably correct and a blueprint for China to follow.

The USSR had undergone rapid state-led industrialisation during the 1930s in a series of programmes called Five-Year Plans. Industry had been set ambitious targets. A mixture of state propaganda to inspire workers to greater efforts to build socialism and state coercion in the form of labour camps had resulted in impressive industrial growth. In Mao's view, a similar process needed to be undertaken in China and, as with the USSR, the focus of this economic growth should be on heavy industry.

Mao indicated in 1949 that China would follow the Soviet example and 'lean to one side', meaning that China could either 'lean' towards (that is, support) the USA or Britain, or 'lean' towards Moscow, but not remain neutral. He chose to make the USSR China's chief ally and was openly hostile towards the Western powers. He maintained in 1949 that Stalin was to be China's teacher and that the USSR had valuable economic lessons for China, even though in the following decade many of Stalin's economic policies would be repudiated or ignored by his successors.

From 1950, there was an influx of Russian economic advisers into China, bringing with them Stalinist central planning expertise and knowledge. They came following the signing of a treaty the previous year by Mao, when he visited Moscow for the first time. The Treaty of Friendship, Alliance and Mutual Assistance was less a product of Maoist ideology and more the result of Mao's economic desperation. Mao's economic ideological beliefs were that China's peasants, if mobilised in their entirety, could build a new socialist society and outperform not only the West but Soviet Russia as well. He was humiliated in Moscow by Stalin, who was naturally suspicious of the new Communist leader.

The treaty gave Soviet advisers extraterritorial exemption (see page 12) from Chinese laws, and they had to be paid in gold and foreign currency for their expertise. The USSR also demanded rare raw materials such as antimony, tin and tungsten to be shipped to the USSR, and Stalin wanted control over the former Russian treaty port, Port Arthur. Mao's original passion for all things Soviet began to sour by the early 1950s, but this did not prevent him from pressing on with Soviet-style policies, based on Stalinist economic ideology, which demanded rapid state-led industrialisation, dictated by a central bureaucracy which imposed targets and quotas for industrial production. Chinese technicians visited Moscow to learn from their Soviet counterparts how to run a centralised **command economy**.

KEY TERM

Command economy
An economy where all economic decisions are made by central government. Businesses (state owned or private) are forced to meet whatever targets or plans are set. The opposite is a market economy, where consumers buy goods and services, and producers decide what to produce based on market demand.

Following the start of the Korean War (see page 163) and the economic blockade of China by the United Nations, the Chinese became economically dependent on the USSR. Owing to a lack of currency, China had to barter with Soviet Russia. China sent large quantities of agricultural products to the USSR, from meat and soya beans to cotton and tobacco, as payment for industrial equipment and expertise. Mao ensured that Chinese industrialisation prioritised heavy industry over light manufacturing, emulating the Soviet Union. In 1949, only 26 percent of all Chinese industry could be described as heavy industry (coal, iron, steel, shipbuilding, railways). The remaining 74 percent was light industry, creating products for consumers such as clothes, food and household items. By 1952, however, heavy industry output accounted for 42 percent of all manufacturing, with Shanghai and Liaoning province accounting for 28 percent of all national manufacturing output in China. Heavy industry was not evenly distributed across China, much of it being concentrated in Manchuria. The more populous south-east had mainly light manufacturing, and most of China's provinces were agricultural. The experience of the Korean War and US military power convinced Mao that large-scale development of heavy industry was necessary for defence. The mass production of tanks, ships, aircraft and munitions would have been impossible without coal, steel and other key heavy industries.

EXTEND YOUR KNOWLEDGE

Maoist ideology
Mao was not an orthodox Marxist. He took the arguments of Karl Marx and attempted to adapt them to the historical conditions that existed in China. Marx focused mainly on Europe in his writing. He appears to have had less understanding about China and certainly did not think it was advisable for a revolution to begin there. Mao disagreed with Marx and orthodox Marxists that the industrial working class was the social group that would bring about a revolution. Instead, Mao believed that the peasants in China and around the world would overthrow capitalism. He argued that if China's vast reserves of peasant manpower could be mobilised at once, then the technological advantages that capitalist powers had would be negated. In his view, the masses were Chinese Communism's secret weapon.

Stalinist ideology
Stalinism was the version of Communist thinking that dominated the Soviet Union from 1928 onwards. It was centred around transforming a largely peasant society into an urban, industrialised socialist country with a large working class. Stalin believed in massive state-led industrialisation, and from 1928 onwards he enacted the Five-Year Plans that Mao later introduced into China.

SOURCE 2

From a speech made by Mao on 17 February 1950 as he left Moscow to return to China, reprinted in the Chinese *People's Daily* newspaper.

This time in Moscow, Comrade Zhou Enlai, the members of the Chinese delegation, and I met with Generalissimo Stalin and other comrades in responsible positions in the Soviet government. It is difficult for me to express in words the complete understanding and deep friendship that was established between us on the basis of the fundamental interests of the people of our two great nations. It is plain to see that the unity of the people of the two great countries, China and the Soviet Union, solidified by treaty, will be permanent and inviolable, and one which cannot be put asunder by anyone. Moreover, this unity will not only influence the prosperity of these two great countries, China and the Soviet Union, but will surely also affect the future of humanity and the triumph of peace and justice all over the world.

During our sojourn in the Soviet Union we have visited many factories and farms. We have seen the great achievements of the workers, peasants and intellectuals of the Soviet Union in their undertaking of socialist construction; we have observed the work-style of combining a spirit of revolution with a spirit of realism and practicality which has been nurtured among the people of the Soviet Union through the teaching of Comrade Stalin and the Communist Party of the Soviet Union. This has confirmed the conviction which the Chinese Communists have always held: that the experience of the Soviet Union in economic and cultural construction and its experience in construction in other major areas will serve as an example for the construction of New China.

SOURCE 3

From a speech by Mao on 30 August 1956, called 'Reinforce the unity of the party and carry forward the party traditions', soon after Stalin was criticised by his successor Khrushchev (see Chapter 6), much to the anger of Mao.

The first thing is to unite with the several dozen Communist parties and with the Soviet Union. Since some mistakes have occurred in the Soviet Union and those things have been much talked about, they have been exaggerated, and now there is the impression that mistakes of that kind are really terrible. There is something wrong with such an outlook. It is impossible for any nation not to commit any mistakes at all, and [since] the Soviet Union was the first socialist country in the world, and has had such a long experience, it is impossible for it not to have made some mistakes. Where are the mistakes of the Soviet Union, such as Stalin's mistakes, located [in the scheme of things]? They are partial and temporary. Although we hear that some [of these] things have been around for twenty years already, they are nevertheless still temporary and partial and can be corrected. The main current in the Soviet Union, its principal aspect, the majority [of its people], was correct. Russia gave birth to Leninism, and after the October Revolution, it became the first socialist country. It built socialism, defeated fascism, and became a great industrial state. It has many things from which we can learn. Of course, we should study the advanced experiences, and not the backward experiences.

ACTIVITY
KNOWLEDGE CHECK

Mao and Stalin

1 Read though the information in this chapter on Mao and Stalin. Study Source 3. Is it an accurate representation of what Mao really thought of Stalin?

2 Source 2 mentions visits to factories and farms. What economic lessons did Mao learn from the USSR?

3 Examine Source 3. Why is Mao attempting to defend Stalin?

4 How far can it be argued that Mao repeated Stalin's 'mistakes' in China?

Modifying Soviet Marxism and 'walking on two legs', 1958

When Stalin died, Mao assumed that he would be the dictator's heir and would lead the Communist world from Beijing. When this did not happen and instead Khrushchev took over from Stalin as the most significant leader behind the Iron Curtain, it gave Mao the opportunity to break with some key Soviet policies. The Chinese First Five-Year Plan (see page 29) had enjoyed only mixed results, and Mao had a more ambitious and more radical economic plan that he hoped would propel China economically ahead of Britain in a decade.

Mao wanted state-led industrialisation, but he believed that soviet-style planning was actually holding back the energies of the Chinese people through bureaucratic state control, leading Mao to believe that administrators became a more important class than the peasants. Instead, he wanted to inspire the population to work hard to build socialism, but remove central planning and simply allow the peasants and workers to respond to Mao's demands for greater output.

Mao's view of what motivated Chinese peasants was quite divorced from reality. Most of them were not motivated out of a passion for building socialism or from a passionate belief in Mao's own genius. Mao referred to his own economic vision as China '**walking on two legs**', meaning self-sufficiency in industry and agriculture. He believed that when peasants worked harder to grow more food, the industrial output of the cities would increase and as a result there would be greater capacity in the economy and more money to invest in the cities and the countryside. Mao had little if any understanding of economics, but at the same time he was immensely controlling over economic policy and did not listen to any dissenting voices.

Mao's focus on the role of China's peasants was one of the fundamental aspects of Maoist Communism. This represented a clear break with Soviet Marxism. Lenin, Stalin and the other leaders of the Soviet Union did not believe that the peasants were a useful revolutionary class and thought they were not only incapable of taking the revolution to the next stage, but might also be manipulated by counter-revolutionaries into undermining it. Mao was certain that it was China's peasants who would build the country's economic future and would eventually challenge foreign capitalist powers.

Land reform and collectives

Mao's policies towards China's peasants were determined by Maoist ideology and were modelled on the practices of the USSR in the 1930s. Mao came to power promising land redistribution and an end to the power of China's landlords who, the Communists claimed, kept the peasants in grinding poverty.

EXTRACT

From *The Tragedy of Liberation* by historian Frank Dikötter (2013). Recent studies, particularly by Dikötter, have suggested that the landowning class that Mao blamed for much of China's problems did not really exist. Instead, there was a broad mix of poorer and more well-to-do peasants.

> Village life of the eve of the communist conquest was extraordinarily diverse. In the north where tightly packed villages with houses made of sun-dried mud bricks were scattered across the plain, wheat was the staple. Most farmers owned the land... Further south along the Yangtze valley, rich deposits of silt allowed farmers to produce abundant crops of rice. Nowhere in this profusion of social diversity could anybody called a 'landlord' be found. The term had been imported from Japan in the late nineteenth century and given its modern formulation [meaning] by Mao Zedong. It had no meaning for most of the people in the countryside, who referred to some of their more fortunate neighbours as 'caizhu', an appelation [name] that implied prosperity but carried no derogatory undertones.

Mao ordered land to be redistributed between the peasants in 1950 with the Agrarian Reform Law. Land, equipment and livestock were confiscated from landowners and those accused of '**landlordism**' were forced to undergo **self-denunciation sessions** in front of their friends and neighbours. Many were attacked or killed at the end of these long sessions by villagers who were often afraid of the party **cadres** who were the ultimate authority in the village. It is thought that within four years a million former landowners were executed or murdered, with others being sent for 're-education' in labour camps where they faced hunger, hard work and brutal conditions. Mao believed that 'land reform' was an integral part of the creation of a **socialist economy**, and that while it would be brutal it was a necessary part of **Communist ideology**.

KEY TERMS

Walking on two legs
At the core of Mao's vision of economic development was the idea of industry and agriculture developing simultaneously. Mao believed increased agricultural efficiency would free millions of peasants to move to cities to work in factories. The communes would produce enough food to feed these workers.

Landlordism
A term used to denounce any Chinese peasants who owned or rented land. They were accused of exploiting the poorer peasants and were often subjected to self-denunciation sessions.

Self-denunciation session
A type of torture involving public humiliation and shaming. Individuals, from landowners to intellectuals and party members, were forced to stand in front of their peers for hours and admit hundreds of invented errors or crimes. The audience would often be forced to perform for party cadres who were present, reaching levels of artificial rage and anger that might spill over into violence towards the person denouncing themselves. Afterwards, the individual might be given a long prison sentence or be executed.

Cadre
A party activist who spread Communist ideas in villages, factories and schools. They also enforced party doctrine on a local level.

Socialist economy
From Mao's point of view, an economy that was completely state controlled, with all resources belonging ultimately to the government. Peasants and workers would all come under the control of the state and be directed to work not for their own personal benefit but for the nation. Individual buying and selling of goods and services was prohibited and prices of items were set not by the market, but by the state.

KEY TERM

Communist ideology
The group of revolutionary ideas (e.g. Stalinism, Maoism) that originate from the ideas of Karl Marx in the 19th century. Communists believe that the defining struggle throughout history is between social classes, and that the oppressed classes (workers, peasants) will triumph, building a utopian society.

The problem that Mao faced after land reform was completed was that a major disruption had occurred in the traditional structure of the Chinese rural economy. Some peasants who farmed full time had lost the land and equipment they needed. Others who were part-time farmers and who supplemented their incomes from other work with small plots now had more land than they could farm. Others had new plots of land and insufficient tools, know-how or livestock. The solution to the problem, in Mao's eyes, was collectivisation (see page 29).

This was a policy that had been carried out in the USSR with disastrous consequences, resulting in famine conditions in the early 1930s and the death of 3–5 million people in the Ukraine. Mao interpreted the huge loss of life in the USSR as a necessary price of revolution, reasoning that those who died were from enemy or counter-revolutionary classes. In some parts of rural China, some peasants began to work collectively as a result of land redistribution, sharing tools, livestock and land. This practice gained official backing and in villages across China, cadres encouraged and enforced sharing, punishing those who refused to allow their neighbours to use their livestock or tools.

Often, tools and vital equipment were broken because they now belonged to nobody and so were not taken care of. Those refusing to share were publicly humiliated and often exposed to violence from their neighbours. Mao's ideological vision of the countryside was one where redistribution would free the peasants from feudalism and capitalism. However, as soon as redistribution happened, peasants rapidly bought and sold land, trading it among themselves. Mao claimed this as evidence that a long protracted war with capitalism in the countryside needed to be fought. By 1953, the disruption to the countryside resulted in famine and the collapse of rural food-producing industries across China. Mao blamed the famine on hoarders and counter-revolutionaries trying to overthrow the regime. Villages were turned into **co-operatives** and all property was lost to the state. As in Russia, the peasants slaughtered all their own livestock to prevent it falling into the hands of the village party cadres.

The government declared a monopoly on all grain, and peasants were required to sell any surplus to the state at a price fixed by the government. The government would estimate what the harvest in a village was likely to be, and the peasants were expected to meet this quota. Often these estimates would be unrealistic. This initiative was designed to keep prices across China uniform in order to prevent speculators or merchants from making a profit. However, famine created a black market for grain as desperate peasants paid high prices for food.

The embrace of capitalism in the 1980s and 1990s

Within three years of the end of the Cultural Revolution (see page 23) in 1976, the economic, political and social assumptions that Maoism had been based on were overturned. In the 1980s and 1990s, a state-controlled version of the **free market capitalism** that had become the new economic orthodoxy in the USA and Europe was introduced.

In December 1978, when Deng Xiaoping announced economic reforms, China was extremely poor following three decades of economic, political and social turmoil. The population was close to a billion and 250 million lived in poverty. Deng was aware that other Asian economies such as Japan, Taiwan and Singapore had developed high-technology industries and highly skilled workforces since the 1960s.

Deng was not inspired by the ideology of the free market in the way that Mao had embraced Stalinism and then developed his own economic ideas in the guise of Maoism. Instead, he was concerned with finding an economic model that would generate prosperity. Creating equality between all Chinese people was one of the founding ideals of the Communist Party, and Deng was aware that rising inequality would have to be accepted and, to an extent, tolerated. The new Chinese capitalism would be based around the Four Modernisations (see page 60), meaning that no area of the Chinese economy would be unaffected by the power of **market forces**.

Deng argued that the true essence of socialism was the ability to bring material abundance to the Chinese people and the final phase of Mao's rule, the Cultural Revolution, had done precisely the opposite. Deng was always suspected by Mao of being a '**capitalist roader**' and a rightist, an accusation that was not necessarily valid. Deng was a capable and reliable party member who carried out Maoist policies faithfully, and during the civil war (see page 25), brutally. The shift to embrace capitalism was based on a desire to find a workable economic policy. China's transition to capitalism happened alongside other economic changes in the world economy at the end of the 20th century. The USA, Britain and other European economies imported cheap goods from overseas

KEY TERMS

Co-operative
Village co-operatives were villages where all the land, tools, livestock and seeds were communally owned and the peasants lost the right to private property.

Free market capitalism
An economic system based on the workings of markets to decide prices, wages and labour costs. The role of government in deciding how goods and services are produced and distributed is limited, regulations on what businesses are allowed to do are kept to a minimum, and taxes on businesses tend to be low.

Market force
A factor that affects the supply of and the demand for goods and services. An example of this might be the price of a product. When cheaper, better-made products enter a marketplace, the demand for them increases and existing producers are forced to compete or lose their markets to the new competitor.

Capitalist roader
A pejorative term for a member of the Communist party who was suspected of deviating from Mao Zedong's thinking and taking the 'capitalist road' to development.

KEY TERM

Consumer credit
Borrowing of money by ordinary consumers to buy goods and services for their own personal consumption. An example might be the purchase of a car with a loan or hire-purchase agreement. Other types of consumer credit include credit cards and store cards.

and their citizens gained greater access to **consumer credit**. This meant that China in the 1980s and 1990s was able to become a manufacturing giant with overseas markets into which to sell its goods.

Deng's reforms

Initially, Deng was cautious with the introduction of industrial capitalism into China, but in the countryside dramatic change was rapidly introduced. The first province to allow market reforms was Guangdong in the south, close to the British colony of Hong Kong and therefore able to access world markets through the island outpost. In the countryside, Mao's communes were broken up. By 1981, 45 percent of the work teams that had been created during the Great Leap Forward were disbanded and 'family work teams' (or simply families, working land allotted to them) replaced them. This figure had leapt to 98 percent by 1983. Despite the fact that these reforms were gradual, they had immediate and dramatic effects. Central planning of agriculture ended. It had contributed to famines by telling farmers to grow crops unsuited to their land or for which there was no demand.

TVEs and SEZs

Farmers were given autonomy to produce whatever foodstuffs they wanted. They were also allowed to have secondary occupations and rear their own livestock. Soon, meat and fish were widely available for a majority of Chinese people and China was able, by the early 1980s, to be a food exporter. New enterprises established by private investors rapidly outperformed state-owned enterprises, and many were based in villages that had been part of Maoist communes. Rural China became industrialised through the establishment of Town and Village Enterprises (TVEs) that were part-run by the state and part-owned by private enterprise. The TVEs brought light industry to villages and, alongside farming, peasant families also produced bicycles and small electrical goods.

The development of Special Economic Zones (SEZs, see page 33) happened at a more gradual pace. The SEZs were modelled on other Asian countries like Taiwan, that created areas for businesses to operate where they benefitted from lower taxation and regulation. This in turn rapidly generated jobs and economic growth and attracted investment from overseas. The creation of SEZs again shows that Deng was willing to place pragmatism over ideology. Inviting capitalist enterprises from overseas was closer to the thinking of Li Hongzhang than Mao Zedong. Deng was still concerned that the Communist Party itself would be threatened by the capitalist changes being introduced, especially if they involved foreign capitalist enterprises. For this reason, the SEZs were situated away from centres of economic and political power.

Throughout the 1980s, as it became clearer that the economic changes that were occurring were unlikely to threaten the Communist Party and instead actually strengthened its control over the country, the anxieties over market reforms declined. Deng encouraged inward investment into China to bring in high-technology industries to share their knowledge and practices. Until September 1983, only foreign-owned firms could operate in the SEZs and therefore benefit from low taxation. By the early 1980s, the number of Chinese workers employed in the SEZs was still relatively low, and the products made there were designed for export markets, meaning that the level of interaction between the majority of the population and the SEZs was low. However, the rate of growth of the SEZs meant that this changed radically throughout the decade.

The SEZs became synonymous with prosperity and also corruption. The more conservative elements of the Communist Party that feared change and hoped to undermine it focused on corruption scandals, particularly a notorious case where businessmen and party officials used the SEZ on Hainan Island to import over US$1.5 billion of cars without paying taxes. The other negative impact of the reforms was the rapid pace of social change. Families and individuals were uprooted from the countryside, and some areas of China boomed while others suffered from unemployment and poverty. SEZs and the prosperity they promised drew millions of Chinese from the countryside.

Shenzhen

In 1979, Shenzhen was a rural backwater with a population of 300,000, with just five miles of road and a dozen buses. In 1980, it became an SEZ and was physically separated from the rest of Guangdong by steel fences, preventing 'dangerous' economic and political ideas from contaminating the rest of the country.

Between 1981 and 1984, Shenzhen's economy grew by 75 percent each year, and the Chinese economy in total grew by 9.6 percent annually from 1981 to 1993. Shenzhen became the model for all future SEZs in China and was seen by Deng as a 'laboratory' for future economic reform, an enclosed space where the economic, social and political impact of economic changes could be tested and monitored. By 1992, it was home to three million workers, many of whom were employed by investors in Hong Kong.

Deng and democracy

In the USA and Europe, capitalism and liberal democracy were intimately connected and a prevailing belief in Western societies was that free markets, free elections and freedom of expression were inseparable. Deng Xiaoping had experimented with support for a pro-democracy movement in 1978, but he never repeated this. He did not believe that democracy was necessary for prosperity to flourish. Instead, he saw China as a chaotic and frequently anarchic state that needed strict order to hold it together. Following the crushing of the **pro-democracy movement** in 1989, the party's conservatives claimed that free market reforms had led to the students' demands, and attempted to halt economic liberalisation. After 1989, Deng became isolated and abandoned by some of his most influential supporters such as Chen Yun, an anti-Maoist party member who had helped Deng to power. In the press and on television, criticism of the SEZs proliferated. However, by 1992 Deng had regained the initiative and announced his intention to allow **financial liberalisation**, starting in Shanghai.

KEY TERMS

Pro-democracy movement
In June 1989, students and protesters occupied Tiananmen Square in the heart of Beijing to demand democratic reforms. The government responded by declaring martial law and attacking the protesters with tanks and troops, killing an unknown number of protesters.

Financial liberalisation
A process whereby the government reduces or removes controls over the banking and investment industry. This means that banks and stockbrokers can buy, sell, borrow and lend in any way that will maximise their profits.

ACTIVITY
KNOWLEDGE CHECK

Deng's reform era

1 Read through the section on Deng's economic reforms. To what extent had Deng broken with Maoism? Did any elements of it remain?

2 In what differing ways do Sources 4 and 5 show market reforms changing China in the 1980s?

SOURCE 4

A Chinese peasant ploughs a rice field with a petrol-driven plough on a former commune near Suzhou in the 1980s.

SOURCE 5

Prisoners making lamps for export in a workshop in a Chinese Youth Detention Centre, Chengdu, 1985. China's young prisoners helped to power Deng's manufacturing boom in the mid-1980s.

A Level Exam-Style Question Section C

'Capitalism was a far more effective ideology than Communism in bringing about economic change in China.'

How far do you agree with this opinion? (20 marks)

Tip

Before you start writing, make sure you are very clear on what capitalism and Communism are. If necessary, create a chart, table or diagram showing the key features of both ideologies.

HOW FAR WERE KEY INDIVIDUALS RESPONSIBLE FOR BRINGING ABOUT ECONOMIC GROWTH IN THE YEARS 1860–1997?

This section examines the role of key individuals in bringing about economic growth in China between 1860 and 1997. It explores the actions and motivations of individuals such as Li Hongzhang and Mao Zedong. Not all of the individuals mentioned in this section were entirely successful in promoting growth, and some were motivated by beliefs other than economic expansion. In the 137-year period under examination, China experienced an enormous, turbulent and often violent upheaval that disrupted economic growth and led to the loss of millions of lives. Several of the key figures who are discussed in this chapter were either partly or wholly responsible for this turmoil, and this should be evaluated against their economic achievements. The journey from a feudal society to a Communist one and from there to capitalist modernity has been more rapid and more bloody in China than in any other society in 20th-century history.

Li Hongzhang

In the history of the economic development of China, Li Hongzhang is as important a figure as Mao Zedong or Deng Xiaoping. The previous section looked at the importance of ideas and ideologies to the economic development of China. This section examines Li's personal contribution to China's economic development in the late 19th century.

Li Hongzhang became known to Western diplomats and businessmen as a moderniser and a skilled administrator who organised resistance to the Taiping Rebellion between 1859 and 1864. He was generally popular with Europeans seeking to open up China to trade, and was even given an honour by Queen Victoria of Great Britain. However, in China he was seen quite differently during his lifetime and afterwards. His career as a bureaucrat was well established by the 1870s, and in 1871 he was appointed **viceroy** of Zhili, the province that surrounds Beijing and was directly ruled by the imperial government, unlike more distant provinces such as Szechuan. There were eight viceroys across China, and they had responsibility for most aspects of provincial life.

KEY TERM

Viceroy
An official with the power to rule a province in China on the emperor's behalf.

This broad swathe of responsibilities gave Li the power to press through modernisations from the provincial capital at Tianjin. He was also made commissioner of the northern ports of China, which meant that he regularly came into direct contact with Western merchants and diplomats and was able to see how their power stemmed from modern technology and commerce. Li was much like other high-ranking officials in the imperial government, in that he sought out ways to benefit himself financially when he introduced new mines, factories and railways to Tianjin.

Many administrators believed there was little point in introducing schemes that would enrich only the general population and not themselves directly. Li built a coal mine, railways, a cotton mill and a steamship company in Zhili, making the province the centre of Chinese industry in the 1870s and 1880s. He also understood the power of communications and introduced the telegraph to China, along with a postal service modelled on the British Royal Mail. Li was above all a pragmatist, believing that China's best interests were served by maintaining good relations with European powers, which he acknowledged were far too powerful to simply dismiss. Previous Qing emperors and their administrators had assumed that no power outside China was civilised enough to defeat the empire, but the two Opium Wars had shattered this myth in Li's eyes.

Li was not an appeaser of Europeans for its own sake. Instead, he knew that a weak China had to build up its power gradually until it could be economically self-sufficient. Only when it had economic power could it successfully develop militarily and force the Europeans and Japanese from Chinese soil. Li was one of the principal architects of the Self-Strengthening Movement (see page 40), and he has been likened to Deng Xiaoping in his willingness to adopt whatever measures were necessary to improve China's economic situation. However, as mentioned above, there was resistance to Li's reforms at the imperial court in Beijing, particularly from the Dowager Empress Cixi.

It was feared that modern technology would sweep away Chinese culture and society, and that traditional Confucian ways of understanding the world would be threatened, along with the careers of imperial administrators who depended on tradition. Li died in 1901, and after the 1911 revolution his reputation was called into question by successive generations of revolutionaries. The intellectuals of the May Fourth Movement (see page 42) saw him as a traitor for 'capitulating' to foreign powers in his dealings with them in the treaty ports, and for his decision to hire foreign generals and mercenaries to fight the Taiping Rebellion.

When Mao came to power, Li was seen as a bourgeois capitalist who was happy to sell China to European and Japanese commercial interests. In both instances, his legacy was interpreted through the prevalent ideology of the day. A more nuanced view of Li is that he was no more corrupt by the standards of the day than any other administrator, and that the major economic reforms that he began in the 1870s were reflected in every significant economic change throughout the following century.

Sheng Xuanhuai

After Li Hongzhang, perhaps the most important figure in the Self-Strengthening Movement was Sheng Xuanhuai. Sheng had a sophisticated understanding of Western-style capitalism. Li was a friend of Sheng's father, and as a young man Sheng served as an adviser to Li. Both men combined their knowledge of China's bureaucracy with an understanding of European-style commerce, finance and industry. However, while Li had an instinctive understanding of how to do business, Sheng had a far broader knowledge of the relationship between banking and industry. He could see that the ability to borrow and lend money in order to invest in industry was the key to the Europeans' success.

China's moneylending by the 1890s did not resemble that of Europe. Instead, traditional moneylenders dominated most of China's finance industry and more often than not they simply used debt to exploit the peasants. Sheng convinced Li that railways, mines and ports could not be built unless large amounts of credit from banks was available. However, until 1897 the only banks that were accessible were Western-owned ones in Shanghai and Hong Kong. This meant that essential investment was still controlled by European powers and inevitably came with strings attached. When the Qing government found itself in debt to Britain, France or Germany, it quickly came under pressure to grant new rights to political or commercial concessions.

Sheng argued that the establishment of a Chinese-owned bank would prevent the Qing government from having to borrow from Europe. He had a wide range of commercial interests by the 1890s, including coal, cotton, steamship and telegraph companies. In 1897, he established the Imperial Bank of China (see page 55). The bank was based on European financial ideas and Sheng was very similar to Li in his belief that European ideas could be grafted on to China, but that they should only serve to strengthen and stabilise the country, not to bring about radical or revolutionary change. Both Sheng and Li believed this was not in any way desirable. They were loyal to the regime, but they resisted as far as they could the tendency of the Dowager Empress Cixi to oppose the European powers.

During the Boxer Rebellion (see page 96), which Cixi supported, both men formed an alliance of provinces called The Mutual Protection of Southeast China. The provincial governors who joined with them refused to obey Cixi's order to declare war on the 11 European, US and Japanese powers fighting the Boxers, knowing that defeat was certain. Sheng, as the minister for telegraphy, prevented the transmission of the message calling for war to be waged against the invaders.

T.V. Soong

One of the most significant and overlooked figures of the Nationalist era of Chinese politics is T.V. Soong (who was Jiang Jieshi's brother-in-law). Soong held a variety of posts from governor of the Bank of China to prime minister of Jiang Jieshi's government. Despite the fact that Soong was a member of the post-revolutionary Guomindang government in Canton and then, after 1928, across the rest of China, there are clear similarities with the pre-revolutionary figures Li Hongzhang and Sheng Xuanhuai. All three men understood the significance of Western capitalist ideas, but it was arguably T.V. Soong who did more to integrate China into the global economy than any other figure until Deng Xaioping in the 1980s.

Soong was educated at Harvard University in the USA, and already had experience of banking and finance, having worked at the International Banking Corporation in New York. In 1917, Sun Yat-sen had enticed Soong to return to China to salvage the financial system in Canton, the heartland of Guomindang power.

In the early 1920s, he introduced a simplified tax system and doubled government revenues in two years. He regulated China's banks, making them safe for depositors to invest their money, and savings rose by 600 percent by 1926. Most significantly, he created a **national debt** for the Guomindang government by selling **securities** to the Chinese people.

KEY TERMS

National debt
The total amount that a country owes to its creditors. Financial markets assume that nations rarely go bankrupt, so a manageable national debt can be a useful way of borrowing money to fund investment or pay for emergencies like war or natural disasters. When it is suspected that a country might actually become bankrupt, the cost of borrowing increases dramatically. Most national debt is raised by the state issuing a bond, which is a government-backed IOU.

Securities
Government-backed investments, such as bonds.

This meant that the Guomindang government had a large and stable flow of finance that it could access. Soong also introduced anti-corruption campaigns and cracked down on smuggling, preventing criminal gangs from importing goods without paying taxes. In 1931, he opened the first bond and stock markets in Shanghai, and set up the National Economic Council which offered loans for projects that boosted economic development in China. However, despite these reforms, economic growth across China during the 1930s was uneven. Rural peasants enjoyed a far smaller share of prosperity than workers in towns and cities, and international competition ate away at China's exports.

In 1902, China had dominated 34 percent of the international tea market; in 1932, this had fallen to just under ten percent. By 1932, 70 percent of China's manufacturing wealth still came from artisan handicrafts, and trade union unrest in major industries like mining resulted in a lot of strikes. This was due to low wages and poor safety at work (there were frequent mining accidents throughout the 1930s). Soong's tax system, while effective, tended to predominantly tax consumer goods. Taxes on imports and commodities like salt put prices up, while the growth of new businesses in China was slow, so **corporation tax** revenues were low. The new middle class that Soong hoped would emerge was small and contributed collectively very little in income tax to the government.

KEY TERM

Corporation tax
Tax paid on corporate profits.

In the mid-1930s, China had a seemingly irreconcilable economic problem – despite Soong's reforms, economic growth was sluggish, but government spending remained high. Fighting a civil war with Mao's Communists and dealing with the threat of Japanese troops on Chinese soil meant that Jiang kept a large and expensive army, which accounted for half of all state spending.

In order to persuade Chinese citizens to buy bonds, Soong had to offer attractive interest rates, meaning that the dividends on bond ownership were high, ensuring that a further 30 percent of government finance went on servicing debt. Soong resigned as finance minister in 1933, in protest at the scale of spending on the army, but his resignation did not improve economic policy in China. Instead, the practice of printing money to pay for Jiang's forces was introduced.

Much of the government wealth poured into the army was stolen by corrupt officers. By the late 1930s, the value of Chinese currency was in decline and inflation was growing as a result of the policy of printing money. Despite Soong's efforts, living standards for Chinese people had not changed very much by the end of the 1930s, with the number of schools, hospitals and rural clinics remaining hopelessly inadequate for China's vast population.

ACTIVITY
KNOWLEDGE CHECK

Western-style economic growth

How significant was T.V. Soong in the development of China's economy? Compare and contrast him with one other key figure discussed in this chapter, and examine both individuals' impact on China's:

- industrialisation
- finance system
- living standards of ordinary people.

Mao Zedong

Much of this book features the significance and impact of Mao Zedong on China. He was a pivotal figure in China's 20th-century history, but in this section we are concerned with the extent to which Mao promoted economic growth between 1949 and 1976.

Several generations of historians have written about Mao and offered competing perspectives on his leadership. Most Maoist or Marxist historians have focused on his ideological struggles with 'class enemies' and attributed to him military genius for his victories over the Nationalists in 1949. The Chinese government in the post-Mao era, following the end of the Maoist personality cult, accept that he was imperfect and mistakes were made, but there has never been full renunciation of Mao by any of his successors. The current generation of post-Maoist revisionist historians, such as Jung Chang, Jon Halliday and Frank Dikötter, have used statistics extensively to present Mao's handling of the economy and the famines that stemmed from it throughout his rule as disastrous.

Mao can be seen as a clear ideological break from the first three individuals studied in this section (Li Hongzhang, Sheng Xuanhuai and T.V. Soong). He quickly began to reverse China's integration with the global capitalist system, believing that it was inherently based on exploitation and the imperial conquest of China by capitalist powers. Instead of the USA and Europe, China's main trading partner in 1949 became the USSR, but within a decade the relationship had soured. China faced the prospect of economic isolation until the early 1970s, when Mao invited US President Richard Nixon to China.

It would be wrong to suggest that Mao did not value economic growth and progress. He believed that China's Five-Year Plans, collectivisation and communalisation, and the Great Leap Forward would all achieve those goals. He had little knowledge of economics and depended on Liu Shaoqi and Zhou Enlai to help create Communist economic plans. He was highly suspicious of both, however, accusing them of having 'rightist' ideas, whereas in reality they believed that change in China needed to happen at a slower and more gradual pace.

The start of the Cultural Revolution (see page 23) introduced chaos into industry, bureaucracy and education. Workers were encouraged to see their managers as anti-Maoist elements who could be ignored or denounced.

Schools and universities were among the first institutions to lose control over their students. Across China over the decade from 1966, education was plunged into crisis, with huge shortages of skilled workers. The Cultural Revolution was so named as it was an attempt to create a new Maoist culture in China and to sweep away 'old' ideas. However, the revolutionaries succeeded in attacking all elements of modern scientific thinking in China, as it was targeted by Red Guards as 'counter-revolutionary'. When Mao met US President Richard Nixon in 1972, on the first visit by a US president to China, he was keen to develop a friendship with the USA. Part of his interest was to arrange a 'technology transfer' from the USA to China, as Chinese research and development by 1972 had slumped.

While Mao declared the Cultural Revolution over by 1968, it really ended in 1976 with his death. The students Mao had encouraged to attack the 'bourgeois' institutions of China were unwilling to end their radical and violent activities, and Mao began to realise that he had unlocked revolutionary energies that even he was unable to control.

Acute economic damage had been done to China by 1969, with **per capita national income** having contracted by three percent. Steel production had fallen by 75 percent, while industrial accidents across China quadrupled. Employees at major state factories ceased working and were often absent for prolonged periods, and electricity production slumped by 30 percent, leaving millions of Chinese families in the dark. Small traders who were able to establish market stalls in the aftermath of the Great Leap Forward were attacked by the Red Guards as they were seen to be counter-revolutionaries.

KEY TERM

Per capita national income
A measure of a nation's wealth, which divides the total national income of a country by its population. It is an inaccurate gauge of living standards as it assumes that all wealth is evenly distributed, whereas in practice there are always inequalities.

While the Cultural Revolution was not quite the human and economic catastrophe that the Great Leap Forward was (see page 21), it created a decade of dislocation, chaos and violence. The combination of this and much of Mao's previous social and economic policy in China from 1949 onwards devastated Chinese agriculture, commerce and industry, leaving the Chinese people in 1976 deeply impoverished, while living in a country of abundant natural resources.

Deng Xiaoping

In the previous section we explored Deng Xiaoping's pragmatic economic policy that focused on economic outcomes over ideological goals. Deng's own personal actions to promote economic growth in China are probably the most successful economic reforms in any country in the 20th century. They produced an average growth rate between 1978 and 1997 of ten percent per annum, and lifted hundreds of millions of Chinese people out of poverty. Even during the economic golden age of the 1950s and 1960s, the USA and Europe could not boast of economic achievements anywhere near those of Deng. He created a hybrid of a capitalist and a state-controlled socialist economy, where markets for goods and services were allowed to exist but major enterprises that were notionally private were in fact controlled by the state. The end goal for Deng had been the creation of an economy that was able to provide for the material needs of the population and therefore prevent internal dissent. In addition to this, the economy needed to be technologically advanced enough to create high-tech military equipment to defend China and project power into the rest of Asia.

So while Deng introduced a hybrid capitalism into China, he cannot be thought of as a capitalist, merely a pragmatist who chose economic tools that suited his overall objectives. It was easy to deal with the potential challenge that the reintroduction of a capitalist class into China might pose to the regime. For most of the period 1978–97, the capitalists in question were based overseas. Many of them were Hong Kong Chinese entrepreneurs, others were Western light-manufacturing businesses that outsourced their production to China.

There were a growing number of wealthy Chinese businessmen and women in China as a result of the reforms, but an insufficient number to represent a social class that might want to create a political party that represented its interests. Deng ensured that while foreign businesses could utilise the SEZs for production, there were strict limits on the amount of overseas foreign investment in China. Put simply, multinational corporations were not able to buy Chinese companies, making sure that foreign power in China was limited. Deng looked back to the era of Li Hongzhang when he considered the power that foreign capitalists could potentially wield over China. The era of reform under Deng allowed for a greater social mobility than China had seen since 1949.

Peasants had been kept out of China's cities for the most part with a permit system that prevented mass migration. It had been important for the Maoist regime to keep them working on the land, or to prevent them fleeing famine and swamping what welfare systems there were in the cities. During the 1980s, the permit system was relaxed and the size of cities under Deng's leadership grew dramatically. The rapid influx of workers to China's cities provided SEZs with a large, cheap workforce that powered a massive expansion in manufacturing in China. By the end of the century, over 100 million peasants had left the countryside for the cities, making Deng's reforms responsible for the largest migration in human history. However, as peasants moved from the countryside to the city they left behind the welfare safety net that had existed in their recently dissolved communes. This meant that while Deng's China was becoming more prosperous overall, wide gaps between rich and poor were emerging.

Deng certainly promoted economic growth and was the most successful Chinese leader in the 19th or 20th century in doing so. However, the benefits were unequal, resulting in poverty, unemployment and poor standards of living for many millions of migrant workers in the new SEZs and China's cities. In the countryside, as communes were dismantled and TVEs were established, services such as schools, clinics and utilities were effectively privatised, leaving peasants (whose incomes were increasing due to market reforms) having to pay for services they had previously accessed for free. In 1995, property ownership was legalised in China's towns and cities, meaning that for the first time since the revolution people could purchase their own homes (normally the state-built apartments they had been living in) with a mortgage from a bank.

As urban populations increased, property values increased and the type of speculation in property that Mao would have deemed 'bourgeois' and 'counter-revolutionary' occurred. This ability of town dwellers to buy and own property dramatically increased disparities between rural and urban incomes. The relative economic backwardness of rural communities was mitigated by workers in the cities who sent money home to their peasant families. Deng's pragmatism might have resulted in unprecedented economic advances for China as a whole, but the introduction of market reforms resulted in increases in inequality. The irony for the Communist Party in the 1990s was that their only hope of stabilising China and preventing it from being divided by the new capitalist prosperity was to encourage the development of a new middle class – the social group that Mao had all but eradicated after 1949.

EXTRACT 3

R. Macfarquhar and M. Schoenhals, in *Mao's Last Revolution* (2008), describe the impact of the economic successes of China's neighbours on Deng's decision-making.

Two years after the Cultural Revolution ended in 1976, the principal survivor of that cataclysm, onetime CCP General Secretary Deng Xiaoping, initiated China's reform era. The enormity of the challenge facing him and his colleagues was visible throughout East Asia. When the CCP had come to power in 1949, its morale was high, determined to transform China economically and socially, Japan was under foreign occupation... Taiwan was a rural backwater to which the defeated remnants of Chiang Kai-shek's [Jiang Jieshi's] Nationalist Party (KMT [GMD]) and army had fled. Within a year, South Korea would be devastated by invasion from the north, and so afterward Chinese troops were contributing to its destruction. As late as the eve of the Cultural Revolution seventeen years later, not much seemed to have changed in East Asia. Only a few observant foreigners had noted the signs of dynamic growth in the Japanese economy. But by the time that Deng returned to power, the Japanese miracle had been emulated in South Korea and Taiwan. The sleepy entrepôts of Singapore and Hong Kong had become flourishing industrial centres. The rampant East Asian tigers had proved that being part of the old Chinese cultural area, let alone Chinese, need not condemn one to poverty. Yet at the historic heart of the area, China itself now lay spread eagled, this time by its own hand, not as a result of foreign invasion or conventional civil war. For Chinese leaders the message was clear; they had to embark upon a policy of rapid economic growth to make up for lost time and relegitimise CCP rule.

ACTIVITY
KNOWLEDGE CHECK

The beginning of Deng's Reform Era

1. Why did Japanese and Taiwanese economic success make China's leaders feel nervous?
2. What do the authors of Extract 3 suggest was the Cultural Revolution's economic impact on China?

The establishment of the first modern bank, 1897

Foreign banks, **piaohao** and **qinzhung** each controlled roughly a third of the market for borrowing in China before 1897, and the emergence that year in Shanghai of the Imperial Bank of China (IBC) radically altered the shape of the financial industry. The bank was the direct product of the Self-Strengthening Movement and the need for large long-term loans in order to finance railways, mines, steamships and factories (a railway line from Beijing to Hankou completed in 1905 cost over US$68 million).

By the 1890s, the Qing government's creditworthiness was in decline, meaning that banks either refused to lend, fearing they would never see their money again, or they imposed steep interest rates to reflect the risk involved. This made the establishment of a major Chinese bank a high priority. Smaller institutions tended to lend many times more money in the form of paper notes that they were able to issue than they actually had in deposits. This made them unstable, and foreign banks had little interest in China's long-term growth – they were more interested in short-term profits. This meant they were unlikely to invest in Chinese industry and railways, as this represented a high **financial risk**.

Foreign banks had little ability to test whether a Chinese company would be creditworthy in the long term, and there were few laws to protect their investments. Therefore, they tended to avoid complex projects like railway-building and they preferred lower-risk short-term lending. When they lent directly to the Qing government, it was agreed that the government would raise special taxes to pay back the loan. Chinese administrators and bureaucrats thought that the power of European banks to raise taxes in China was possibly the beginning of the end for China itself. Therefore, breaking the control of European powers over Chinese banking was seen as a matter of national survival.

Li Hongzhang had first proposed a Sino-American bank in 1876 to finance industrialisation, but it was opposed by conservatives along with other national bank schemes for two decades. Only the support of Prince Gong in 1897 made the project possible. When the Imperial Bank of China opened, it differed from the piaohao and the qinzhung in that it already had substantial sums of government money (nearly US$5 million) deposited with it that could be lent to borrowers, making it the biggest Chinese lender. Within two years, it had issued US$8 million in loans. The bank was an extension of the Self-Strengthening Movement, in that it rejected all traditional Chinese moneylending practices. It modelled its regulations on the Hong Kong and Shanghai Banking Corporation, appointed a British banker as its first general manager and gave other senior posts to Europeans. Other European powers hoped to merge the bank with their own lending institutions, but Sheng Xuanhuai rejected offers from France and Austria, stating that the point of the bank was to remain independent from foreign control. The IBC was also able to lend money to foreign corporations, including Standard Oil in the USA, and it had a close relationship of lending and co-operation with the piaohao and the qinzhung.

The crises of the Imperial Bank of China

In 1899, the outbreak of the Boxer Rebellion was disastrous for the bank as its branches in Tianjin and Beijing were destroyed as symbols of European ideas (even though they were intended to prise the grip of European commerce from China). Large amounts of cash were looted from the banks at the same time that a second crisis occurred. The bank, which had the right to issue its own currency, discovered that large amounts of counterfeit notes were being circulated in Shanghai, dramatically reducing the value of IBC-issued money. It was particularly harmful as IBC rules stated that each note was equivalent to its value in silver, and customers could exchange a note for silver when they wanted. Counterfeit notes therefore threatened to bankrupt the bank. The result was a collapse in confidence in the IBC, and the first 'run' on a bank in China occurred in 1903. The source of counterfeit notes was traced to smugglers in Japan, though it is unclear whether Japanese banks or the Japanese government had any involvement. The bank's longer-term problem was its failure to secure enough deposits from the Chinese people. This meant that it always lent more than it could afford to, and while the bank never failed, it was never able to replace banks like the Hong Kong and Shanghai Banking Corporation and become the main lender in China.

KEY TERMS

Piaohao
A network of small moneylenders that the government relied on to pay wages and allow money to circulate around China.

Qinzhung
A small moneylender who offered loans to farmers and small businesses and benefitted from the arrival of European powers in China.

Financial risk
The likelihood that an investment will fail. Banks will often not lend to a business that appears to be too likely to fail or is being set up in an unstable environment or country.

EXTEND YOUR KNOWLEDGE

Piaohao and qinzhung moneylenders

China had a history of banking and paper money dating back nearly 2,000 years, and from the 10th century onwards there was a wide variety of local, regional and national financial institutions that protected the deposits of savers and lent money to borrowers. In Shanxi province in the early 19th century, a local network of moneylenders called piaohao or 'ticket offices' emerged. Instead of moving large amounts of currency around and potentially attracting bandits, savers and moneylenders could take a 'note' from one piaohao and redeem it at another. By the 1880s, there were 475 branches in all 18 provinces, showing that China had a need for complex banking and credit systems, even though much of the country was not industrialised.

The other type of small local moneylender was the qinzhung, which lent money to businesses and farmers, often without a deposit. The piaohao business grew when the Qing government adopted it as a means of circulating money, but the qinzhung boomed when foreign trade came to China, as thousands of small businesses required loans in order to trade with European powers.

The piaohao and the qinzhung were only able to conduct transactions within China. International finance from the 1860s to the 1890s was monopolised by European banks and finance companies (many of which were subsidiaries of British or European trading companies). The Hong Kong and Shanghai Banking Corporation and the British Indian Oriental Bank dominated merchant and investment banking in China, and no institutions on the scale of these lenders existed in China to compete with them. The British were followed by the French, with the Compte d'Escompte de Paris and the Banque de L'Indochine, and Germany with the Deutsche Bank.

By the 1890s, a financial 'scramble for China' appeared to be underway as branches of foreign banks emerged in towns and cities across the country. Each bank was unrestricted in how it operated due to the policy of extraterritoriality, and their power was considerable. They helped China conduct its business with the rest of the world, through remittances (money transfers), and were able to issue their own currency. After the Sino-Japanese War in 1894, they grew more powerful because the government turned to them to borrow money to pay war debts to Japan. Between 1853 and 1894, however, the Qing government had taken out 43 loans from foreign banks, making China one of the most indebted countries in the world (in the three years that followed the war, the government again borrowed US$350 million).

China Development Finance Corporation

The China Development Finance Corporation was the creation of T.V. Soong. It attempted to succeed where previous innovations such as the Imperial Bank of China had failed, by providing the finance to modernise China. Both Soong and Jiang Jieshi were conscious that China was not capable of attracting foreign investment during the 1930s without sacrificing China's sovereignty in the way that the Qing government had. They wanted to bring overseas investment to China to build railways, infrastructure, factories and mines, but were reluctant to hand any more political power to foreign governments. They decided to approach the League of Nations for help.

China had been one of the founding members of the League in 1920, and in 1931, after protracted debates within the Guomindang, Jiang wrote to the League's finance minister Joseph Avenol, requesting expert help in establishing a new finance organisation to develop Chinese industry that meant China would not be dependent on foreign loans. Instead, the new organisation was intended to attract inward investment on a more equal basis, ensuring that China did not have to give away political control in return. Soong invited Jean Monnet, a French international financier and one of the founding members of the League of Nations, to China in 1932. Monnet was experienced in stabilising struggling economies and had already helped to rescue the Polish economy in 1928. During the four years he was in China, he specialised in finding joint investment opportunities for European and US businesses. He introduced Chinese banks and lenders to foreign investors who could collaborate on industrial projects. Monnet and Soong developed the China Development Finance Corporation during this period. It was a means of connecting foreign investment and Chinese investment in a way that limited the political control that overseas businesses had been able to exert in the past.

The Great Leap Forward

In 1958, Mao's Second Five-Year Plan began. It was referred to in government circles initially and then across the country as the Great Leap Forward. The gradual souring of relations with the USSR and Mao's fear of the capitalist powers of the West and Japan led him to plan a dramatic transition to a fully industrialised and socialist economy within a decade. He hoped that, by mobilising the entire population, he could propel China into prosperity and power in a few years. Mao believed that China's most powerful resource was its vast population. This alone could compensate for lack of industry and finance, and could enable the country to compete with the USSR and the Western powers in the Cold War within a generation. The key was to organise and mobilise the masses.

Mao proposed a fundamental break with **Marxist Leninism** at this point. The leaders of the USSR argued that the industrial working class was the most important social group in the creation of a socialist society, but Mao argued that if China's peasants were mobilised in vast numbers to create a socialist society, they would achieve far more than the USSR had done. The fact that Mao had decided to use economic policy to pursue an independent course within the Communist sphere, rejecting the USSR, represents a key turning point in Chinese history.

The next stage of ideologically charged land reform in the countryside was the creation of communes. These large organisations were merged collectives, incorporating thousands of peasants who were often removed from agricultural work to perform manual labour hundreds of miles from home. They were regimented into work battalions and companies, using the same structure as an army – Mao frequently wrote that China was engaged in a 'war' with nature and the environment. The abolition of all private land and the removal of all kitchen utensils and cooking from private homes (peasants were forced to eat in communal village canteens) were attempts by Mao to abolish the traditional 'bourgeois' structures of Chinese peasant life. He hoped to erase concepts of individual property ownership and private life to transform Chinese peasants into revolutionary citizens. Money was replaced by work points that could be exchanged for food. This approach, combined with the diversion of food to towns and cities and to China's supporters overseas (countries as diverse as North Korea and Albania), led to a famine that some historians believe killed over 40 million people.

The belief that the energies of millions of Chinese peasants and workers unleashed at the same time could be a short-cut to the creation of socialism in China did not just affect the country's peasants. At the same time, in China's towns and cities, the Communist regime encouraged the creation of backyard steel-smelting furnaces, assuming that this would be a quick and simple way to mass produce large amounts of high-quality metal. Mao had no understanding of the science of metallurgy or the industrial processes necessary to create steel that could be used commercially. In August 1958, Mao demanded that steel production double in a year; however, he wanted backyard smelting to provide this increase. He believed it was possible to create high-grade steel from scrap metal, and Chinese workers and peasants were forced to chop down thousands of trees and use their own belongings as furnace fuel.

Mao was easily deluded by other party members who convinced him the furnaces would work, because this was consistent with the ideological assumptions he already held. When Mao discovered that backyard furnaces could not work, he continued with the policy, believing that revolutionary morale was more important than the quality of the steel produced. Mao's critics had been silenced in the Hundred Flowers Campaign, an attack on China's intellectuals in 1956 where he encouraged them to speak out and then arrested them in their thousands (see page 58). As a result, there was no one to speak out against the mistakes of the Great Leap Forward. Mao was suspicious of experts and believed that voices of moderation and concern were counter-revolutionary. On large-scale projects such as irrigation and river diversion, there were few, if any, expert engineers or geologists. Instead, peasants and workers were employed and tens of thousands died of overwork, hunger and accidents. A decision to kill as many small wild birds as possible (it was thought that they were pests and ate grain) in the Wild Birds Campaign led to an epidemic of crop-eating locusts across China.

KEY TERM

Marxist Leninism
The variant of Marxist ideas adopted by Vladimir Lenin and Joseph Stalin in Russia. Lenin believed that following a Communist revolution, the state would have to build up heavy industry for decades and with it, the size of the working class.

EXTEND YOUR KNOWLEDGE

The Hundred Flowers Campaign

When Mao witnessed the chaos that followed the decision to denounce Stalin in the USSR and Eastern Europe in 1956, he became concerned about critics of his own policies in China. He believed that most Chinese people were fiercely loyal to him, but that a small number of rightist troublemakers existed.

Assuming that these malcontents operated within the party and academia, he devised a plan to encourage them to show themselves. Mao encouraged criticism of the party, knowing that real loyalists would never speak out against him, and that scientists and engineers would also benefit from working in a more open society by being able to experiment with new ideas without the threat of denunciation.

The new spirit of openness was referred to as the 'Hundred Flowers Campaign'. Mao described it as 'letting a hundred flowers bloom and a hundred schools of thought contend is designed to promote the flourishing of the arts and the progress of science.' He misjudged the anger in China over the hardships and violence that the party had inflicted on the population since 1949, and a barrage of criticism resulted, much of it directed personally against Mao.

Deng Xiaoping was given the job of rooting out 'rightist' troublemakers and half a million people were arrested, with many being deported to the remotest parts of China to carry out hard labour. The outpouring of anger left Mao struggling to regain control of the party, but it also gave him the opportunity to silence criticism of him and the regime.

EXTRACT

Historian Frank Dikötter, in his book *Mao's Great Famine* (2011), discusses the beginnings of the commune system and its use in major irrigation projects.

Located a hundred kilometres south of Beijing in the dry and dusty countryside of North China, marked by harsh winters, spring floods and an alkaline soil that hardly yielded enough grain for villagers to survive on, Xushui, a small county of some 300,000 people quickly came to the attention of the Chairman [Mao]. Its local leader Zhang Guozhong approached the irrigation projects like a field campaign. Conscripting a workforce of 100,000 men, he divided farmers along military lines into battalions, companies and platoons. He cut off links with the villages and had the troops live in the open, sleeping in makeshift barracks and eating in collective canteens. Zhang's approach was highly effective and attracted the attention of the leadership in Beijing in September 1957... By collectivising the villagers into disciplined units responding to the call with military precision, Zhang had simultaneously solved the problem of labour and that of capital. Where other counties faced labour shortages as the men abandoned the fields to work on irrigation schemes, he deployed his troops as a continual revolution, tackling one project after another, one wave coming in as another crested.

EXTEND YOUR KNOWLEDGE

The Lushan Conference and the impact of Mao's ideology

In 1959, the party met at Lushan to discuss the impact of the Great Leap Forward. Mao was expecting universal praise from the delegates, but the atmosphere was muted. Marshal Peng Dehuai, China's minister of defence, openly criticised Mao and was dismissed from his post as a result. The conference greatly unsettled Mao, who became increasingly suspicious of the party. Criticisms of the Great Leap Forward did not stop however, and by 1962 Mao had been sidelined by the party. He lived for the next four years in relative obscurity until staging a return to power in 1966 with the Cultural Revolution.

The Great Leap Forward had an enormous impact on the economy. The birth rate halved in five years and even though there was widespread famine, Mao's regime refused to accept any overseas aid. The size of the Chinese economy decreased for the first time in the 20th century as a result of the Great Leap Forward, and the Communist Party demolished nearly 40 percent of all homes in China. Mao's ministers, aware of the death toll the famine was causing, argued that the peasants were making the necessary sacrifices for the revolution. Foreign Minister Chen Yi said in late 1958 that 'Casualties have indeed appeared among workers, but it is not enough to stop us in our tracks. This is the price we have to pay, it's nothing to be afraid of. Who knows how many people have been sacrificed on the battlefields and in the prisons? Now we have a few cases of illness and death: it's nothing!'

SOURCE 6 Chinese peasants on a commune in Yenan province during the Great Leap Forward, 1958.

The Four Modernisations

In 1978, when Deng Xiaoping abandoned the idea of equality for all citizens as a prime economic goal, he adopted the notion of 'xiaokang', or an 'ideal society that provides for the people'. This represented a significant break with Maoist orthodoxy and signalled the start of a new economic era in China. This could not be achieved without significant modernisation, and while Deng's predecessor, Mao, had sought technological modernisation for China, this was combined with immense chaos and upheaval which had significantly reduced standards of living by Mao's death in 1976.

The central aim of the Cultural Revolution era under Mao had been the 'intensification of class struggle'. Mao, for a mixture of his own personal ends and ideological rigidity, had left China in chaos, but the modernisations of Deng Xiaoping had an entirely different objective. Official state propaganda that had once featured Mao and extolled the virtues of the Cultural Revolution changed. Instead of Red Guards brandishing *The Little Red Book* of Mao Zedong's thoughts, propaganda posters featured scientists, workers and engineers, all engaged with building China's future.

In 1975, the fourth National People's Congress met. It was the first time a congress had taken place since 1964, and it was the first one since the start of the Cultural Revolution. The Congress was seen by the party as close to being a parliament, but one that was not democratically elected or representative of the population. Zhou Enlai first mentioned the Four Modernisations, and Deng would later use this announcement as the basis of his own reform programme. The areas that would be modernised, Zhou stated, were agriculture, industry, national defence and science and technology.

Zhou, Deng and other modernisers were elected by party delegates at the congress to take control of China as the aftermath of the Cultural Revolution still affected the country. They were chosen largely because of their pragmatism and moderation, and as a bid to keep Mao's wife Jiang Qing from taking control. However, following the first mention of the Four Modernisations, Deng's more complex task was winning over the Marxist theorists within the party (Deng understood Marxism on a practical level, but he was not a theorist or intellectual). Deng finally managed to bring the party under control in June 1975 by establishing the Political Research Office, meaning that he was able to control the discussion of reform across the party. Deng and Zhou's Four Modernisations were completely at odds with Mao's three principles, which were:

- opposing revisionism (preventing a return to capitalism)
- stability and unity (supporting Mao Zedong's thought)
- improving the national economy (collectivisation and central planning).

By pretending to be loyal to Mao's vision, but selectively ignoring all the aspects of it that hampered reform, Deng and Zhou were able to push through reform. As Mao was frail and dying, he was unable to confirm or refute his position on Deng and Zhou's leadership, though the official line was that they had Mao's backing. This meant that there was no one in the party who could mount a serious challenge to the Four Modernisations.

Military modernisation

In January 1975, Deng had become deputy chairman of the Central Military Commission, gaining power over the People's Liberation Army. He believed that the high point of China's post-revolutionary military power had been in the late 1950s, and that the Cultural Revolution had caused chaos within its ranks which must be redressed if China was to be a great power in Asia again. Initially, the main emphasis for Deng was on making the army efficient again (he described it as 'overstaffed' and 'bloated'), and ensuring that the factional disputes of the Cultural Revolution era in the army came to an end. The army was instructed to take orders only from the party.

Economic modernisation

In this and in the previous section, we have looked at how Deng brought modernising reforms to the communes and gave peasants the autonomy to sell surpluses and grow the crops they wished to. Here we will focus on Deng's reforms to industry. One of Deng's first priorities was to deal with the Chinese transport system in the aftermath of the Cultural Revolution, particularly the railways (for more details on Deng's approach to the railway network, see page 23). The iron and steel industry was in chaos with idle factories and foundries across China, and Deng used Mao's three principles to argue that it should be reformed using 'stability, unity and improving the national economy'. By June 1975, the state council set up an Iron and Steel Leading Group, which within a year had begun to revive the industry. The key to ending the chaos was simply to allow the managers and workers at industries to go back to work without the threat of denunciation or self-criticism.

Science and education modernisation

The system of education had all but collapsed as a result of the Cultural Revolution. Universities had fallen victim to much of the violence of the Red Guards, who were mainly students claiming to represent the true ideas of Mao. Most education for high-school and university students came to an end during the revolution and, instead, intensive study of Mao's works was the only learning that was permitted. Many teachers and academics had been imprisoned, killed or sent to work on communes in the countryside to 're-educate' them in peasant or proletarian values. Deng ended the attacks on teachers and used Mao's three principles to restore order to schools and universities.

Not only did an entire generation miss out on formal education, but scientific research and engineering also came to a halt. The fear of political denunciation caused many researchers to abandon their work. In September 1975, at Deng's instruction, Hu Yaobang wrote a report stating that there were to be no more attacks on scientists for carrying out research, and no areas of scientific learning would be considered politically unsuitable.

A Level Exam-Style Question Section C

'Ideologies, not individuals, drove economic change in the years 1860 to 1997.'

How far do you agree with this opinion? (20 marks)

Tip

This question requires you to balance the influence of individuals and ideologies, but remember that the two are connected. A well-rounded essay will draw comparisons between individuals and ideologies, but it will also see connections between them.

EXTRACT 5

From *The Penguin History of Modern China* by J. Fenby (2010). Here Fenby discusses the development of Special Economic Zones in China in the 1980s.

> The SEZs grew at an average of 30 per cent annually - that is doubling [in size] in three years - as they pumped out exports. Investment poured in through Hong Kong and Taiwan. Companies in the British colony moved investment over the border, employing millions... by 1990 Guangdong would account for a fifth of all China's exports and almost two fifths of its growth came from export industries, its private companies amassing more capital than its state or cooperative sectors.

EXTRACT

From *The Search for Modern China* by J. Spence (1999). Here Spence examines the achievements of Li Honghzhang and the Self-Strengthening Movement.

> In the 1880s Li went on to develop arsenals in Tianjin, which manufactured the bullets and shells for the Remington and Krupp guns that he now began to buy from abroad. A start was soon made on manufacturing the Remington rifles themselves with purchased American equipment. Li developed a national telegraph system by linking the international cables - which had terminated at Shanghai - first to Tianjin and then to Peking [Beijing]; branch wires were then extended to many large inland cities. He also directed the construction of new dock facilities in the south Manchurian city of Lüshun and a seven-mile stretch of railway line to carry coal from the Kaiping mines to a nearby canal, whence it could be shipped to Tianjin and used by the new fleet. Originally the cars were pulled down the tracks by mules, but in 1881 one of Li's assistants used Western scrap parts to build China's first steam engine, which was employed successfully on the line.

EXTRACT

From *Mao's Crusade: Politics and Policy Implementation in China's Great Leap Forward* by A. Chan (2001). Chan describes how Mao's government set targets for heavy industry output.

> The projected production of iron and steel [in Guangdong Province], which became an obsession later in the year, was modest. The target for pig iron (excluding indigenous iron) was a mere 22,000 tons, although three iron and steel plants with a combined annual production capacity of 160,000 tons were planned and expected to be completed within the year. At the closing session [of the Third Plenum of the Provincial Planning Conference January 1958], Wen Minsheng, the party secretary in charge of industry, attacked the so-called 'rightist opportunists', and the 'lazy fellows' who were said to be lethargic, and indifferent toward the Leap. Those who had allegedly set targets low deliberately to gain bonuses were not spared.

THINKING HISTORICALLY

Change 8a, b & c (II)

Judgements about change

If two professionals were asked to track a patient's health over time, one might approach this task by measuring heart rate, weight and cholesterol, while the other professional might assess the patient's mental well-being, relationships and ability to achieve their goals. Both are valid approaches, but result in different reports.

What is true in this medical case is true in historical cases. Measuring change in something requires: (a) a concept of what that something is (for example: What is 'health'? What is an 'economy'?); (b) judgements about how this thing should be measured; and (c) judgements about what relevant 'markers of change' are (how we distinguish a change from a temporary and insignificant fluctuation).

Historians have differed in their accounts of economic change and development in China in the 19th and 20th centuries, and debated the appropriateness of the term 'economic growth' to characterise the story of the economy in this period.

Look at Extracts 5–7 about economic development in China between 1860 and 1997 and answer the following questions:

1. Do all three extracts suggest that the state played an important role in China's industrialisation in the period 1860–1997?
2. Do all three extracts suggest that change was successfully implemented during the years 1860–1997?
3. Do all three extracts agree that economic change happened for ideological reasons during the years 1860–1997?
4. Do the authors show that economic development was equally successful throughout the years 1860–1997?
5. Generalising from these examples, to what extent do historians' judgements about economic change depend on what historians decide to look at and how they decide to measure change?

Conclusion

This chapter has focused on the impact of ideas and individuals in the economic development of China in the 19th and 20th centuries. By the end of the 20th century, it was clear that enormous progress had been achieved and China was emerging as an economic superpower. However, for much of the period 1860–1997, attempts to economically develop and modernise China had either struggled to succeed or had resulted in economic and human catastrophe (for example the Great Leap Forward). The Self-Strengthening Movement, China's post-1911 modernisers, the Guomindang, Mao and then Deng all embraced foreign economic and industrial ideas to differing degrees.

In addition, each of these attempts to bring about economic change in China can be seen as key turning points in the country's history. In each instance, there was a struggle between traditional Chinese economic, social and political practices and the transformative ideas from European and American capitalism and later Soviet communism.

A consistent concern for all of China's rulers throughout the era was that economic weakness would result in political and military weakness, and a backward and poor China would be defeated in war and colonised. The victory of Communism in 1949 did not stop China's new rulers from finding foreign economic ideas and philosophies. Communism was a European concept, devised by the 19th-century German revolutionary Karl Marx. Mao also sought advice and help from the USSR throughout much of the 1950s, and modelled China's Five-Year Plans on those of the USSR. In this chapter, however, we have seen that Chinese rulers often adapted Western economic and industrial ideas to China's own specific circumstances. The Self-Strengthening Movement sought to exploit European technologies but did not want to embrace any economic, social or political idea that would cause the Qing dynasty itself to change, modernise or introduce democratic government. Qing mandarins were able to undermine self-strengthening reforms through a commitment to traditional Confucian beliefs. However, a century later, when Deng Xiaoping introduced economic reforms using elements of capitalist thinking into post-Maoist China, they were far more successful, even though

Communism, a far more overtly anti-capitalist ideology, had been the dominant force in Chinese life for three decades.

Throughout the period covered in this chapter, key figures had a significant impact on the development of China's economy and industry, though in some instances, such as Mao's economic policy in the 1950s, they significantly damaged the economy. The extent to which individuals and ideologies changed the Chinese economy is difficult to gauge, and requires historians to carefully evaluate the available evidence. Each individual discussed, from Li Hongzhang to Deng Xiaoping, had a complex relationship with the economic ideologies that shaped China throughout the period of study.

ACTIVITY
SUMMARY

Ideologies and individuals behind economic growth

1 Who do you think was the most significant individual in the industrial development of China throughout the period 1860-1997? Read the chapter to find evidence to support your argument.

2 What was the role of ideology in developing China?

3 'Mao Zedong's economic ideas had the greatest impact on China's industrial development.' Use the information in this chapter to decide how far you agree with this statement.

4 How far do you agree with the view that industrialisation of China 1860-1997 was brought about by ideologies, not individuals?

WIDER READING

Dikötter, F. *Mao's Great Famine*, Bloomsbury (2011)

Harvey, D. *A Brief History of Neoliberalism*, OUP (2005)

Jisheng, Y. *Tombstone: The Great Chinese Famine, 1958-1962*, Penguin (2012)

Spence, J. *The Search for Modern China*, Norton (1999)

3.3 Opening up China to foreigners, 1860–70

KEY QUESTIONS

- What was the significance of the Treaty of Tianjin (1860)?
- How important for China was the growth in foreign trade?
- To what extent was China influenced by other languages and cultures?

KEY TERMS

Celestial Empire
An old name for China. 'Celestial' means heavenly and the term is linked to the description of the Chinese emperor as the son of heaven.

Kowtow
A traditional Chinese mark of respect performed before the emperor. It involved bowing and kneeling so that one's forehead touched the floor. This prostration demonstrated the Chinese belief that no one was the equal of the imperial emperor.

INTRODUCTION

The first British attempt to open up the whole of the **Celestial Empire** to foreign trade and representatives in 1793 ended in failure. The British diplomatic representative refused to perform the traditional **kowtow** and was dismissively rejected by the emperor; a subsequent mission in 1816 was similarly rejected. China had hoped that in spurning the chance of establishing trade relations, Britain and the West would drop their interest in China. China had minimal knowledge of the West and the central part played by commerce in the developing industrial economies and, as such, was unprepared for the Westerners' determination to open the Chinese market beyond the confines of Guangzhou where limited foreign trade had existed for centuries. Opium, produced in British-held India, was imported into China as the British attempted to reduce its trade deficit with China. The importation of opium would balance out the exports to Europe of Chinese porcelain, silks and tea, which in a relatively short space of time had become a British obsession. Resistance by the Qing dynasty to the opium trade led to a British declaration of war. The First Opium War resulted in a humiliating defeat for the Chinese navy. The Qing dynasty had hoped that a show of strength would deter the British, yet its comprehensive defeat opened the way for further foreign incursions into China. In 1842, the Treaty of Nanjing ended hostilities and partially opened China to foreign trade.

EXTEND YOUR KNOWLEDGE

The First Opium War (1839–42)
Attempts by Qing officials to seize British opium and to halt the opium trade in China led Britain to declare war. Britain's naval supremacy led to a crushing defeat for China, which was compelled to surrender. The Treaty of Nanjing was signed to end the war, and it opened up five Chinese ports to foreign trade. Not only was this a heavy defeat for China, it also showed Chinese ignorance of the West, its intentions and its military strength. It marked the beginning of a century during which China was unable to assert itself in the face of foreign demands for economic and territorial rights.

1860 – Burning of Summer Palace

Ratification of Tianjin Treaty

1861 – Self-Strengthening Movement begins

Establishment of Zongli Yamen

1861–74 – Tongzhi Restoration

1862 – Tongwen Guan School of Combined Learning opened in Beijing

1863

1864 – Defeat of Taiping Rebellion

Tongwen Guan schools open in Guangzhou and Shanghai

1865 – HSBC opens

Jiangnan arsenal established in Shanghai

WHAT WAS THE SIGNIFICANCE OF THE TREATY OF TIANJIN (1860)?

Foreign trade, which had previously been **cartelised** to a limited number of imperial-approved Chinese traders, had been broken open by the Treaty of Nanjing in 1842, under the terms of which five ports – most notably Shanghai – were opened to British merchants. Britain was also given the right of extraterritoriality within these ports. A follow-up treaty the following year established the principle of most-favoured nation. This provision meant that any concession, privilege or immunity given to one 'most-favoured' foreign power must also be extended to the other foreign powers enjoying the same designation. China had hoped this would limit foreign demands, but in reality it prevented it from playing the foreign powers off against one other and weakened China significantly. A contemporary US diplomat suggested that the most-favoured-nation clause destabilised China, allowing other foreign powers to pick up the fruit when others had shaken the tree.

Also as a result of the Nanjing Treaty, Hong Kong, then a barren desolate island, was ceded to Britain in perpetuity. Britain was also awarded a substantial indemnity to compensate for the losses suffered by its opium merchants during the war. China had hoped that with the terms of the Treaty of Nanjing met, the **barbarians** could be restricted to the five coastal treaty ports. The Qing regime was attempting to handle the Europeans in the same manner as China had traditionally dealt with invading forces, such as the Mongols and the Manchus in the 13th and 17th centuries respectively. Marauding peoples and cultures had been assimilated without any loss of Chinese national identity. However, China had fatally misinterpreted Britain's intention. Unlike the marauders of old, 19th-century Westerners directly challenged the way in which China was governed by disregarding Confucian tradition and instead imposing their own system, based on free trade.

China had hoped that the Nanjing Treaty would be the extent of foreign presence and influence. As a consequence, the treaty did not succeed in opening China to the degree that Britain hoped, and Western trade with, and within, China remained limited. In the following years, it became clear that the British opposed attempts to limit Western influence to the treaty ports. Trade did not expand as Britain had hoped, as Qing officials were unenthusiastic to co-operate and Chinese citizens had either little interest in foreign goods or insufficient wealth with which to purchase them. For Britain to assert its trade interests, it determined to open up more of China and waited for an opportunity to act. France was keen to follow Britain's lead and develop trade with China. Britain and France did not have to wait long for provocation. China still viewed itself as superior to the barbarians and continued to adopt an antagonistic stance. In contrast to Britain and France, China did not consider that any renegotiation of the 1842 treaty was required. Two incidents in 1856 gave Britain and France the justification to resume hostilities and push for further concession from the Qing. A ship flying the British flag, the *Arrow*, registered in Hong Kong, was boarded by Chinese officials and the crew were arrested on grounds of piracy and smuggling. Britain protested and the crew were eventually released, but with neither an apology nor assurances that ships under British protection would not be boarded again. This was sufficient grounds for Britain to declare war on China, in which it was supported by France, which had also been wronged by the murder of a French Catholic missionary.

KEY TERMS

Cartelised
Having trade or industry limited to a small group of enterprises dominating an area.

Barbarian
A pejorative term applied to peoples or races said to be uncivilised and primitive. In 19th-century China, it was an insult applied to Westerners.

The Second Opium War erupted and a combined British and French force bombarded and occupied Guangzhou before an Anglo-French fleet sailed north to attack Tianijn and threaten nearby Beijing. In the face of superior military forces, the Chinese surrendered and signed the Treaty of Tianjin in 1858.

EXTEND YOUR KNOWLEDGE

The Second Opium War (1856–60)
Britain felt that China had prevented the terms of the 1842 Treaty of Nanjing being fully enforced and engineered an opportunity to restart hostilities in order to secure a more advantageous agreement. War broke out again in 1856 and by 1858 a combined Anglo-French force had easily defeated China. An agreement was put in place to be ratified by the Xianfeng emperor in 1859. However, when the British and French came to Tianjin to secure the emperor's ratification, they found the city's defences rebuilt. Chinese forces inflicted heavy casualties on the British and French troops and the war began again. The Chinese military was again overwhelmed and the original treaty was made harsher and additional terms were added. The Tianjin Treaty was ratified in full in 1860.

The effects of the Treaty of Tianjin were always going to be felt more than the Treaty of Nanjing. Now, not only the British but also the French would have to be satisfied. Recognising China's weakness, Russia and the USA also pushed for trade agreements. The treaty gave foreign powers the right to house their ambassadors in the capital, and Christian missionaries were permitted to travel freely and spread their gospel throughout the realm (having previously been restricted to the treaty ports). China was also forced to open up ten further treaty ports, including four on the Yangtze River, most notably Nanjing, as well as others in Manchuria, Shandong, Guangdong and Taiwan. The taxes on shipping foreign goods in the interior of China were lowered, foreign ships were given the right to enter any Chinese port, the opium trade was legalised, Christianity was to be tolerated and an indemnity of $4 million demanded. China had learnt little from the humiliation of the First Opium War and fared no better in the Second Opium War, which was significant as it demonstrated the failure of China's attempts to check foreign influence and its inability to militarily oppose Britain and France. China's inability to resist the Western powers encouraged other industrialised powers, such as Russia and the USA, to press territorial and trade claims safe in the knowledge that China was in no position to offer effective opposition.

ACTIVITY
KNOWLEDGE CHECK

The terms of the Treaty of Tianjin

1 What were the terms of the Treaty of Tianjin? Rank them in terms of significance.

2 Write two or three sentences justifying which term of the treaty you believe to be the most significant.

3 Why was the Treaty of Tianjin likely to alter China's attitude to the Western world?

The international impact of the Treaty of Tianjin, 1860

However, this was not the end of the Second Opium War. In the negotiations of the 1858 treaty, it had been agreed that the treaty would be ratified in 1859. When British and French diplomats travelled to Tianjin, the emperor defiantly opposed the establishment of embassies in Beijing. The forts of Tianjin had been repaired and the river on which it stands had been obstructed by chains and sunken objects. Britain and France, with the consent of Russia and the USA, therefore reassumed hostilities and attacked Tianjin in 1859. The British-led fleet attempted to clear the river but met a spirited Chinese resistance and suffered heavy casualties. Qing officials overinflated this victory and sought to repudiate the Tianjin Treaty, believing the Westerners to have been defeated and put in their place.

Repulsed by the Chinese, Britain sent a team of negotiators overland to Beijing, but they were taken prisoner and some were executed. Britain determined to teach China a harsh lesson it would not soon forget. An armed force of about 20,000 troops broke Tianjin's defences and marched on Beijing. The Summer Palace – a complex of palaces, museums, libraries and gardens in Beijing known for its extensive collection of architecture and other works of art – was looted and burnt to the ground. This act was partly punishment for the treatment of the British negotiators, partly a cold-hearted act of war, but mostly a clear message to China that it had no alternative but to comply with the foreign powers. As well as the original treaty being ratified in 1860, an additional Convention of Beijing was negotiated and added to the existing agreement. The emperor apologised for the treatment of the British envoys. A further indemnity to cover war expenses of $8 million was inserted, as was a clause permitting Chinese emigration on British ships (mostly to be '**coolie**' labour on projects in the Americas). Tianjin was also opened as a treaty port and the British colony of Hong Kong was enlarged by the ceding of the Kowloon peninsula on the Chinese mainland. The Russians, although not directly involved in the fighting, took advantage of the situation to seize territory north of Korea, where they soon established the port and city of Vladivostok. The network of treaties that would beset China until the Second World War (1939–45) had been established.

KEY TERM

Coolie
An unskilled manual labourer. Most Chinese emigration in the 19th century took the form of 'coolie' labour.

SOURCE

'What we ought to do in China', a cartoon by John Tenniel published in the British satirical magazine *Punch* in 1860. The cartoon depicts an unruly, backward and uncivilised Chinese dragon threatened by a powerful and morally just British warrior on horseback.

SOURCE 2 Ruins of the Imperial Summer Palace near Beijing, 1860. The burning of the Summer Palace was the final act of the Second Opium War, and all but a few of the palace's buildings, temples and palaces were looted and destroyed by a combined Anglo-French force.

EXTRACT 1

From W.A.P. Martin, *The Awakening of China* (1907). Martin was an American missionary to China and also translated a number of Western texts into Chinese.

The summer palace was laid in ashes to punish the murder of a company of men and officers under a flag of truce; and it continues to be an unsightly ruin. The Emperor fled to **Tartary** to find a grave [he would be dead within the year], and throne and capital were for the first time at the mercy of an Occidental [Western] army. On the accession of Hsien-feng [Xianfeng], in 1850, an old counsellor advised him to make it his duty to 'restore the restrictions all along the coast.' His attempt to do this was one source of his misfortunes. Supplementary articles were signed by which China relinquished her absurd pretensions, abandoned her long seclusion, and, at the instance of France, threw open the whole empire to labours of Christian missions. They had been admitted by **rescript** to the five ports, but no further.

KEY TERMS

Tartary
An old term for a broad area across northern and central Asia.

Rescript
An official announcement.

ACTIVITY
KNOWLEDGE CHECK

The significance of the Treaty of Tianjin, 1860

1. Source 1 was published in Britain. How might a Chinese cartoon have differed in its depiction of Britain and China?
2. To what extent does Source 2 reflect the expectations of the cartoonist who drew Source 1?
3. In which ways does Extract 1 blame the emperor for China's humbling? Do you agree?
4. How was the Second Opium War likely to alter China's perceptions of foreigners?

The challenge to conservative Chinese attitudes after the Second Opium War

The Treaty of Tianjin and its supplementary treaties were significant for China both domestically and internationally. While the negative consequences of the agreement were clear, it had a significant, if only temporary, benefit. It can be traced back to Britain's decision to destroy the Summer Palace. In 1860, Lord Elgin, in command of the British land forces, wanted to destroy the entire **Forbidden City**. However, British officials deemed this too grand an insult to inflict upon China, fearing that the dishonour incurred by the destruction of the Forbidden City would be enough to end the Qing regime. Therefore, the devastation of the Summer Palace was the lesser of two evils: a demeaning punishment for sure, but not a fatal blow to the Qings' continued existence. The reason for British leniency was simple. By 1860, China had acquiesced to all the Westerners' demands. If the Qing dynasty was to fall, perhaps jeopardising the whole structure of imperial China, the territorial concessions, trading rights, agreements and privileges that Britain and the rest of the Western powers had so painstakingly extended might be endangered. The foreign powers would have to re-negotiate terms with whatever regime rose up in the place of the Qings, most likely the Taiping rebels who had long been agitating for the empire's demise. This unpredictability ran counter to colonial interests. After having defeated China and secured its continued subjugation and compliance in a network of unequal treaties, it made sense for the West to uphold the Qing regime to protect its gains and work towards developing trade, which had always been Britain's priority. As it transpired, in the years following the Second Opium War, the West fulfilled a duplicitous role: that of exploiter and saviour.

China had been in the grip of domestic rebellion since 1850, and the Qing had been unable to subdue this and simultaneously defeat the foreigners. Now with China defeated and the Westerners' demands met, Britain, France and the USA went from being adversaries to allies of the Qing. However, the price of Western friendship was submission to the unequal treaties. Imperial China saw this as a price worth paying. Thus, a foreign army fighting on behalf of the Qing empire came into being, the Ever Victorious Army. This army led the successful defence of Shanghai in the face of a Taiping attack in August 1860. Imperial China was wedded to the foreign powers that constricted it.

KEY TERM

The Forbidden City
Consisting of almost a thousand buildings in Beijing, this was the home of the emperors as well as the ceremonial and political centre of Chinese government for almost 500 years until the Qing dynasty collapsed in 1911.

EXTEND YOUR KNOWLEDGE

Ever Victorious Army (1860–64)
After the signing of the Tianjin Treaty, a ragtag group of a couple of hundred Western mercenaries was formed to protect Shanghai from the Taiping Rebellion. Under the command of the American, Fredrick Townsend Ward, the Taipings were repulsed. A British major, Charles Gordon, took over command in 1862 and the epithet of Ever Victorious Army was bestowed on the army, which had grown to 5,000 men. They fought as part of the larger imperial army and played a key role in subduing the Taipings.

EXTEND YOUR KNOWLEDGE

Taiping Rebellion (1850–64)
Discontent in the wake of China's humbling in the Second Opium War led to the formation of a movement under the leadership of Hong Xiuquan, a failed imperial examination candidate who converted to Christianity and believed he was Jesus' younger brother. The rebellion supported social reform, the empowerment of women and the overthrow of the Confucian system. It scored many victories over the Qing armies but was eventually defeated when British, French and US forces came to the aid of the imperial government.

The defeat that China suffered against Britain and France served as an awakening in some quarters. Prince Gong, the emperor's brother, was left to negotiate the peace after Emperor Xianfeng had fled the capital. By ratifying the Tianjin Treaty and acquiescing to the Convention of Beijing, Gong accepted a political and diplomatic reality that the Qing had been attempting to resist since the late 18th century. Qing officials believed that China was superior to foreign powers and, therefore, dealings with the foreigners could only happen when foreign representatives came before the Chinese throne. By being permanently housed within the capital, foreign powers were now accorded equal status to China. The era of Chinese isolation, born of its sense of moral and cultural superiority – namely that China could meet all of its own needs – had come to an abrupt halt. Not only had it become evident that China could not simply ignore the foreigners at its door and their requests for greater economic freedoms, but also it had become evident that the adoption of Western means and even the active military support of Western regimes was central to China's ability to withstand domestic rebellion and sustain itself.

EXTRACT 2
From historian J. King Fairbank, *The Great Chinese Revolution*, 1800–1985 (1986).

In retrospect it seems that the abolition of opium had been mainly a Chinese but also a Manchu policy, to save the people, but when Britain proved invincible, appeasement became the necessary Manchu policy, to save the dynasty. From this time the Manchus' grip on China began to slip, though they were clever enough to get the foreigners' support and survive for another seventy years, until 1911.

ACTIVITY
KNOWLEDGE CHECK

The challenge to conservative Chinese attitudes after the Second Opium War

1. Explain why, after the Second Opium War, Britain and the other Western powers had come to support the Qing dynasty.
2. Why had China opposed the introduction of foreign ambassadors to Beijing?
3. Why was China unlikely to obstruct the Tianjin Treaty of 1860?
4. How does Extract 2 suggest the Second Opium War was pivotal in 19th-century Chinese history?

A Level Exam-Style Question Section B

How significant was the Treaty of Tianjin in the years 1860–70? (20 marks)

Tip

This is a broad question. In order to answer it competently, you will need to look at the domestic and international impact of the agreement. You will also need to evaluate the effect on Chinese attitudes as well as the material effects of the treaty itself.

The Self-Strengthening Movement

With the internal rebellions successfully defeated, China could now take the necessary steps to address its declining status. The defeat in the Second Opium War brought into focus issues that had been growing since China's first defeat two decades earlier. Simply put, China had been overrun by Western powers. China had objected to the Tianjin Treaty, but when it had resisted its ratification the Westerners inflicted another humiliating defeat that resulted in yet more terms being added to the agreement. The country had descended from a lofty isolation to having its interior opened up by conquering foreigners in the space of 50 years. A growing opinion in the upper echelons of the Qing government was that modernisation needed to happen: the Self-Strengthening Movement (see Chapter 2). Yet this realisation was mostly justified as a necessary evil, a means of expunging Western influence, in essence, borrowing parts of Western development and learning to defeat it. The intrinsically conservative Chinese court, therefore, concluded that the basic foundation of imperial China was sacrosanct and not in need of reform. With a new emperor, Tongzhi, the **mandate of heaven** was restored in the eyes of the elite; all that was needed was Western-style militarisation. Also, by focusing on military improvements, the Qing dynasty deflected attention and criticism from its own handling of affairs, most notably its obstruction of foreign trade and inability to understand the nature of Western interest in China. Self-strengthening managed to sustain the Qing dynasty by suggesting that salvation, through militarisation, was at hand.

The shortcomings of China's military had been cruelly exposed during the Opium Wars and reinforced by the difficulties in overcoming internal rebellions. The contrast between the hapless imperial Chinese army, which had been unable to defeat the Taiping rebels, and the British and French armies that had defeated China so comprehensively in 1860, was stark. Accordingly, the Jiangnan arsenal in Shanghai was commissioned in 1865; this and another built in Nanjing became the first Chinese mass producers of ships, guns and cannon. Also noteworthy were the Tianjin machine factory and the Fuzhou navy yard. Promising students of domestic and international affairs were sent to further their learning abroad. The Self-Strengthening Movement gathered pace in the following decades, but its emphasis was universally militaristic. Therefore, the rest of industrial development, such as electricity and rail construction, tottered behind. It can be said that the Treaty of Tianjin led to the Self-Strengthening Movement, a recognition that China in its current state was weaker than the Western powers, but the path of reform that it chose lacked the robustness, breadth and, subsequently, the success of its Meiji counterpart in Japan (see Chapter 4).

Internationally, China's reputation was tarnished following the Tianjin Treaty. The glorious kingdom of old appeared to be collapsing, the embattled Qing faced enemies within as well as abroad. China had dragged its feet in abiding by the terms of the Treaty of Nanjing, and this impudence had been punished severely in the Second Opium War. China had the resistance beaten out of it. The humiliation of the Tianjin Treaty must have been harder to swallow considering that Qing China could not defeat the Taiping and Nian Rebellions without the intervention of the conquering imperialists eager to protect their gains. From this point on, Western presence and influence in China would steadily grow and the memory of isolation faded.

KEY TERM

Mandate of heaven
An ancient Chinese belief that the right to rule was granted by heaven, based on the ruler's ability to rule justly. According to this belief, Chinese emperors were heaven-ordained. Natural disasters were often interpreted as an emperor losing his mandate. In some quarters, China's subjugation under the unequal treaties from the 1840s onwards constituted a loss of mandate.

SOURCE 3

From Feng Guifen, *On the Manufacture of Foreign Weapons* (1861). Feng was a Qing scholar who advocated self-strengthening. In order to achieve modernisation, Feng supported the adoption of Western technology and military systems. This tract was written in the immediate aftermath of China's defeat in the Second Opium War, when China's military shortcomings were made clear to the world.

Why are the Western nations small and yet strong? Why are we large and yet weak? [...]

We have only one thing to learn from the barbarians, and that is strong ships and effective guns... Funds should be allotted to establish a shipyard and arsenal in each trading port. A few barbarians should be employed, and Chinese who are good in using their minds should be selected to receive instruction so that in turn they may teach many craftsmen...

Intelligent and brilliant scholars have exhausted their time and energy in such useless things as the stereotyped examination essays, examination papers, and formal calligraphy... We should now order one-half of them to apply themselves to the manufacturing of instruments and weapons and to the promotion of physical studies... The intelligence and ingenuity of the Chinese are certainly superior to those of the various barbarians; it is only that hitherto we have not made use of them... There ought to be some people of extraordinary intelligence who can have new ideas and improve on Western methods [...]

Some have asked why we should not just purchase the ships and man them with [foreign] hirelings, but the answer is that this will not do. If we can manufacture, repair, and use them, then they are our weapons. If we cannot manufacture, repair, or use them, then they are still the weapons of others... In the end the way to avoid trouble is to manufacture, repair, and use weapons by ourselves... only thus can we become the leading power in the world; only thus can we restore our original strength, redeem ourselves from former humiliations, and maintain the integrity of our vast territory so as to remain the greatest country on earth.

... during the past twenty years since the opening of trade, a great number of foreigners have learned our written and spoken language, and the best of them can even read our classics and histories [...] On the other hand, our officers from the governors down are completely ignorant of foreign countries. In comparison, should we not feel ashamed? The Chinese officers have to rely upon stupid and preposterous interpreters as their eyes and ears. No wonder that we understand neither the foreigners nor ourselves.

A Level Exam-Style Question Section A

Study Source 3 before you answer this question.

Assess the value of the source in identifying the Treaty of Tianjin's effect on Qing attitudes to modernisation in the 1860s as well as the potential flaws of the Self-Strengthening Movement.

Explain your answer, using the source, the information given about its origin and your own knowledge about the historical context. (20 marks)

Tip

Be sure to analyse economic, political, military and cultural consequences of the treaty.

ACTIVITY
KNOWLEDGE CHECK

Self-Strengthening Movement

1. Compile two lists, identifying the strengths and limitations of the Self-Strengthening Movement.
2. Why was investment in Western technology opposed by the more conservative members of the Qing court?
3. Imagine you are a progressive moderniser in China. Write a memorandum to the emperor, arguing for the adoption of more Western ways and methods.

HOW IMPORTANT FOR CHINA WAS THE GROWTH IN FOREIGN TRADE?

Among the most significant effects of the Treaty of Tianjin was the opening up of further ports to foreign trade. This allowed Britain, with the enthusiastic support of France, to redress the limitations of the 1842 Treaty of Nanjing. Western opinion held that, in order to profit from China, it was necessary to open further ports and for a culture of free trade to take root. The four ports opened on the Yangtze allowed foreign trade to spread inland from the coast. Further coastal outlets were established, allowing more access to imported European goods (see Figure 3.1). British people had developed an insatiable appetite for Chinese tea, and silks and porcelain were sought-after luxury consumer items. The problem for Britain was that the Chinese market was not as receptive to Western goods. The Qianlong emperor's letter to King George III was not mere bravado: it represented the reality that due to its international seclusion, China knew nothing of the West and there was not much call for foreign manufactures. In Indian-grown opium, Britain succeeded in finding a product for which there was a ready market in China. The Treaty of Tianjin legalised the trade and for the next 20–30 years it would play a hugely prominent role in China's finances. Now, silver flooded out of China to pay for the opium, and Britain's trade deficit turned into huge profit.

EXTEND YOUR KNOWLEDGE

The Qianlong emperor's letter to King George III (1793)
In 1793, a British delegation headed by Lord McCartney had attempted to reach a trade agreement with China. However, the mission was not successful and the delegation was dismissed without any progress being achieved. In a letter to the British throne, the Qianlong emperor wrote that China had no need of Western-produced goods (see Source 3, page 135). The emperor hoped that this would end Britain's interest in China.

Foreign trade as a concept was initially alien to the Chinese people, but gradually raw cotton began to be imported and, over the coming decades, textile mills were established in major Chinese cities such as Shanghai, producing cloth for domestic use as well as export. The greater significance of the growth in foreign trade was the broadening of China's horizons. China began to learn the ways of the West, a process sometimes referred to as using the barbarians' ways to defeat the barbarians. Unfortunately for China, in the wake of the Treaty of Tianjin, it was too weak and too ignorant to repel foreign exploitation. Imports entered China via the ports which, due to extraterritoriality (see page 12), were under British rule. The British authorities in the ports were able to set a low fixed tariff of five percent. This failed to protect the fledgling Chinese industries as the tariff was sufficiently low to encourage the mass import of British goods which now flooded China. Obviously, the manufactured goods from Britain were of a superior quality to those produced in China. The opening of treaty ports also brought more foreign businesses and merchants to China and furthered China's awakening from years of isolation. The opening of treaty ports and growth of foreign presence and trade can be seen as the beginning of the slow modernisation of China.

A final effect of the growth of foreign trade was the evolution of a new Chinese commercial class: **compradors**. They were Chinese who assisted foreign firms in their commercial dealings, becoming valuable assets to them. Although contracted to foreign firms, they became China's first entrepreneurs, investing in foreign firms, and sometimes their wealth exceeded that of their employers. They also had a wealth of knowledge of, and access to, traditional trade routes which enabled foreign firms to establish roots in China. Most importantly, in the long term, compradors served as role-models and guides to budding Chinese businessmen. This growing entrepreneurialism was strengthened by extraterritoriality within the treaty ports, which gave more freedoms and less bureaucracy.

KEY TERM

Comprador
From the Portuguese word meaning 'buyers', compradors were Chinese agents who worked for foreign firms that had entered China since the 1840s. They helped foreign firms who could not speak Chinese. The compradors can be seen as the first capitalist class in China.

Foreign influence did not fully infiltrate China's internal economy because its influence did not go beyond the treaty ports. British investment in China was focused on firms established within the treaty ports. For the most part, the interior of China remained much the same. Peasants were too poor to purchase industrial goods and many provinces were prone to periods of famine. The Qing government passively observed developments, reacting to them rather than taking the initiative. Its belief remained consistent: self-strengthening would be achieved through militarisation alone. Thus China lacked the centralisation and governmental drive for mass industrialisation. The Qing regime was frequently beset by internal dissent arising from resentment against the corruption, inefficiency and cowardice in its dealings with the foreign powers. Conservative circles at the Qing court opposed major growth of foreign trade as it was deemed incongruous with Confucian values and the Chinese essence. On the other hand, more progressive, forward-looking Chinese economic reformers were of the opinion that the ruling Qing class needed to be more active in supporting modernisation in order to sustain the viability of the empire. Rather than aiding its liberation, China's tentative industrialisation failed to address inherent structural frailties and gave Western powers more opportunities to exploit.

KEY TERM

Tongzhi Restoration (1860–74)
A process named after the Tongzhi emperor, who succeeded Xianfeng in 1860. It was closely linked to the Self-Strengthening Movement. China attempted to strengthen the empire which had been increasingly discredited from the 1840s, culminating in the Second Opium War.

As increased commerce was the main goal of the Western powers, the growth in foreign trade that followed the Treaty of Tianjin afforded China the ability to develop in peace. Indeed, the decades following the Second Opium War mark what has been known as the **Tonghzi Restoration**. For the next 30 years, foreign powers did not need recourse to war in order to achieve their aims. Foreign commerce grew in a more stable environment in which the Taiping and Nian Rebellions had been defeated and China acknowledged its place in the treaty system.

EXTRACT 3

From historian M. Wright, *The Last Stand of Chinese Conservatism* (1973).

Not only a dynasty but also a civilization which appeared to have collapsed was revived to last for another sixty years by the extraordinary efforts of extraordinary men in the 1860s. This was the T'ung-chih [Tongzhi] Restoration... In every sense of public life, the government acted in accordance with the well-known pattern of a restoration - a period in which the decline of a dynasty is arrested and for a time reversed.

EXTRACT 4

From J. King Fairbank and M. Goldman, *China: A New History* (2006).

That the Qing managed to survive both domestic and international attacks is due largely to the policy and leadership changes known as the Qing restoration. By 1861 the Manchu dynasty's mandate seemed truly exhausted. The diehard anti-Western faction in charge of Qing policy had been defeated by the Anglo-French occupation of Beijing in 1860, which secured final acceptance of the unequal treaty system. [...] This more flexible policy began a restoration of Qing power. ('Restoration' - zhongzing - was a traditional term for a dynasty's 'revival at midcourse'.)

ACTIVITY
KNOWLEDGE CHECK

The growth of foreign trade

1 Why did the growth of foreign trade have such a significant impact on China in the 1860s?

2 What effect do you think foreign trade would have on China's attitude to, and relations with, Western powers?

3 Was the Tongzhi Restoration the beginning of the end for Qing China, or did it rather give a declining dynasty another 60 years it would not otherwise have had?

4 To what extent do you agree with the interpretations proposed in Extracts 3 and 4?

The British in Shanghai and penetration of the Yangtze valley

Britain's interests in China had never been territorial in nature. It did not have the means to colonise China, the largest country in the world. British actions in China were trade-related. Britain selected Shanghai as one of the five ports to be opened up in the Treaty of Nanjing that concluded the First Opium War. Of the ports opened by the terms of the Nanjing Treaty, for geographic and logistic reasons only Shanghai had prospered, as its position at the mouth of the great Yangtze River optimised access to the Chinese interior. In a time before rail travel, control of the internal waterways was central to Britain's hopes of realising its Chinese trade aspirations. Shanghai enabled Britain to establish lines of trade into central China, opening the massive Chinese market to British merchants and businesses. Shanghai had not only geography in its favour, but also the fact that it was already an established fishing port.

In 1845, Britain established a settlement in Shanghai. The settlement, to the north of the walled city, was under British law and in 1849 was joined by a French settlement and a few years later by one in the name of the USA. The British and US settlements merged in 1863 to form the Shanghai International Settlement; China retained sovereignty over the walled city. Foreign nationals, primarily Britons, flooded into the settlement. Their numbers were further swollen by thousands of Chinese fleeing the Taiping Rebellion, which was strongest around the Yangtze River to the west of Shanghai. The settlement had its own police, fire and armed services as well as administrative offices: a famous sign in a public park barred Chinese and dogs from entering. The settlement began to take the form of well-to-do British society, with golf and race courses, cricket and tennis clubs, swimming pools, theatres, schools and churches, not to mention bars, brothels and cabarets. The opium trade flourished and international banks sprang up as international trade and business grew. The Hong Kong and Shanghai Banking Corporation (HSBC) was established in 1865. Shanghai soon superseded Guangzhou as the centre of internal Chinese commerce and trade.

From Shanghai, treaty ports were opened up westwards on the Yangtze River, including Nanjing and Hankou. Britain hoped that it could now use its base in Shanghai to penetrate the Yangtze valley and unlock the potential of a market numbering many millions. By opening the Yangtze valley, Britain also established stable conditions for trade nearer to centres of production and consumption, thereby cutting transit costs. Within years, various inlets on the river would specialise in exporting petroleum, rice, cotton and tea. Opening up the Yangtze also allowed for the navigation of tributary rivers. Although this development offered potential, the British never fully achieved its trade objectives in China. The treaty ports developed into glistening examples of modernity in terms of Western institutions and architecture, but Chinese culture and outlook, on the whole, lagged behind. Foreign trade failed to significantly alter the character of China's economy and it remained a primarily agricultural and self-sufficient country. In essence, this was the final instance of China's isolation and seclusion. Before too long, Britain would no longer be the prime foreign power operating in China, and the nature of foreign powers' interest in China would take a territorial turn. However, during the 1860s, British presence in Shanghai and the penetration of the Yangtze valley offered China insights into British ways of trade, diplomacy, administration and militarism. It is telling that the international community successfully defended Shanghai against the Taipings in 1862, and their victory foreshadowed the dawning reality that to assert its rights and maintain its sovereignty, China would have to incorporate Western ideas and developments into its oriental Confucian methodology.

Figure 3.1 Taiwan and the Yangtze River, and the treaty ports that were opened as a result of the Tianjin Treaties of 1842 and 1860. By enjoying control of the Yangtze, Britain was able to further its trade interests in China.

ACTIVITY
KNOWLEDGE CHECK

The British in Shanghai and the penetration of the Yangtze valley

1 Why had Shanghai grown under British influence?

2 Work in pairs. One of you should play the role of a member of the Shanghai International Settlement and the other a Chinese producer of porcelain. Discuss whether foreigners should be allowed to penetrate the Yangtze valley.

3 With reference to Figure 3.1, why was the Yangtze River central to Britain's ambition of exploiting China's internal markets?

TO WHAT EXTENT WAS CHINA INFLUENCED BY OTHER LANGUAGES AND CULTURES?

The spread of foreign-language schools teaching English and French

China's defeat in the Second Opium War and the subsequent Tianjin Treaty of 1860 had convinced the Qing court that its weakness and backwardness made some degree of modernisation imperative. From 1860 to 1870, as the terms of the Treaty of Tianjin were enacted, China was opened up to foreigners. In order to sustain its position and not be further humiliated and exploited, China became increasingly acquainted with Western technology as a means to self-strengthen. Western technology on top of a base that remained consistent with Chinese culture, traditions and morals, would enable China to become independent of its oppressors and re-assert itself internationally, while retaining its Chinese character. Central to this aspiration was the requirement to increase the learning of Western languages, primarily English and French. Obviously, such learning would serve China well in terms of international diplomacy, and this was the stimulus for the spread of foreign-language schools. Initially limited to translating the Tianjin Treaty and Beijing Conventions to prevent further manipulation at the hands of unscrupulous and incompetent interpreters, foreign-language schools would develop a wider and more ambitious scope.

That is, of course, not to say that the concept of education did not already exist in China, but it was unrecognisable from the approaches adopted in the West. Indeed, the civil service exams, the **jinshi,** had existed since the Tang dynasty (618–896 CE) and remained pretty much unchanged. Bright candidates were identified and instructed to apply locally; if successful, they entered regional and then national examinations. The knowledge required to pass the exam was focused on the study of Chinese classics and **calligraphy**. If the jinshi was obtained – and only two percent of all applicants were successful – the position holder would be called into the service of the government. In that sense, China chose its civil servants on merit long before examinations were introduced into its Western equivalents. However, more significantly, by 1860 this meant that Chinese scholars and officials were ignorant of Westernised diplomacy, technology and culture and, consequently, the Qing court was wholly deficient in its dealings with the West.

Those in favour of Western-influenced reform included Prince Gong, who was responsible for the establishment, in 1862, of the first foreign-language school in Beijing: the **School of Combined Learning (Tongwen Guan)**. The school never educated more than 200 students at any time, but hired Western tutors to give instruction in English, French, Russian and Japanese. It soon grew to cover astronomy and mathematics as well as chemistry, medicine and international law. After 1869, an eight-year programme was developed; the first three years were dedicated to the learning of foreign languages, and scientific and more general studies were available thereafter. The school struggled to attract the cream of the Chinese youth, as Manchu families focused on their children passing the jinshi civil service examinations, which had no Western content. The spread of foreign-language schools was a key component of the Self-Strengthening Movement, and in 1863 new Schools of Combined Learning were commissioned for Shanghai and Guangzhou. The Shanghai school offered a broad classical education along with mathematics, science and foreign languages, and offered places to 50 students. The Guangzhou school took in fewer students and was less open to Western ideas. The immediate impact of the schools was notable for introducing organised Western learning to China, albeit on a limited scale.

KEY TERMS

Jinshi
Literally meaning 'presented scholar', this was the qualification needed to work for the Chinese government and the third and highest level to be attained following examination in the capital city. Applicants had to display knowledge of the Four Books and Five Classics, which were written at equivalent times to the New and Old Testaments respectively.

Calligraphy
The writing of characters is an art which has developed over many centuries in China. It is displayed in museums just as paintings are.

School of Combined Learning (Tongwen Guan)
A school established in Beijing in 1862 and funded by the Chinese government. It primarily taught foreign languages but also developed to cover a broad scientific curriculum.

SOURCE

From Prince Gong, a memorial to the Chinese throne (1866). Memorials to the throne were official communications to the emperor which court administrators read aloud to him. They were the means of bringing developments or ideas to the emperor's attention. Gong was the uncle of the Tongzhi emperor and had been the lead Chinese negotiator at Tianjin in 1860. He was a supporter of Chinese modernisation and advocated the opening of the Beijing Tongwen Guan and its sister institutions in Guangzhou and Shanghai.

The school has now been in operation nearly five years, and the students have made fair progress in the languages and letters of the West. Being, however, very young, and imperfectly acquainted with the letters of their own country, their time is unavoidably divided between Chinese and foreign studies. Should we, in addition, require them to take up astronomy and mathematics, we fear they would not succeed in acquiring more than a smattering of anything.

The machinery of the West, its steamers, its firearms, and its military tactics, all have their source in mathematical science. Now at Shanghai and elsewhere the building of steamers has been commenced; but we fear that if we are content with a superficial knowledge, and do not go to the root of the matter, such efforts will not issue in solid success.

Your Majesty's servants have accordingly to propose, after mature deliberations, that an additional department shall be established, into which none shall be admitted but those who are over twenty years of age, having previously gained a degree in Chinese learning. For we are convinced that if we are able to master the mysteries of mathematical calculation, physical investigation, astronomical observation, the construction of engines, the engineering of watercourses, this, and only this, will assure the steady growth of the power of the empire.

ACTIVITY
KNOWLEDGE CHECK

The impact of the spread of foreign-language schools

1 Using Source 4, compile a list of reasons explaining why foreign-language schools were so strongly promoted by Prince Gong and Chinese modernisers.

2 Why do you think there was considerable opposition to the establishment of these schools in the years 1860–70?

3 Produce an A4 poster advertising the Beijing Tongwen Guan to prospective applicants.

Apart from the Schools of Combined Learning, the other noteworthy providers of foreign-language and Western studies were the schools set up at the Jiangnan arsenal and the Fuzhou navy yard. It was at these small schools that European instructors hoped the students would imbibe the principles of Western technology and learning. The schools operated with the arsenal and shipyard to teach practice as well as theory. At Fuzhou, more than 100 pupils from local gentry families aged 14 and under were enrolled upon its foundation in 1867. The school was split into French and English divisions, both instructing pupils in subjects such as naval construction, geometry, calculus, trigonometry, physics and mechanics, as well as French and English respectively. A smaller centre educated mostly those who had previously worked in English foundries in Hong Kong and Shanghai and offered English, simple maths and the principles behind steam-powered ships.

Students at the Jiangnan arsenal school received an education in western maths and sciences while simultaneously learning about Western machinery. There was also a translation department, and within it a school for training translators, producing books in Chinese on Western science and technology. In 1869, the Shanghai School of Combined Learning relocated to the arsenal. The influence and impact of foreign-language schools across China went beyond the number of the students it enrolled. They introduced a generation of Chinese students to Western learning. Although viewed with disdain by the traditional elites who rejected them for presenting a challenge to Confucian orthodoxy, foreign-language schools were a reaction to the reality in which China now found itself. Western learning and the presence of English and French instructors ended China's international seclusion more permanently and completely than the signing of the Treaty of Tianjin or the conventions that followed.

ACTIVITY
KNOWLEDGE CHECK

Western education within a Confucian framework

1 In what ways would conservative Chinese have criticised Western education as being incompatible with Confucian values?

2 Do you believe that Western education would improve or worsen Chinese relations with, and attitudes to, the West? Explain your answer.

SOURCE

From a memorandum to the emperor from Li Hongzhang in 1863, requesting that Combined Schools of Learning be opened in Shanghai and Guangzhou. Li was a regional governor and one of the foremost promoters of self-strengthening within the Qing court. He was one of the most significant figures in Chinese politics from the 1860s onwards.

That which the Westerners are good at, such as mathematical studies, the principles of science and the techniques of manufacturing and surveying, have all been the subject of specialisation and practical treatment and have been written up in books... Can the Chinese be inferior to the Westerners in ingenuity and intelligence? If there are men well versed in the Western language and one person can teach another, then all the skilful techniques of steamships and firearms can be gradually mastered.

SOURCE

From Feng Guifen, *On the Adoption of Western Learning* (1862). Along with *On the Manufacture of Foreign Weapons* (Source 3), this exemplifies Feng's progressive economic thinking. Although a proponent of self-strengthening, Feng believed in the traditional political and social order grounded in Chinese ethics and Confucian thinking.

Books on mathematics, mechanics, optics, light, chemistry, and others all contain the ultimate principles of understanding things. Most of this information is unavailable to people in China...

I have heard that with their new methods the Westerners have found that the movements of the earth conform closely to those of the heavens. This can be of assistance in fixing the calendar... I have heard that the Westerners' method of clearing sand from harbours is very effective... This can be of assistance to keep the water flowing. Also, for agricultural and sericultural [silk-farming] tools, and things required for the various crafts, they mostly use mechanical wheels, which require little energy but accomplish much... There are many intelligent people in China. Surely there are some who, having learned from the barbarians, can surpass them...

ACTIVITY
KNOWLEDGE CHECK

The impact of Western ideas on Chinese education

1 In which ways do Sources 5 and 6 suggest Western education would be beneficial to China?

2 How useful to the historian are Sources 5 and 6 in evaluating the idea that the imposition of Western ideas was universally welcomed in China?

3 How and why did figures such as Li Hongzhang and Feng Guifen attempt to combine Western learning with Confucian thinking?

4 Are there aspects of Western society and culture that would have been helpful to strengthen China which Sources 5 and 6 do not notice? If so, why might this be?

Growing awareness amongst the elite of other cultures and ideas

After the shock of its forced reintroduction to the Western world in the years from 1860 had been digested, it dawned upon the Qing elites that China's position within the world order was changing. Progressive self-strengtheners felt that China was in desperate need of modernisation and that unless this was commenced post-haste, imperial China would spiral downwards in terminal decline. On the other hand, conservative elements remained sceptical of the relevance of foreign institutions to China. They remained firm in the belief that Confucian thinking was superior to anything the barbarians could possibly offer, and that recent defeats were only attributable to the West's superior weaponry. Thus with military modernisation achieved, China could check the West without any need to reform its dynastic regime. To facilitate this, some Western learning and science would have to be adopted, but these would be grafted onto the existing Confucian model.

From a negligible starting point, a growing awareness of other cultures and ideas slowly began to emerge. One of the main reforms which engendered this awakening was the establishment of the **Zongli Yamen** in 1861. This became the government department responsible for managing relations with foreign nations. It was the first development of government that can be attributed to the impact of the West and the Treaty of Tianjin. The Zongli Yamen's primary function was to execute foreign policy rather than create it; that honour remained the exclusive prerogative of the emperor (during this period, the Dowager Empress Cixi) in consultation with the Grand Council. The curious status of the Zongli Yamen can be illustrated by its accommodation. As relations with Westerners were still deemed of secondary importance, the Zongli Yamen was established in a modest disused government building in Beijing, but given an impressive frontage to impress foreign visitors. This illustrated the realisation that relations with the foreign powers were to become a fixed feature of Chinese politics from this point, while still clinging to the structure of traditional dynastic imperial China.

KEY TERM

Zongli Yamen
Under the terms of the Treaty of Tianjin, China was forced to accept foreign ambassadors. The Zongli Yamen was set up to formalise relations with foreign powers.

Upon its formation, the Zongli Yamen, with Prince Gong at its head, focused on familiarisation with international law, itself a marked development from the insular response to defeat in the First Opium War, when China tried to remain as isolated from foreign powers as possible. Where previously defeat had been seen as an exception to the norm of Qing dominance, defeat in the Second Opium War was seen as evidence of decline and decadence in the face of Western strength of arms. Each military defeat was followed by a treaty that was unfavourable to China. What had become abundantly clear was that China was just as overpowered diplomatically as it was militarily, its military weakness mirrored by diplomatic ignorance on a bewildering scale. Imperial negotiators easily backed down on significant issues like tariff control, extraterritoriality and the most-favoured-nation principle, but fought tenaciously to resist such relatively innocuous proposals as foreign embassies and abandoning the kowtow for foreign visitors. The translation of Henry Wheaton's *Elements of International Law* was commissioned by the Zongli Yamen in 1862, as Chinese diplomats became aware that there was more to Western foreign policy than military might. The translation was completed in 1864 and Prince Gong soon used it to score a diplomatic victory when a ship of the Prussian navy captured three Danish merchant ships in Chinese waters. In Europe at that time, Prussia and Denmark were at war, but using his newly acquired knowledge, Prince Gong pointed out that Prussian aggression was in violation of international law. The Danish merchants were freed and China was compensated to the tune of $1,500. Subsequently, the translated text was distributed throughout the country. This triumph proved to be the exception rather than the rule, but it demonstrated the benefits of China becoming more aware of the international community.

EXTEND YOUR KNOWLEDGE

Elements of International Law (1836)
Written by Henry Wheaton, a US lawyer and diplomat, this formed the basis of international diplomatic law. Its translation began the process of Chinese assimilation into international society.

British advisers Robert Hart, the Inspector General of Customs in the employment of the Qing, and Thomas Wade, the British minister in Beijing, both submitted papers to the Zongli Yamen in the mid-1860s advocating industrial developments like rail and steam travel, mining and modern education, but most prominent among their recommendations was familiarisation with, and adoption of, Western diplomatic practices. In response, the Zongli Yamen authorised a delegation to undertake an informal fact-finding mission across Europe in 1866 under Hart's leadership. The tour took in all the capital cities of the countries with whom China now had relations through the tangled web of the unequal treaties. The delegation was not successful: although the delegates visited Paris, London, Berlin, Stockholm, Copenhagen and St Petersburg, their attention was mostly taken by aesthetic marvels such as tall buildings, gaslights and lifts; the subtler refinements of European democracy largely passed them by. This is symbolic of the period as a whole. There was growing awareness of foreign cultures and ideas, but it was more dipping a toe in the water than total immersion.

Even though a growing number of Chinese citizens travelled internationally during the 1860s and brought Western learning back with them, this would take generations to permeate China to any meaningful degree. New ideas would slowly seep into urban areas, but rural China and the lives of the vast majority were unaffected. The effect of proximity with, and knowledge of, foreign cultures only served to exacerbate disaffection with the Qing dynasty, which was increasingly viewed as an obstacle against the modernisation, and thereby salvation, of China. Every success and achievement of Western society seemed to highlight a commensurate weakness in China.

EXTEND YOUR KNOWLEDGE

Imperial Maritime Customs Service (1854–1911)
This was the institution responsible for collecting customs duties payable on business transacted in the treaty ports. It soon grew to cover domestic customs and postal administration, harbour and waterway management, weather reporting, and anti-smuggling operations. It conducted loan negotiations, currency reform, and financial and economic management. It was largely staffed by Westerners, primarily British but also significant numbers of French, Americans and Japanese.

China undertook to send another international mission in 1868 in response to fears that US and European traders and merchants wished to accelerate the opening of China to foreign trade. The delegation was led by the retiring US Minister to China, Anson Burlingame, who lent his name to the mission. As the head of the Chinese delegation, he was welcomed grandly in the USA as the son of the world's newest culture and representative of the world's oldest. He secured US assurance that the pace of modernisation would not be forced. Similar agreements were achieved with Britain, Germany and Russia. The mission, however, did not prove to be much of an achievement, as when the Tianjin Treaty was due for renegotiation in 1868, Britain refused to make concessions to make the treaty any less unequal. This brush with Western diplomacy did not immediately benefit China, but it paved the way for more formal and standardised relations with the Western powers. It was part of a long learning process that necessitated the end of China's international seclusion and familiarisation with the West as a means of modernisation and preservation of China's autonomy.

ACTIVITY
KNOWLEDGE CHECK

The Zongli Yamen

1. In which ways did the Zongli Yamen contribute to the modernisation of Chinese politics?
2. Explain why the Zongli Yamen was accommodated in modest premises and not a more palatial building.
3. Assess the significance of the two Chinese foreign missions headed by Hart and Burlingame.

The impact of missions and missionaries

SOURCE

Herman Knackfuss, *Peoples of Europe, guard your dearest goods* (1895). This German painting represents a prominent school of thought in the West, present since the mid-19th century, that the Christian countries had a duty to civilise the East and neutralise an alien threat to Western society.

ACTIVITY
KNOWLEDGE CHECK

Different cultures in the West and East

1. Why do you think pieces of propaganda like Source 7 became increasingly common from 1860 onwards?
2. How far is Source 7 representative of Western understanding of China?
3. How might contemporary Chinese have disagreed with the message presented in Source 7?

There was perhaps no clearer immediate exemplification of Western influence than the impact of missions and missionaries. Missionaries from Europe and the USA brought the teachings of the Christian faith to China. Some had entered China prior to the First Opium War, but Britain's victory ushered in an era of accelerated missionary activity. Missionaries came with the intention of saving China by converting its people to Christianity. Such an air of superiority manifested itself in a condescending attitude to China and its Confucian culture. The preaching zeal of the missionaries was ill-suited to a sensitive and defensive China that resented being humbled at the hands of the Western powers and the opening-up to foreigners that this precipitated. Nevertheless, it is clear that missions and missionaries had a profound effect on China in the 1860s.

The Treaty of Tianjin of 1860 included a provision, at French insistence, to give missionaries freedom of travel. They had hitherto been confined to the treaty ports, but military might had secured them wider rights to preach and they poured into the Chinese interior. The poverty of the Chinese peasantry offered opportunities for missionary activities with the social groups most receptive to the Christian message – non-Manchu poorer Chinese, ethnic minorities and women. For all these groups, Christian missionaries offered an alternative vision and challenged Confucian orthodoxy. As with economic and industrial developments, the presence of missionaries was largely met by a wall of resistance and cynicism. After centuries of isolation, it would take time for China to accept foreign visitors and their ideas. Previously, foreigners had kowtowed to the emperor and come before the Dragon Throne as tributaries adopting a subservient posture to the Qing. Now missionaries had been granted extraterritoriality and secured legal rights and protection for Chinese converts that were not afforded to non-Christian Chinese. Chinese converts renounced central Confucian tenets such as concubinage, foot-binding and ancestor worship. Missionaries drew the ire of those most loyal to the status quo: the educated gentry. Scholarly patriotic indignation fused with ugly xenophobia, which had grown in reaction to the Tianjin Treaty, in a fierce defence against Christian evangelism. Thus Christianity became associated with Chinese efforts, whether Christian or not, at reforming the Qing regime.

ACTIVITY
KNOWLEDGE CHECK

The appeal of Christianity in China

1 Make a list of the benefits Christian missionaries brought to different sections of Chinese society.

2 How did Christianity pose a threat to the established Confucian order?

Indeed, it was not the religion of the devout missionaries that had the most significant effect on China – numbers of converts remained low, a negligible percentage of the total population – but rather the cultural, educational and social ways they brought with them. That is not to say that no Chinese converted to Christianity. By the turn of the century, approximately 700,000 Chinese had converted to Catholicism and 100,000 to Protestantism. Protestant missionaries, in particular, were prodigious printers and produced huge quantities of literature to be distributed, mostly free of charge. Due to the large amount of illiteracy in China, it was common for pamphlets and leaflets to be read aloud at public gatherings. The message of Christian tracts and Bibles spread rapidly and thousands converted, notable amongst them Hong Xiuguan, who later went on to lead the Taiping revolt. The Taipings were associated with Christianity, and the fervent nationalism and traditionalism that had defeated the uprising prevented Christian ideas from taking root. The Taiping Rebellions had served to increase suspicion of Christianity as a direct threat to the Qing dynasty. Salacious accusations were thrown at missionaries and converts: Christians were said to mutilate pregnant women, rape female Chinese converts and engage in incest. As wild and unfounded as these accusations were, through endless repetition an intense anti-Christian and, in effect, anti-Western folklore developed. It was not all one-way, and missionaries' patronising habit of involving themselves in regional political cases in support of converts or in a populist attempt to win converts to Christianity only increased hostility. Indeed it was this practice, largely carried out by Catholics, that swelled the number of converts. It is fair to say that a higher percentage of Protestants were genuine in their conversion than Catholics, who tended to be attracted by legal and material benefits. For this reason, a high number of Catholic converts were drawn from the seedier, even criminal, parts of Chinese society.

The social and educational impact of missionaries

The impact of Christian missionaries was particularly felt in the realm of education, and it was natural enough that much missionary zeal was directed at China's youth. The masses were illiterate, impressionable and convertible. Although present since the Treaty of Nanjing in 1842, missionary schools sprang up inland and along the coast following the opening of new treaty ports in 1860. Curriculums differed from region to region and there were distinct Protestant and Catholic variants. Catholic education focused on Chinese classics and **proselytising**. Protestant schools taught a more rounded, secular curriculum including maths, the sciences, history and geography. They performed the function of educating Chinese people sufficiently to take up English-speaking positions within the treaty ports. However, the educational nature of missionary work had a greater effect on China's awakening and development than just educating its children. Missionaries played a significant role in the translation of Western works that filled gaps in Chinese knowledge and learning. Works on astronomy, algebra, geometry and calculus were translated and made accessible to the educated Chinese classes, as well as information on Western learning and the Western world in general. Through this familiarisation, the missionaries contributed to China's development by providing information and education to a society ripe for reform. Although failing to reach the majority of China's population, the missionary schools undoubtedly gave basic learning to thousands of Chinese who would have previously had no access to organised education. Many of those educated in missionary schools from 1860 to 1870 would study at higher levels, frequently abroad, and go on to play important roles in China's modernisation. Missionary distribution of literature and propaganda weakened the Qing by presenting an alternative to Confucian dogma. As awareness of the West became more widespread, the emperor's grip on China grew ever weaker. The more China was defeated and humiliated, the more attractive and relevant the theories and knowledge of the West became.

KEY TERM

Proselytising
The act of converting to Christianity.

Missionaries also played an important social role. Missions provided famine relief and also provided refuges for the curing of opium addicts (opium addiction had become rife since the Qing had been defeated in the Opium Wars). Famine had become a more regular occurrence as the population had doubled over the previous century. Missionaries also made efforts to care for the deaf and blind. Orphanages, which served the double purpose of looking after destitute children while simultaneously spreading the Christian message, saved many lives. In their achievements, missionaries showed the deficiencies of imperial China, which appeared incapable of adapting to the changing world and its own growing population.

The subservience of women within China was one of the most fundamental aspects of Confucianism, and it was here that the efforts of Protestant missionaries were directed. Tradition dictated that women should be submissive before their parents and husbands. They enjoyed minimal opportunities for expression or social activity beyond their own family unit. Also female access to formal education was strictly forbidden. Women were prohibited from entering the civil service examinations and were not allowed to serve in any official capacity. Women in Confucian society were subjected to concubinage, infanticide and foot-binding. Therefore, the challenge that Christianity posed to Confucius appealed to women, as the most disenfranchised social class. In stark contrast to their Chinese sisters' subjugation, the most striking sign of Western female emancipation was that a large number of missionaries were women. These women were all literate, many were teachers or physicians, and they believed in sexual equality to a degree totally alien to Chinese tradition. They criticised female infanticide and arranged marriages, and decried the practice of foot-binding. From 1860 to 1870, it slowly become customary for Chinese women to ritually unbind their feet on joining the church. Female converts received the same opportunities as males in Protestant schools.

A Level Exam-Style Question Section A

Study Source 8 before you answer this question.

Assess the value of the source in revealing Chinese society's view of Christian missionaries and the Westerners' perception of China from 1860 to 1870.

Explain your answer, using the source, the information given about its origin and your own knowledge about the historical context. (20 marks)

Tip

You will need to evaluate why educated Chinese held the views referenced in the source and the influence they held in China. You should also analyse the background to the establishment of Christian missions in China and also the positive and beneficial works conducted by European missionaries.

SOURCE 8

John Griffith, quoted in R. Thompson, *John Griffith: The Story of Fifty Years in China* (1906). Griffith was a leading British Protestant missionary who resided in China 1855–1912. In this excerpt from his biography, he is debating the effect of Christian missionary work on the educated Chinese classes and the gentry in particular. He also discusses his encounters with other social classes within Chinese society.

It is impossible not to displease them. To preach is to insult them, for in the very act you assume the position of a teacher. To publish a book on religion or science is to insult them, for in doing that you take for granted that China is not the depository of all truth and knowledge. To establish hospitals and other benevolent institutions is to insult them, for there is in the idea a reflection on the native skill and charity. To propound progress is to insult them, for therein you intimate that China has not reached the very acme of civilisation, and that you stand on a higher platform than they. This is the way the literati think and feel with respect to foreigners and everything that is foreign; and the anti-foreign, anti-progressive, exclusive, self-satisfied, proud, and supercilious spirit of this class is the resisting medium in China.

Behind the literati are the people. These are, on the whole, quiet, industrious, and harmless. With respect to foreigners, the people seem to me to be passive, except when roused to antagonism and hatred by their superiors. It would be too much to say that they like us or desire intercourse with us; but it would be equally wide of the mark to say that they are ill-disposed towards us. Of course I am not now speaking of those who have come into close contact with us, and who have been benefited by us religiously or otherwise. Among these there are many thousands who are warmly attached to us, who desire sincerely that China should come into warmer and more intimate relations with the nations of the West, who readily acknowledge our superiority in many respects, and who pity the blindness of those who set their faces so resolutely against all progress.

The Tianjin massacre of 1870 and its immediate consequences

The differences between Christianity and Confucianism and the reaction of Chinese resistance to missionary overtures of conversion caused frequent violence and bloodletting. The most infamous of all was the Tianjin massacre of 1870. The location was no surprise: Tianjin had been the scene of the humiliating 1860 treaty and had been occupied by the French and British in 1856 and again in 1860. The English and French stationed thousands of troops within the city to ensure China abided by the treaty's terms. Simmering resentment was inflamed by the construction of tall churches that disregarded the Chinese belief of feng shui. The gentry organised anti-missionary activities and, in 1868, an attack on a mission station in Yangzhou was met by a disproportionate British response: warships were sent to Nanjing to demand compensation and the execution of the perpetrators. Such harsh reprisals riled the Chinese population and it was in this context, combined with irritation at the continued presence of foreign soldiers and missionaries, that the Tianjin massacre came to pass.

EXTRACT 5

From historian P. Cohen, *Discovering History in China: American Historical Writing on the Recent Chinese Past* (1984).

In part, too, the missionary was attacked because the manner in which he made his presence felt after 1860 seemed almost calculated to offend. By indignantly waging battle against the notion that China was the sole fountainhead of civilisation and, more particularly, by his assault on many facets of Chinese culture per se, the missionary directly undermined the cultural hegemony of the gentry class. Also, in countless ways he posed a threat to the gentry's accustomed monopoly of social leadership. Missionaries were the only persons at the local level, aside from the gentry, who were permitted to communicate with the authorities as social equals; in addition, they enjoyed an extra-territorial status that gave them greater immunity to Chinese laws than the gentry had ever possessed.

[...]

Missionaries were the first foreigners to leave the treaty ports and venture into the interior, and for a long time they were virtually the only foreigners whose day-to-day labours carried them to the farthest reaches of the Chinese empire. For many Chinese in the last century, therefore, the missionary stood as a uniquely visible symbol against which opposition to foreign intrusion could be directed.

ACTIVITY
KNOWLEDGE CHECK

Opposition to Christianity within educated Chinese society

1 In which ways does Extract 5 explain why conservative Chinese circles opposed Christianity and missionaries?

2 Using Extract 5, do you believe that Christian missionaries were more welcomed or reviled in China from 1860 to 1870?

The Tianjin massacre

In 1869, the French insensitively constructed a church and orphanage, Notre Dame des Victoires, on the site of a razed Buddhist temple. The orphanage offered payment in exchange for orphans. Sick and dying children were baptised to offer them eternal salvation, but this was not understood by the Chinese, who thought high mortality rates were the result of Western barbarism. Rumours abounded that the hearts and eyes of children were used for Western medicine. A riot loomed and an official investigation that absolved the orphanage of any guilt failed to appease the crowds. A furious French diplomat demanded that the protesters be dispersed and fired his pistol at the local magistrate, missing him but killing his servant. This caused the mob to erupt in full-blown riot. The church and orphanage were both burnt to the ground, the French diplomat and his assistant were murdered, as were ten nuns, two priests and two French officials. Three Russians were mistaken for French citizens and killed, and British and US churches were destroyed. Foreign gunboats were dispatched to Tianjin and complaints by foreign powers compelled the Zongli Yamen to open negotiations. Li Hongzhang, the governor of the region, went to Tianjin and proposed the execution of eight leaders and exiling of a further 20 for hard labour. A delegation was sent to France to issue an official apology, the local magistrate was dismissed and an indemnity to compensate loss of lives and properties was set.

The massacre did not end attacks on missionary stations and churches. The evangelical nature of the missionaries' work continued to antagonise Chinese sensitivities and there emerged a cycle of attacks followed by Western reprisals, the execution of the ringleaders and indemnities. The aftermath of the Tianjin massacre illustrated the relationship between China and the Western powers. With the slightest provocation, foreign powers imposed their will without Qing resistance. Within a decade, missionary work had gone from being restricted to the treaty ports to asserting Christian beliefs nationally in the face of established tradition, with Western gunboats eager to address any perceived dishonour.

A Level Exam-Style Question Section B

'From 1860 to 1870, China transformed from a Confucian society to a Western one.'

To what extent do you agree with this opinion? (20 marks)

Tip

This question requires you to evaluate not only the changes that occurred in China in this decade but also their limitations. Consider what changed and what remained the same.

ACTIVITY
KNOWLEDGE CHECK

The Tianjin massacre

1 To what extent do you believe the Tianjin massacre of 1870 was inevitable?

2 Who do you believe was to blame for the Tianjin massacre?

THINKING HISTORICALLY **Cause and consequence (7a & b)**

Questions and answers

Historians ask different questions, depending on what they think is important, and the questions that interest us are what define the history that is written. These questions change with time and place. Different historians will also come up with different answers to the same questions, depending on their perspectives and methods of interpretation, as well as the evidence they use.

Below are three historians who had different areas of interest.

Thomas Carlyle	Karl Marx	Sir Charles Oman
• A political historian who lived in the 19th century • Was interested in the idea that great men shape history	• An economic and political historian who lived in the 19th century • Was interested in the role of the lower classes and how they contributed to historical change	• A military historian who lived in the late 19th and early 20th centuries • Was interested in the minute detail of warfare, including how armies were organised and what tactics were used

These are some key events in the opening of China to foreigners, 1860–70:

The Taiping Rebellion and its suppression	The Second Opium War ending in the destruction of the Summer Palace	The Tianjin massacre
The Self-Strengthening Movement	The opening of more treaty ports	The creation of the Zongli Yamen
The establishment of the Tongwen Guan	The presence of Catholic and Protestant missionaries	The Tongzhi Restoration

Working in groups of between three and six, answer the following questions.

1 Which of these events would have been of most interest to each historian? Explain your answer.

2 Each take the role of one historian and devise a question that would interest them about each of the events.

3 Discuss each event in turn. Present the questions that have been devised for each historian and offer some ideas about how they would have answered them.

4 For each event, decide as a group which question is the most interesting and worthwhile of the three.

Answer the following questions in pairs.

5 Identify the different ways in which each historian would approach writing an account of the opening of China to foreigners, 1860–70.

6 In what ways would Carlyle and Marx differ in their explanations of the significance of the Tongwen Guan (the foreign-language schools)? What would be the focus of their arguments?

Answer the following questions individually.

7 All three historians might produce very different accounts and explanations of the same piece of history. Of the three, whose account would you prefer to read first? Explain your answer.

8 Do the differences in these accounts mean that one is more valid than the others?

9 Explain why different historical explanations are written by different historians.

10 Explain why different explanations of the same event can be equally valid.

Conclusion

By 1860, Qing officials still clung to their faith in their own cultural superiority. However, this faith was shaken by the ease with which China had been militarily overrun and outclassed by Britain in the Second Opium War. As a result of the Treaty of Tianjin (1860), the China of 1870 had undergone significant developments and was very different from the China that had blundered into the Second Opium War a decade earlier. The Treaty of Tianjin was indicative of a more defined Western approach to China. The French secured further freedoms for missionaries and the British opened more ports to foreign trade. The Yangtze valley was opened for trade, offering the British access to internal Chinese markets. The potential to open the Chinese market was not fully achieved during the 1860s, but the foundations were laid for further opportunities in the decades that followed. China's hope of restricting foreign influence to the treaty ports, in the expectation that in time it would wither and die, had failed.

However, the 1860s was not solely a decade of China resisting change. China embarked on the Self-Strengthening Movement, a modernisation process to strengthen China's defences by mastering Western techniques: to use Western methods to defeat the West in the hope that victory would expel un-Chinese elements. However, the Qing refused to countenance any challenge to its Confucian core. The domestic developments that occurred during the 1860s were, for the most part, due to Western religious and economic influence. Missionary work introduced the concepts of public health and education, which transformed the lives of many Chinese. Christianity also attracted thousands of converts and posed a growing challenge to the Confucian order. Similarly, the promotion of English and French teaching evidenced that other cultures could benefit the Chinese nation. The Schools of Combined Learning, developed following China's defeat in the Second Opium War, altered the focus of Chinese education and, in time, society. Western-style curriculums were introduced to strengthen and modernise China. In addition to this, the Zongli Yamen sponsored delegations to travel to Europe and the USA to broaden Chinese horizons and gain an appreciation of Western practices. Yet, as evidenced by anti-Western violence such as the Tianjin massacre, there was no widespread acceptance of the primacy of Western civilisation.

It was symbolic that the tumultuous 1860s began with the Tianjin Treaty and concluded with a massacre of Christian missionaries in the same city. It was a clear sign that attacks against Western institutions would not be tolerated and reprisals would be swift and brutal. By the end of the 1860s, imperial China was in a state in flux. Trapped between an adherence to tradition and the willingness of foreign powers and Chinese progressives to support reform, its leaders were torn between the two.

ACTIVITY
SUMMARY

Opening up China to foreigners, 1860–70

1. Explain how Chinese attitudes to foreigners had altered throughout the 1860s.
2. Make two lists covering developments in China 1860–70. One list should cover ways in which China was weakened and the other should detail methods by which China strengthened itself.
3. Using these lists, do you believe the 1860s was a decade of Chinese humiliation or progress?
4. Plot a graph for the years 1860–70. Mark the years on the *x*-axis and use the *y*-axis to measure the level of anti-foreign sentiment in China. Reference all the major events of the decade.

WIDER READING

Cohen, P. 'Christian missions and their impact to 1900', in J. Fairbank, *The Cambridge History of China*, Vol.10, Cambridge University Press (1978)

Fairbank, J.K. *The Great Chinese Revolution 1800–1985*, Harper and Row (1986)

Fenby, J. *The Penguin History of Modern China: The Fall and Rise of a Great Power, 1850 to the Present*, second edition, Penguin (2013)

Hsü, I. *The Rise of Modern China*, fifth edition, Oxford University Press (1995)

Kuo, T. and Liu, K. 'Self-strengthening: the pursuit of Western technology' in J. Fairbank, *The Cambridge History of China*, Vol.10, Cambridge University Press (1978)

Spence, J. *The Search for Modern China*, W.W. Norton and Company (1991)

3.4 Defeat and humiliation, 1894–1901

KEY QUESTIONS

- What was the significance of the Sino-Japanese War of 1894–95?
- What was the impact of the Triple Intervention?
- What was the significance of the Boxer Rebellion, 1898–1900?

INTRODUCTION

The geographical proximity of China and Japan meant that they developed along similar cultural lines, notably in adhering to Confucian beliefs and remaining secluded from the Western world. As observed in Chapter 3, this isolation came to an end in the mid-19th century when the industrialised Western nations sought to impose themselves economically and territorially on China and Japan. Through the West's complete military dominance, several crippling unequal treaties were inflicted upon China and Japan. How the countries reacted to this affront was indicative of the ways in which relations between the two great oriental powers would change in the late 19th century.

Japan undertook to free itself from Western shackles by achieving economic and military parity with its oppressors. Under the Meiji Restoration, the adopted approach was to combine Western industrial technology with the Japanese spirit. Japan began an intense period of industrialisation and institutional restructuring along Western lines, and within a generation had renegotiated the unequal treaties and proved that industrialisation was not the monopoly of the West.

EXTEND YOUR KNOWLEDGE

Meiji Restoration

Japan had suffered similarly to China at the hands of Western powers. Beginning in 1854, a series of unequal treaties were imposed on Japan, most notably by the USA, Britain, France, Russia and Prussia (the largest of the German states). Japan decided that to reverse these treaties and establish itself as a world power, it would have to modernise in the style of the West. Japan embarked on a programme of political and industrial reform called the 'Meiji Restoration' (after the Japanese emperor at that time). A constitution was introduced, along with a parliament, elections, religious freedom and compulsory education. Industrialisation transformed Japan's economy and it developed its military, basing its army on that of Prussia and its navy on Britain's. The Meiji Restoration was far more successful than the Self-Strengthening Movement that took place in China at the same time.

1894-95 - Sino-Japanese War

1897 -
May: China leases Qingdao to Germany

1894 | 1895 | 1896 | 1897

1895 -
17 April: Treaty of Shimonoseki
23 April: Triple Intervention

While some attempts were made to modernise China through the Self-Strengthening Movement (see Chapter 2), they were half-hearted and far less wide-reaching than achieved in Japan. Therefore, China continued to labour under foreign subjugation. In comparison, Japan was compact and able to centralise behind a strong national government and military. China's sprawling land mass and numerous separate regional identities were ill-suited to effective unity. In addition, the ultra-conservative Dowager Empress Cixi resisted overtures to Western-style development and reform of the ruling system. She thought China's traditions and culture were superior to those of the Western barbarians, and she also feared that giving ground to the West would weaken her own position of power. This proved fatal to China's well-being and ultimately to the Qing dynasty.

As Japan grew stronger, its attitude to China hardened. Japan began to look at China as a way of establishing its new-found independence and confidence. If Western powers were building empires as indications of industrial might, then why should Japan not do the same? China, geographically close and too weak to defend itself, was an ideal place for Japan to achieve its interests. Japan lacked key raw materials such as coal, iron and oil, while China had them in abundance. Japan could use these to power its own industrial revolution at home. Also, if Japan could occupy parts of China, it could resettle its people, as Japan's population was growing at a rate that was difficult to sustain given the limited land size of the country. Where China had failed to modernise extensively, Japan now sought to exploit. What better way was there for Japan to announce its arrival on the world stage than by upsetting the established Confucian order and supplanting China as the dominant regional power? Japan first showed its intent with the Riyaku Islands, a Chinese **tributary state**, which they seized control of in 1875. This was the first sign of what a contemporary Japanese politician likened to plucking fruit off a withered tree.

KEY TERM

Tributary state
A state that is subordinate to a more powerful neighbour. Subservience was shown through the sending of tributes, normally gold or another wealth indicator. The Japanese severed the relationship between China and the Riyaku Islands, and less than a decade later the French achieved the same in Vietnam. Britain emulated this in Burma and another protectorate fell. China's loss of these tributary states was an indicator of the traumas it was soon to suffer.

WHAT WAS THE SIGNIFICANCE OF THE SINO-JAPANESE WAR OF 1894–95?

Causes and consequences of the Sino-Japanese War, 1894–95

Today, Korea is split into North and South, with a Communist North bordering a US-supported capitalist South. However, until the 20th century, it was a single state. Korea had long since been under the suzerainty of China and paid tribute three or four times annually, but Japan attempted to increase its influence. Japan's actions were not just expansionist but also conceived with its own defence in mind. Korea, at the south-easternmost tip of the Chinese landmass, resembled an arrow aimed directly at the heart of Japan. With China bowing to the demands of the Western powers, Japan was very aware of Russia's creeping influence in Korea, and wanted to act before any further Chinese capitulations gave Russia extraterritoriality that would threaten Japan's borders and national security. For Japan, attack was also a form of defence. It was also hoped that Korea's coal and iron ore deposits would support Japan's growing industrial base.

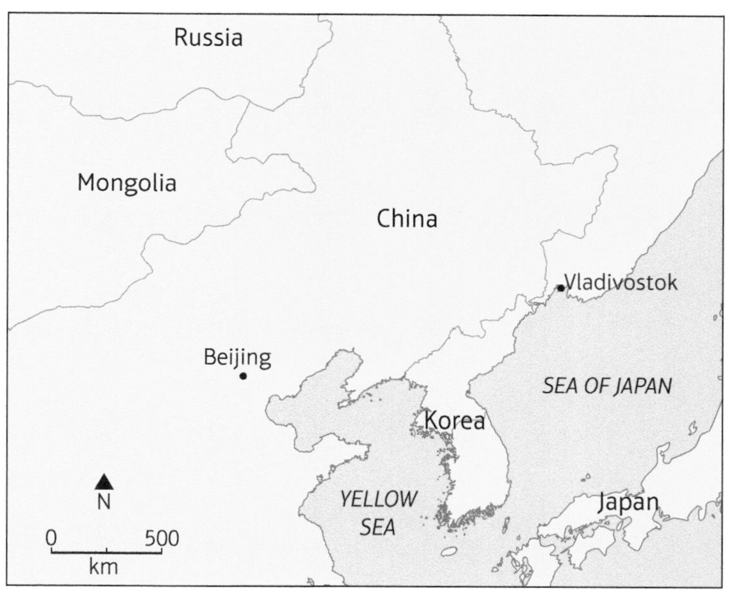

Figure 4.1 Korea's position between China and Japan. Russian proximity and interests in Korea were seen as threats by both China and Japan.

1898 –
Boxer Rebellion begins
March: China leases Dalian and Lushun to Russia
May: China leases Guangzhou to France

1901 –
7 Sep: Signing of Boxer Protocol

1898 | 1899 | 1900 | 1901

June: Britain extends size of crown colony of Hong Kong
11 Jun–21 Sep: Hundred Days Reform
20 Jun–14 Aug: Siege of foreign legations
July: China hands over Weihaiwei to Britain
21 Sep: Conservative coup d'état launched by Dowager Empress Cixi, forcing Guangxu Emperor into seclusion

ACTIVITY
KNOWLEDGE CHECK

Significance of Korea

Write two or three sentences explaining:

1 the historical importance of Korea, as a tributary state, to China

2 how the Meiji Reformation threatened the established order.

Like China and Japan, Korea had existed in isolation to the extent that by the 19th century it was known internationally as 'the Hermit Kingdom'. Ignoring Korea's tributary status to China, Japan sought to assert itself. In 1875, a Japanese warship attempting to land was shelled by Korean forces. In retaliation, Japanese marines managed to land and killed everyone in sight. It was Japan's first use of its Imperial Navy and it had stood up to the test, proving itself ruthless and efficient. Japan rubber-stamped its victory by imposing a Western-style unequal treaty, the Treaty of Ganghwa, in 1876 which, while not giving Japan extraterritoriality, did open up Korea to trade.

This was always unlikely to be the limit of Japanese incursions into Korea. In the 1880s, a pro-Japanese coup d'état (military takeover) in the Korean capital was surprisingly put down by Chinese and Korean troops under the command of Yuan Shikai, and China increased its military presence in Korea. Even more surprisingly, the coup d'état did not lead to war between China and Japan, and the Tianjin Convention was signed in 1885. This convention held that neither China nor Japan could deploy further troops to Korea without notifying the other of their intention. The convention lasted the best part of a decade.

EXTEND YOUR KNOWLEDGE

Treaty of Ganghwa

This treaty was the culmination of Japanese-Korean hostilities. Having had unequal treaties inflicted in the 1850s and 1860s, Japan was now strong enough militarily to impose a similar agreement on Korea, forcing it to open ports to foreign trade. Its proximity to Korea allowed it to act quickly and decisively before any European power could. The treaty was significant in displaying how effective the Meiji Reformation had been. Japan had succeeded in creating a modern, industrialised navy that easily overcame Korean resistance. Japan now occupied Korea. The arrow pointed at Japan had been reversed and pointed at China. This threatened China, as Korea provided a base from which an attack on China could be launched. By occupying Korea, Japan had supplanted China's traditional dominant role. Additionally, these events upset the traditional Confucian order. China, which had long enjoyed the role of dominant regional power, in effect a big brother, was seeing its influence challenged by the younger brother, Japan. The Meiji Reformation had given Japan a modern Western-style military that enabled it to act like a Western power. Japan did not respect China's traditional role and treated China with the same disdain the Europeans had.

EXTEND YOUR KNOWLEDGE

Tianjin Convention

This convention showed that the era of Chinese domination of Korea was effectively at an end. The Confucian order was again being challenged and China was not strong enough to fulfil the role of older brother. The agreement treated China and Japan as equals. However, the fortunes of China and Japan were shifting; Japan was very much in the ascent, while China slumped. The reason for China's approval of the convention was simple: it was not strong enough to repel Japan. Where the Meiji Restoration had given Japan military might, the Self-Strengthening Movement had yet to have a similar effect on China. The Tianjin Convention was, therefore, a Chinese attempt to buy time until it could defeat Japan. In effect, Japan had demonstrated that it had surpassed China in terms of military power.

However, this did not end the unrest in Korea, and the nationalist Tonghak Movement emerged and grew in popularity. The movement grew in opposition to internal corruption and exploitation and resentment at Korea's compliance with foreign powers, be it China, Japan or the West, and in 1894 a full-blown uprising broke out. However, the result of this insurrection was not an assertion of Korean sovereignty. The king requested Chinese assistance to put down the rebellion and Li Hongzhang (see page 50) obliged, sending Chinese reinforcements after having informed Japan in accordance with the Tianjin Convention. Not to be outdone, Japan also sent troops, and on 25 July war erupted between China and Japan.

Contemporary world opinion held that China would easily defeat Japan, a view that was shared throughout China. China's navy was larger and it was still regarded as stronger than Japan's. However, Japan's navy, although smaller, was more modern and its officers were trained in the Western ways of industrialised naval warfare. The Japanese opened fire on, and sank, a Chinese vessel ferrying reinforcements to Korea. War was formally declared on 1 August. Japan bombarded the port of Weihaiwei on 10 August and captured the major city in northern Korea, Pyongyang, on 16 September. Chinese troops evacuated Korea and set up a defensive line in Manchuria. Soon after, the outcome of the war was decided at the mouth of the Yalu River, where the Beiyang fleet under Admiral Ding Ruchang was defeated. The Chinese fleet withdrew to shelter at Weihaiwei; Li likened it to a tiger withdrawing to its lair, suggesting that the war was far from over. Between October and December, Japan succeeded in occupying Korea, landed troops on Taiwan and crossed over to the Chinese mainland, seizing the Liaodong peninsula in southern Manchuria. Ding failed to live up to Li's hopes and the fleet was destroyed after Japan seized the port of Weihaiwei from the landward side and then turned the port's guns on the fleet. Li's tiger turned out to be toothless. Ding committed suicide and his fleet was in little better shape. China sued for peace, but it was to be a peace hard earned. Through military and naval incompetence and defeat, China had lost a lot of bargaining power.

EXTEND YOUR KNOWLEDGE

Tonghak Movement

The Tonghak Movement was a religious and nationalist grouping that emerged in the 1860s in the face of the progress of Western ways and ideas. Literally meaning 'Eastern learning', it was firmly opposed to Western learning, notably Christianity. The Tonghaks promoted equality and wanted to turn Korea into an independent paradise free of foreign presence. Their movement was put down by China and their leaders were executed. Following this, the Sino-Japanese War erupted and the Tonghak goal of independence was as far away as ever, with a more powerful Japan replacing China as the foreign power in control.

The war had severe consequences. Firstly it confirmed that China was in a state of decline. China was shown to the world as weak, incompetent, corrupt and arrogant almost to the point of delusion. The Self-Strengthening Movement had failed and China had been defeated, not by a European power but by an Asiatic one. China's eclipse by Japan as East Asia's major power was complete, and reform to China's system of government was required. Soon after, China embarked on the Hundred Days Reform (see page 97) in an attempt to halt this decline. The defeat discredited the Qing dynasty and its international prestige plumbed new depths.

China also suffered the indignities of territorial losses and reparations. These indemnities, in turn, prevented further investment in modernisation. They would also have one further consequence. China's weakness was evidenced for the world to see and the Western powers, not satisfied with their mid-century gains, exploited this mercilessly in what became known as the 'scramble for China' (see page 16).

As humiliation after humiliation was heaped upon China, domestic resentment both at the foreigners and, more so, the impotence of the Qing dynasty bubbled away and soon manifested itself in the bloody Boxer Rebellion.

What had begun as an attempt to assert Chinese suzerainty over Korea ended with China losing land, influence and respect. It was an unmitigated disaster.

EXTEND YOUR KNOWLEDGE

Scramble for concessions

This was the name given to the methodology used by the industrialised colonial powers to further their expansionism in China. It was brought about in the aftermath of the Sino-Japanese War of 1894–95, in particular the Triple Intervention. The term mimics the 'scramble for Africa', when most of the African continent was partitioned between Britain, France, Portugal and Belgium. Unlike Africa, where Britain colonised several areas, China was a sovereign state, so territories were turned into spheres of influence rather than colonies. Within spheres of influence, economic and trade privileges were determined by an external power. The process was also informally known in Western circles as 'carving the melon', relating to the ease with which the imperialist powers secured their interests.

EXTRACT

From O. Arne Westad, *Restless Empire: China and the World Since 1750* (2013).

The Sino-Japanese War of 1894-95 was the first war China fought with its new Western-type army and navy. It was also the first conflict between China and Japan in three hundred years, and the beginning of an enmity that was to define China's foreign relations for a century to come. But in a curious way the war itself and the two decades that followed stand astride these two distinct periods in the Sino-Japanese relationship: China and Japan may have engaged in a bloody and terrible war, but the admiration that many Chinese felt for Japan's successes in building a new type of state and army was not diminished by China's losses. On the contrary, the sacrifices that China had to make were often blamed on the Qing dynasty and its inability to follow the examples set by Japan. To some Chinese, the Japanese model was in a perverse way validated by its victory: What should not happen and therefore could not happen in a Confucian world - that a younger brother beat and denigrated his older brother - had happened nonetheless. It was visible proof of China's decline and decadence. For people from Korea to Burma, the war redefined power in their region and turned the known order upside down.

EXTRACT 2 From H. McAleavy, *The Modern History of China* (1968).

This was certainly the darkest moment of Li Hung-chang's [Li Hongzhang's] career. His beloved Huai Army was in ruins, and its sister navy no longer existed. Cries for vengeance were heard from one end of the land to the other; respectable mandarins addressed memorials to the Throne in which they declared the satisfaction it would give them to dine on his flesh; a figure of speech, no doubt, but an uncomfortable thing to have to listen to.

ACTIVITY
KNOWLEDGE CHECK

Threats to the Qing Empire

1 Put the following factors into a table, and for each factor clearly explain how it weakened the Qing Empire:

   a) the success of the Meiji Reformation

   b) Japan's lack of raw materials

   c) Japan's growing population

   d) the failure of the Self-Strengthening Movement

   e) China's belief in its superiority over Japan

   f) the presence of European powers in China.

2 Using Extracts 1 and 2, make a list of the reasons why the Sino-Japanese War was so disastrous for China. Add these factors to the table you created above.

The Treaty of Shimonoseki and the loss of Taiwan and Korea

The price for peace exacted by Japan in the Treaty of Shimonoseki was atrocious. Forebodingly for China, the negotiations took place in sight of the mighty Japanese navy. China conceded every territorial claim and was forced to recognise Korea's full autonomy and independence; the payment of tributes and formal subservience to China were immediately stopped. China also ceded the Liaodong peninsula in Manchuria as well as Taiwan and the Pescadores Islands. A war indemnity in excess of US$100 million was squeezed out of China, and Japan was accorded further privileges with more ports being opened up for trade. Japan was also given the right to manufacture goods on Chinese territory. It was the most chastening of all the unequal treaties. The terms would have been harsher yet had Japan not been embarrassed when an extremist attempted to assassinate Li Hongzhang.

ACTIVITY
KNOWLEDGE CHECK

The Treaty of Shimonoseki

1 What was the significance of China having to sign the treaty within sight of Japan's navy?

2 Imagine you are a Chinese student in favour of modernisation. Write a speech arguing that Japan should be a role-model for China to follow.

The effects of the Sino-Japanese War

As already argued, the war was a calamity for the Chinese from start to finish. Firstly, it signalled the failure of the Self-Strengthening Movement to bridge the gap between China and the fully industrialised powers. That is not to say the movement did not achieve anything (see pages 40 and 71), but its accomplishments imbued the Chinese with confidence – over-confidence, as it turned out. China had invested in its military forces, strengthened its army and developed its navy, but they were no match for the Japanese forces. Although China could call on combined armed forces a million strong, the majority were untrained and poorly armed and thus of limited value. A contemporary French military adviser disparagingly, but fairly accurately, referred to China's military forces as 'a rude medieval militia, called out now and then for a holiday parade'. China underestimated Japan's military capacity while simultaneously over-inflating its own strength, with disastrous effects.

China enjoyed a numerical advantage in troops and a firepower advantage at sea. However, the industrialised professional army and navy of Japan pummelled the Chinese into submission. An example of this related to the unfortunate and ill-fated Admiral Ding, and indicated chronic incompetence. Japanese commanders were well versed in military tactics and their ships, although smaller, were faster, more manoeuvrable and better armed than China's. Ding, on the other hand, owed his position of power to his loyalty to Li Hongzhang rather than any naval acumen, and relied wholly on the expertise of his European assistants. His ineptitude was best evidenced at the naval battle at the Yalu River, as he magnificently took his place on the bridge of his flagship, only to realise that neither he nor his British master gunner could understand a word the other was saying. The farce and absurdity of Ding attempting to conduct the war by sign language to his gunner only ended when an errant shell from a Chinese ship incapacitated both men. This was indicative of a navy whose weaknesses were also exacerbated by corruption. For example, in some reported instances, the money allocated for explosives was misappropriated and the shell casings were filled with sand.

The end of the Confucian order

The war shook Qing China to its roots, mostly because defeat came as such a surprise. The Confucian order dictated that China was the pre-eminent regional power and Japan existed in its orbit. Accordingly, the Chinese held their culture as superior to that of Japan. A British adviser to the Qing court, Robert Hart, noted that confidence was high and that out of every 1,000 Chinese only one believed that mighty China would be troubled by little Japan. This view of their own racial and cultural pre-eminence also guided the Chinese view of Westerners, who were often characterised as barbarians. China's implementation of the Self-Strengthening Movement was hindered by a belief that China only needed more and better, but that the basic structure and fabric of Chinese society remained superior to all others and was not in need of major reform. The superiority of the Meiji Reformation is clearly shown in Japan's victory over China. News of the treaty resulted in protests and demands for economic and governmental reform in Beijing from those assembled for the jinshi (civil service) exams. The Confucian order had been overthrown and the Qing dynasty, enfeebled and in terminal decline, would be no more within two decades. In the little time it had remaining, Qing China was overrun by foreign powers and became unable to defend itself.

The war established Japan as a major player on the world stage. Japan had followed the German example of militarism and imperialism by using war as a means of defining itself. Its army and navy were modelled on the foremost military and maritime powers at the time – Germany and Britain respectively – and had turned Japan into a destructive war machine. Japan gave further notice of its capability by defeating Russia in a war in 1904–05 to strengthen its claims in Manchuria. Manchuria had always been Japan's main goal; it offered a source of required minerals and resources for industry. Not only did it serve as a market for Japan's manufactured goods but, largely unsettled and underpopulated, it could accommodate Japan's excess population. China's weakness made the lure of Manchuria's treasures and possibilities more irresistible, and this is explored in Chapter 5.

SOURCE

From Hilary A. Herbert, 'Military Lessons of the Chino-Japanese War' in the *North American Review* (1895). Herbert was the US Secretary of the Navy and, therefore, in charge of one of the most advanced navies in the world. The *North American Review* is the oldest literary magazine in the USA. The article demonstrates the realisation in the West of the Meiji Reformation's success in Japan.

Japan has leaped, almost at one bound, to a place among the great nations of the earth. Her recent exploits in the war with China have focused all eyes upon her, and the world now comprehends the startling fact that this small island kingdom, so little taken account of heretofore in the calculations even of students and statesmen, has within a few decades stridden over ground traversed by other nations only within centuries. We estimate the rate at which bodies move by their relations to other bodies, and it often happens that when the eye is fixed upon two objects, both moving in the same direction, the greater speed of the one causes the other to seem to be standing still. So, to the casual observer, it is with China and Japan. The common impression is that while Japan has been making phenomenal progress, China has been stagnating.

SOURCE 2 *Punch* cartoon, 'China: Jap in a China Shop' (1894). A satirical British cartoon of the Sino-Japanese War (1894–95) in which Qing China was defeated and forced to cede territories and pay a large indemnity of 340 million silver taels to Japan.

ACTIVITY
KNOWLEDGE CHECK

China after the Sino-Japanese War

1. How did the Sino-Japanese War upset the regional hierarchy in South-East Asia?
2. How do Sources 1 and 2 suggest Japan would now act in relation to China? Explain your answer.
3. Why might many Chinese have looked upon Japan as a model to follow?

WHAT WAS THE IMPACT OF THE TRIPLE INTERVENTION?

The Triple Intervention and concessions to France, Russia and Germany

Japan's victory came as a surprise to the Western powers and it presented a challenge. Since the 1860s, Europeans had faced no organised opposition to their presence in China. Now, however, Japan had secured a base on the Asian mainland: the Liaodong peninsula, and this upset the status quo. Russia and Germany were particularly vocal in opposing Japanese expansion to the mainland.

The Triple Intervention that followed has traditionally been viewed as a Russian initiative, and it is true that Japan's victory and subsequent territorial gains on the mainland threatened Russia's eastern Siberian frontier. The Liaodong peninsula also contained the strategic ports of Dalian and Lushun, which were the warm-water ports (i.e. they did not freeze in winter) that Russia so craved. Should Japan annex the territory, Russia's maritime aims would not be achieved. Germany also supported mediation, nominally to uphold China's sovereignty, but in reality it instigated the intervention to further its own interests. Active involvement in the Far East benefited Germany on many counts: it would allow it to establish a presence in China, it would divert Russian attention away from its western border, shared with Germany, and it would give Germany an invaluable naval base in the region. Any Japanese territorial encroachment would dash German hopes of gaining influence.

Russia and Germany were similar in that their involvement was not based on any support for China. They concluded that concessions would be far easier to squeeze out of China in gratitude for making Japan stand down, but that it would be trickier to uphold their interests should Japan permanently ensconce itself in the area. The French were obliged to support Russia as a result of the Franco-Russian agreement of 1894. They were also wary of German aspirations and thought that joint action would uphold France's own interests.

EXTEND YOUR KNOWLEDGE

Franco-Russian agreement of 1894
In the late 19th century, a complicated alliance system emerged as European nations signed various agreements to protect and further their own interests while blocking the hopes of their rivals. One such agreement was the Franco-Russian agreement. France had been defeated by the Germans in the Franco-Prussian War, 1870–71, and a united and rapidly industrialising Germany threatened Russian interests in Eastern Europe. Although France had economic interests in Russia, it did not have territorial ambitions in Manchuria and supported intervention only because, like Russia, it distrusted German intentions.

Faced by the deflated Qing regime, Japan pushed its claims and demands forcibly. However, being challenged by three of the pre-eminent world powers was an entirely different matter. The combined might of Germany, Russia and France united in 1895 and demanded that Japan relinquish the mainland territory it had seized through the Treaty of Shimonoseki. Thus, when the Triple Intervention was presented, Japan was compelled to accept and withdrew from Liaodong, returning it to China in return for the war indemnity owed being increased by a further £30 million. Any Chinese gratitude to the intervening powers would be short-lived and, in effect, all China had achieved was to ensure that further territorial losses would be to the European powers and not Japan. Indeed, the losses accrued from the effect of the Triple Intervention far outstripped the value of the Liaodong peninsula, whose annexation had necessitated Chinese appeals for European mediation in the first place.

The confidence created by the Self-Strengthening Movement had been destroyed by annihilation at the hands of the Japanese. This was now compounded in another series of humiliations that took the form of territorial concessions at the hands of the European powers. The Qing Empire's ability to retain its own territory was fatally challenged.

First to strike was Germany, eager to press its imperial claims. In response to this humbling at the hands of the European powers, virulent anti-Western xenophobia increased. One such instance, the murder of two German Catholic missionaries in western Shandong province, provided Germany with a pretext to push its claims. A German naval force entered the port of Qingdao and trounced the Chinese garrison, and German forces took control of the whole province, obtaining mining and railway-building rights into the bargain.

In December 1897, a Russian fleet entered Lushun. Russia claimed to be protecting China from Germany and Japan, but its aim was clear to see: an all-year warm-water port. Russia signed an agreement, after the Chinese delegates had been bribed, to lease Dalian and Lushun for 25 years. Russia was also granted permission to begin the construction of the South Manchurian Railway.

The actions of Germany and Russia were calculated. China's degeneration was made known to the world in the wake of its defeat in the Sino-Japanese War, and its only option was to submit. France followed the Russian and German example and sent its navy into Guangzhou Bay. It was leased the bay and given spheres of influence in Guangdong, Yunnan and Guanxi provinces in the south and south-west. France was also granted the right to build a railway linking its colony of Indochina (modern Vietnam, Cambodia and Laos) to the Chinese mainland.

The damage wrought by the Triple Intervention offset any advantage Li Hongzhang had hoped to win by soliciting foreign intervention against Japan. China had become an observer in its own internal affairs. The Triple Intervention also had a notable effect on Japan: it felt robbed. The military was praised for its conduct in the war, but the government was castigated by Japanese nationalists for its craven submission to Germany, Russia and France. This consolidated the dominance of the armed forces and they increasingly controlled the direction of Japanese foreign policy. Japan accelerated its militarism and signed a treaty with Britain in 1902 to prevent such a humbling ever befalling it again.

EXTRACT 3 From J. Grasso, J. Corrin and M. Kort, *Modernization and Revolution in China* (1997).

Japan's decisive victory was a great blow to Chinese national pride. It was bad enough that the emperor had to give way to Europeans. Being crushed by the 'dwarf bandits' of Japan, inhabitants of an island backwater that had always sat in the celestial shadow of the Peacock Throne and had borrowed heavily from Chinese civilization, was a humiliation beyond endurance.

Of more significance, Japan's victory seemed to portend the demise of the Qing dynasty. Out of fear that chaos might ensue at its collapse, Western powers began the dreaded scramble for concessions and special 'spheres of influence' to safeguard their interests. In particular, Japan's foothold on the Asian mainland frightened Russia, which coveted the ice-free port of Dalian at the southern tip of the Liaodong Peninsula. The Russians convinced the French and Germans to join them in forcing Japan to remove herself from the peninsula on the grounds that such foreign presence threatened the integrity of Beijing. This so-called Triple Intervention sufficed to push an angry Japan off the mainland. But the European tigers turned out to be more dangerous and territorially ravenous than the Japanese wolf they had chased away.

A Level Exam-Style Question Section B

How accurate is it to say that the Triple Intervention hindered China far more than it helped? (20 marks)

Tip

At the core of this question are the long-term implications of the Triple Intervention. Consider not only the European powers but also the effect on Japan.

ACTIVITY
KNOWLEDGE CHECK

The Triple Intervention

1 Draw a spider diagram for France, Russia and Germany, showing what each had gained through the Triple Intervention.

2 With reference to Extract 3, how did the Sino-Japanese War and the Triple Intervention threaten Chinese sovereignty?

The role of Britain and the granting of a new concession: Weihaiwei and Hong Kong's New Territories

As seen in Chapter 3, Britain developed and nurtured its imperial interests in China from the Opium Wars onwards. Britain had become the foremost expansionist power in the modern world, and its colonial experiences dictated policy in China. With the new century dawning, China's enfeeblement made partition (splitting China into smaller independent states) by the international powers logistically achievable. However, this was a policy Britain was keen to avoid. Britain's attitude was straightforward: if China's sovereignty was upheld and there was the appearance at least of national unity, British trade interests would be protected. Britain's interests in China had only ever been economic, not territorial. The commonly held view in Britain was that it should not overextend the Empire, since any opposition to British rule could easily spread to other British colonial possessions and threaten the Empire in its entirety. Robert Hart, a contemporary British diplomat in China, proclaimed that he desired a strong (meaning independent) China, and for Britain to be a friend to it. Any annexations to other colonial powers jeopardised British trade by potentially excluding British investment and trade, and it was this view that dictated British policy at this juncture which dovetailed neatly with the US **'Open Door' policy**.

KEY TERM

'Open Door' policy
A laissez-faire proposal to assist the opening of Chinese markets to foreign commerce and goods while retaining China's national sovereignty and integrity in order to promote economic stability. It was guided by the long-standing US desire to stay isolated from European colonisation and to prevent war by increasing inter-reliance through mutually beneficial trade.

Britain needed to think on its feet when its preference for trade freedom was jeopardised first by the aggressive expansionism of Japan and then by the Triple Intervention of Germany, Russia and France. The 'scramble for concessions' that followed forced Britain's hand and, not wishing to be outdone, Britain demanded, and received, the port of Weihaiwei. This countered the naval presence of Germany in Shandong and Russia in Liaodong. Weihaiwei was leased for as long as Port Arthur (as Lushan had been renamed) remained in Russian possession. Britain also obtained rail and trade rights in the Yangtze valley.

However, of considerably more significance were the New Territories. Hong Kong had been ceded to Britain back in 1842 (see Chapter 3), and the 1860 Treaty of Tianjin had added to it the Kowloon peninsula on the Chinese mainland, adjacent to Hong Kong. However, the colony was given a new lease of life during the 'scramble for concessions', when it was increased in size over tenfold by the acquisition of the New Territories stretching further inland from the Kowloon peninsula. The New Territories were leased for 99 years, only being returned to China at the expiration of the lease in 1997 (see Chapter 7). The New Territories provided fertile farmland for the fledgling colony, served as the industrial base for Hong Kong and also housed the surplus population resulting from population growth and immigration to the area.

EXTRACT 4 From J. Keay, *China: A History* (2008).

The concessions now in demand were commercial as well as territorial and included mining rights, transport systems and industrial ventures, any of which might become a nucleus of extraterritoriality as well as a source of income. Affording the Chinese a foretaste of the game of Monopoly, the competitors – the warship, the corporate top-hat, etc. – chased each other round the empire's perimeter snapping up properties, utilities, railways and investment funds, while scooping a share of the indemnities in lieu of passing 'Go'...

By 1898, such was the competition between the foreign powers, and such internally the centrifugal drift of authority to the provinces, that there was a real danger of China sharing Africa's fate and being scrambled over and partitioned. Russian railway tracks were ensnaring the whole of Manchuria; the Japanese had already detached Taiwan; the Germans were expanding their presence in Shandong; the British and the Americans controlled traffic into the productive interior via the Yangzi; and the French were eyeing up the commercial potential of the Red River into Yunnan. No one wanted to be left out. On the other hand, fragmentation was clearly not in the interest of those with the most investment at risk, such as the British. Yet to prevent it, they saw no alternative to matching the other powers move for move, thus raising the stakes.

To counter the Russians in Lushun and the Germans at Qingdao, in 1898 the naval base of Weihaiwei, more or less midway between the two, was snapped up by the British. They also leased more of the Kowloon peninsula – Hong Kong's so-called New Territories – to supply and secure that colony. ... Not to be outdone, the French leased a port west of Hong Kong and obtained mineral rights in Guangxi and Yunnan. Meanwhile the United States again led the way in levelling the playing field by demanding that any concessions extended to one be open to all.

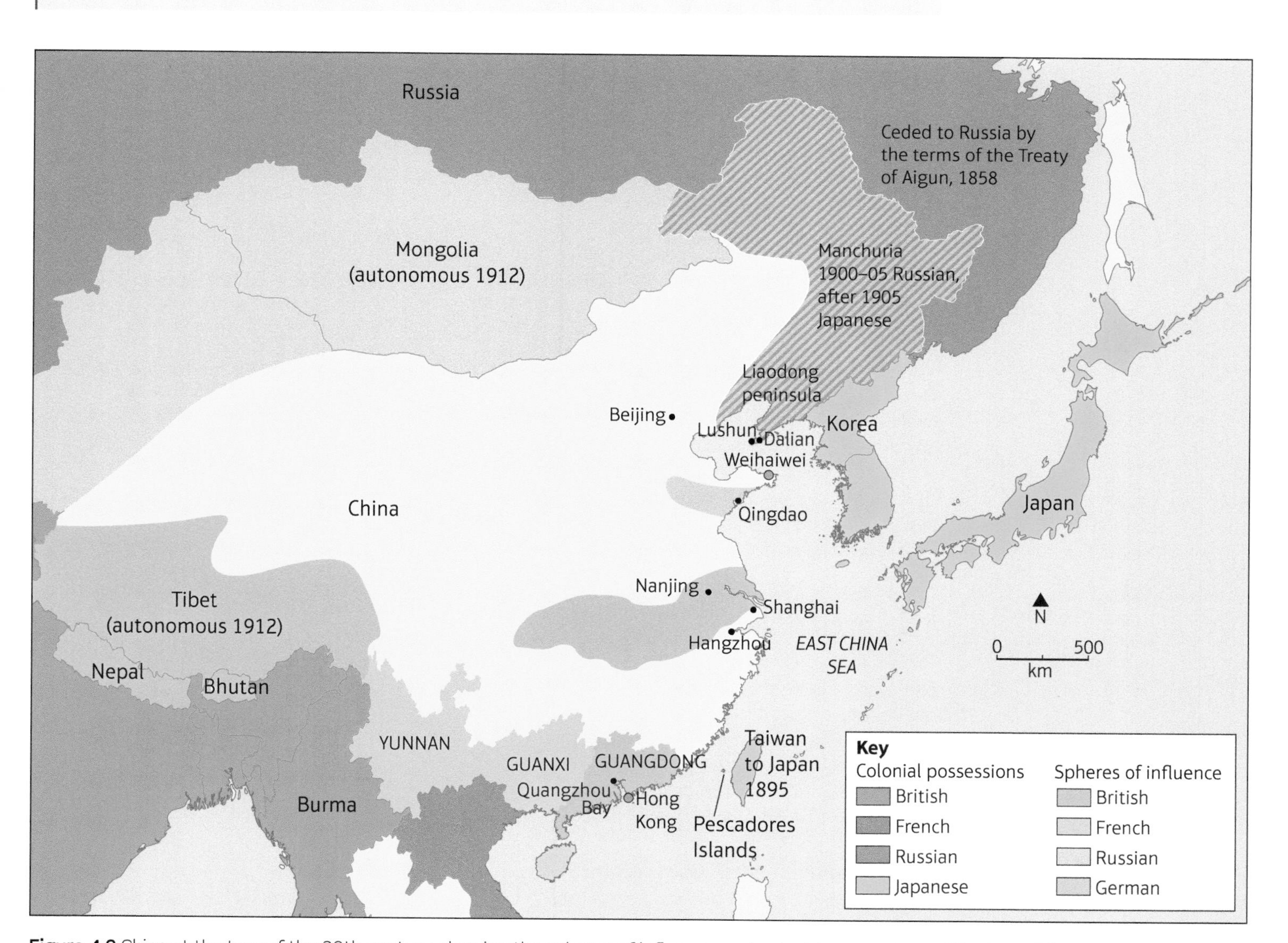

Figure 4.2 China at the turn of the 20th century, showing the spheres of influence and colonial possessions of the imperial powers.

SOURCE

From a memorandum by Joseph Chamberlain MP, Secretary of State for the Colonies (1900) to the British cabinet in support of the 'Open Door' policy. The memorandum is anti-Russian and paints a picture of Russian interests threatening to 'shut' the open door in northern China.

We should, without urging it, let it be known that we shall put no obstacle in the way of German expansion in Shantung [Shandong], nor in the way of the gratification of Japan's ambition in Corea [Korea]. But, in return, we should obtain written assurances recognizing our claim to predominant interest and influence in the Yang-tsze [Yangtze] Valley. We are not likely to ever want to take possession of any territory in the interior ourselves; but we ought to try for some understanding which will keep off all others, and make it easy to maintain the 'Open Door' in at least this, the most important portion of the Chinese empire.

ACTIVITY
KNOWLEDGE CHECK

Britain's attitude to China

1 What does Source 3 say about Britain's colonial attitude towards China?

2 Why, according to Extract 4, did Britain make territorial demands of its own following the Triple Intervention?

3 Make a list of the benefits offered to Britain by Weihaiwei and Hong Kong.

WHAT WAS THE SIGNIFICANCE OF THE BOXER REBELLION, 1898–1900?

Causes of the Boxer Rebellion

The 19th century was one of turmoil, upheaval and degradation for the Qing dynasty and, by association, for China. It was fitting that such a challenging century would come to a close with drama and a crowning dishonour. The Boxer Rebellion was the result of continued failures: the failure of the Self-Strengthening Movement; the ensuing defeat in the Sino-Japanese War and Chinese corruption and impotence in opposing the territorial demands of the colonial powers; and the 'scramble for concessions'. All these ignominies resulted in the growth of Chinese nationalism, which manifested itself, naturally enough, in the form of anti-foreigner sentiment and opposition to the Qing dynasty.

The immediate outcome of the 'scramble for concessions' for China was a period of self-reflection and a time to reconsider its position in the world. The distrust of foreigners was a firmly held belief in China following the country's emasculation. However, there was a clear schism regarding attitudes to the Qing dynasty. Progressives, such as Kang Youwei and his acolyte Liang Qichao, advocated sweeping reforms following broadly the Japanese model laid out in the Meiji Restoration. At the other end of the spectrum were those who felt that too much of China's Confucian essence had already been sacrificed and that the further Westernisation of China would only bring more deterioration and possible loss of the mandate of heaven.

The attitude of Empress Cixi

The progressives found a patron in the form of the emperor, Guanxu. On the other hand, the emperor's aunt, the irrepressible ex-regent the Dowager Empress Cixi, was ultra-conservative. She had tentatively supported the Self-Strengthening Movement's technological and military reforms, but vehemently opposed any reform to the political system. However, following the 'scramble for concessions', Cixi was merely the ex-regent, while Guanxu was the political voice of the Qings. Guanxu saw reform as the only way to preserve imperial China, and this put him on a collision course with Cixi, who felt that reform meant a loss of power for the Qing dynasty.

The Dowager Empress Cixi (1835–1908)

Cixi became one of the Xianfeng emperor's concubines in 1851 and in 1856 bore a son. Her ability to read and write, uncommon for women in that age, allowed her to gain an intimate knowledge of state affairs as she assisted Xianfeng in his ailing years. Upon the death of Xianfeng in 1861, his five-year-old son the Tongzhi emperor ascended the throne. Cixi performed the role of regent with Xianfeng's widow until Tongzhi reached adulthood. However, Tongzhi died of smallpox, childless, in 1875 and Cixi deftly manoeuvred to ensure she was reinstated co-regent with her four-year-old nephew Guangxu becoming emperor. In 1881, the Xianfeng emperor's widow died, leaving Cixi unchallenged as regent, the dowager empress. She ruled until her nephew married in 1889, reassuming the regency in 1898 after she had plotted his removal. Guanxu was placed under house arrest until his death in 1908. Cixi was famed for her Marble Boat at the Summer Palace, the renovation of which was paid for by the diversion of funds intended for modernising the Chinese navy. The dowager empress boasted amazing resilience and a predatory instinct for maintaining her personal power.

It appeared that Cixi's long-term stewardship over China had reached its end when Guanxu married and ascended the throne. Guanxu threw his weight behind Kang and Liang (see page 96) and, in 1898, China embarked upon a path of radical reform known as the Hundred Days Reform. The reformers sought to halt the cultural and economic decline: the education system was to be put on a more Western footing, with practical topics being given more coverage at the expense of the traditional literary composition, and this required the reorganisation of all existing schools. Additionally, a Western-inspired university was set up in Beijing. The press was to benefit from freedom of publication, banks and a chamber of commerce were to be opened and the modernisation was to be rolled out to the army and navy too. Finally, government departments were to be established to promote and support mining, agriculture, medicine and trade. The reformers also targeted the structure of the government, which was in desperate need of overhauling and modernisation in order to remain viable, and wished to set up a national legislative assembly and a constitution.

EXTEND YOUR KNOWLEDGE

The Hundred Days Reform

In 1898, China lost its last chance of effective reform and modernisation. China's defeat in the Sino-Japanese War signalled the end of China's role as the dominant power in South-East Asia. Japan had clearly overtaken China economically, industrially and militarily. As a fellow Asian country, defeat to Japan was particularly hard to swallow. To China, Japan now fulfilled an interesting dual threat: on the one hand, it was the main threat to China, but on the other hand it offered a path of reform to follow. On 11 June 1898, Emperor Guanxu signed an imperial decree supporting sweeping reform, and the Hundred Days Reform began. The reformers supported modern, European education, the introduction of democratic institutions like a National Assembly (Parliament) and the abolition of extraterritoriality. All of the proposed reforms had been successfully carried out previously in Japan. However, the Hundred Days Reform caused a conservative backlash led by Cixi, who effectively led a coup d'état against Guanxu, removed him from office and renewed her regency over China. The Hundred Days Reform had been brought to an end. The ideas made popular during the Hundred Days Reform re-emerged after Cixi's death.

However, any hope of redemption and modernisation was soon to be dashed, and those who stood to lose the most from the Hundred Days Reform acted to protect their own positions and power. Guanxu had intended to imprison Cixi to prevent her derailing the modernisation process. However, Cixi again proved her adroitness by moving more quickly: she succeeded in imprisoning Guanxu with the help of her household guard. Guanxu remained under house arrest for the rest of his life, and any hope of imperial modernisation and renewal was snuffed out. Cixi, once again, declared herself regent and Kang and Liang fled to the safety of Japan. Six other reformers, Kang's brother amongst them, were not so fortunate and were executed. The drive for reform never fully evaporated, and when those who had staged the coup against Guanxu, notably Cixi, had died, the demands for modernisation and reform again resurfaced. Tragically, however, it was far too late to save the Qing dynasty.

The defeat of the reformers reinvigorated the elderly dowager empress, who now resumed her position at the top of the autocratic dynasty. Soon, the inevitable happened: opposition to the foreign powers who had established settlements in China developed and spread.

It is hardly surprising that the rebellion began in Shandong, a province that had suffered many humiliations. It was here, at Weihaiwei, that Admiral Ding's fleet had been forced into complete surrender in 1895; three years later it was handed over to the British. Germany had also established a military presence on the peninsula, taking over the port of Qingdao. Consequently, xenophobic tendencies began to grow amongst the indigenous Chinese, and a group emerged, the Fists of United Righteousness, or Boxers as they were known to foreigners. Mainly consisting of poorer peasants, the Boxers opposed Western influence. They directed their ire against Christianity and, more specifically, against Chinese converts and the ease with which they had discarded centuries of traditional beliefs. They resented the building of railways and churches for upsetting the natural order feng shui, and claimed that such desecration of the land brought bad luck.

Practised in martial arts, the Boxers began to attack anything of Western origin. They claimed to have supernatural powers and their mystical faith held that they could not be harmed by Western weapons: bullets would simply deflect off them. One Boxer woman, 'Lotus' Huang, boasted unique spiritual powers, and cooks in the Boxer camps claimed to feed troops from pots that magically refilled themselves. Sadly for them, such superstition and hocus pocus did little but buoy them on to their slaughter: obviously, when the bullets flew, the Boxers died.

EXTEND YOUR KNOWLEDGE

Fists of United Righteousness (Boxers)

This group's thinking was shaped by Buddhism and support for traditional Chinese values in the face of foreign influence, foreign trade and extraterritoriality. The Boxers identified three targets: the Great Hairy Ones (foreigners); the Secondary Hairy Ones (those Chinese who had either converted to Christianity or were involved in foreign economic projects); and finally the Tertiary (third) Hairy Ones (those who used foreign products). The Boxers attracted a wide following, particularly amongst the impoverished peasants. The traditional boxing that they practised promoted physical health and spiritual enlightenment. Boxers tended to be young and many were female. Separate groups were organised along military lines and each cell had an absolute leader. The Boxer Rising in 1900 gained the support of the Dowager Empress Cixi, but culminated in defeat in Beijing at the hand of a combined army of the Western powers. The Boxers who had risen to reclaim China from the foreigners had been put down and those same foreigners imposed another harsh agreement, the Boxer Protocol (see page 101), on the beleaguered Qing Empire.

SOURCE 4 A popular Chinese song at the time of the uprising. It was also displayed as a wall poster in villages and towns across China, 1898–1900. It was a form of propaganda. Methods such as this were central to the Boxers being able to spread their beliefs and to attract support to their cause.

Divinely aided Boxers,
United-in-Righteousness Corps
Arose because the Devils
Messed up the Empire of yore.
They proselytize their sect,
And believe in only one God,
The spirits and their own ancestors
Are not even given a nod.
Their men are all immoral,
Their women are truly vile.
And if you don't believe me,
Then have a careful view:
You'll see the Devil's eyes
Are all a shining blue.
No rain comes from Heaven.
The earth is parched and dry.
And all because the churches
Have bottled up the sky.
The gods are very angry.
The spirits seek revenge...
En masse they come from Heaven
To teach the Way to men.
Gods come down from the hills,
Possessing the bodies of men,
Transmitting their boxing skills.
When their martial and magic techniques
Are all learned by each one of you,
Suppressing the Foreign Devils
Will not be a tough thing to do.
Rip up the railway tracks!
Pull down the telegraph lines!
Quickly! Hurry up! Smash them—
The boats and the steamship combines.
The mighty nation of France
Quivers in abject fear,
While from England, America, Russia
And from Germany naught do we hear.
When at last all the Foreign Devils
Are expelled to the very last man,
The Great Qing, united, together,
Will bring peace to this land

SOURCE 5

From the Dowager Empress Cixi's declaration of war against the Western powers (1900). Cixi's reasons for declaring war were controversial. Her explanation in this declaration was plainly anti-foreign, but it has also been argued that by supporting the uprising, Cixi wanted to deflect any criticism from her and the governing Qing dynasty.

For more than 200 plus years, the Court had always acted in deep kindness, those foreigners came from faraway, our ancestors had always treated them with respect. During the reign of Emperor Daoguang and Emperor Xianfeng, foreigners began to be allowed to trade with China, and yet they begged for the permission to preach the teaching of Christ, since the teaching was for the good of the people, the Court also granted permission. The foreigners have been aggressive towards us, infringed upon our territorial integrity, trampled our people under their feet... They oppress our people and blaspheme our gods. The common people have suffered greatly at their hands, and each one of them is vengeful. Thus it is that the brave followers of the Boxers have been burning churches and killing Christians.

SOURCE 6

From a Boxer proclamation, distributed across China to encourage peasants to stand up to the foreign oppressors. It was published in 1900.

Hear ye, townsmen and villagers... The Catholics and Protestants have been maligning what we hold sacred; they have bullied the officials and oppressed the black-haired people of China. Gods and men are angry with them but the people keep their counsel, so we have trained ourselves in the sacred boxing of righteousness and harmony to protect China, drive out the foreign invaders and check and kill the members of the churches so as to avoid the subjugation of the masses. After the publication of this proclamation we instruct all villagers, wheresoever they may be, to drive away any converts with haste and burn their churches and other buildings so there is no trace left of them.

SOURCE 7

From Sir Robert Hart, *These from the Land of Sinim* [China] (1901). Hart was a former British diplomat and was head of the Chinese Imperial Maritime Customs Service, 1863–1910. He received the high honour of the award of the Red Button from the Imperial Court. The book was a memoir and commentary on China. Here, he is writing about China at the time of the Boxer Rebellion of 1898.

Sixty years of treaty relations have culminated in this Boxer movement; how to account for such a finale? The Chinese are a proud – some say a conceited – people but they have good reasons for their pride. There is pride of race, pride of intellect, pride of civilisation, pride of supremacy; and this inherited pride, in its massive and magnificent setting of blissful ignorance, has been so hurt by the manner of foreign impact that it has overwhelmed the other good points of Chinese character; it is not simply the claim for equality by foreigners, or the demonstration of physical superiority or the expansion of contact under compulsion, or the dictation of treaties, that have hurt that pride. It is something in those treaties which keeps open the raw wound and prevents healing.

The most important, and from the foreign standpoint the most essential, stipulation in the treaties is that which extra-territorialises the foreigner in China. By it the foreigner is not subject to any Chinese tribunal and can only be dealt with by officials of his own country. It leads to the supposition that he is not only to be judged by his own laws, but is absolved from any laws of China. These laws are of two kinds, the one being the written laws of the Chinese Empire and the other the unwritten laws, the practices, prejudices and superstitions of a locality. These in their turn are just as binding on all the people there. They are more likely to produce ill-feeling if violated.

A foreign official is brought in by missionaries, for instance, and his intervention obliges Chinese officials to enforce the sale of a certain plot of ground to the missionaries against the wishes of the neighbours. Then the mission proceeds to put up a lofty building on it, thereby, in the estimation and to the consternation of the whole population, irretrievably ruining the luck of the neighbourhood and the fortunes of the inhabitants. To the foreigner, the native objection is not only something to be laughed at, but is a superstition to be fought against and swept away.

This is just the style of action which carries with it the sure seed of a future riot followed by demands by the foreigners for gunboat protection.

A Level Exam-Style Question Section A

Study Source 7 before you answer this question.

Assess the value of the source for revealing the nature of Chinese society in the late 19th century and the reasons for the Boxer Rebellion.

Explain your answer, using the source, the information given about its origin and your own knowledge about the historical context. (20 marks)

Tip

When answering this question you must include relevant factors that are not referenced in the source. Good examples here would be the Tianjin Convention (1860), the Sino-Japanese War and the Treaty of Shimonoseki (1894–95), the Triple Intervention (1895) and the Hundred Days Reform (1898).

ACTIVITY
KNOWLEDGE CHECK

The Boxer Rebellion

1 Use Sources 5 and 6 to make a list of reasons the Boxers gave for hating the West.

2 How useful is Source 5 for the historian studying the causes of the Boxer Rebellion?

3 Why did the Boxers particularly target Chinese converts to Christianity?

4 What do Sources 5, 6 and 7 say were the Boxers' aims?

Events and consequences of the Boxer Rebellion

The Boxers represented a shift in opinion against colonialism. Thus, it was a genuinely patriotic movement responding to the political and economic duress under which China laboured. With hindsight, it was clear that the Boxers were doomed from the start and, by giving her imperial support, Cixi also consigned imperial China to the past, although that took another decade to become apparent. As heartfelt and determined as the uprising was, it was never likely to succeed. It lacked the charismatic direction that would characterise the future leaderships of Sun Yat-sen, Jiang Jieshi and Mao Zedong, and while it was clear what they opposed, it was less clear what they hoped the outcome of the rebellion would be.

The Boxers had been committing atrocities in Shandong during the 1890s, with approximately 30,000 Chinese Christians being killed. By 1900, their numbers had swollen to several hundred thousand, and churches and railways were burnt and destroyed, telegraph poles were cut and missionaries murdered. The greatest infamy took place in Taiyuan, the capital of Shanxi province, where the governor had promised to shelter missionaries and their families from the Boxers. However, he lied, and when they arrived they were all promptly put to death. The Boxers then entered Beijing and besieged the foreign **legations**; a Japanese diplomat and the German minister were assassinated. It was hoped that if the legations were destroyed and the colonialists in them killed, China would be free of the yoke of foreign oppression. A British relief force of 2,000 was beaten back and the fate of the besieged appeared to be sealed. Despite a vast superiority in numbers, the Boxers lacked the leadership to achieve their aims, and the half-hearted support of the Qing dynasty did little to help.

KEY TERM

Legation
A diplomatic representative lower in stature than an ambassador. Legations were established in China in 1860 as a term of the Tianjin Treaty. Situated in Beijing, the legation quarter negotiated directly with the Qing dynasty's minister and representatives.

Cixi hoped to use the Boxers to rid China of the hated foreigners and gave her backing to the uprising. She felt it wiser to agree with the Boxers, who raged against official corruption and co-operation with the West. Cixi played the anti-foreigner card and supported the rebellion to deflect the Boxers' rage from herself. She ordered Qing troops to assist the uprising, but this order was ignored by powerful regional bosses such as Li Hongzhang, Zhang Zhidong and Yu'an Shikai, who saw the rebellion as folly. The Western powers conferred and sent a joint army to relieve the besieged legations. An Eight Nation Army numbering 20,000 troops, mostly Japanese, Russian and British, landed in Tianjin and marched to relieve Beijing, fighting peasant Boxers all the way. Needless to say, the Boxers' mysticism did not withstand the Western powers' progress and the siege was lifted on 14 August.

EXTEND YOUR KNOWLEDGE

Legations
Legations were resented and targeted during the Boxer Rebellion as a symbol of foreign domination. After the uprising was put down, the legations resumed their role and survived well into the 20th century. Foreign diplomats were moved out of the legation quarter fully in 1959 and the complex was vandalised by Red Guards during the Cultural Revolution and altered beyond recognition by developers in the 1980s.

ACTIVITY
KNOWLEDGE CHECK

The Dowager Empress Cixi and the Boxer Rebellion

1 Compile two lists detailing the advantages and disadvantages of Cixi backing the Boxer Rebellion.

2 How useful are Sources 7 and 8 (see opposite) in explaining Cixi's decision to support the Boxer Rebellion?

3 Was this decision wise?

A Level Exam-Style Question Section B

To what extent was the defeat of the Boxer Rebellion the result of the limited support of the Qing dynasty? (20 marks)

Tip
Split the main body of this essay into clear paragraphs, each focusing on a different factor explaining the Boxers' defeat. Contrast the factors against each other to determine which was the most significant. In questions like this, it is crucial to reach a firm judgement and not to sit on the fence.

After the Eight Nation Army entered Beijing, chaos broke out. The Dowager Empress Cixi and her entourage of imperial eunuchs, lackeys and sycophantic advisers beat a retreat westwards out of Beijing to Xi'an. With the imperial court no longer present, those who were left behind bore the brunt of the invading Eight Nation Army's fury. Civilians were murdered, shops, warehouses and valuable antiquities were looted, and punitive expeditions were launched from Beijing against cities and towns thought to have been loyal to the Boxer Rebellion.

It appeared that the very fabric and existence of the Qing regime hung in the balance. Cixi had gambled, lost and fled in disarray. Nevertheless, she had probably achieved some popular support for having stood up to the West, however half-hearted and haphazardly.

The defeat of the Boxer Rebellion was followed by another crippling and humiliating peace treaty – the Boxer Protocol. In a time of crisis, Cixi recalled the veteran diplomat Li Hongzhang from semi-retirement to lead the negotiations for China. It was a thankless task for Li, and he died within a year of the treaty's signing. The Boxer Protocol demanded apologies for the murder of the Japanese diplomat and a memorial was to be constructed to commemorate the assassinated German ambassador. The Legation Quarter was turned into a foreign quarter where Chinese people were no longer to enjoy rights of residency. Many fortifications separating Beijing from the sea were razed to the ground. Each of the participating foreign powers was given access to the sea and allowed to station troops in Beijing. A reorganised Ministry of Foreign Affairs was to be established. Leaders of the rebellion, both Boxers and courtiers, were to be executed or banished. Official jinshi examinations (see page 76) were suspended for five years in areas where foreigners had been harassed, memberships of anti-foreign societies were prohibited, and last, but by no means least, the Chinese were burdened with a staggering indemnity amounting to 450 million taels. The Boxer Protocol decreed that payments would continue until 1940. The indemnity was shockingly high, especially as China's entire annual income amounted to approximately 250 million taels. When including interest rates, by 1940 China had paid close to one billion taels.

The Boxers had represented a nostalgic and romantic, but ultimately fruitless, way of thinking. They held that China could be purged of foreign influence and, in essence, history and progress could be reversed. Their disregard for modern weapons and ways of war were grounded in superstition and myth. However, the Boxers are easier to understand than the Qing dynasty. Any serious attempt to free China of foreign suppression would have required unity, commitment, organisation and leadership, but in all these areas the Boxer Rebellion was lacking. Attacking foreign influence without any real chance of defeating it was a provocative and ill-thought-out move. Cixi was also unable to fully command the loyalty of her underlings, and her call-to-arms was summarily ignored by those who felt the Boxer Rebellion was doomed to failure.

The reason that China remained a unitary state was because the Western powers deemed it better for international trade and regional security that China's sovereignty was upheld. It was felt that another round of territorial concessions could lead to war between the competing powers, a broadly accurate assessment given that the Russo-Japanese War of 1904–05 was fought over Chinese land, Manchuria. Therefore, the major powers gradually began to abide by the 'Open Door' policy espoused by the USA and supported heartily by Britain. The size of China made it more convenient to open up the country to trade and exploit it economically than to commit thousands of troops and vast sums of money in governing the areas.

SOURCE

From Putnam Weale's diary, *Indiscreet Letters from Peking*, published in 1900. Putnam Weale was the pen name of Bertram Simpson, an Englishman employed by the Chinese Customs Service who was present during the Boxer Rebellion. He is seen by some historians as a man of dubious character, and there is some doubt about the credibility of his diary as a whole. His diary was highly critical of British diplomats.

And now when we wander even in our own streets - that is, those abutting immediately on our compounds of the Legation area - a new nickname salutes our ears. No longer are we mere *yang kuei-tzu*, foreign devils; we have risen to the proud estate of *ta mao-tzu*, or long-haired ones of the first class. *Mao-tzu* is a term of some contemptuous strength, since *mao* is the hair of animals, and our barbarian heads are not even shaved. The *ta* - great or first class - is also significant, because behind our own detested class press two others deserving of almost equal contempt at the hands of all believers in divine Boxerism. These are *ehr-mao-tzu* and *san mao-tzu*, second and third class coarse-haired ones. All good converts belong to the second class, and death awaits them, our servants say; while as to the third category, all having any sort of connection, direct or indirect with the foreigner and his works are lumped indiscriminately together in this one, and should be equally detested. The small talk of the tea-shops now even says that officials having a few sticks of European furniture in their houses are *san mao-tzu*. It is very significant, too, this open talk in the tea-shops, because in official Peking, the very centre of the enormous, loose-jointed Empire, political gossip is severely disliked.... Now everyone can do as he likes.

It is, therefore, becoming patent to the most blind that there is going to be something startling, something eclipsing any other anti-foreign movement ever heard of, because never before have the users of foreign imports and the mere friends of foreigners been labelled in a class just below the foreigners themselves. And then as it became dark to-day, a fresh wave of excitement broke over the city and produced almost a panic... At last all the Legations shivered, and urgent telegrams were sent to the British admiral for reinforcements to be rushed up at all costs.

But too late - too late; ... For the Chinese Colossus, lumbering and lazy, sluggish and ill-equipped, has raised himself on his elbow, and with sheep-like and calculating eyes is looking down on us - a pigmy-like collection of foreigners and their guards - and soon will risk a kick - perhaps even will trample us quickly to pieces. How bitterly everyone is regretting our false confidence, and how our chiefs are being cursed!

A Level Exam-Style Question Section A

Study Source 8 before you answer this question.

Assess the value of the source for revealing the ideology of the Boxers and the reasons why anti-Western feeling had grown so extreme in the years 1894–1901.

Explain your answer, using the source, the information given about its origin and your own knowledge about the historical context. (20 marks)

Tip

Consider the source's attribution and the author's purpose in writing his diary. How representative is this of Chinese society?

The significance of the Boxer Rebellion

The significance of the Boxer Rebellion can be measured in several ways. Its effect on China was profound. Military defeat was something with which China was becoming increasingly familiar, but this loss was more. It signalled the last stand of conservative China. It was the manifestation of the xenophobic discontent that had simmered, and sometimes boiled over, since China was opened up by the Treaty of Nanjing in 1842. The rebellion's defeat forced China to accept the foreign presence as permanent. Growing from this, China would pick up the baton of the Self-Strengthening Movement. In addition to economic and military modernisation, there were now attempts to reform the political system. Accompanying these developments, a form of Chinese nationalism began to grow. It was no surprise that, half a century later, the CCP commemorated the Boxers as heroes fighting the spectre of foreign domination (see Chapter 6 for the CCP's view of foreign domination). This nationalism would continue to fitfully express itself under Jiang Jieshi (see Chapter 5), but would become an entrenched part of the national psyche after the civil war ended and the People's Republic of China (PRC) was proclaimed in 1949. The Cultural Revolution (1966–70) borrowed the fervent anti-foreigner hatred of the Boxers (see Chapter 6).

The Qing dynasty was upheld by the foreign powers, but this had little do with its own merits. Rather, it was the only regime capable of maintaining any semblance of national unity. The survival of imperial China was the result of the foreign powers seeking to consolidate their economic and colonial interests. However, the Qing dragon had lost its flame. The reforms, though they came, were too little, too late to prolong the dynasty for long. Nationalist opposition had grown from the Taiping (see page 70) and Boxer Rebellions as well as from resentment at foreign domination, which had many unsavoury effects, not least of which was the flood of opium imported to China. This resulted in an increase to the number of addicts to about 40 percent of the entire population. The rampant addiction issues in China intensified criticism of the Qing dynasty's weakness, and the huge indemnity with which China had been saddled as a result of the Boxer Protocol had lost the Qing a lot of respect within China. With the Dowager Empress dead and in her place a two-year-old emperor (his father served as regent), the Qing dynasty was unable to survive and, in 1911, it succumbed to revolution. The Qings were deemed to have lost the mandate of heaven. Therefore, the Boxer Rebellion was significant because it turned the demise of imperial China from an 'if' to a 'when': it inadvertently heralded a new century of modernisation and nationalism.

The uprising also had an international significance, as it led to Japan's rise from regional upstart to fully fledged member of the international community. The 20,000-strong Eight Nation Army sent to liberate Beijing consisted primarily of Japanese troops. This was an indication of the high importance Japan would increasingly grant China (see Chapter 5). Within five years, Japan had gone to war with, and routed, Russia over rights in Manchuria. The conquest of China, or at least significant portions of it, lay the foundation for Japan's imperial expansionism, and became its foremost priority. Japan's more prominent role and prioritisation of expansionism weakened the USA's preferred 'Open Door' policy.

EXTEND YOUR KNOWLEDGE

The emergence of terror as a tactic

The barbarity and bloodthirstiness of the Boxer Rebellion are worthy of comment. The technological advances that changed the face of modern warfare gave insurgents the firepower to inflict serious damage. Civilians were the main victims of war. The Boxers slaughtered foreigners and Chinese converts mercilessly, no quarter was given. During the Boxer Rebellion, 136 Protestant missionaries and 53 children were killed, in addition to nearly 50 Catholic nuns and priests. An estimated 30,000 Chinese Catholic converts and 2,000 Protestant converts suffered the same fate. Havoc was wrought among the civilian population as a tactic of war. Savagery was not the monopoly of the Boxers however, and the international force that relieved Beijing looted, pillaged, murdered and raped. In some instances, they were joined by those who had just been besieged, meaning that war was no longer the exclusive preserve of the armies who actively fought it. A British journalist, present at the time, suggested that Western civilisation was just a veneer over savagery. Foreign troops raped and looted at will and a US general concluded that for every one Boxer killed, 50 innocents were also slain. Villages suspected of having supported the Boxers were burned to the ground. Japan took these abuses to a new level during its occupation of China from 1931 onwards, and terror became a lasting feature of Japan's means of waging war.

EXTRACT 5

From J. Grasso, J. Corrin and M. Kort, *Modernization and Revolution in China* (1997).

The Boxer episode, in the long term, proved to be a lethal blow to the Qing dynasty. For purposes of political stability, the dowager empress was allowed to return to power behind her bamboo screen. The court also initiated an extensive reform program that might have succeeded in meeting twentieth-century demands for modernisation. However, the imperial reformist impulse came too late. By 1900 the patriotic consciousness of China's gentry and other new social forces (namely the compradores, a Portuguese term meaning 'general manager' who represented foreign firms doing business in China, and military men) had been aroused. Being sensitive about a regime that was Manchu, and having tired of half-hearted attempts at reform, China's elites became infatuated with revolution along Western lines. By 1911, in the midst of massive popular demands for revolutionary change, the fall of the Qing, when compared to the world's other major historical upheavals, amounted to little more than the proverbial whisper.

EXTRACT 6

From M. Rossabi, *A History of China* (2014).

[T]he humiliation of paying reparations was damaging for the Qing's pride and image. The indemnities were also sizable, exacerbating the chronic financial problems of the Qing court. Many Chinese now turned against the government, while foreigners began to distrust the court. Foreign states, which earlier might have supported the Qing for fear that its collapse would lead to chaos and endanger their economic interests, now were less willing to bolster the court.

SOURCE

From Zou Rong, *The Revolutionary Army*, published in 1903. Zou was one of many Chinese students who studied in Japan. He was heavily influenced by Japan and the steps it had taken to modernise. He blamed the ruling Qing dynasty for China's shortcomings and, in 1903, aged only 18, he wrote *The Revolutionary Army*, in which he urged his countrymen to rise up in revolution. On his return from Japan, he resided in the foreign quarter in Shanghai, which was administered by British law (extraterritorially). The Qing brought charges against Zou for publishing inflammatory materials. British officials resisted Qing pressure for Zou to be put to death and he was sentenced to two years' imprisonment. Ironically, he fell ill in prison and died, aged 19, in 1905.

I do not begrudge repeating over and over again that internally we are the slaves of the Manchus and suffering from their tyranny, externally we are being harassed by the Powers, and we are doubly enslaved. The reason why our sacred Han race [the Han ethnic group made up over 90 per cent of China's population], descendants of the Yellow Emperor [a legendary figure, said to have ruled China 2697-2597 BC and to have established its civilisation], should support revolutionary independence, arises precisely from the question of whether our race will go under and be exterminated.

With the rapid advances in science, the superstitious doctrine whereby a man becomes an emperor through the gift of heaven and the spirits can be destroyed. With the rapid advance in world civilization, the system whereby the rule of a single man in a despotic form of government can cover the whole country may be overthrown. With the rapid advances in wisdom, everybody will be able to enjoy his or her natural rights. If today our great Han people are to throw off the bonds of the Manchus, to retrieve all the rights we have lost, and is to take its place among world powers (for we wish to preserve in its entirety our natural equality of status and independence), we cannot avoid carrying out a revolution and safeguarding our right to independence. ... with the utmost deference I offer to my most revered and beloved 400 million countrymen of the great Han people to prepare them for the path they are to follow.

- China is the China of the Chinese. Countrymen, you must all recognize the China of the Chinese of the Han race.
- Not to allow any alien race to lay their hands on the least rights of our China.
- To expel the Manchus settled in China or kill them in order to revenge ourselves.
- In each area and province a deputy to a general assembly is to be elected by vote in public elections. From these deputies, one is to be elected by vote to serve as provisional president to represent the whole country.
- The whole population, whether male or female, are citizens.
- All men have the duty to serve as citizen soldiers.

- Everybody in the country, whether male or female, is equal. There is no distinction between upper and lower, base and noble.
- A free and independent state has full rights and equality with other great states in the matter of war and peace, treaties and trade, and all other matters pertaining to an independent state.
- The law of the constitution shall be modelled on the American constitutional law, having regard for Chinese conditions.
- The law of self-government shall be modelled on the American law of self-government.
- Likewise in all matters of a national character, negotiations, the establishment of official departments and the determination of the official duties in the state American practice will remain a criterion.

ACTIVITY
KNOWLEDGE CHECK

The significance of the Boxer Rebellion

1. Why has the Boxer Rebellion been called the conservatives' last stand in China?
2. Using Extracts 5 and 6 and Source 9, draw a five-columned table called 'What was the most significant effect of the Boxer Rebellion?' The columns should be headed: 'The indemnity', 'The increase of Chinese nationalism', 'Increased foreign presence and influence', 'The loss of Chinese support for the Qing' and 'The distrust of foreign powers'. Write arguments in favour of each factor.
3. Write a paragraph explaining which factor was the most problematic for the Qing dynasty.
4. How useful is Source 9 in assessing the level of discontent in China following the Boxer Rebellion?

A Level Exam-Style Question Section B

How far do you agree that the defeat in the Sino-Japanese War was the most humiliating defeat suffered by China in the period 1894–1901? (20 marks)

Tip

Make sure you cover the whole of the specified time period, and do not include information not relating to this timeframe. Why has the examiner chosen these dates?

THINKING HISTORICALLY **Interpretations (6a)**

Ever-changing history

Our interpretations of the past change as we change. This may be because our social attitudes have changed over time, or perhaps a historian has constructed a new theory, or perhaps technology has allowed archaeologists to discover something new.

Work in pairs.

1. Make a timeline that starts with the Boxer Rebellion and ends 50 years in the future. Construct reactions that illustrate the point that time changes history. In the future box you can speculate how people might react to the event in 50 years' time. Below is an example:

1898-1901	1911	1936	1968	2067
Event: Boxer Rebellion	Qing court official: 'The beginning of the end of imperial China.' A Christian missionary: 'China's awakening. Christians and foreigners will no longer be tolerated in China.'	A GMD Nationalist: 'A humiliation, China's lowest point.' A Communist participant of the Long March: 'A heroic stand against imperialism.'	A Red Guard: 'A revolutionary inspiration against foreign presence.' A Western historian: 'An example of outdated and simple-minded superstition.' A British MP: 'It prevented full partition like that imposed in Africa.'	?

2. Answer the following questions.
   a) Identify three factors that have affected how the Boxer Rebellion is interpreted over time, or might affect it in the future.
   b) If a historian was to write a book proposing a radically new interpretation of the Boxer Rebellion, how might other historians react? What would affect their reaction?
   c) How will the future change the past?

Conclusion: defeat and humiliation, 1894–1901

The period 1894–1901 in China is one of its most tragic chapters, associated with defeat and humiliation at the hands of the Western industrial powers. However, the confidence with which China entered this period belied the grave consequences that would befall it.

China had been opened up by Britain and France, and Russia had followed suit. The unification of Germany in 1871 brought another pressure to bear, but these could be tolerated. What proved unendurable was receiving the same dismissive treatment from Japan. While Japan had never been a Chinese possession, it lay within China's orbit and had long been influenced by Chinese civilisation, particularly Confucius. It had always been assumed that China, with its long and distinguished history, was the prevailing power in East Asia and superior to Japan, but that supposition was to be challenged.

Both powers had been similarly disadvantaged and humbled at the hands of foreigners in the mid-19th century, but whereas Japan flourished under the Meiji Restoration, China's Self-Strengthening Movement proved an illusory imitation. In China, modernisation was solely applied to the military, and it fell prey to the incompetence, lack of vision and corruption of politicians. The remodelled Huai army and Beiyang fleet were no match for Japan and collapsed during the Sino-Japanese War, 1894–95. The outcome of the war altered the balance of power in South-East Asia: Japan had eclipsed the role of China, symbolically taking such protectorates as Taiwan and Korea. This upsetting of the Confucian order fully exposed the decay of the Qing dynasty to the world.

European colonialists had happily walked the path blazed by Britain in the aftermath of the Opium Wars, and had secured prominent treaty ports throughout China (see Chapter 3). Yet British interests were based on practicality, and China was generally considered a lower priority than their other territorial holdings. Thus, what they desired in China was influence and rights rather than direct rule. Japan, however, had no other imperial demands and focused on China, for territorial concessions on the Asian mainland were central to Japan's continued growth. Korea was to be a stepping stone to Manchuria, where Japan hoped to satisfy its expansionist ambitions.

Japan gained that foothold in the form of the Liaodong peninsula in south Manchuria, but this encroachment onto territory coveted by the Great Powers, especially Germany and Russia, was not to be tolerated. In the short term, Japan's plans were thwarted by the Triple Intervention, which brought to bear the threat of the combined military might of Germany, Russia and France. Compelled to backtrack, Japan seethed as it watched its cherished acquisition fall into Russian hands in 1898. At the same time, Germany, France and Britain had all profited from China's weaknesses by securing further concessions.

Japan felt cheated and pushed on with its militarisation in order to be able to stand up to the Western powers. Japan's growth depended on sourcing more raw resources like oil and coal, which were abundant in China. China's weakness, so clearly demonstrated during the Sino-Japanese War, made further Japanese attacks inevitable. The culmination of this was Japan's occupation of Manchuria in 1931, its drive for further territory in the subsequent years leading to its attack on Pearl Harbor in 1941.

Ironically, the seeds of salvation were sown during China's darkest hour. Although they had been defeated and their leaders executed on the orders of those they had wished to banish from China, the Boxers were the first sign of resurrection. Their bravery and determination grew into Chinese nationalism, a patriotic love of country and culture, and a firm purpose to reclaim Chinese sovereignty throughout the realm. They also contributed to the demise of the Qing dynasty and with it imperial China. Although reforms followed, they were not sufficient to pacify the Chinese population, and within a decade revolution would engulf China, setting it on a new and different way forward.

SOURCE 10 '*En Chine: Le gâteau des rois et... des empereurs*' ('China – the cake of kings and... of emperors'). Cartoon published in *Le Petit Journal*, a French magazine, in 1898 depicting the attitude of the imperial powers to China. Characters representing Britain, Germany, Russia, France and Japan contemplate dividing up China between them. An exasperated and forlorn Chinese figure looks on helplessly.

ACTIVITY
SUMMARY

Defeat and humiliation, 1894–1901

1 Draw a table called 'The influence of foreign powers in China', with five columns. Dedicate one column each to Britain, France, Russia, Germany and Japan and list their territorial possessions.

2 a) Using bullet points, list every reason from 1894 to 1901 that contributed to the growth of Chinese nationalism.

b) Rank the top three of these factors and justify your view.

3 Study Source 10. How would this have surprised:

a) the majority of the Chinese population before the Sino-Japanese War?

b) Japanese negotiators at the Treaty of Shimonoseki?

c) French, Russian and German diplomats prior to the Triple Intervention?

d) Americans who supported the Open Door policy?

e) the Boxers before laying siege to the Legation Quarter in Beijing?

WIDER READING

Grasso, J., Corrin, J. and Kort, M. *Modernization and Revolution in China*, M.E. Sharpe (1997)

Jowett, P. *China's Wars: Rousing the Dragon, 1894–1949*, Osprey (2013)

McAleavy, H. *The Modern History of China*, Weidenfeld and Nicolson (1968)

Putnam Weale, B.L. *Indiscreet Letters from Peking*, The Echo Library (2006)

Rossabi, M. *A History of China*, Wiley Blackwell (2014)

3.5 The Japanese threat, 1931–41

KEY QUESTIONS

- What was the significance of the Manchurian Crisis of 1931–33?
- Why did all-out war break out between Japan and China in 1937?
- What was the impact of the war of 1937–39?

INTRODUCTION

After the Boxer Rebellion had been suppressed, the Qing court began to introduce reforms. Foot-binding was prohibited (although it took another generation for the practice to die out), and the civil service examinations that had existed practically unchanged for a thousand years were abolished. By 1909, provincial assemblies had been established, elected by limited suffrage. Japanese influence over China had grown since the Treaty of Shimonoseki, notably following Japan's victories in Manchuria in the Russo-Japanese War (1904–05). This in itself was an indignity for the Chinese, as a war had been fought on its mainland in which it was not involved.

The reforms introduced within China in the first decade of the 20th century failed to stem the tide of opposition to the Qing dynasty. Many reforms were aimed at industrialisation, and textile mills, mines and factories, often financed by foreign investment, all followed. However, by 1911 the Qing dynasty had lost the support of most of the nation. The Dowager Empress Cixi had died in 1908 and on her deathbed named as her successor the two-year-old nephew of the also deceased Emperor Guangxu. This did nothing to strengthen the Qing dynasty, and alienated those Chinese who felt that rule by another regency until the emperor reached adulthood would slow down reform and modernisation.

In 1911, the Qing dynasty fell to a revolution inspired by Sun Yat-sen. From 1911 to 1949, China was a republic, although in its early years it was divided under rival regional warlords. The revolution did not succeed in warding off foreign interest. Further disgrace, at the hands of the foreigners, was heaped on China in 1915 when Japan issued the Twenty-One Demands. In the previous year, Japan had entered the First World War on the side of the Allies, in part to take over German interests in Shandong, which it swiftly achieved. If accepted, the Twenty-One Demands would have made China a virtual Japanese protectorate. Only the protestations of the Allied Nations and the USA prevented the more expansionist elements of the demands being implemented. However, the Treaty of Versailles that concluded the First World War confirmed that German interests in China would be passed to the Japanese and not returned to Chinese control.

1931 –
19 Feb: Jiang Jieshi appeals to League of Nations to intervene against Japanese invasion
18 Sep: Mukden Incident

1932 –
Jan-Mar: Fighting between China and Japan in Shanghai
18 Feb: Proclamation of Japanese puppet state, Manchukuo

1933 –
Feb: Japan rejects Lytton Report
Mar: Japan leaves League of Nations
May: Treaty of Tanggu recognises Japanese control over Chinese provinces of Manchuria, Rehe and Hopei. Peiping and Shanghai demilitarised

1934–35 –
Long March

1935 –
June: He-Umezu Agreement leads to creation of East Hebei Autonomous Council

1931 1932 1933 1934 1935

By the 1920s, Japan enjoyed control over the Shandong peninsula and considerable tracts of Manchuria. However, the **Wall Street Crash** of 1929 and ensuing unfriendly US trade legislation meant that to support its fledgling industrial economy, Japan looked to China, where raw materials were plentiful and there was room for the population of Japan to spread. Sun's successor as leader of the Guomindang (GMD; see Chapter 1), Jiang Jieshi, launched a successful military campaign and by 1928 had brought China under the central control of the Guomindang.

KEY TERM

Wall Street Crash
In 1929, the stock market in Wall Street, New York, crashed and as a result the US economy and all those associated with it fell into depression.

EXTEND YOUR KNOWLEDGE

Sun Yat-sen (1866–1925)
Sun Yat-sen was a Chinese revolutionary hero of the late Qing period, who became a symbol first of the 1911 revolution and later of the Chinese Republic (1912–49). He was educated in the USA, converted to Christianity and qualified as a doctor in Hong Kong. Disillusioned with Qing rule, Sun gave up medicine and turned his attention to politics. His views led to him spending much of his life in exile abroad. He was heavily influenced by Japan and also travelled to the USA, raising funds from expatriate Chinese. He founded a revolutionary party, the Tongmenghui (later the Guomindang) in Japan in 1905 (see page 19).

Sun's beliefs were derived from the Three People's Principles: nationalism, democracy and welfare. He returned to China in 1912 as the elected provincial president. However, without any effective military support, he had to negotiate with Yuan Shikai, the military leader of the North, and relinquished the position of president. Sun became convinced that the only way to unite China was through a military campaign. However, in 1925 Sun died of liver cancer. He was one of the few figures to be equally revered in both Mao's People's Republic of China and Jiang's Republic of China in Taiwan.

EXTEND YOUR KNOWLEDGE

Jiang Jieshi (1887–1975)
Jiang Jieshi was also known as Chiang Kai-shek. After rising through the ranks of the Guomindang, Jiang succeeded Sun Yat-sen as leader in 1925. Finding himself on the right of the party, he launched the Northern Expedition 1926–28 against Chinese warlords in the North, to unite China under Guomindang rule. He also broke the united front with the Communists by ordering the slaughter of thousands of Communists in Shanghai. Jiang's distrust and hatred of the Communists led him to view them as the prime threat to China's safety. As Japan began to extend its rule in China, Jiang maintained that the Communists posed a greater threat than Japan.

By 1937, he ended hostilities against the Communists to fight Japan, a war that by 1939 had become part of the Second World War. After the end of the Second World War, the civil war between the Guomindang and the Communists resumed until Jiang and his supporters were finally forced to flee the mainland for Taiwan. There Jiang remained, forming the Republic of China and establishing friendly relations with the West, particularly the USA, and Japan. Jiang ruled in Taiwan, without elections, until his death in 1975.

1936 –
Nov: Signing of Anti-Comintern Pact between Germany and Japan
Dec: Xi'an Incident ends Chinese Civil War; GMD and CCP declare united front against Japan

1937 –
7 July: Marco Polo Bridge Incident
Aug–Nov: Fighting in Shanghai

1937–38 –
Dec–Jan: Rape of Nanjing

1938 –
Mar–Apr: Battle of Tai'erzhuang, China defeats Japan
Oct: Fall of Wuhan
Nationalists establish Chongqing as capital after retreating from Wuhan

1940 –
Establishment of collaborationist Reorganised National Government
USA imposes heavy economic sanctions on Japan

1941 –
7 Dec: Japan bombards US Pacific Fleet at Pearl Harbor

1936 1937 1938 1939 1940 1941

WHAT WAS THE SIGNIFICANCE OF THE MANCHURIAN CRISIS OF 1931-33?

The global economic downturn triggered by the Wall Street Crash in 1929 presented industrialised Japan with a grave economic challenge. Exports were hit hard, particularly after 1930 when the USA raised its import tariff considerably. Faced with this, an ever-growing population and a relative lack of raw materials, Japan had to act. It cast its eye enviously towards China once more. Japan already boasted influence in Manchuria through control of the South Manchurian railway and accompanying industries, not to mention the military presence of the Kwantung Army. Manchuria, the ancestral home of the now deposed Qing dynasty, was sparsely populated; indeed the Qings had actively prevented mass Han immigration to the region. It was also an area rich in raw materials and arable land. With China still too weak to resist, Japan made its move. Those favouring war with China acted in accordance with the Tanaka Memorial, arguing that Japan's very existence was at risk unless it expanded into China. Japan's policy was not pure imperial aggression, but rather it was born out of economic necessity, the domestic situation in China and military might.

By 1928, Jiang Jieshi had succeeded in unifying most of China, and this threatened Japanese dominance in Manchuria. Therefore, the Japanese assassinated the warlord in Manchuria – Zhang Zuolin – in the hope that his son would prove more compliant to Japanese demands. They were disappointed as Zhang Xueliang proved to be loyal to China.

Basking in his victory in uniting China under his Guomindang (GMD) rule, Jiang turned his attention to the Communists. He saw the eradication of the Communist threat as more significant for China's well-being than the threat posed by a standing Japanese military presence in Manchuria. He called Japan 'a disease of the skin' and the Chinese Communists (CCP) 'a disease of the heart'. Jiang believed the disease of the heart had to be tackled before the disease of the skin. This proved to be all the incentive the Japanese military needed to push its territorial and economic designs.

The Mukden Incident

As Manchuria directly bordered the Japanese protectorate of Korea, it was the logical area for Japan to concentrate its imperial efforts. It should be noted that Japan itself was far from united regarding its attitude to China. The military supported the Tanaka Memorial, whereas the Tokyo government supported a more diplomatic approach. Knowing that the government was to announce a more prudent and patient line, the Kwantung Army acted first. On 18 September 1931, the Kwantung Army blew up a segment of the South Manchuria railway and promptly blamed Chinese saboteurs for damage to Japanese holdings. The city of Mukden was quickly overwhelmed, and without waiting for government approval, the Kwantung Army, supported by Japanese forces in Korea, occupied official buildings. As the Kwantung Army consolidated its gains, the Japanese government was compelled to fall into line: the military tail was wagging the Japanese dog.

EXTEND YOUR KNOWLEDGE

The Kwantung Army

The Kwantung Army was home to radical militarists who favoured the overthrow of the civilian government in favour of a military dictatorship. In the 1920s and 1930s, as the balance of power in Japan shifted towards militarism, the Kwantung Army began to act independently. In 1928, it planned and carried out the assassination of the Manchurian warlord, Zhang Zuolin. Then in 1931, without official sanction, it engineered the Mukden Incident that led to the invasion of Manchuria. The Kwantung Army fought Chinese forces continually and also clashed with the USSR prior to and during the Second World War, suffering heavy casualties. The army was disbanded following Japan's defeat at the end of the Second World War.

EXTEND YOUR KNOWLEDGE

The Tanaka Memorial

The Tanaka memorial was written by Baron Tanaka, Japan's Prime Minister from 1927 to 1929. It advocated the conquest of Manchuria to lead to the invasion and occupation of the whole of China. Japan would then attack throughout South Asia and eventually threaten the USA. There is doubt whether the document existed, and there now appears to be consensus that it was a forgery. Nevertheless, Japan's foreign policy from the 1930s onwards did mirror the Memorial. Japan first attacked Manchuria, then expanded its influence in China. During the Second World War, Japan invaded French Indochina and British-held Singapore. In 1941 it attacked Pearl Harbor, leading to war with the USA. Wartime US propaganda referred to the Tanaka Memorial as the Japanese *Mein Kampf*.

EXTRACT 1

From O. Arne Westad, *Restless Empire: China and the World since 1750* (2013).

Believing that Zhang Zuolin stood in the way of this process [making Manchuria an independent Japanese-dominated nation], local officers of the imperial army placed a bomb under his Japanese-made railway carriage and blew their former ally sky-high, demonstrating to all how far some Japanese were willing to go to fasten their country's grip on Manchuria. While Tokyo was increasingly losing full control of its army's actions abroad, the Japanese government feared the rise in Chinese nationalism and the vigorous new regime of Chiang Kai-Shek [Jiang Jieshi]. It also feared the effects of the global depression on Japan and its development aims. Japan's response was to do as much as it could to preserve Manchuria as its exclusive zone of influence, even if that meant fighting future wars over it.

Within a generation Japan had gone from being the foremost inspiration in creating a new state and society to being the main threat to China's existence. In the 1920s and 1930s there were still people around on both sides who called for the relationship to be less confrontational and more cooperative. ... But as imperial Japan moved to secure its role as a great power at China's expense, the voices of cooperation became fewer and increasingly reviled by their compatriots. Much of the Chinese nationalism, as it was formed in the interwar years, became ingrained with a vision of Japan as China's deadly enemy, a vision that persists among many Chinese today. Instead of a new East China in which China and Japan were partners, as so many had dreamed about in the nineteenth century, the region in the next century became a nightmare of conflict, a nightmare that by the 1930s seemed to have no end.

SOURCE 1

Political cartoon by Erich Schilling in *Simplicissimus* (1933): 'Oh! Japsi, you ought to tell your old aunt that you want to play war again.' *Simplicissimus* was a German satirical magazine. First published in 1896, by 1933 it had become an instrument of the Nazi Party. Contributors such as Schilling toed the Nazi party line and became propagandists for the Nazi regime.

SOURCE 2

Eduard Thony in *Simplicissimus* (1933): 'Japan is forced to punish China for its provocative behaviour.' The cartoon shows Japan as the aggressor looking for excuses to invade. Like Schilling (Source 1), Thony kept his position at *Simplicissimus* by becoming loyal to the Nazi Party. Until the signing of the Anti-Comintern in 1937, Germany was an ally to China and supplied it with military instructors (see page 123).

ACTIVITY
KNOWLEDGE CHECK

Jiang Jieshi's view of the threats posed by the CCP and Japan

1. Explain why the Japanese occupation of Manchuria and the Kwantung Army posed such a threat to Chinese security.
2. Using Extract 1, Sources 1 and 2 and your own knowledge, how far do you agree with Jiang Jieshi that 'the Japanese are a disease of the skin' and 'the Communists are a disease of the heart'?

Jiang Jieshi's response

Jiang's response to Japanese hostilities reflected his personal beliefs more than those of the Chinese Republic. Although many Chinese had looked to Japan for inspiration regarding how to readjust China's international standing within the modern industrial context, there was now widespread protest against Japanese aggression and imperialism. Public opinion demanded resistance, and a National Salvation movement emerged amongst the population to hinder Japanese expansionism. However, this did not receive backing from Jiang's government, who felt that the wisest response was to acquiesce until the Communists had been eliminated and a united China could turn its attention to Japan.

Jiang's priority in this period was the annihilation of the enemy within: the CCP. At the time of Japan's invasion of Manchuria, Jiang was embroiled in a campaign to destroy the Communists. Jiang commanded Zhang Xueliang to withdraw his troops, believing that Chinese forces in the region were no match for the advancing Japanese. Jiang refused to call a truce with the CCP and continued to see the Communists as his main threat domestically, hoping to use the League of Nations to protect China from Japanese incursions.

EXTEND YOUR KNOWLEDGE

Zhang Xueliang (1901–2001)
Zhang Xueliang was the warlord commander of Manchuria who ascended to the position after his father's assassination by Japanese agents. Japan expected Zhang to be intimidated into compliance, but instead Zhang developed a lifelong hatred of Japan. He was known as the Young Marshal, to distinguish him from his father, the Old Marshal. In 1928, he swore allegiance to Jiang Jieshi and the Republic of China. Zhang was ordered to evacuate his native land as Japan invaded in 1931, losing land and his personal fortune, which only intensified his loathing of Japan.

A noted playboy who was addicted to opium and morphine, he undertook a curative tour of Europe and on returning to China was put in charge of the anti-Communist campaign. However, he saw the Japanese as the enemy, and wanted to push them out of his native Manchuria. In 1936, he was responsible for the kidnap of Jiang (see page 119) to force him to accept a united front to oppose Japan.

EXTEND YOUR KNOWLEDGE

The League of Nations
The forerunner of the United Nations, the League of Nations was set up in 1919 following the end of the First World War. It attempted to support self-determination and to uphold the post-war consensus. Its main aim was to prevent another world war. The League hoped to utilise the armed forces of its member states and economic sanctions to prevent foreign aggression. However, it proved weak and ineffective: the international community's distaste for war meant that it proved powerless in standing up to aggressive regimes such as Germany, Italy and Japan. The Manchurian Crisis exemplified the League's impotence in the inter-war period.

China appealed to the League of Nations in the wake of Japan's invasion, and the League set up the Lytton Commission to investigate the matter. The commission reported that Japan was guilty of aggression and that China's sovereignty had been compromised without any popular support within Manchuria. Japan ignored the judgement and walked out of the League of Nations, never to return. With the West in the grip of recession, there was little appetite for the League to enforce its will through costly military force. China had been betrayed by the League, which had refused to defend China's national integrity. Jiang's hope of achieving a status quo with Japan by means of the League demanding Japan's withdrawal from Manchuria had been lost. The Chinese population reacted to Japan's invasion of Manchuria by boycotting Japanese goods; Japanese sales in China were cut by two-thirds. Japan had not anticipated this response and outwardly declared it an act of aggression, though privately it was worried by this demonstration of Chinese nationalism and the effect it would have on the ailing Japanese economy. Japan determined to end the boycott through military might.

SOURCE

D. Low, *The Doormat* (1933). This cartoon was printed in the *Evening Standard*, a London-based UK national newspaper, and shows the noble League of Nations being trampled over by the Japanese army. The diplomats in charge of the League are doing nothing to stop Japan. Low was a firm supporter of the League of Nations, although not its leadership.

THE DOORMAT.

SOURCE

'The League of Nations is a League of Robbers!' 6 October 1932. This is a telegram from the Chinese Soviet Government the Jiangxi Soviet (also known as the Chinese Soviet Republic), a self-governing region within China under the control of the CCP in the 1930s, representing the views of the Chinese Communist Party. The Communists wanted to stand up to Japanese aggression. This nationalism appealed to many Chinese in regions under Japanese rule.

Workers, peasants, and soldiers of all China! Exploited masses of the whole country!

The Provisional Central Government of the Chinese Soviet Republic long ago told the popular masses of the whole country that the League of Nations is a League of Robbers by which the various imperialisms are dismembering China. The principal task of the Lytton Commission of Enquiry sent to China by the League was to prepare the dismemberment of China and the repression of all the revolutionary movements that have raised the flag of the Chinese Soviets.

Now the Commission of Enquiry of the league of imperialist robbers – the Lytton Commission – has already published its report regarding the dismemberment of China. This report is an admirable document shown to the Chinese popular masses by the imperialists regarding the dismemberment they propose to inflict on China, and yet the Kuomintang [Guomindang], which is selling out and dishonouring the country, as well as the government which is the emanation of the Kuomintang, have accepted it completely!

The Lytton Report is the bill of sale by which imperialism reduced the Chinese people to slavery! The Soviet Government calls on the popular masses of the whole country to participate in an armed uprising under the direction of the Soviet Government, to wage a national revolutionary war in order to tear to shreds the Lytton Report, and to oppose all the new projects of the imperialists for dismembering China, repressing the Chinese revolution, and attacking the Soviet regions and the Soviet Union. Let us hurl out of China, Japanese imperialism and all other imperialisms in order to obtain the complete liberation and independence of the Chinese people! Let us defend the Soviet Union with arms in our hands, let us establish a close alliance between the toiling masses of China and of the Soviet Union.

The Soviet Government proclaims to the workers, peasants, and soldiers of the whole country, and to all the exploited popular masses, that if we really want to wage national revolutionary war and oppose the dismemberment of China by the imperialists, we must first overthrow the reactionary domination of the Kuomintang, these scavengers who pick up the scraps of the imperialist dismemberment of China, and who are repressing the national war!

A Level Exam-Style Question Section A

Study Source 4 before you answer this question.

Assess the value of the source for revealing Chinese attitudes to Japan and the different approaches of the GMD and CCP to repelling the invading Japanese in 1933.

Explain your answer, using the source, the information given about its origin and your own knowledge about the historical context. (20 marks)

Tip

When analysing the usefulness of this source, consider to what extent it was representative of Chinese public opinion.

EXTRACT 2 From J. Fenby, *Generalissimo Chiang Kai-shek and the China He Lost* (2005).

The commission produced a report that was generally favourable to the Nationalists. Though conceding some rights to Japan, it pronounced Manchuria an integral part of China, said the Mukden Incident could not be regarded as legitimate self-defence, and described Manchukuo as a Japanese creation, not an independent state. Tokyo, it found, had violated the Covenant of the League. When the report was debated at the League's headquarters in Geneva, Japan cast the only negative vote, and quit the international body. It knew that, whatever the Lytton team had decided, neither China nor the League was going to take action. A Japanese report even had Chiang [Jiang] remarking: 'If Japan will be satisfied with Manchuria, well, we aren't happy about it but we can pretend they aren't there.'

EXTRACT 3 From F. Northedge, *The League of Nations: Its Life and Times 1920–1946* (1986).

Nevertheless, the Report was clear that without a declaration of war, a large area of what was indisputably Chinese territory has been forcibly seized and occupied by the armed forces of Japan and has, in consequence of this operation, been separated from and declared independent of the rest of China... As events were to show, the Japanese had no intention of isolating Manchuria from their relations with China; on the contrary, they meant to master both Manchuria and China and the two together under their own control. Lacking this insight into the Japanese frame of mind (and the fact that such an outcome hardly seems to have been thought of by the Lytton commission shows how readily Japanese professions of innocence were taken at their face value), the Report's proposals for a settlement now seem little more than well-intentioned daydreaming.

ACTIVITY
KNOWLEDGE CHECK

The League of Nations

1. What did Jiang hope to accomplish by appealing to the League of Nations after Japan invaded Manchuria in 1931?
2. With reference to Extract 2 and your own knowledge, write a paragraph explaining why Chinese public opinion differed from that of Jiang Jieshi with regard to opposing Japan.
3. How useful is Extract 3 in explaining why the League of Nations did not act more forcefully to Japan in 1933?
4. How useful to the historian is Source 3 in showing the West's response to Japan's invasion of China?

The loss of Manchuria

By 1932, Manchuria had been conquered. Key cities such as Harbin were occupied and the last Qing emperor, Puyi, was installed as chief executive of the newly renamed Manchukuo ('the land of the Manchus'). Manchukuo continued to exist until the end of the Second World War in 1945. By appointing Puyi, Japan was attempting to give Manchukuo a Chinese character and, therefore, legitimacy. However, in reality it was nothing more than a puppet regime that existed under the total control of the Kwantung Army.

Japan began to develop Manchukuo as a colony: roads were built (see Chapter 1), an airline was set up, and Japanese department stores were opened in the province. Although some Chinese troops switched allegiance to Japan, domestic opposition persisted. The loss of Manchuria was a humiliation on a scale even beyond that endured during the period of Qing decline. While the concessionary leases granted by the Qing to Western powers in the 19th century were long-lasting, they were not permanent. In contrast, Japan had invaded Manchuria, renamed it Manchukuo and, although in name and theory it was an independent nation, it was to be a Japanese colony in perpetuity. Chinese volunteers fought guerrilla campaigns and attacked isolated Japanese garrisons, railway interests and Japanese citizens residing in China. This, in turn, provoked a brutal Japanese response and large-scale anti-bandit campaigns were launched. Eventually, the campaigns wore down the opposition and Jiang Jieshi's government gave no support. Jiang remained convinced that

China was not yet strong enough to resist Japan, and had to go on the defensive until either China had strengthened itself or Japanese aggression threatened European interests enough to trigger foreign intervention on China's behalf. By 1937, however, organised opposition to Japanese rule in the region had been largely quelled.

SOURCE 5 The Chinese Manchu emperor's State Visit to Tokyo, Japan, 6 April 1935. Postcard depicting Puyi, the puppet emperor of Manchuria. The flag of Manchukuo is printed at the top of the card. Materials such as this were produced to try to show Manchukuo as a legitimate state with popular support, in contrast to the findings of the Lytton Report (see page 113).

ACTIVITY
KNOWLEDGE CHECK

The establishment of Manchukuo

1 Produce a newspaper article detailing events in Manchuria/Manchukuo 1931-33. Your article should be from the perspective of one of the following:

  a) a Manchu supporter of the Qing Empire now resident in Manchukuo

  b) a Guomindang official justifying Jiang Jieshi's actions

  c) a critic of Jiang Jieshi's decision to eliminate the Communists before opposing Japan.

2 With reference to Source 5 and your own knowledge, why did the following things occur?

  a) Japan appointed the former Qing emperor to lead Manchukuo.

  b) Puyi accepted the role.

3 Why was China unable to resist the establishment of the puppet state of Manchukuo in 1932?

4 Write three to four sentences justifying your answer to question 3.

As Japan consolidated control of the puppet state of Manchukuo, it acted decisively in Shanghai to end the boycott of Japanese goods. As was the case in Mukden, Japanese intelligence officers conspired to create a situation to justify conflict. A group of Japanese monks were beaten by a Chinese crowd, giving the Japanese Imperial Navy the excuse they needed to begin military operations. The attack had been organised by a Japanese agent who paid Chinese thugs to attack the monks. Japanese marines landed but were opposed by GMD troops. The Japanese then ordered an aerial bombardment and the destruction was vast. The GMD forces fought ferociously and stalled Japan. War raged through Shanghai for five weeks, ending only when the Japanese deemed that China had been taught a lesson. More than 70,000 Japanese troops occupied Shanghai. Chinese casualties spiralled into the thousands, unemployment soared to beyond 300,000, farmland and railways were ruined, upwards of 200,000 citizens fled the city and there was a huge downturn in trade. The GMD army that had so heroically defended Shanghai was ordered away from the city against its wishes. Jiang did not believe the army's chiefs were fully loyal. The victorious Japanese went on a rampage of rape, looting and murder through Shanghai. Shanghai was devastated. The damage to factories, houses, shops and schools was estimated at US$1.5 billion. The resulting armistice stipulated that a neutral zone be drawn around the city.

Public opposition to Japanese occupation grew, but Jiang did not think that China was strong enough to defeat Japan yet. Therefore he adopted a position of appeasement in the face of ever greater aggression. Jiang remained steadfast in his belief that Japan could not be effectively resisted until the CCP had been eliminated as a political force. Only then would a united China be powerful enough to turn its attention to Japan.

EXTEND YOUR KNOWLEDGE

The Fukien Rebellion (1933-34)

Under the leadership of General Cai Tingkai, the GMD 19th Route Army was redeployed from Shanghai to Fukien province to put down the Communists. However, as demonstrated by their determined defence of Shanghai, the 19th Route Army saw the invading Japanese and not the CCP as their enemy. In Fukien, instead of fighting the Communists, they negotiated and formed a new government.

Jiang Jieshi sent sizeable forces to the region to suppress the rebellion. Although it had earned a good reputation in the Shanghai fighting, the 19th Route Army could not realistically stand against the rest of the GMD army. The rebellion was rapidly brought to an end. The affair was significant in demonstrating Chinese disunity. Jiang's assessment that the Japanese were a disease of the skin but the Communists a disease of the heart and, therefore, more urgent, was not shared. There was a deep-seated feeling that it was in China's national interest for Jiang to end the anti-Communist campaigns and form a united front with the Communists to stand and fight the Japanese invaders.

The Treaty of Tanggu, 1933

With Manchuria now effectively run by Japan and Shanghai demilitarised, Japanese aggression continued. The Kwantung Army in Manchuria crossed the border into neighbouring Rehe province and claimed the area, citing the suppression of domestic unrest as central to Manchukuo's self-preservation. After securing Rehe, the marauding Japanese advanced south-westerly to occupy Hopei province. With no organised military resistance coming from the Nationalist government in Nanjing, Wang Jingwei, a senior member of the GMD, and Jiang Jieshi authorised the Tanggu Treaty in May 1933 to halt hostilities. The treaty recognised Japanese control of Manchuria, Rehe and Hopei. An area encompassing Tianjin and Peiping (the name of Beijing between 1928 and 1949) was demilitarised and Japan had secured its interests in northern China. Jiang had surrendered Chinese sovereignty to avoid a full-scale war with Japan.

The treaty was vilified by most Chinese and was another humiliation for China. The fact that the treaty was signed under the intimidating presence of Japanese warships was ominous. The treaty may have achieved peace in the short term, but only through China bowing to Japanese demands. It was unlikely that Japan was satisfied, and indeed Jiang's yielding, as well as Japan's growing economic reliance on Chinese resources, only encouraged further Japanese incursions.

EXTEND YOUR KNOWLEDGE

Wang Jingwei (1883–1944)

Wang Jingwei was a Chinese politician who played a role in the 1911 revolution and became a prominent figure in Sun Yat-sen's Guomindang. He hoped to become leader of the GMD after Sun died, but was outmanoeuvred by Jiang Jieshi. He remained in the GMD but had frequent disagreements with Jiang. When all-out war broke out in 1937 (see pages 121–22), Wang became pessimistic in the face of early Japanese successes and advocated that China should seek peace.

In 1940, Wang Jingwei defected and was appointed to lead the Reorganised National Government, a Japanese puppet regime (see page 123) set up to rival the nationalist government of Jiang Jieshi. Wang was denounced by Jiang as a traitor. Wang said that collaboration with Japan was the only way to protect the Chinese people from war.

In 1943, Japan returned rule of Shanghai's foreign concessions to the Reorganised National Government, but this did not help Wang gain support, and the view of him as a traitor persisted until his death in 1944.

SOURCE 6 From a telegram sent to the Chinese government by a federation of citizen groups in 1933.

Every member of our federation is risking his life to resist the Japanese. What risk is Wang Jingwei taking as he curries favour with the Japanese, and unhesitatingly and shamelessly signs the traitorous Tanggu Truce, and that on the heels of the Shanghai Ceasefire Agreement? He has added another blot on his already disgraceful reputation.

ACTIVITY
KNOWLEDGE CHECK

The Tanggu Treaty

1 What were the terms of the Tanggu Treaty?

2 What effect do you think the Tanggu Treaty would have on Japan from 1933 onwards?

3 How useful is Source 6 for the historian studying Chinese public opinion in regard to Jiang Jieshi's reaction to Japanese aggression?

Conclusion

The Manchurian Crisis was significant for many reasons. It set Japan on a course of territorial expansion and regional domination that led to the bombing of the US fleet at Pearl Harbor in 1941. The Chinese unity proclaimed by Jiang Jieshi in 1928 was a false dawn for those Chinese desiring the restoration of past glories. Although Jiang had claimed supremacy over most of the Chinese mainland, his power was concentrated in the south, and he was preoccupied with eliminating the Communists as rivals to his power. He also believed that China was too weak to defeat Japan, so he appeased Japan to buy time until China was strong enough to defend itself or until Japan's expansionism led to war with the USSR or USA, both of which Jiang Jieshi thought likely. However, in the short term, his refusal to halt attacks against the Communists and to concentrate his attentions on the invading Japanese led to significant land losses. It is indicative of Jiang's priorities in this period that the Japanese invasion of Manchuria began when he was leading a campaign against the Communists.

The indignities associated with the 1930s were far greater than China had ever experienced: China ceded control of Manchuria and watched helplessly as the deposed last Qing emperor, Puyi, was installed as chief executive of the newly created Manchukuo. Rehe also fell under Japanese control and areas around Shanghai and between Peiping and the Great Wall had been demilitarised. The Treaty of Tanggu was more a confirmation of Japanese conquests than an indication of lasting peace ahead. Economic weaknesses at home had emboldened the Japanese military. The government, which had previously been lukewarm in its support for the army's actions in China, fell in line after initial successes proved popular.

There were many factors that suggested Japanese expansionism would continue. Japan gained control over several Chinese provinces. China's weakness also served to give Japan's military more influence over the civilian government in Tokyo in relation to leading policy in China. In addition, Japan's economy relied heavily on China's resources and land, and the League of Nations was not prepared to defend China. However, in the short term, a peace had been negotiated and Jiang, once more, drew up plans to eliminate the Communists.

EXTRACT 4

From O. Arne Westad, *Restless Empire: China and the World since 1750* (2013).

From the 1920s on, the Guomindang leader Chiang Kai-Shek [Jiang Jieshi] had regarded Japan as the foremost threat to China's unity and integrity. While admiring Japanese fighting skills and organizational abilities, Chiang realized that these very qualities could be turned against China if Tokyo so decided. From 1931 on, Chiang knew that a war was coming, and he wanted to postpone it for as long as possible, giving his regime time to complete the unification of China and gain foreign allies. Though much maligned then and now, Chiang's strategy made eminent sense: He knew better than anyone else just how weak China was compared with Japan, and that the only way in which his nationalist project could be saved was through buying time. Throughout the early 1930s, against considerable opposition from friends and foes alike within China, Chiang clung to his strategy. He would not fight a full-scale war with Japan until he absolutely had to, and then, he predicted, there would be a long war in which China's very survival would be at stake. It was a war China could not fight without unity, weapons, and foreign assistance.

ACTIVITY
KNOWLEDGE CHECK

The significance of the loss of Manchuria

1. Why was the loss of Manchuria in 1933 more significant than any other territorial loss suffered by China since 1860?
2. According to Extract 4, why did Jiang not lead a more robust campaign against Japan until 1933?

WHY DID ALL-OUT WAR BREAK OUT BETWEEN JAPAN AND CHINA IN 1937?

Increased hostilities, 1933–37

Jiang Jieshi was willing to tolerate the puppet state of Manchukuo as long as there were no further Japanese incursions. In doing so, he hoped Japan would be satisfied and would leave the rest of China alone. Jiang believed this would give his government time to achieve the stability required to focus on the total annihilation of the Chinese Communists. If the Communists no longer threatened Jiang's leadership, he could then turn his attention to combatting Japan. However, the plan backfired in two ways. Firstly, the Japanese were not content with their gains up to and including the Tanggu Treaty, and pushed for further territory, and secondly, Jiang was unable to destroy the Communists.

Japan was emboldened by China's feeble response to its aggression. Japan was also pressured by its own economic demands, as well as being aware that at some stage China must resist. Therefore, Japan determined to act before China grew resilient. Accordingly, Chahar province, which neighboured conquered Rehe, was annexed. Also, in June 1935 the He-Umezu Agreement dictated that all GMD activities must cease in Hopei province. This agreement was then formalised by the creation of East Hebei Autonomous Council, which proclaimed independence from the Republic of China. Although nominally under the control of Chinese separatists, like Manchukuo, it amounted to nothing more than a Japanese puppet regime. Jiang's response was one of resignation rather than opposition, and he persisted in his anti-Communist campaigns. This was not cowardice on Jiang's part, he was a Chinese nationalist and he was not prepared to tolerate Japanese aggression indefinitely, but he believed China would only be strong enough to resist Japan when the Communists had been defeated. Jiang's cold logic was not popular with the Chinese population, yet to follow the anti-Japanese policies of his critics would provoke war. For their part, the Communists proved irrepressible and escaped total destruction through the legendary Long March, a 6,000 mile flight to the north-west of China. The cries became louder: 'Why must Chinese fight Chinese?'

It is impossible to know when, or even if, Jiang Jieshi would have changed his tactics. He was not a collaborator, but his preoccupation with the CCP showed no signs of abating until forces beyond his control compelled him to agree to a united front with the Communists against Japan.

EXTEND YOUR KNOWLEDGE

Unity in nationalist China

In the final years of the Qing dynasty, as central government control declined, various regimes began to govern themselves. This continued until Jiang Jieshi came to power in 1925 and determined to bring these outlying regions under control. He successfully led the Northern Expedition, which concluded in 1928, meaning that China was more united than it had been since the Qing dynasty. However, there was not total unity. Manchuria was now under Japanese rule; Outer Mongolia was under Soviet influence and Xinjiang's Uighurs also favoured self-rule. Tibet looked to British troops in India to help retain its autonomy. Of all the opposition he faced, Jiang viewed the Communists as his greatest threat because their ideology would not accept being ruled by Jiang and the GMD in the long term.

SOURCE

Edgar Snow was a US journalist who was sympathetic to Mao and the CCP. He travelled to China in 1936 with a letter of introduction to Mao. His book, *Red Star Over China* (1938), was the first and only authorised account of Mao's life, of the Long March and of the men and women who formed the Communist Party. Mao and Snow became lasting friends.

The Young Marshal formally presented to the Generalissimo the program for a national front, cessation of civil war, alliance with Russia, and resistance to Japan. Chiang Kai-Shek [Jiang Jieshi] replied, 'I will never talk about this until every Red soldier is exterminated, and every Communist is in prison. Only then would it be possible to cooperate with Russia.' A little before this the Generalissimo had rejected a Russian offer of a mutual-defense pact... A flame of strong nationalist feeling swept through the country, and the Japanese demanded the suppression of the National Salvation movement, which they held responsible for the anti-Japanese agitation. Nanking [Nanjing] obliged. Seven of the most prominent leaders of the organization, all respected citizens, including a prominent banker, a lawyer, educators, and writers, were arrested. At the same time the government suppressed fourteen nationally popular magazines. Strikes in the Japanese mills of Shanghai, partly in patriotic protest against the Japanese invasion of Suiyuan, were also broken up with considerable violence by the Japanese, in cooperation with the Kuomintang [Guomindang]. When the other patriotic strikes occurred in Tsingtao [Qingdao], the Japanese landed their own marines, arrested the strikers, and occupied the city. The marines were withdrawn only after Chiang had agreed virtually to prohibit all strikes in Japanese mills of Tsingtao in the future...

In November, under pressure from his own officers, Chang Hsueh-liang [Zhang Xueliang] dispatched his famous appeal to be sent to the Suiyuan front. 'In order to control our troops,' this missive concluded, 'we would keep our promise to them that whenever the chance comes they will be allowed to carry out their desire of fighting the enemy. Otherwise they will regard not only myself, but also Your Excellency, as a cheat, and thus will no longer obey us. Please give us the order to mobilize at least a part, if not the whole, of the Tungpei Army [Zhang's Manchurian army that now served as part of the main GMD army], to march immediately to Suiyuan as reinforcements to those who are fulfilling their sacred mission of fighting Japanese imperialism there. If so, I, as well as my troops, of more than 100,000, shall follow Your Excellency's leadership to the end.' The earnest tone of this whole letter, the hope of restoring an army's lost prestige, were overwhelmingly evident. But Chiang rejected the suggestion. He still wanted the Tungpei Army to fight the Reds.

EXTEND YOUR KNOWLEDGE

The Long March

By late 1934, the CCP's base, the Jiangxi Soviet, had been surrounded by Jiang's GMD forces. Unable to stand and fight as they were outnumbered and outgunned, the CCP audaciously broke through the GMD cordon and fled their pursuers. Events such as the crossing of the Dadu River went on to enter the folklore of CCP history, and the campaign solidified Mao Zedong's leadership over the CCP. Although the march devastated the Communists, who suffered approximately 80 percent casualties, they survived. The march lasted 13 months and traversed numerous mountain ranges and large rivers. It ended in Yan'an, an area which was transformed into the CCP's new base.

A Level Exam-Style Question Section A

Study Source 7 before you answer this question.

Assess the value of the source for revealing the nature of Chinese society in the 1930s and the Chinese public's desire to end the civil war and declare war on Japan.

Explain your answer, using the source, the information given about its origin and your own knowledge about the historical context. (20 marks)

Tip

In this question, you must determine the usefulness of the source. How useful do you think this source would be? What are its strengths and what are its limitations?

EXTEND YOUR KNOWLEDGE

The Xi'an Incident

By late 1936, Jiang was close to fulfilling his destiny of destroying the CCP. He readied a campaign to be led by the Young Marshal, Zhang Xueliang. However, Zhang seethed with resentment at Japan (see page 112), and would rather have attacked the Japanese than the CCP. To this end, he began non-hostility negotiations with the Communists. Jiang went to Xi'an to confront Zhang. A plot emerged, and Zhang and local leaders took Jiang hostage until he agreed to end the civil war and form a united front with the CCP against Japan. Jiang requested he be shot, but Zhang said he was not wanted dead, he was wanted to lead the struggle against Japan. An agreement was reached that Jiang would end the civil war and release all political prisoners and, in return, the Communists would agree to fight under him. Faced with no alternative, Jiang agreed to the truce and he was released on 25 December 1936. He flew back to the capital, Nanjing, to a rapturous reception. Jiang had certainly been backed into a corner, but he survived and clung on to power.

EXTEND YOUR KNOWLEDGE

Zhou Enlai (1898–1976)

Zhou Enlai was a long-standing revolutionary hero of the CCP. Western educated and a talented politician, he served with Jiang at the Whampao Military Academy in the early 1920s and led the CCP in negotiations at Xi'an in 1936. Zhou's diplomatic skills came to the fore as a united front was formed. Zhou went on to serve as Mao's ever-loyal lieutenant for the next 40 years and died a national hero in 1976.

EXTRACT 5 P. Jowett, *China's Wars: Rousing the Dragon, 1894–1949* (2013).

Following skillful negotiation from Chou [Zhou], Chiang [Jiang] seemed to become more receptive to the plan for the United Front. An agreement of sorts was reached and Chiang was allowed to fly back to Nanking [Nanjing] on 25 December... Under the agreement Communist troops would serve in the Nationalist Army but would be kept in their own units. Although segregated into their own divisions they would be under the orders of the Nationalist high command. Although the agreement had been signed by Chiang under duress he realized that the kidnappers did represent a large section of public opinion. The public's growing outrage against the Japanese and their dismay at Chiang's soft attitude towards the aggression may well have forced him to agree to the United Front.

EXTRACT 6 H. McAleavy, *The Modern History of China* (1968).

There are few events in modern history so important as this famous mutiny. The war between China and Japan, the destruction of the British, French and Dutch empires in South-east Asia, even, if we remember that America came into the western conflict only when Hitler declared war on her after Pearl Harbor, the liberation of Europe from the Nazis, all of these owe in some measure to the transactions of those December days in Sian [Xi'an]... The wave of hysterical enthusiasm that swept across the country at the word that the Generalissimo was safe and sound must have reassured Mao and his friends that they had been right in their assessment of his value. It showed too, and the point is worth remembering to Chiang's [Jiang's] credit, that the Chinese people, infuriated as they so often were by his policy of appeasement, knew, as the Japanese military knew, that he had endured the unendurable solely in the desperate hope of buying time, until a modernized, united, non-Communist China could emerge to take her proper place among the nations.

ACTIVITY
KNOWLEDGE CHECK

The Chinese public's view of Jiang Jieshi

What insights do Extracts 5 and 6 give about why Jiang's decision to resist Japan altered the Chinese public's perception of him?

The Marco Polo Bridge Incident

China was now united, but this did not amount to a declaration of war on Japan. Jiang still wanted to buy as much time as possible to continue strengthening the Chinese military. The Chinese public took a different view and demanded an immediate halt to the erosion of Chinese sovereignty in northern China. It was a firmly held principle amongst the Chinese people that China would eventually recover control over Manchuria, Rehe, Chahar and Hebei, but that could wait, and for now, any further Japanese aggression would be confronted. The Chinese public had demanded unity and got their wish, but what form the resistance to Japan would take was unknown. Jiang knew that China's military prowess was dwarfed by Japan's. Although China was now united, its army's weaponry was not standardised, and most of its troops were under-trained and under-equipped. Should war break out, China would be unable to withstand Japan, and would be unable to defeat it without foreign support. Should foreign intervention not be forthcoming, Jiang hoped to win by exhausting Japan's stretched resources. It was a desperate ploy, but the only realistic option available to Jiang.

The spark that lit the fuse leading to the declaration of war was no more than a minor skirmish at the Marco Polo Bridge, ten miles outside Peiping. On the night of 7 July 1937, Japanese garrison troops, allowed in the area due to the Boxer Protocol (see page 101), were challenged by Chinese troops. The Chinese opened fire, a Japanese soldier was reported lost but later turned up unharmed; there were no casualties. The next day, Japanese troops demanded that they do house-to-house searches in the area, and again there was a brief clash. The confrontations escalated and by late July, the Chinese Army in Peiping was losing control. They had already suffered thousands of casualties in air strikes against the city as well as fighting around Peiping, and on 29 July Japanese forces occupied the city. By 8 August, it was firmly under their control and garrisoned by 3,000 troops. The Chinese were given an ultimatum to withdraw all forces from Peiping. Neighbouring towns were overrun by the Japanese and, in some instances, troops of the Kwantung Army killed all the Chinese in sight. Previously, the issuing of a Japanese ultimatum had resulted in a humiliating yielding by Jiang Jieshi, but not this time. Jiang, in keeping with the united front, declared enough was enough. China would not permit any further loss of sovereignty. Japanese aggression and Chinese resolve saw China descend into war. For their part, Japan had grown confident in dealing with China, and their military leaders had thought China would be crushed within three months.

EXTRACT 7

From J. Fenby, *Generalissimo Chiang Kai-shek and the China He Lost* (2005).

In a message to the Communist military commission, Mao said a moment of truth had been reached at which it was imperative to enforce 'the policy of total resistance by the whole nation'. From his side, Chiang [Jiang] declared: 'No territory must be lost and no sovereign rights impaired.' In Tokyo, where the Emperor pressed for a 'war-ending' battle, Hirohito's brother, Prince Takamatsu, summed up the military mood as: 'We're really going to smash China so that it will be ten years before they can stand up straight again.' A message to Berlin, from von Falkenhausen reported: 'This is... total war.'

Six years after the Mukden Incident, the long-awaited war between Japan and China had begun. It came several years too soon for Chiang, whose development and defence plans were far from fruition. But a failure to fight and the abandonment of northern China would have posed a potentially fatal threat to the Generalissimo. For their part, the Japanese expected a short war which could be confined to the north and would give them mastery there.

The fight for Shanghai, August–November 1937

Resolved to stand and fight, Jiang determined to strike. He decided to deploy his best-trained and best-equipped forces in an attack on Shanghai. It was a bold and unexpected move, and while it would turn into disaster for China, it did succeed in sucking Japan into a prolonged conflict it could ill-afford.

For the first time on the offensive, the campaign began calamitously for Jiang as his air force, ordered to bomb the Japanese fleet in Shanghai harbour, entirely missed their targets and hit civilian areas in the city and the French concession. Casualties were in the thousands. However, it was indicative of Jiang's approach. He had wilfully disobeyed the demilitarised status forced on Shanghai in 1932 (see page 116) and had opened up a second front in the conflict. Japan was now engaged in northern China as well as Shanghai.

After an inauspicious start to the campaign, Nationalist troops bravely resisted the Japanese. At the height of conflict, Jiang ordered upwards of 500,000 troops into Shanghai, where they outnumbered the 200,000 Japanese occupiers. The Japanese launched air and artillery attacks on civilian targets. Nationalist morale, however, remained high. A contemporary Japanese politician explained that victory had different meanings in Japan and China, and that for the Chinese anything other than an immediate retreat constituted a victory. As far as Japan was concerned, the resistance it faced and casualties it suffered were unacceptable.

Despite Chinese tenacity and grit, Japanese superiority in arms began to tell. A naval landing put 30,000 Japanese troops in the rear of the Chinese and the fate of Shanghai was sealed. Casualties had sky-rocketed, with an estimated 300,000 Chinese fatalities compared to approximately 70,000 Japanese dead and 25,000 injured. More than 100,000 Chinese sought refuge in the foreign concessions and over a quarter of a million fled the city. What began as an orderly retreat soon descended into a frantic flight for survival. The conquering Japanese enjoyed the fruits of victory: rape, looting and other sadistic pleasures.

The Shanghai campaign was a catastrophe for Jiang. The loss of life and property was astronomical. GMD forces had been defeated and retreated in blind panic in the direction of the capital, Nanjing, which was now vulnerable to attack. However, Jiang had succeeded in diverting Japan from consolidating its northern possessions, and the Chinese tiger had finally shown its teeth. The Japanese would no longer enjoy any walkover victories and could not bully China into conceding further territory or influence. Japan had hoped to deliver a swift and decisive beating to the Chinese, who would promptly surrender and acquiesce to Japanese demands. This had not happened, and now Japan was involved in a drawn-out war.

A Level Exam-Style Question Section B

How far do you agree that the actions of Jiang Jieshi in 1937 were more in China's national interest than his response to the Japanese invasion of Manchuria in 1931? (20 marks)

Tip

In this question, you will need to evaluate how Sino-Japanese relations had altered in the years 1931–37. You should also consider the transformation in Chinese domestic politics and how this may have influenced Jiang, as well as defining what is meant by 'national interest'.

ACTIVITY
KNOWLEDGE CHECK

The reasons for all-out war, 1937

1 What reasons does Extract 7 give for the attitudes in China and Japan to all-out war?

2 Write a speech that Jiang Jieshi could have delivered on the outbreak of war in 1937. You will need to explain his actions since 1931 with regard to Japan and the CCP. Be careful: by 1937 Jiang was in a united front with the Communists and would avoid any public verbal criticism of his new allies.

3 Create a two-column table with the title 'Was the fight for Shanghai a disaster for China?' One column should be used to argue it was and the other should evaluate why it was not a total failure. Compare your table with that of a classmate and discuss. Together, reach a judgement of whether the fight for Shanghai was a disaster for China.

WHAT WAS THE IMPACT OF THE WAR OF 1937–39?

The seizure of the coast

Initially, Jiang's fears that China had not had sufficient time to prepare for war appeared vindicated as the Japanese army seized the port of Tianjin, apart from the foreign concessions. Japanese forces also occupied Xiamen, an island off Fukien province from where the capture of Fuzhou, the province's major port and capital, was launched. Soon after, Shantou was bombed and occupied, and there was alleged use of poison gas. It was added to the catalogue of Japanese coastal possessions. This left Guangzhou as the sole port held by the GMD Nationalists in the whole of China. It fell with little real resistance in October 1938. Japan now enjoyed complete naval supremacy. It occupied all the Chinese coast and major ports. In addition, it controlled China's most fertile farmland and several vital industrial centres, which it now used to bolster its own economy.

The rape of Nanjing

The resolute defence of Shanghai had ended in a frenzied retreat to the extent that the carefully planned line of fortifications at Wuxi was easily breached. This left the way open to Nanjing, the capital of Nationalist China. The safety of the city was entrusted to the politician and former warlord, Tang Shengzhi, known as the Buddhist General. Tang publicly swore to protect the city to his last breath. However, three days of heavy bombardment weakened his resolve and he fled the city, which flew into panic. Some Chinese soldiers murdered citizens to obtain civilian clothing in which to merge with the masses and attempt to escape. When Japanese forces entered the city, a prolonged series of atrocities ensued, collectively known as the 'rape of Nanjing'. Why this happened has never been fully established. Perhaps it was because with the fall of the capital, Japan wanted to send a strong psychological message to the rest of China. Perhaps it was just consistent with total war and terror tactics. Or perhaps it was Japan taking revenge for the unexpected stoutness of the opposition they had faced in Shanghai. Whatever the reason, what followed was brutality on an unprecedented scale.

Thousands perished attempting to cross the Yangtze to escape. On the first day of the Japanese occupation, 24,000 surrendered Chinese troops were massacred, and inhabitants of Nanjing were murdered indiscriminately. Women, including children and senior citizens, were raped. Thousands were burned or buried alive, disembowelled or mutilated. Medical experiments were conducted and some Japanese troops used live Chinese people as targets for bayonet practice. One particularly gruesome episode reported in the Japanese press involved two bloodthirsty Japanese lieutenants who competed to be the first to behead a hundred Chinese. It was not clear who won, so the contest was extended to 150. Foreshadowing the genocide visited upon European Jewry during the Holocaust, the Japanese army viewed the Chinese race as subhuman and deserving of every atrocity imaginable. The rape of Nanjing lasted almost seven weeks. The death toll surpassed that reached in Shanghai and it is unlikely that the full number of casualties will ever be determined.

EXTRACT

From J. Fenby, *Generalissimo Chiang Kai-shek and the China He Lost* (2005). Jonathan Fenby is a journalist who, after a career in the UK writing for publications such as *The Guardian* and *The Economist*, worked as the editor of the *South China Morning Post*, 1995–2000. In 2000, he returned to the UK and wrote several books about China.

As the Nationalist capital, Nanking [Nanjing] was obviously an important target where the Japanese wanted to achieve maximum humiliation of their adversary. But the sustained mass bestiality can better be explained – if it can be rationally explained at all – by the tensions that had built up in the army since the Shanghai battle erupted, by the knowledge of the Japanese troops that they were heavily outnumbered by the Chinese in the city, by the callousness bred in the previous four months – and, above all, by the dehumanisation of the Chinese which had become part of the psyche of the Imperial Army. The invaders saw the people around them as lower than animals, targets for a bloodlust which many, if not all, their commanders felt could only spur their men on to fight better. In his diary, one soldier described the Chinese as 'ants crawling on the ground... a herd of ignorant sheep'. Another recorded that while raping a woman, his colleagues might consider her as human, but, when they killed her, 'we just thought of her as something like a pig'.

It seems certain that the Emperor in Tokyo knew at least the outline of what was going on. His uncle was in command, and Japanese newspapers reported the execution contests among officers as if they were sporting events. Hirohito still hoped that China could be defeated with one big blow, which Nanking might provide. Japan's terms for a settlement were toughened to include indefinite stationing of troops in China and reparations as well as recognition of Manchukuo and cooperation against the Communists. 'We must strengthen our resolve to fight through to the end with China,' the Foreign Minister told a meeting of the Imperial Conference. Tokyo withdrew recognition of the Nationalist government which, it said, was to be 'eradicated'.

SOURCE

A letter written by Ernest H. Forster to Tokuyasu Fukuda, 1937. Forster was a US missionary who continued to work throughout the rape of Nanjing. Fukuda was the Japanese attaché to the embassy, a high-ranking Japanese official in Nanjing at the time.

LETTER TO MR. FUKUDA,

December 15, 1937

Sir:

Owing to the large number of wounded soldiers and civilians in Nanking [Nanjing], we have organized a local branch of the International Red Cross Society to deal with the situation.

We have appealed for recognition from the International Red Cross Society in Shanghai and from the Red Cross Society of China.

We now request your good offices in securing for us permission from the Japanese Military Authorities in Nanking to carry on this humanitarian work.

We herewith enclose a list of the membership of our Committee.

With kind regards, I am

Yours cordially

ERNEST H. FORSTER

Secretary

ACTIVITY
KNOWLEDGE CHECK

The rape of Nanjing

1 According to Extract 8, why did Japan launch the rape of Nanjing?

2 How useful to the historian is Source 8 in determining the nature of the fall of Nanjing?

The effect of the war

After the fall of Nanjing, Nationalist forces fell back to Wuhan. The Japanese attempted to encircle the Chinese forces. A major campaign was fought in Xuzhou, to the north-east of Wuhan, where Japan encountered stiff resistance. Japanese forces suffered a severe defeat at the Battle of Tai'erzhuang where, under the leadership of Li Zongren, GMD forces inflicted upwards of 10,000 Japanese casualties. The victory shattered the illusion of Japanese invincibility, and although the city of Xuzhou was eventually evacuated, on the whole the battle strengthened Chinese determination.

However, with Xuzhou in Japanese hands, the way to Wuhan was clear. Drastic action was required. Jiang decided to destroy the dikes at Huayuankou and flood the Yellow River to slow the Japanese advance. He ordered this without forewarning the villages that stood in the path of the water. Over 30,000 square miles were flooded, and thousands of villages were obliterated. At least half a million people drowned and three million were made homeless. However, the move succeeded in delaying the Japanese advance by three months. This was in line with Jiang's strategy of 'trading space for time' whereby Jiang hoped that by withdrawing and conceding territory he would buy sufficient time for China to be strong enough to militarily resist Japan. Some assistance came from the Soviet Union, which formed a volunteer air force to help the Nationalists. Jiang had turned to the USSR for military aid after Germany recalled its advisers as a condition of the Anti-Comintern Pact signed between Germany and Japan. The Soviet airmen engaged the Japanese and inflicted significant losses, but nevertheless Wuhan fell in October.

EXTEND YOUR KNOWLEDGE

The Anti-Comintern Pact (1937)

This pact was an anti-Communist alliance signed between Germany and Japan in 1937. Although it did not directly affect China, it had repercussions on Chinese affairs. As a result of the continued conflict with China, Japan insisted that Germany recall its military advisers. Germany had a tradition of supplying military aid to China, with such luminaries as Hans von Seeckt and Alexander von Falkenhausen having served as advisers, but this was now suspended. Jiang requested Soviet help to fill the void left by Germany, and the USSR responded by forming a volunteer air force and also engaging Japanese troops in northern Manchuria.

The early stage of the war was a bleak time for China. In fact, it drew to an end the era of humiliation extending back to the mid-19th century. The Japanese were renowned around the world for their brutal terror tactics. Hell had descended on China. Civilians were murdered by the thousand, prisoners of war were treated without mercy, women and children were raped. The Chinese military was overwhelmed and constantly retreating. Ports and cities fell like dominoes: Peiping, Shanghai, Guangzhou, Nanjing and Wuhan, to name just the most significant. This was in addition to Manchukuo and the East Hebei Autonomous Government. A collaborationist Mongolian regime was established under Japanese tutelage and a pro-Japanese Provisional Government of the Republic was based in Peiping. After the fall of Nanjing, the Reorganised National Government was established in 1940. Wang Jingwei, Jiang's one-time deputy, gave the puppet regime some semblance of legitimacy by agreeing to become its leader. Wang, for his part, had come to believe that defeat by Japan was inevitable and collaboration offered the only possibility of preventing untold devastation. From his seat in Nanjing, he decried Jiang as a traitor who would only bring further suffering upon China. He claimed that Jiang only cared about maintaining his power rather than the fate of the Chinese nation and population.

Given their predicament, Chinese morale was surprisingly high. It may have taken Jiang Jieshi the best part of a decade to stand up to Japan, and he had been coerced into the united front, but now his mind was made up and he stood defiantly in the face of Japanese hostility. Jiang's determination was admired by the Chinese public and his personal position and prestige were higher than they had been in years. With Wang Jingwei out of the way, no longer a rival and universally denounced as a traitor, Jiang enjoyed total domination of the Guomindang. Although on the back foot and having endured far in excess of a million casualties, he had successfully induced Japan to commit more troops and resources than it could sustain indefinitely. Jiang knew Chinese salvation and victory could only be achieved through endurance and by waiting for Japan to over-extend and exhaust itself.

ACTIVITY
KNOWLEDGE CHECK

Jiang Jieshi's strategy

1 Why did Jiang Jieshi adopt a policy of 'trading space for time'?

2 Why did Wang Jingwei declare Jiang Jieshi a traitor to the cause of Chinese nationalism?

Change (8a, b & c (I))

Imposing realities

1 Explain why the conversation in the cartoon above would not have happened.

The shape of history is imposed by people looking back. People who lived through the 'history' did not always perceive the patterns that later historians identify. For example, some people living through the industrial revolution may have understood that great change was taking place, but they would not have been able to understand the massive economic, social and political consequences of industrialisation.

2 Consider relations between China and Japan during the Second Sino-Japanese War.

a) Who would have made the decision for China to resist Japanese aggression?

b) Could anyone have challenged this decision?

c) Explain why someone living in China during the 1930s would have been unable to make a judgement about the beginning of a new era.

3 Who living at the present time might regard the Second Sino-Japanese War as an important event?

4 What does this image tell us about the structure of history as we understand it?

The retreat to Chongqing

Jiang Jieshi retreated down the Yangtze and selected Chongqing as his next seat of government. Jiang held that the southern provinces of Sichuan, Yunnan and Guizhou would be the base of China's deliverance. Chongqing, in Sichuan province, was sufficiently inland not to be immediately under threat from Japan. It was no spur-of-the-moment decision on Jiang's part, he had considered it a viable location since using it as a base to launch his previous anti-Communist activities. Jiang's thinking indicates that, from the outset, he thought modern cities like Wuhan and Nanjing would fall.

A consistent strategy had been implemented that, wherever, possible industries and facilities would be relocated westwards to Chongqing, out of captured areas. Prior to the fall of Nanjing, 15,000 cases of art treasures had been moved out of the city. Factories had been dismantled in Shanghai and approximately 150 of them were transferred deep into the interior. In total, 2,000 enterprises were transported downriver. The Shanghai Machine Works was the first to be re-established in Chongqing, followed swiftly by a steel mill and a power plant successfully uprooted from Wuhan. Textile factories and other key industries were also relocated. Government offices also migrated en masse, as did thousands of students and intellectuals who did not wish to live under Japanese occupation.

Despite these dramatic improvements, Chongqing remained a backward city. It was also poor – it produced relatively little and there was hardly any modern transport. It was hot and humid in summer and bitterly cold in the winter. It must have been a shock for those fleeing the modern Chinese cities that were now under Japanese rule. The surge of refugees stretched food and supplies to their limits and food shortages were commonplace. The economy creaked under the pressure, and inflation ran high. Compulsory grain purchasing was commissioned and a new taxation programme in Nationalist-held areas proved unpopular. It gave rise to mass corruption and was riddled with inefficiencies.

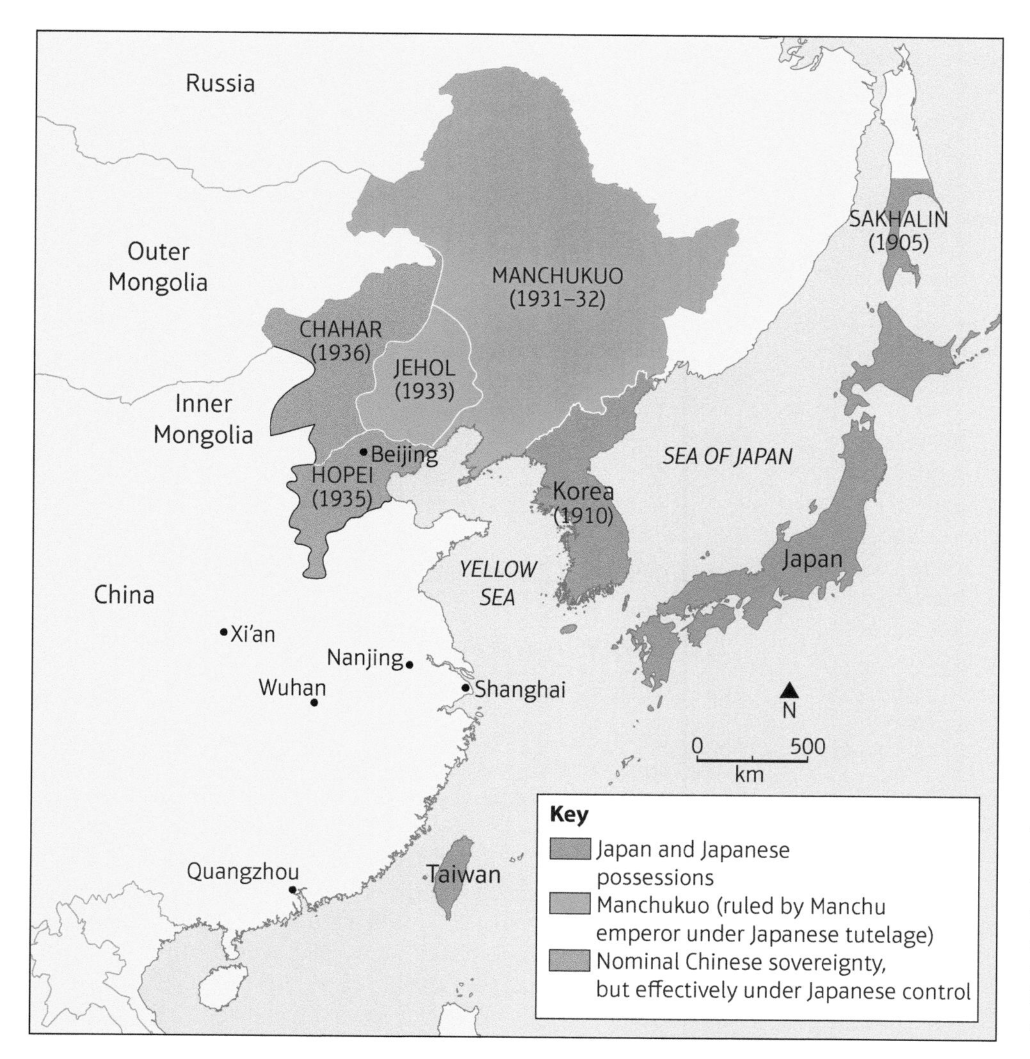

Figure 5.1 The extent of Chinese land losses to Japan by 1940. Korea and Taiwan had become Japanese possessions after the Treaty of Shimonoseki. In 1931, Manchuria was taken over by Japan. Rehe and Chahar soon followed, while Hopei and Shanghai were demilitarised. The capital, Nanjing, fell in 1937 and the same fate befell the next designated capital, Wuhan, in 1938.

The military was also in a rundown state. Bereft of German assistance and advice, Jiang had managed to compensate by securing Soviet aid, which took the form of 50,000 rifles, 10,000 machine guns, nearly 100 tanks and about 900 aircraft, along with instructors and pilots. By 1938, Jiang had introduced conscription to make up for the huge losses suffered. Not only that, but the GMD had lost the majority of its competent officers and Jiang continued to question the loyalty of the Communists. In May 1939, Japan began an aerial bombardment of Chongqing, similar in nature to that endured by Great Britain during the Blitz. Thousands were killed and damage to property was considerable, but a network of underground tunnels enabled Chongqing to withstand the attacks. In conclusion, although severely beaten and pushed back, and faced with problems both economic and military, the Nationalists stood and established Chongqing as the centre of government.

The role and importance of the USA, 1940–41

Jiang's strategy was based on the belief that Japan could not defeat and conquer all of China, and that all China needed to do was hold out until foreign intervention saved it. Jiang recognised that Japan's expansionist foreign policy would eventually lead to a war with a foreign power. At times, it looked as if the Soviet Union would fulfil this role, but increasingly the USA became China's most likely ally and saviour. US suspicions had grown in response to the expansionist nature of Japan's foreign policy. Japan's growing navy and determination to become the dominant power in South-East Asia now put US interests in the Philippines at risk, as well as US naval bases in Hawaii.

As Japanese–US hostilities grew, the USA began to offer financial support to China. If the preservation of China harmed Japan, the consensus held that it must benefit the USA. War credits were issued, as were loans ranging from US$25 million to US$50 million to be used to stabilise the economy. The Nationalist air force had been decimated in the war and Chongqing, under a prolonged aerial assault, had fewer than 70 planes, just under half of which were not equipped to fly at night. In contrast, Japan had a thousand modern planes at its disposal. Jiang sought to redress this balance by using his US adviser, Claire Chennault, to negotiate the purchase of a hundred of the latest P-40 fighter planes from the USA. In addition, Chennault was permitted to recruit a volunteer service of pilots to fly in combat and train Chinese pilots. The planes became known as 'The Flying Tigers' because of the teeth painted on them. They inflicted serious damage, incentivised by a US$500 bonus for every Japanese plane shot down. As the pilots were 'volunteers', this was not considered a declaration of war against Japan.

In an attempt to check Japanese aggression, the USA imposed economic sanctions. After Japan invaded French Indochina in 1940, the USA promptly froze Japanese assets in US banks. It also stopped exporting oil, iron and technology to Japan. US sanctions showed the extent of Japan's dependence on the USA. Increased US assistance for China from 1940 was the beginning of the realisation of Jiang's hopes: Japan would bring about its own defeat.

SOURCE 9 Second World War poster of Uncle Sam shaking hands with a Chinese soldier, the flags of China and the USA, and a poster of Sun Yat-sen.

ACTIVITY
KNOWLEDGE CHECK

The role and importance of the USA, 1940–41

1. According to Source 9, what linked the USA and China?
2. How useful is Source 9 in portraying the US view of China in the period 1931–41?

The significance of 7 December 1941 for China

Japan, boxed into an economic corner, found alternative iron and oil sources as well as rubber in British-held Malaya and the Dutch East Indies, respectively, and planned to seize control of the Westerners' colonies. Knowing this would elicit an immediate reaction from the US Pacific Navy as it would threaten the USA's regional interests, notably the US colony of the Philippines, Japan launched the infamous attack on Pearl Harbor in Hawaii, where the US Pacific Fleet was based. Japan launched a surprise aerial bombardment of the base. The US Navy suffered severe losses: five battleships were sunk, and a dozen other ships suffered the same fate. Over 100 planes were destroyed and 2,400 servicemen were killed. In response, the USA declared war on Japan. After a decade of facing Japanese aggression alone, Jiang Jieshi had been proved right and Japanese expansionism had led to foreign intervention. China and the USA were now allied against the common enemy of Japan. Financial aid was forthcoming in the form of a US$500 million loan and a further US$630 million 'Lend-Lease' package that would provide China with military supplies. After Japan pressured Britain to shut off the Burma Road for three months, China was cut off from receiving supplies. This was overcome by an enormously ambitious undertaking: US pilots flew supplies in over the Himalayas. The Nationalist Army was bolstered by having a US chief of staff, and the 'Flying Tigers' squadrons were increased and reorganised. This extra help was only possible due to the attack on Pearl Harbor on 7 December 1941.

After the signing of the Nazi-Soviet Pact in 1939, the last of the USSR's assistance to China (see page 123) was withdrawn. China had stood alone against Japan for almost two years. The USA's entry into the Second World War secured China's long-term safety: all China had to do was hold out until Japan was defeated. Forty percent of all Japanese troops were stationed in China, far more than Japan had ever anticipated. On the outbreak of war in 1937, Japan believed victory would be won within a few months. Japan's fate was sealed by its inability to quickly and decisively defeat China, combined with its provocative and antagonistic approach towards the USA. Military victory over Japan took four more years, but on 7 December 1941 Chinese survival was guaranteed. As it transpired, Jiang Jieshi was correct: Japan's defeat, however far off, was inevitable. By bombing the US fleet at Pearl Harbor, Japan had provoked war with a country on whom it was significantly dependent for raw resources, and which out-produced it industrially by a ratio of 9 : 1. Manchuria, envisaged as Japan's industrial base for war, at the peak of its steel production in 1943, was out-produced by Pittsburgh alone, by 40 times.

EXTEND YOUR KNOWLEDGE

Burma Road

By 1939, China's coastline was under Japanese control. Also in 1939 a Soviet pact with Germany was signed, and one of the provisos was that the Soviet Union would desist from offering any assistance to China. The only route for China to import food, resources and war materials was through Burma, on China's south-west, which had been under British control since the 19th century. In 1939, Britain became involved in the Second World War and was unable to fight Germany at the same time as Japan. Therefore, when Japan applied pressure for the Burma Road to be closed, Britain had no alternative but to comply, and China was left without an import route. When Japan overran Burma in 1942, the route was sealed. However, by then, the USA had entered the Second World War by declaring war on Japan after Pearl Harbor. The alliance system now saw the USA undertake an ambitious plan to fly supplies into China over the Himalayas. The Burma Road was reopened in 1945 after Japan was forced out of Burma.

The Japanese threat, 1931–41: conclusion

The roots of the Japanese threat to China can be traced back to the late 19th century, but the threat grew greater throughout the 20th century. Japan's Twenty-One Demands of 1915 were an ominous sign of further aggression to follow: an attempt to extend Japanese influence and extraterritoriality in the knowledge that China was too weak to resist and foreign powers were uninterested in, or incapable of, intervention. Although expansionist and imperialist in nature, Japan's actions were no different in essence to British and US actions in Africa and Latin America, respectively. However, this changed in 1929 when the Wall Street Crash precipitated a global economic crisis that hit Japan hard.

The downturn in Japan's economy resulting from the Wall Street Crash necessitated a change in philosophy. China became central to a programme of expansion dictated by Japan's need for raw resources to feed domestic industries. Japan's government lacked the courage to stand up to the hawkish might of the Imperial Army. The Army acted independently and its initial victories were so popular with the Japanese population that the government dared not oppose it. A clear example of this was the Mukden Incident, which was expressly counter to government wishes. However, Jiang's refusal to oppose Japan until the CCP had been destroyed encouraged Japan to bully China into more territorial concessions. The period between the Mukden Incident in 1931 and the Marco Polo Bridge Incident in 1937 ranks as one of the most abject in China's history.

Japan's disrespectful handling of China in these years had many effects. It strengthened Chinese nationalism, and eventually led to the united front and all-out war. It was a war that Japan had miscalculated seriously and, ultimately, fatally. Although dominant in terms of industry, armed forces and economy, Japan had grown overconfident in the wake of Chinese weakness. Japan was never able to fully subdue China, whose vast land mass and population made full occupation an impossibility. The Communists deserved their share of praise for victory over Japan. The CCP provided a constant anti-Japanese nationalist rhetoric, which increased their support and upheld national morale. More importantly, the CCP could have tried to assassinate Jiang Jieshi in 1936, but they pushed for a united front to repulse Japan. The CCP also recognised that Jiang was the only figure with the required prestige to lead a national resistance.

Jiang's basic premise, that to emerge victorious all China had to do was to survive long enough for Japan to bring about its own defeat, was correct. A disregard for Chinese pride and resilience led to Japan overinvesting resources and troops in China while simultaneously agitating the USA. The erroneous policy advocated by the autarchic approach led to the momentous decision to attack Pearl Harbor. This declaration of war ironically ensured China's survival and eventual deliverance. China was bolstered by US aid, and trade embargoes on Japan hit its military capacity severely, which ultimately led to Japan's demise. Sunday 7 December 1941 must have been a great day for Jiang Jieshi: however distant it might prove to be, there was light at the end of the tunnel.

A Level Exam-Style Question Section B

'China's best option was to wait for Japan to self-destruct.' To what extent do you agree with this assessment of China's handling of Japan in the years 1931–41? (20 marks)

Tip

In answering this question, you need to give a balanced consideration of the whole of the period stated. Consider factors such as the territorial and military losses up to 1939 and US intervention at the end of 1941, both of which heavily influenced Jiang Jieshi's strategy.

THINKING HISTORICALLY Cause and consequence (7c)

The value of historical explanations

Historical explanations derive from the historian who is investigating the past. Differences in explanations are usually about what the historians think is significant. Historians bring their own attitudes and perspectives to historical questions and see history in the light of these. It is therefore perfectly acceptable to have very different explanations of the same historical phenomenon. The way we judge historical accounts is by looking at how well argued they are and how well evidence has been deployed to support the argument.

Approach A	Approach B	Approach C
A united front is caused by decisions taken by politicians. It is imposed from the top by great men. Ordinary people then fall into line and do whatever they are told.	A united front is a mass movement of similar peoples with similar ideas. The small aspects of commonality all add up together to cause unity in times of war.	A united front is the inevitable unifying of people who share a common language and interests. Civil war is an unnatural and temporary state. It only happens when groups of people are manipulated by politicians.

Work in groups of between three and five (you will need an even number of groups in the class).

In your groups, devise a brief explanation of the creation of the united front between the Guomindang Nationalists and the Chinese Communist Party in 1936 (see pages 118–119). The explanation should be between 200 and 300 words and match one of the approaches above. Present your explanation to another group, who will decide on three things:

1 Which of the approaches is each explanation trying to demonstrate?

2 Considering the structure and the quality of the argument and use of evidence, which is the best of the three explanations?

3 If you choose a 'best' explanation, should you discount the other two? Explain your answer.

ACTIVITY
SUMMARY

The Japanese threat, 1931–41

1 Using your knowledge of the period 1931–41, explain:

   a) why China was ripe for Japanese exploitation

   b) why the USA entered the war

   c) why the USA's declaration of war was so significant to China.

2 Was Jiang Jieshi justified in his decision to focus his attention on the destruction of the CCP rather than resisting Japan?

3 For each of the following factors, write a paragraph explaining to what extent the outbreak of the Sino-Japanese War was caused by:

   a) Japanese aggression

   b) Chinese nationalism

   c) the Second World War.

WIDER READING

Fenby, J. *Generalissimo Chiang Kai-Shek and the China He Lost*, Simon & Schuster (2005)

Gray, J. *Rebellions and Revolutions: China from the 1800s to the 1980s*, Oxford University Press (1990)

Jowett, P. *China's Wars: Rousing the Dragon, 1894–1949*, Osprey (2013)

Spence, J. *The Search for Modern China*, W.W. Norton and Company (1991)

Stewart, G. *China 1900–76*, Heinemann (2006)

Westad, O.A. *Restless Empire: China and the Modern World since 1750*, Vintage Books (2013)

3.6 The Sino-Soviet split, 1958–69

KEY QUESTIONS

- Why was there a breakdown of relations between the Soviet Union and China, 1958–60?
- Why did Mao feel threatened by the Soviet Union?
- What was the significance of military confrontation between the Soviet Union and China in 1969?

INTRODUCTION

Chinese distrust of Russia dated back to tsarist times, when Russia had preyed on China's vulnerability to take control of territory including Manchuria and Port Arthur. Even after the CCP's victory over the GMD in the civil war, relations between the two now Communist nations remained cold. The Soviet leader, Joseph Stalin, rejected Mao's **sinified** vision of a peasant-based movement and thought him a caveman Marxist. In recognising the People's Republic of China (PRC) on its proclamation in 1949, Stalin was recognising a political reality and in no way accepting Mao's ideology. Mao decided to support Communist Russia in ideological opposition to the capitalist USA (see Chapter 2). The PRC required economic support and the USSR was prepared to give it. In 1950, the Sino-Soviet Treaty of Friendship, Alliance and Mutual Assistance was signed.

KEY TERM

Sinified
Made Chinese.

EXTEND YOUR KNOWLEDGE

Sino-Soviet Treaty of Friendship, Alliance and Mutual Assistance (1950)
The USSR lent China US$300 million and technicians and technology to assist economic development. Mao thought the agreement was exploitative in loaning rather than gifting assistance to China. Soviet requests for joint mineral mining rights in the Chinese regions of Xinjiang and Manchuria were reminiscent of the unequal treaties of the 19th century.

Nikita Khrushchev replaced Stalin in 1953 and there followed a brief period during which relations between the USSR and the PRC improved. Khrushchev pumped more assistance into China in the form of industrial enterprises and technical assistance. He offered better trade relations between the two and even gave up Russian rights in Xinjiang and Manchuria. However, this upturn in relations did not last. The split began in earnest in 1956, when Khrushchev delivered his 'Secret Speech' to the 20th Congress of the Communist Party. In it, he savaged Stalin's rule as despotic and criticised the systematic purges that had decimated the Communist Party of the Soviet Union (CPSU). Therefore, by 1958, Sino-Soviet relations were strained for the following reasons:

1958 – Soviet demands to China
Hostilities between PRC and Taiwan nearly lead to war

1958–62 – Great Leap Forward

1959 – Lushan Conference and purge of Peng Dehuai

1960 – USSR withdraws economic assistance from PRC

1961 – China and Albania sign alliance after USSR withdraws assistance to Albania

1962 – Sino-Indian War
Cuban Missile Crisis

1963 – Nuclear Test Ban Treaty

- a Soviet rejection of China's peasant-based vision of Communism
- Mao's belief that the USSR was attempting to impose unequal agreements in a similar way to the tsarists of old
- Mao's rejection of de-Stalinisation and **peaceful coexistence**.

KEY TERM

Peaceful coexistence
A revisionist idea that Communism should not promote or support worldwide revolution. It deviated from Marx, believing instead that capitalism's injustices would, in time, lead to the workers rising against it.

EXTEND YOUR KNOWLEDGE

Secret Speech
In 1956, three years after Stalin's death, Khrushchev delivered his Secret Speech to the Soviet Communist Party. He attacked Stalin's style of leadership and the effect it had on the USSR. A process of de-Stalinisation began during which Khrushchev attempted to restyle Communist rule. He attacked the 'cult of personality' that Stalin had cultivated. However, the cult of personality applied equally to Mao in China, who portrayed himself as the spearhead and inspiration of Chinese Communism. Khrushchev also rejected worldwide revolution and believed that, in the short term, socialism would peacefully coexist with capitalism. Mao claimed this was a betrayal of Communist principles, and the seeds of the Sino-Soviet split had been sown.

WHY WAS THERE A BREAKDOWN OF RELATIONS BETWEEN THE SOVIET UNION AND CHINA, 1958-60?

While the roots of the breakdown in Sino-Soviet relations can be traced back to Stalin and then Khrushchev's denunciation of Stalin in 1956, it grew in intensity from 1958 until 1969, when war between the two nearly broke out. Khrushchev had issued his Secret Speech without consulting the Chinese and it was this, as much as the ideas expressed, that provoked such fierce Chinese criticism. Mao was sensitive to political developments in other countries that affected China. Khrushchev's criticisms of Stalin, many of which equally applied to Mao, constituted a challenge to Mao's rule, and relations began to decline as a result.

The significance of Russian demands in 1958

Mao's view was that in order for China to be strong, it must be self-reliant, because foreign powers could not be trusted. China's dealings with foreign powers had been marked by exploitation forced on China due to its weakness. Mao's belief in self-reliance had been strengthened by the 1950 Sino-Soviet Treaty of Friendship, Alliance and Mutual Assistance. Given China's economic weakness in 1949, Mao had no alternative but to seek the USSR's assistance. He had hoped to be treated as an equal, but he felt the agreement favoured the Soviet Union. Mao's distrust of foreign powers dictated the nature of his reaction to Russian demands in 1958.

In 1958, Khrushchev headed a Soviet delegation to China regarding the prospect of Sino-Soviet defence collaboration. Khrushchev put forward the idea of a joint Pacific naval fleet. Mao hoped for a Soviet fleet manned by Chinese officers, while Khrushchev wanted the fleet to be headed by Soviet officers. Mao, haunted by China's history of domination by foreign powers, rejected Khrushchev's

1964 - Malinovsky Affair

1966 - Cultural Revolution begins

1967 - USSR and the PRC recall their ambassadors

1968 - Brezhnev Doctrine

1969 - Military confrontation between USSR and PRC

1964 1965 1966 1967 1968 1969

seemingly innocuous proposal and turned it into a flashpoint. Khrushchev requested a longwave radio station based in China to control Russia's Pacific submarine fleet. He also wanted permission for the Soviet navy to carry out repairs in Chinese ports, as well as granting their sailors leave on Chinese territory. Mao interpreted all of this as an attempted violation of Chinese sovereignty. Khrushchev's demands confirmed Mao's fears: the USSR was not a fraternal ally, but was trying to exert influence consistent with that of an imperial power. Khrushchev was surprised by Mao's reaction and dropped the idea, but a chance to strengthen relations between the two pre-eminent Communist powers had been lost.

This disagreement was representative of a divergence in the Soviet Union and the PRC's understanding of the Cold War, the ideological conflict that had emerged between capitalism and Communism after the Second World War. The Soviet Union sought to help China by directing its naval activities in the Pacific. Khrushchev assumed that China would follow the USSR's lead and accept its requests. However, Mao distrusted Russia's intentions and saw this as an example of great-power chauvinism, a renewal of the subjugation of its sovereignty that China had experienced in the mid- to late 19th century (see Chapters 3 and 4). Mao's reaction, although volatile, was understandable. For years he had been requesting Soviet assistance in weapon development, namely nuclear weapons and submarines capable of launching them. He felt that Khrushchev had been stalling in giving China the technicians and technology to develop its military strength and nuclear capability. Mao's interpretation of the Soviet demands in 1958 was that Khrushchev did not trust him with nuclear weapons, hence his preference for a joint approach under Soviet direction. Mao felt patronised and wanted to show the world that China was capable of adopting an independent approach. Therefore, he asserted Chinese sovereignty and questioned the assumption that China and the Soviet Union had identical goals. Mao's decision to stand up to the USSR helped to mobilise China behind him at a time when China was in the midst of collectivisation (see Chapter 2) and moving Chinese economic development in a different direction from the Soviet Union. A constant theme of the Sino-Soviet split was China trying to emerge from the shadow of the Soviet Union as a world power in its own right, with its own goals and ambitions.

EXTEND YOUR KNOWLEDGE

Cold War (1945–91)
The Cold War began soon after the Second World War ended, as the alliance that had defeated Nazi Germany split into mutually hostile camps, with the West led by the USA and Eastern Europe led by the USSR. In 1949, the CCP won the civil war and China became Communist. Naturally, China sided with the USSR. Both Communists and capitalists believed their system of government was superior and hostilities continued, to varying degrees, until the collapse of Communism in Europe between 1989 and 1991.

During his tirade at Khrushchev over the USSR's demands in 1958, Mao, a chain-smoker, continually blew smoke in Khrushchev's face. This disrespectful action showed that he saw himself as superior. Mao had upheld Chinese sovereignty against perceived Soviet attempts to control China's navy, and his deferential attitude towards Stalin had been replaced by a more antagonistic approach to Khrushchev. This change can also be seen by measuring Mao's reaction to Khrushchev's demands in 1958 against his willingness to combat the USA in the Korean War in 1950 (see page 163) at the request of Stalin. Mao found it easier to assert himself with Khrushchev than he had with Stalin, and the demands of 1958 gave Mao the opportunity to demonstrate his disdain for Khrushchev.

EXTEND YOUR KNOWLEDGE

Great-power chauvinism
The belief that the superpowers' dealings with developing nations do not happen on an equal footing. Mao believed that great powers only helped others in order to help themselves. His suspicion was based on China's experiences of the previous century. For Mao, great-power chauvinism was a contemporary variant of the unequal treaties. The USSR's demands of 1958 reinforced his belief that foreign powers were only interested in what concessions they could squeeze out of China.

ACTIVITY
KNOWLEDGE CHECK

The significance of Russian demands, 1958

1. List the reasons why Mao took exception to the demands of 1958. For each reason, write briefly how Mao would have justified his thinking.
2. The Russian demands of 1958 worsened Sino-Soviet relations. Using one colour, list reasons why Khrushchev was to blame for this, then use a different colour to list reasons why Mao was to blame.
3. Write a speech from the CCP perspective, stating why the Russian demands of 1958 increased Chinese distrust of the USSR.

Mao's resentment of Khrushchev's demands in 1958 was exacerbated by his suspicion that Khrushchev was reluctant to supply China with nuclear weapons. Mao believed that only when China had its own nuclear weapons would it be able to protect itself and lead the international fight against capitalism. Emboldened by his rejection of Soviet demands in 1958, he sought to engineer an occasion to test the USSR's promise of assistance.

Jiang Jieshi and the GMD had fled to the island of Taiwan after their defeat in the civil war, and were provocatively within the reach of the PRC. Mao believed it was China's destiny to take over Taiwan and reunite it with the mainland under Communist rule. The USA had supported Taiwan since 1949 and recognised it, not the People's Republic, as the legitimate government of China. It had promised to use its navy to defend Taiwan. Mao feared the Taiwanese islands of Quemoy and Matsu, close to the Chinese mainland, could be used as springboards for a GMD invasion of mainland China, no doubt backed by its US supporters. In 1958, Mao ordered a bombardment of the islands, and the Taiwan Crisis ensued.

Although Khrushchev had been pugnacious in publicly warning US President Eisenhower that an attack on the PRC constituted an attack on the Soviet Union, in private discussions with the CCP he recommended caution. The USSR was afraid to risk a local conflict escalating into a global war, and the USA appeared willing to uphold Taiwanese sovereignty. Mao decided to back down, and tension in the region eased. However, it was another strain on Sino-Soviet relations. Mao viewed Khrushchev as a traitor and a coward for not supporting China more strongly, and Khrushchev's view of Mao as a rash maverick was no more flattering. Mao's ideas were not, according to the USSR, grounded in political reality. His blasé attitude towards provoking nuclear war was a huge threat. If the USA and the USSR were locked in a game of chess, Mao was trying to move the USSR's pieces according to his own needs and ruin Khrushchev's plans of avoiding a nuclear confrontation.

ACTIVITY
KNOWLEDGE CHECK

The Taiwan Crisis, 1958

1 Create a mind map to show Mao's possible intentions throughout the Taiwan Crisis.

2 Using this, what did Mao hope to achieve through bombing the islands of Quemoy and Matsu?

3 In what ways do Extracts 1 and 2 differ and agree in their interpretations of the Taiwan Crisis?

EXTRACT

From J. Chang and J. Halliday, *Mao: the Unknown Story* (2005). Jung Chang is a Chinese-born British writer, best known for her family autobiography *Wild Swans*, documenting the lives of three female generations of her family in China. Jon Halliday, her husband, is an Irish-born historian.

Mao wanted a fleet of his own, and to build his own ships. In order to give himself an excuse to turn down the Russian proposal for co-operation, he staged a tantrum. ... He then distorted Moscow's proposal into an issue of sovereignty, accusing the Russians of 'wanting to control us' through a 'joint fleet'. 'It boils down to you don't trust the Chinese...' In among the bluster, Mao inserted his real demand: 'You must help us to build a navy! ... We want to have two or three hundred [nuclear] submarines.'

Khrushchev was alarmed by Mao's outburst, as Mao had hoped he would be, and rushed to Peking [Beijing] in secret on 31 July [1958]. ... To keep the pressure on, Mao strongly hinted that otherwise the Russians might be drawn into a war: 'Now that we don't have a nuclear submarine fleet, we might as well hand our entire coast over to you, for you to fight for us'. Then, to hammer this point home, as soon as Khrushchev departed, Mao manufactured a war situation ...

This time his target was nuclear submarines and other high-tech military know-how. On 23 August Mao opened up a huge artillery barrage against the island of Quemoy, the springboard to Taiwan, blanketing the tiny island with over 30,000 (mainly Russian-made) shells. Washington thought Mao might really be going for Taiwan. No one in the West suspected his true goal: to force the USA to threaten a nuclear war in order to scare his own ally – a ruse unique in the annals of statecraft.

EXTRACT

From Frank Dikötter, *Mao's Great Famine* (2010). Dikötter is a Dutch historian specialising in modern Chinese history.

Over the years Mao had taken the measure of Khrushchev. Now he bossed him around, dismissing the need for a submarine base and brushing aside a request for a radio station. The Soviet delegation went home empty-handed. But this was not the end of it, as Mao was determined to take the initiative in world affairs. A few weeks later, on 23 August, without advance warning to Moscow, Mao gave the order to start shelling the offshore islands of Quemoy and Matsu in the Taiwan Strait, controlled by Chiang Kai-Shek [Jiang Jieshi], triggering an international crisis. The United States responded by reinforcing its naval units and arming a hundred jet fighters in Taiwan with air-to-air missiles. On 8 September Moscow was forced to take sides by throwing its weight behind Beijing, proclaiming that an attack on the People's Republic of China would be considered an attack on the Soviet Union. Mao was jubilant. He had forced Khrushchev to extend the protective mantle of nuclear power to China while at the same time wrecking Moscow's bid to reduce tensions with Washington. ...

But the real reason for the bombing of the islands had nothing to do with international relations. Mao wanted to create a heightened sense of tension to promote collectivisation: 'A tense situation helps us to mobilise people, in particular those who are backward, those middle-of-the-roaders... The people's communes should organise militias. Everyone in our country is a soldier.' The Taiwan Strait crisis provided the final rationale for the entire militarisation of the country.

SOURCE

From Dr Li Zhisui, *The Private Life of Chairman Mao* (1994). Li Zhisui was Mao's personal physician from 1954 until Mao's death in 1976. Mao often discussed personal and political matters with him. In 1988, Li emigrated to the USA, where he published his memoir of his time in Mao's service. The book was, and still is, banned in the PRC, where officials have maintained it is mainly fabricated.

It was Mao's challenge to Khrushchev's bid to reduce tensions between the Soviet Union and the United States, his demonstration of China's importance in the triangular relationship among China, the Soviet Union, and the United States. Seeing Khrushchev's efforts at world peace as an attempt to control him and China, Mao deliberately tried to trip up the game. Mao was convinced that Chiang Kai-Shek [Jiang Jieshi] wanted the United States to drop an atom bomb on Fujian province, and Mao would not have minded if it had. His shelling of Quemoy was a dare to see how far the United States would go. He shelled the islands for weeks. Then on October 6, at Mao's instruction, the Communist party announced a one-week cease-fire. On October 13, the cease-fire was extended for two more weeks. When the American fleet moved in to protect the Straits of Taiwan, Mao ordered the bombardment resumed. On October 25, a new policy was proclaimed. If American ships stayed away, the communists would give the cannons a rest on even-numbered days and bomb Quemoy, and the island of Matsu, on odd-numbered ones.

Mao knew that 'comrades' like Khrushchev - and some within China, too - thought he wanted to retake Taiwan. But that was never Mao's intention. He did not even want to take over Quemoy and Matsu. 'Quemoy and Matsu are our link to Taiwan,' he said. 'If we take them over, we lose our link. Doesn't everyone have two hands? If we lose our two hands, then Taiwan is no longer in our grip. We let it slip away. The islands are two batons that keep Khrushchev and Eisenhower dancing, scurrying this way and that. Don't you see how wonderful they are?'

For Mao, the shelling of Quemoy and Matsu was pure show, a game to demonstrate to both Khrushchev and Eisenhower that he could not be controlled and to undermine Khrushchev in his new quest for peace. The game was a terrible gamble, threatening the world with atomic war and risking the lives of tens of millions of ordinary Chinese.

A Level Exam-Style Question Section A

Study Source 1 before you answer this question.

Assess the value of the source for revealing the reasons behind the Sino-Soviet split and Mao's objectives during the Taiwan Crisis of 1958.

Explain your answer, using the source, the information given about its origin and your own knowledge about the historical context. (20 marks)

Tip

While the source offers a theory in answer to the question, you should use the rest of this chapter to identify and evaluate other contributing factors such as ideological and personal differences.

The clash of personalities between Khrushchev and Mao

There were pronounced differences between the Marxism-Leninism adopted by the USSR and Mao Zedong Thought, Communism sinified to suit Chinese circumstances. Tension grew in the wake of Khrushchev's de-Stalinisation of 1956 and developed into a split following the Soviet demands of 1958 and Mao's reaction. The split was intensified by the clash of personalities between Khrushchev and Mao, the two chief Communist leaders, who were not known for their tact or diplomacy. Mao had little respect for Khrushchev. Mao viewed him as a bureaucrat and administrator who was derailing the achievements of Communism to date through ideological misinterpretations. Mao considered himself the rightful leader of world Communism and an intellectually superior Marxist to Khrushchev. Khrushchev's support for peaceful coexistence with capitalism differed from Mao's view of worldwide revolution to destroy it. Mao accused Khrushchev of **revisionism** as evidenced by Khrushchev's lukewarm support for Mao's bombings of Quemoy and Matsu in 1958. In contrast, Khrushchev felt Mao was irresponsible, hot-headed and unaware of the practical effects of the revolutionary ideas he advocated. Khrushchev thought Mao naive in believing that the USSR and PRC's combined populations, outnumbering that of the USA, gave them the tools required to destroy capitalism. Khrushchev argued that the world had moved on and numbers were not the determining factor in conflict, as nuclear weapons could annihilate millions.

KEY TERM

Revisionism
Thinking that revolves around the revision of fundamental Marxist principles. It adjusts Communism to suit circumstances, so change becomes less radical and militant and more gradual, and is evolutionary rather than revolutionary in nature. For Mao, revisionism represented a loss of revolutionary fervour and a betrayal of Marxism. He used the term to insult Khrushchev as well as opponents at home.

Fresh in Khrushchev's memory was the 40th anniversary of the October Revolution in Moscow, in 1957. Mao had been at his most belligerent, belittling the Americans as paper tigers and saying that nuclear war would annihilate capitalism, leaving the world Communist. When Italian Communist Party delegates asked how many Italians could expect to survive a nuclear conflict, Mao replied likely none, and asked why Italians were so important to humanity. His flippancy unnerved many delegates.

EXTEND YOUR KNOWLEDGE

The sinification of Marxism
In conventional Marxism, Communism is reached after the proletariat (the industrial working class) overthrows capitalism. However, this was not possible as China did not have widespread capitalism and only a small percentage of the population worked in industry. Mao sinified the Chinese revolution by basing it in the peasantry, by far China's largest social group, and not the proletariat. Mao's support for permanent revolution also differed significantly from Soviet practice.

Mao continually demanded Soviet assistance in developing nuclear weapons, but while Khrushchev agreed to help China develop its nuclear capability, he began to reconsider this decision almost immediately in the face of Mao's reckless attitude to nuclear war. Mao rejected out of hand Khrushchev's support for peaceful coexistence. Khrushchev's refusal to countenance all-out war, on the grounds of causing a nuclear war, was interpreted by Mao as ideological heresy. Khrushchev also resented what he saw as Chinese duplicity. While Mao accepted the USSR as the head of world socialism and requested its military assistance, he also criticised it and accused it of revisionism.

SOURCE 2

From a letter the Qianlong emperor wrote to King George III (1793) (see page 73).

> As your Ambassador can see for himself, we possess all things. I set no value in objects strange or ingenious, and have no use for your country's manufactures.

SOURCE 3

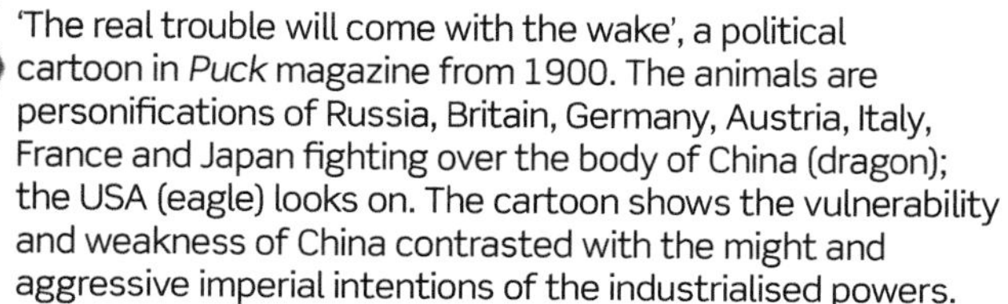

'The real trouble will come with the wake', a political cartoon in *Puck* magazine from 1900. The animals are personifications of Russia, Britain, Germany, Austria, Italy, France and Japan fighting over the body of China (dragon); the USA (eagle) looks on. The cartoon shows the vulnerability and weakness of China contrasted with the might and aggressive imperial intentions of the industrialised powers.

EXTRACT 3

From G. Kucha and J. Llewellyn, 'The Boxer Rebellion', on the Alpha History website.

> By the end of 1899, gangs of Boxers were stalking around western Shandong, attacking foreigners and Chinese Christians. Buildings constructed, owned or used by foreigners were burned or torn down. Some Chinese were even assaulted or murdered for owning or carrying a Bible, English-language books or items obtained from Europeans. The Boxers also busily distributed anti-foreign propaganda in the form of art, posters, poetry, song and rumour.

SOURCE 4

Lu Shaofei, 'He says himself, he's already got a new appearance!' (1931–38). The Japanese man holding the mask represents Japan's aggressive policy towards China.

THINKING HISTORICALLY Cause and consequence (6c)

Connections

Work in groups or individually and answer the following:

1. Read Source 2.
   a) What did Mao think of capitalism and Western values?
   b) How is this similar to the Qianlong emperor's view of the West?
2. Look at Source 3. Why was the PRC suspicious when the Soviet Union made its demands in 1958?
3. Read Extract 3. To what extent was the Boxer Rebellion's attitude to foreigners an earlier version of the anarchic xenophobia of the Cultural Revolution?
4. Look at Source 4. How might this be seen as similar to the PRC leadership's belief regarding the intentions of foreigners?
5. Make a list of other similarities between imperial China and the PRC. How did an understanding of the weaknesses of the Qing Empire affect the attitudes and actions of the CCP?
6. Why is it important for historians to see these links across time and be able to explain how causal factors can influence situations much later in time?

Mao's accusation of revisionism focused on Khrushchev's handling of Marshal Tito, the president of the Federal Republic of Yugoslavia. Diplomatic relations between the USSR and Yugoslavia had been terminated by Stalin in reaction to Yugoslavia's co-operation with the West and assertion of its independence from Moscow. Khrushchev reopened relations with Yugoslavia and attempted to woo it back to the Communist camp under Soviet direction. Khrushchev granted other socialist countries the right to interpret Marxism in a different way, and promised equal relationships between all satellite states and the Soviet Union. Khrushchev's keenness to establish unity throughout the Communist bloc was interpreted as weakness by Mao. Mao believed Stalin was justified in excluding Yugoslavia, and favoured a hard line against those who deviated from revolutionary principles. Khrushchev's reconciliatory attitude was consistent with peaceful coexistence and an exemplification of his revisionism. He was prepared to accept models of government fundamentally different from Communism. He even supported socialist parties who favoured a parliamentary route to power over revolutionary struggle. Mao saw this as a betrayal of Communism; for him it was the duty of Communist nations to support revolutions in capitalist countries. This difference of opinion symbolised the clash of personalities between Khrushchev and Mao.

EXTEND YOUR KNOWLEDGE

Marshal Tito and the Federal Republic of Yugoslavia

Tito had led the Communist resistance in Yugoslavia during the Second World War. As Yugoslavia was more active in liberating itself than other soon-to-be Communist nations, who largely depended on Soviet assistance, it considered itself independent. Tito's path of nationalism and self-interest led to a breakdown in relations with the USSR. Khrushchev put considerable effort into bringing Yugoslavia back to the socialist fold. Given Yugoslavia's opposition to Stalin and links with the West (Yugoslavia's independence from the USSR had attracted Western aid), it came in for growing criticism from China. Often, criticism of Yugoslavia was masked criticism of the perceived revisionist leanings of Khrushchev.

Mao disliked Soviet influence over Chinese economic development (see page 29) and sought independence from Moscow. Mao believed himself Stalin's heir as the leader of world Communism and disapproved of the paternalistic support and assistance the USSR offered. Mao wanted to adopt a more revolutionary approach to economic development than that adopted by the USSR. He also felt that the USSR was insufficiently revolutionary to fully understand his ideas, and did not think Khrushchev his equal to disagree with his ideas. So although Soviet assistance to China had grown since Khrushchev became Soviet leader, the relations between the two nations had, if anything, deteriorated. Mao felt disrespected and took it as a personal insult that Khrushchev had not consulted with the Chinese leadership before making his Secret Speech in 1956, and the impact of de-Stalinisation exacerbated the clash of personalities between Khrushchev and Mao. De-Stalinisation and Khrushchev's attack of the cult of personality presented Mao with a dilemma. While Mao had resented Stalin's condescending handling of the PRC, his objections were not based on Stalin's style of rule. Mao believed in the use of purges, and saw them as the essential tool in rooting out revisionism. Indeed Khrushchev's criticisms of Stalin could easily be applied to Mao. Like Stalin, Mao had organised purges of the CCP to eliminate opponents, and he had also cultivated a cult of personality where he attempted to portray himself as separate from the CCP and solely responsible for the success of the revolution. Mao was held up as a god-like figure, and in 1961 his followers collated his speeches into *The Little Red Book.*

EXTEND YOUR KNOWLEDGE

The Little Red Book

A compilation of Mao's speeches on 33 topics, intended as a blueprint for how Chinese people should live. It was compulsory reading for the People's Liberation Army (PLA), and was included in the curriculum of Chinese schools. Millions of copies were distributed throughout China and it became a secular (non-religious) bible, often used to settle family and professional debates. It focused the revolution and revolutionary ideals firmly on the person of Mao. During China's radical peak in the 1960s, it became the symbol of the attack on revisionism within the CCP and traditional ideas in society.

Mao's disregard of Khrushchev can best be seen by looking at Khrushchev's visit to China in 1958 to discuss the Soviet demands for USSR-PRC naval co-operation in the Pacific and the installation of a Russian radio station on Chinese territory. The visit got off to an inauspicious start. In the height of summer, Khrushchev was accommodated in a hotel that had no air conditioning and was plagued by mosquitoes. Mao arranged a meeting in his swimming pool. The difference between Mao, the proficient swimmer, and Khrushchev, who could not swim, was stark: Mao swimming lengths with Khrushchev flapping round with a rubber ring. Mao was playing power politics – showing Khrushchev who was boss and what the pecking order should be. He came to see Khrushchev as a buffoon and not on his level as either ideologue or statesman. This, combined with Mao's opposition to Khrushchev over his conciliatory approach to Tito, the idea of peaceful coexistence, Khrushchev's attack on the cult of personality, the proposal of naval Sino-Soviet co-operation in the Pacific and the unenthusiastic response to Mao's bombardment of the Taiwanese islands in 1958, created a mutual enmity between Khrushchev and Mao that widened the rift of their personality clash.

ACTIVITY
KNOWLEDGE CHECK

The personality clash between Mao and Khrushchev

1 Draw a mind map listing all the factors about which Mao and Khrushchev disagreed. Explain clearly how each factor served to deteriorate relationships further.

2 Write a paragraph detailing which factor you believe was most significant in worsening the personality clash between Mao and Khrushchev. Justify your opinion by not only arguing in favour of your chosen factor, but also explaining why this factor is more significant than the others.

3 Do you think Sino-Soviet relations would have deteriorated if leaders other than Mao and Khrushchev had been in power? Explain your thinking.

The breakdown of relations, 1959-60

The Great Leap Forward (see Chapter 2) signalled the full split in Sino-Soviet relations. Mao begrudged the patronising attitude of the USSR: that to achieve Communism there was no workable alternative to the Soviet line. He hoped to sinify economic development in China. Although the Chinese economy had grown during the First Five-Year Plan, Mao saw limitations such as growth of only three percent in the agricultural sector. He blamed China's reliance on the techniques and thinking of the Soviet Union. Mao believed that the Five-Year Plans should be changed from the Soviet model to better fit the needs of China. This was significant to the Sino-Soviet relationship. Mao supported ideas that had been advocated by Stalin and later discredited by the Soviet leadership, namely the forceful collectivisation of the peasants and the establishment of **communes**. Through presenting an alternative to the heavy industrial-based economic model practised by the USSR, Mao challenged Soviet leadership of the direction of world Communism. The USSR criticised China for deviating from the Soviet model, and Khrushchev mocked communes as old-fashioned, unworkable and erroneous in practice. Mao's support for communes and immediate world revolution were the basis of Khrushchev's accusation that Mao had a poor understanding of Marxism.

KEY TERM

Commune
A community, that can vary in size, where everything is shared. Cooking, childcare and care of the elderly are communal and jobs are assigned by commune leaders. In the PRC, there was a large collectivist drive to establish communes and it became official policy in 1958. Chinese communes consisted of 4,000-20,000 households, and by 1962 there were more than 50,000 communes in China.

Mao believed that communes would accelerate socialist development and achieve the transition to Communism. He boasted that the realisation of Communism in the PRC was close, and that the PRC could avoid some of the detours and pitfalls suffered by the USSR and present an alternative, short cut to Communism. This bold claim threatened the ideological dominance of the USSR and its leadership of world Communism. Mao proposed a complete rejection of the ideas behind the First Five-Year Plan, namely a dedication to heavy industry and a reliance on technical expertise in favour of that which the PRC had in surplus: unskilled labour. In doing so, he thought that China could bypass the capitalist stage of development and move straight to Communism. Mao saw himself as an adventurist at heart, willing to question established thinking in a way the bureaucratic, procedural USSR could not.

To achieve Communism, Mao sought to make China self-reliant, to rely on mass mobilisation and to adopt the slogan 'better red than expert'. He excitedly boasted that the East wind was prevailing over the West and, with no empirical evidence apart from sheer population size, it was claimed that China would overtake the UK in terms of steel production within seven years.

The withdrawal of Soviet economic assistance from China in 1959 has been identified as a landmark in the Sino-Soviet split. It was obviously the most visible evidence of a deterioration in relations, but in reality it was the next logical step in a chain of events that had ended Sino-Soviet friendship.

Already accused by Deng of being spies (see page 139), Soviet economic advisers were increasingly ignored and sidelined as Mao and the PRC moved Chinese economic development in a different direction from that of the USSR. Mao placed the empowering of the masses at the core of the Great Leap Forward, in contrast to the role of Soviet economic advisers who had been crucial to the First Five-Year Plan.

The USSR's help had gone as far as it was going to go. Khrushchev had given the PRC more assistance than Stalin had, but he wanted this support to establish a model that could proceed without indefinite Soviet financial assistance. Mao rejected that advice but wanted more Soviet help in developing a nuclear deterrent, and Khrushchev hesitated, fearing Mao's intentions. Khrushchev also feared that if he supplied China with nuclear weapons, the USA might arm its own allies with nuclear weapons. This would be potentially fatal, as any nuclear weapons supplied to West Germany, a key US ally, would be within range of the USSR. Khrushchev was not prepared to risk this escalation. It is clear that at the heart of Mao's thinking lay the immediacy of conflict between capitalism and socialism. So at the same time as Khrushchev was publicly calling for peaceful coexistence, Mao advocated conflict.

As the Great Leap Forward progressed, it became clear that it was struggling to achieve the greatness Mao had envisaged. However, any criticism of the plan was associated with Soviet revisionism. The story of Peng Dehuai's demise illustrates the point. Peng was a veteran revolutionary and the minister for defence who had undertaken a tour of the PRC in 1959 and had seen the impact of the Great Leap Forward. He knew the plan had clear faults and that the revolution in terms of production had not delivered the great agricultural surplus required to facilitate faster industrialisation. Mao's idea of 'walking on two legs' (see pages 45–46) had failed. In the summer of 1959, an extended meeting of senior CCP officials was held in Lushan (see page 58). Its objective was to discuss the progress of the Great Leap Forward which had begun in 1958. It was at the Lushan Conference that Peng put his concerns to Mao. Mao reacted furiously, accusing Peng of attacking his leadership – not least because prior to his fact-finding tour, Peng had travelled to the USSR and rumours were rife that Peng had shared his concerns with the Soviet leadership. It was also claimed that Khrushchev had proposed supporting Peng as an alternative to Mao as leader of the PRC. Although it has not been determined that such a plan was put forward, association with the USSR had contributed to Peng's disgrace. Peng was subsequently dismissed from positions of power and opposition to the Great Leap Forward was simultaneously silenced. However, Mao's suspicion of Russia deepened.

In fact, the Great Leap Forward was reinvigorated by the purge of Peng and lasted another two years. With Mao now leading the PRC further away from the Soviet path, criticising the Soviet Union and Khrushchev in particular, relations with the USSR soured. In 1960, with China in the midst of economic insecurity caused largely by the Great Leap Forward, Khrushchev withdrew all economic assistance to China. Soviet experts hurriedly left China, taking blueprints with them, including those relating to the development of nuclear weapons. Factories initially set up with Soviet expertise closed, and joint projects were discontinued as the problems with the Great Leap Forward intensified.
This withdrawal of assistance shattered the view of a united Communist front. It widened the Sino-Soviet rift significantly. A theoretical dispute about peaceful coexistence had slowed Soviet military assistance to China, but this had grown into outright disagreements over economic models of development and the withdrawal of Soviet economic assistance. Although Khrushchev may have stopped short of proposing that Peng should overthrow Mao, as Mao had suspected, it was clear that the USSR no longer supported Mao in any meaningful way. Sino-Soviet relations had broken down.

SOURCE

From Mao Zedong 'On Sino-American and Sino-Soviet Relations' (27 January 1957). In this speech to the CCP, Mao advocated developing independently of the USA and viewing the USSR critically. He discussed the inevitability of ideological clashes between different Communist parties. The timing of the speech is critical, as it is from a time when Mao was seeking to sinify China's economic development and implement the Great Leap Forward.

We still need to learn from the Soviet Union. However, we shall learn from them rather selectively; only accept the good stuff, while at the same time avoiding picking up the bad stuff. There is a way to deal with the bad stuff, that is, we shall not learn from it. As long as we are aware of their mistakes, [we] can avoid committing the same mistake. We, however, must learn from anything that is useful to us and, at the same time, we must grasp useful things all over the world. One ought to seek knowledge in all parts of the world. It would be monotonous if one only sticks to one place to receive education.

ACTIVITY
KNOWLEDGE CHECK

The breakdown in relations, 1959–60

1. In what way did:
   a) the USSR see the Great Leap Forward as a threat
   b) the PRC deviate from the Soviet model?
2. What do you think Mao means by 'the good stuff' and 'the bad stuff' in Source 5? Create a two-columned table and complete it with your thoughts.
3. List all the reasons why Sino-Soviet relations broke down in the years 1959–60. Highlight each factor caused by the USSR in one colour and all those caused by China in another colour.
4. Looking at your highlighted list above, do you believe the USSR or the PRC was more responsible for the breakdown in Sino-Soviet relations?

Private insults, public disagreements

Sino-Soviet friendship was over by the end of the 1950s. A clear ideological rift had emerged in the middle of the decade and had been exacerbated by its application to Chinese domestic affairs, notably the Taiwan Crisis and Soviet demands (both 1958), which showed Soviet support for peaceful coexistence and Soviet dominance over Chinese military affairs, respectively. The Sino-Soviet split was heightened by the animosity existing between Mao and Khrushchev. The private insults and public disagreements that followed were due to the combative attitudes of the protagonists as well as the distance emerging between the Soviet and Chinese models. As the application of Communism in China began to diverge increasingly from the traditional Soviet template, both Khrushchev and Mao began to defend their interpretation, each denouncing the other in the process.

The relationship deteriorated rapidly and insults and slurs were frequent. The most recurrent accusation levelled at Khrushchev was that he was a revisionist, a traitor to the revolutionary cause. The evidence that the Chinese used to substantiate their claims was Khrushchev's reluctance to support Chinese shelling of the Taiwan islands in 1958. China's suspicion that the USSR's revolutionary fervour had wavered was confirmed by Khrushchev's friendly attitude to Yugoslavia. Indeed throughout the period 1958–69, the CCP's verbal attacks of Yugoslavia for its revisionism were a veiled criticism of Khrushchev and the USSR.

Khrushchev was accused by Deng Xiaoping, General Secretary of the CCP, of perpetuating great-power chauvinism, meaning that the USSR treated the PRC condescendingly as a junior partner. Deng echoed Mao's sentiments that the Sino-Soviet relationship exploited China. He claimed that Soviet advisers in China as per the terms of the Sino-Soviet agreement of 1950 were, in fact, spies. Deng argued that only Communist revolution would free the world from the shackles of capitalism and that now that the USSR had the means to spread revolution, such as nuclear weapons, it instead negotiated peaceful coexistence with the West. The USSR desired to use its nuclear capability as a deterrent to avoid nuclear war; China instead wanted to use it as an accelerant to launch world revolution. For Deng, as Mao's mouthpiece, this was heresy. Khrushchev was willing to sacrifice the principles of Lenin to secure the gains made by the USSR since the end of the Second World War. China alleged that this was another example of the USSR putting its own national interests above those of the international Communist movement. The USSR's refusal to actively support the PRC's shelling of Quemoy and Matsu, and reluctance to provide the PRC with nuclear weapons, were proof that the USSR would not unquestioningly help Mao achieve his aims.

The final Chinese charge levelled at the USSR was that it believed only itself capable of correctly interpreting Marxism, and its approach to China was tyrannical and arbitrary. By the early 1960s, Mao referred to Khrushchev as a redundant old boot that should be disposed of and forgotten about.

Khrushchev was no more complimentary about Mao. Mao's reaction to the Soviet demands of 1958 had infuriated Khrushchev, as did his insistence that the USSR speed up its nuclear assistance. Khrushchev felt Mao saw an insult when none was meant, and that China should be more grateful for the help it had received from the USSR. Khrushchev openly questioned Mao's understanding of Communism. He believed that Lenin's views on world revolution were from a pre-nuclear era and that common sense and compassion for humanity should be used as a deterrent to avoid nuclear war. As long as the USSR had nuclear weapons, the USA would not attack, and nuclear war could be averted.

Mao's refusal to interpret the geopolitical situation similarly was evidence to Khrushchev of Mao's ideological naivety. Khrushchev labelled him a Trotskyist, an irresponsible advocate of world revolution with no understanding of the implications of such a war. In one instance, in the presence of the Soviet diplomatic delegation at a Sino-Soviet summit, Khrushchev began rhyming the Chinese representatives' names with various Russian expletives. Another clash happened in the wake of the Romanian Communist Party Congress in 1960, where Khrushchev called Mao a nationalist, an ultra-leftist and dogmatist, and disparagingly likened Mao to a Buddha spouting muddled philosophies. As far as Khrushchev was concerned, Mao was a dangerous extremist oblivious to any interests other than his own and, therefore, a great risk to world security. An angry Soviet Union Communist Party Congress in 1961 saw Khrushchev call Mao an Asian Hitler and a living corpse.

SOURCE 6

CCP propaganda poster published during the Cultural Revolution (1966–70). It shows Mao as a next-generation Communist leader, taking the mantle of Marx and Engels, the founders of Communism, and the USSR's first two leaders, Lenin and Stalin. Khrushchev's absence is indicative of the low standing in which he was held by the PRC from 1958 onwards.

Sino-Soviet relations did not improve under Khrushchev's successor, Leonid Brezhnev, so it is hard to conclude that the mutual dislike between Khrushchev and Mao was the sole reason for the split. The volatile and abrasive personalities of Khrushchev and Mao undeniably worsened Sino-Soviet relations. They also put conciliation beyond reach, but this does not wholly explain the reason for the split.

Mao received far more assistance from Khrushchev than he had ever secured from Stalin, a task Mao likened to taking meat out of a tiger's mouth. Yet he did not respect Khrushchev and thought him weak. He saw the USSR's limited support for China's bombardment of Quemoy and Matsu for fear of provoking the USA as further evidence that the Soviet Union put its own faith in peaceful coexistence above Communist principles. This suspicion of Soviet intentions was present when Mao interpreted the Soviet demands of 1958 as an attempt to negate China's sovereignty. The insults that flew freely between the Soviet and Chinese camps made rapprochement unlikely.

The Great Leap Forward saw full Chinese divergence from the heavy-industry economic model followed by Russia and signalled the end of Sino-Soviet friendship, and this was confirmed in 1960 when the USSR withdrew economic assistance. This confirmed the reality that the USSR held no influence over China, but by withdrawing financial assistance Khrushchev was also trying to send a message to Mao that the USSR would not accept Chinese opposition to, or criticism of, Soviet models of development.

ACTIVITY
KNOWLEDGE CHECK

The breakdown in Sino-Soviet relations

1. How might supporters of Mao and supporters of Khrushchev have disagreed about their interpretations of Source 6?
2. Create a graph to analyse Sino-Soviet relations from 1958 to 1961. On the *x*-axis, plot the events chronologically and on the *y*-axis measure the state of Sino-Soviet relations from 0 to 10, with 0 being good and 10 being the worst.
3. Which events in this period had the greatest impact on your graph? Explain their significance.
4. Using the examples from your graph, write a paragraph summarising how each of these factors contributed to the Sino-Soviet split: ideological differences, clash of personalities and national defence.

A Level Exam-Style Question Section B

To what extent was the Sino-Soviet split in the years 1958–60 caused by ideological differences? (20 marks)

Tip

It is imperative to present a consistent line of argument throughout your essay. For example, if you feel that ideological differences were responsible, when evaluating the personality clash between Mao and Khrushchev you need to justify why it was not as significant as ideologies.

WHY DID MAO FEEL THREATENED BY THE SOVIET UNION?

On the foundation of the PRC in 1949, Mao saw the USSR as his only hope of foreign assistance. However, following the Sino-Soviet agreement of 1950, relations soured so much that where Mao once saw friendship he now saw opposition and potential conflict. Ideological disputes intensified as the USSR and the PRC clashed over the Great Leap Forward. Mao saw the USSR's criticism of his economic ideas as an attempt to reassert its influence over the direction of the Chinese revolution. The meeting of Peng Dehuai and Khrushchev made Mao suspect that the USSR hoped to replace him with a leader more open to its objectives. Mao accused Peng of collaborating with the USSR. From this point until his death in 1976, Mao associated domestic opposition with Soviet revisionism and the threat it posed to China. While this served a domestic purpose by instantly discrediting those targeted by Mao, it was also representative of his deep-seated mistrust of foreign powers and their intentions.

Mao was born when China was in the midst of foreign exploitation in the form of the unequal treaties (see Chapter 3) and this influenced his views. The anti-foreign prejudices of his youth were reinforced in adulthood by leading the CCP in war against Japan (see Chapter 4) and his resentment of Stalin's negative attitude to Chinese Marxism. The dichotomy for Mao was that he wanted Soviet economic and military assistance but did not want to bow to Soviet influence and demands.

When Khrushchev issued the demands of 1958, Mao compared the demands to Western abuses of Chinese sovereignty in the late 19th century. Mao told Khrushchev that never again would foreign powers enjoy sovereign rights on Chinese soil. Mao's distrust of the USSR grew when Khrushchev refused to endorse China's bombing of the Taiwanese islands in 1958. Mao interpreted this as an attempt to impede his domestic aims, in this instance the unification of Taiwan with the People's Republic under Communist rule. Subsequently, Khrushchev hesitated in helping the PRC develop its nuclear capacity. As Mao believed nuclear weapons were central to China being able to defend itself, Soviet backtracking on helping China amounted to obstructing China's progress. If nuclear war broke out, Mao contested, China would be reliant on the USSR, which reduced China's autonomy.

ACTIVITY
KNOWLEDGE CHECK

The problem of Soviet influence

1 During the First Five-Year Plan, a popular CCP slogan had been: 'The Soviet Union today is our tomorrow'. Why did Mao wish to distance himself from the USSR from 1958?

2 How did Mao justify labelling the Soviet Union, and Khrushchev in particular, as 'revisionists'?

Perceived Russian threats to Mao's position, 1961-68

Russian influence in Xinjiang, the westernmost Chinese province, had existed since the early 20th century. In 1961, at the height of the famine resulting from the Great Leap Forward, non-ethnic Chinese in the Muslim-dominated region emigrated in droves across the border into the USSR to enjoy the improved living conditions on offer in the USSR. From 1961 to 1962, approximately 70,000 left China and the CCP stepped in to limit migration. At the same time, the CCP accused the Soviet Union of attempting to destabilise and even detach Xinjiang from the PRC. With his economic programme discredited, Mao felt the future of the PRC was at risk, and Soviet actions in Xinjiang had confirmed his fears. As a means of defending his ideology and asserting Chinese influence worldwide, which would strengthen the PRC's legitimacy (their right to rule), Mao attempted to present China as a realistic alternative to the USSR. Mao acted quickly when dissent against Khrushchev emerged within the East European Communist bloc, and he also tried to appeal to the newly decolonised African nations.

In order to assert China's credentials internationally and offset Soviet intervention in Chinese affairs, Mao sought influence over the international movement. Mao hoped for fledgling Communist nations to take their ideological lead from China rather than the Soviet Union. Therefore, Khrushchev's firm stance against the Stalinist tendencies within the Albanian Communist Party offered a unique opportunity that Mao was happy to exploit. Led by the Stalinist hardliner Enver Hoxha, the Albanian Communist Party had grown increasingly distant from the USSR following Khrushchev's Secret Speech. Like Mao, the Albanians took exception to Khrushchev's attack on Stalin and to his conciliatory approach to Yugoslavia. In response to this criticism, the USSR withdrew financial assistance. Mao promptly extended financial support to Albania. This gave the PRC a foothold in Eastern Europe and a platform from which to heap criticism on the USSR. It allowed the USSR and the PRC to attack each other by denouncing their satellites. Soviet attacks on Albanian dogmatism were, in reality, directed at the PRC, and Chinese accusations of Yugoslav revisionism and co-operation with the West were really targeted at the Soviet Union.

The significance of Albania was that Mao had succeeded in presenting a viable alternative to the Soviet Union, making it clear that not all Communist powers advocated peaceful coexistence and de-Stalinisation. Similarly, it presented China as a rival to the Soviet Union in the leadership of world Communism. While the Sino-Albanian alliance was only significant in the short term, it served to ratchet up the Sino-Soviet split considerably. Hoping to exert a wider influence, China rivalled the USSR in the developing world. Mao's promotion of self-reliance and permanent peasant-based revolution found favour in South America as well as Africa, where many nations were emerging independent from decades of European rule. Khrushchev offered economic aid to these new countries. China's proposals were more radical, arguing for anti-imperialist revolution. China pledged generous aid packages and thereby presented itself as a friend and inspiration to the developing world. In doing this, Mao hoped to divert Soviet attention from intervening in Chinese affairs.

SOURCE 7

CCP poster 'Long live the eternal and unbreakable friendship in battle between the peoples of China and Albania!' (1969). Propaganda promoting China's role on the world stage was common. Here, Chinese and Albanian workers are portrayed on an equal footing.

SOURCE 8

CCP poster 'The Soviet Union is our example' (1953). The message of this poster, produced as China began its First Five-Year Plan, was that to develop successfully, China should emulate the USSR. The worker is shown wearing Western clothes and is clearly following Soviet thinking.

ACTIVITY
KNOWLEDGE CHECK

China rivalling the USSR

1 In what ways did assisting developing countries strengthen Mao?

2 Compare Sources 7 and 8. Identify the similarities and differences in the presentation of Sino-Soviet and Sino-Albanian relations.

3 Make a list of all the reasons why China had allied with Albania.

4 Write an extended paragraph arguing why Mao wished to present the PRC as a rival to the USSR.

The Sino-Indian War

The Sino-Soviet split became even clearer in 1962, when tension between the People's Republic and India spilled over into armed conflict. Tibet suffered the worst of the famine resulting from the Great Leap Forward and unrest was suppressed in 1959. The horrors inflicted on the Tibetans, generally recognised in the West as a form of genocide, attracted worldwide condemnation. India felt uneasy with the number of hostile (Chinese) troops on its eastern border. In itself, this does not appear to have much relevance to the Sino-Soviet split, but it led to further deterioration of an already fractious relationship. China expected full Soviet support for two reasons:

- China was fighting to revise the Chinese-Indian border set by the British, the foremost practitioner of imperialist exploitation to which Communism was ideologically opposed.
- China was a Communist ally and India was not.

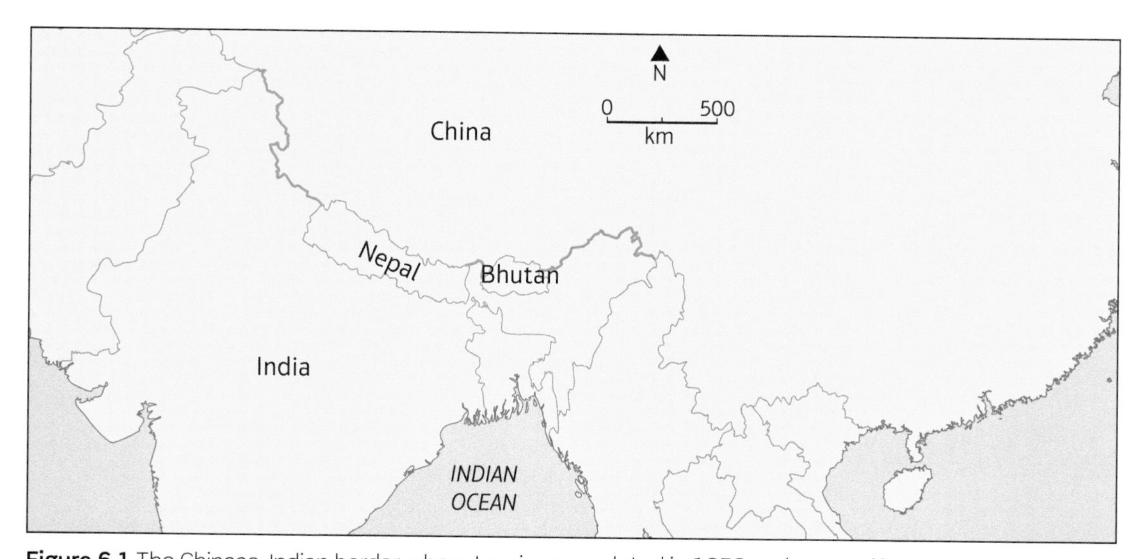

Figure 6.1 The Chinese-Indian border where tensions escalated in 1959 and erupted into war in 1962.

However, the conflict occurred in a context of ideological dispute plus personal animosity between Mao and Khrushchev. Khrushchev did not help matters by accusing the Chinese of incompetence in their handling of Tibetan opposition, with the Dalai Llama, the spiritual Buddhist leader of the Tibetans, escaping to India in 1959. Khrushchev referred to the hostilities at this time as sad and stupid. Also in 1959, Khrushchev had met with President Eisenhower in the spirit of peaceful coexistence and did not want to antagonise the USA by supporting China when the West's support for Tibet was well known. Therefore, when war erupted the USSR remained neutral. Nevertheless, Khrushchev enjoyed good diplomatic relations with India and had supplied it with MiG21 fighter planes.

The war began in October 1962. Fighting only lasted a month, but Indian troops were overpowered and China claimed disputed areas before ceasing military action. The conflict deepened the rift in Sino-Soviet relations and when the USSR offered to mediate between the two nations, the PRC accused it of rank hypocrisy as it had armed India with fighter planes. As with the bombings of the Taiwanese islands in 1958, Khrushchev had not supported Mao's aggressive policies. Khrushchev opposed Mao as he posed a threat to the peaceful coexistence that Khrushchev cherished. By doing so and by continuing to work on improving Sino-US relations, Mao felt Khrushchev was isolating China and monopolising power between the USSR and the USA.

The Cuban Missile Crisis and the Nuclear Test Ban Treaty

The clearest example to Mao of Russia's attempts to neutralise China was Khrushchev backtracking on providing help for the Chinese development of nuclear weapons. Nuclear weapons contributed to further discord between the USSR and China from 1962 to 1963. As the Sino-Indian War played out, the USSR and the USA came close to war during the Cuban Missile Crisis.

In 1961, the USA had launched an unsuccessful invasion of Communist Cuba. Khrushchev decided to install Soviet nuclear weapons in Cuba to deter the USA, thereby putting the entire USA in range of nuclear attack. Kennedy, the US president, ordered a blockade of Cuba, resisting those of his military who advocated air strikes. Kennedy demanded that Russian warships heading to Cuba with nuclear warheads turn back. Khrushchev eventually relented, the ships turned back and war was avoided.

Mao believed nuclear war was inevitable and even desirable; Khrushchev on the other hand did not want to start the Third World War. When Khrushchev recalled the missiles that were en route to Cuba, he averted the outbreak of nuclear war, but as far as Mao was concerned he had acted like a coward. Cuba had been the opportunity to start a nuclear war with America and begin the fight to bring about the end of capitalism. In the face of US military might, Khrushchev had capitulated. For his part, Khrushchev believed Mao to be reckless bordering on insane, and intent on bringing about nuclear Armageddon whatever the cost. Khrushchev wanted to avoid repeating the death and destruction of the Second World War. He advocated a more gradual approach and believed that Communism could only be achieved through class struggle. Sino-Soviet relations continued to deteriorate in the face of another clear ideological disagreement.

EXTEND YOUR KNOWLEDGE

Cuban Missile Crisis (October 1962)

Although not directly affecting China, this widened the Sino-Soviet split, as Mao wanted nuclear war to trigger worldwide Communist revolution and overthrow capitalism. Khrushchev's withdrawal demonstrates the distance between the Soviet theory of peaceful coexistence and China's preference for nuclear war. In response to Chinese accusations of cowardice, Khrushchev affirmed he was scared of world war, particularly nuclear war, and that anyone who did not share this feeling was a fool. It was clear that he viewed Mao as such a fool. Khrushchev's willingness to compromise with the USA was lauded in the West, but in China his actions were seen as confirmation of Soviet revisionism.

ACTIVITY
KNOWLEDGE CHECK

The Cuban Missile Crisis

What differences did the Cuban Missile Crisis show between Khrushchev and Mao's respective ideas: peaceful coexistence and world revolution?

As it transpired, the fallout of the Cuban Missile Crisis was more diplomatic than nuclear, and in 1963 the USA, USSR and UK signed the Nuclear Test Ban Treaty, agreeing to cease over-ground nuclear tests and to slow down the proliferation of nuclear weapons.

Bitter insults were again exchanged. The clause within the treaty to prevent countries without nuclear weapons from acquiring them led Mao to accuse the USSR of protecting its own nuclear deterrent while preventing China from developing the same capacity. Khrushchev believed Mao favoured US-Soviet nuclear conflict in order to elevate China's position and prestige on the world stage.

A year later, in opposition to the test ban treaty, after salvaging documents shredded by Soviet experts on their recall to the USSR during the Great Leap Forward, the PRC successfully detonated its first atomic device. Mao claimed this as a victory for Chinese ingenuity and mockingly claimed Khrushchev deserved a big medal for his role in withdrawing Soviet assistance and spurring the PRC on to triumph.

SOURCE 9

From an open letter from the Soviet government, originally published in *Pravda* on 14 July 1963. *Pravda* was the newspaper of the Communist Party of the Soviet Union and was an accurate representation of the leadership's view.

Some responsible Chinese leaders have also declared that it is possible to sacrifice hundreds of millions of people in a war. ... 'The victorious peoples will create with tremendous speed on the ruins of destroyed imperialism a civilization a thousand times higher than under the capitalist system, and will build a really beautiful future.' It is permissible to ask the Chinese comrades: do they realize what sort of 'ruins' a world nuclear and rocket war would leave behind? ...

It is permissible to ask the Chinese comrades: what means do they propose for the destruction of imperialism? We fully favour the destruction of imperialism and capitalism. Not only do we believe in the inevitable demise of capitalism, but we are doing everything to achieve this through the class struggle, and as soon as possible. Who must decide this historic question? First of all, the working class, guided by its vanguard – the Marxist-Leninist party, the working people of each country. ...

Everyone knows that under present conditions a world war would be a thermonuclear war. The imperialists will never agree to quit the scene voluntarily, to put themselves into the coffin of their own free will, without having resorted to the extreme methods at their disposal. Apparently those who describe the thermonuclear weapon as a 'paper tiger' are not fully aware of its destructive power.

... We ourselves produce thermonuclear weapons and have manufactured them in sufficient quantities. We know their destructive power full well. And if imperialism starts a war against us, we shall not hesitate to use this formidable weapon against the aggressor. But if we are not attacked, we shall not be the first to use it.

Marxists-Leninists strive to ensure durable peace not by supplications to imperialism, but by rallying the revolutionary Marxist-Leninist parties, by rallying the working class of all countries, by rallying the peoples fighting for their freedom and national independence, by relying on the economic and defence might of the socialist states.

We might ask the Chinese comrades, who offer to build a beautiful future on the ruins of the old world destroyed by thermonuclear war: did they consult, on this issue, the working class of countries where imperialism is in power? The working class of the capitalist countries would be sure to tell them: are we asking you to unleash war and destroy our countries in the process of destroying the imperialists.

A Level Exam-Style Question Section A

Study Source 9 before you answer this question.

Assess the value of the source in revealing the nature of the Sino-Soviet disagreements regarding peaceful coexistence and why the relationship deteriorated.

Explain your answer, using the source, the information given about its origin and your own knowledge about the historical context. (20 marks)

Tip

Keep in mind all the reasons you have learned explaining the Sino-Soviet split. Why are some of them not discussed in the source? How might Chinese commentators have disagreed with the Soviet statement?

ACTIVITY
KNOWLEDGE CHECK

Soviet intervention in Chinese affairs

1 With reference to Source 9, was Mao justified in branding Khrushchev a coward for supporting peaceful coexistence?

2 Fully explain all the reasons mentioned in Source 9 and throughout the topic for Khrushchev's opposition to Mao's views on nuclear conflict.

3 Why did Mao want China to have nuclear weapons? Why did Mao perceive the USSR's slowness in providing nuclear assistance as a threat to his position?

In 1964, there was a brief opportunity for reconciliation in Sino-Soviet relations as Khrushchev was removed from office. Mao hoped the CPSU had accepted his criticisms of Khrushchev and this had influenced his removal. However, this was not the case and, in fact, it soon became clear that Brezhnev shared his predecessor's disapproval of Mao's tactics. A piece of diplomatic blundering in 1964 prevented any lasting improvement in Sino-Soviet relations. Marshall Rodion Malinovsky, the USSR's Defence Secretary, drunkenly remarked to a Chinese military delegate that the PRC should follow the USSR's lead. He went on to explain that the Russians had removed their fool, Khrushchev, and China should follow suit by deposing their fool, Mao. An indignant Chinese representation, led by Zhou Enlai, refused to accept Brezhnev's apology that Malinovsky had merely been drunk and instead claimed it was the drink that enabled Malinovsky to speak his mind freely. If anything, it was just a Soviet ruse to test the Chinese delegation's loyalty to Mao. It was unshakeable and Mao, sensitive to how easily Khrushchev had been ousted, concluded that the whole Malinovsky affair was designed to lay the seeds of a potential anti-Mao coup.

The Cultural Revolution

The Great Leap Forward had been the economic expression of Mao's philosophy; the Cultural Revolution was its political demonstration, aiming to purge Chinese society of traditional and capitalist elements. After the failure of the Great Leap Forward, Mao tried to reassert his political influence. He believed revisionist ideas held China back and were responsible for the failure of the Great Leap Forward. Through the Cultural Revolution, Mao hoped to destroy old Chinese culture, habits, customs and ideas (labelled the 'Four Olds'). He also wished to purge the CCP of revisionism, which he openly associated with the USSR. Mao and his supporters often labelled domestic opponents identified in the campaign as 'Chinese Khrushchevs'. Another aim of the Cultural Revolution was to remove any Western or foreign influence. The Cultural Revolution (1966–70) saw the Sino-Soviet split widen to the extent that war between the USSR and China appeared ever more likely by the end of the decade. If not yet a war of nuclear weapons, a war of words was underway.

EXTEND YOUR KNOWLEDGE

The Cultural Revolution (1966–70)

This was a Maoist campaign aimed at purging revisionists from the CCP and eliminating the Four Olds: old culture, old habits, old customs and old ideas. Mao hoped that by achieving this he would keep Communism in China pure. Mao was 73 when the Cultural Revolution began and he wanted to ensure that this purity would continue after his death. The Cultural Revolution was to be carried out by the Red Guards, politicised Chinese teenagers empowered by the CCP to lead the campaign as violently as they saw fit. All areas of society were targeted. Schools and universities were closed as students joined the Red Guards. Government departments ceased to function and the economy suffered as a result. During the Cultural Revolution, the Sino-Soviet relationship descended from animosity to the brink of nuclear war.

The Cultural Revolution was the perfect example of continuing/permanent revolution, one of the key tenets of Mao's ideology, which declared that a revolution must not just be a one-off event but rather an organic, ongoing process keeping the movement pure of revisionism and counter-revolution. Mao thought that bureaucracy and a reliance on expertise, as practised by the USSR and present in the PRC, ran counter to achieving Communism. In contrast, the Soviet Union was founded by the October Revolution of 1917 and since then the state bureaucracy had become integral to the operation of the USSR. The USSR condemned the anarchy of the Cultural Revolution. At the same time, Mao rooted out alleged Soviet sympathisers, capitalist roaders and bureaucrats within the CCP.

Mao became convinced that the USSR was plotting a pre-emptive attack on China. Soviet criticism of the Cultural Revolution convinced Mao that China was still susceptible to the actions of foreign powers and he therefore proceeded to rail against Soviet influence throughout the PRC. Red Guards renamed the Beijing road on which the Soviet embassy was located 'Struggle Against Revisionism Street' and the Chinese-Soviet Friendship Hospital part-funded by, and operated with the help of, the USSR was rebranded the 'Antirevisionist Hospital'. In 1967, both nations recalled their ambassadors.

KEY TERM

Prague Spring
This was a brief period in 1968 when the Czechoslovakian leader, Alexander Dubček, tried to liberalise the country from Soviet domination.

As the Cultural Revolution grew ever more militant, so the chance of Soviet intervention increased. By 1968, the Soviet Union had developed a new foreign policy: the Brezhnev Doctrine. It stated that the USSR would forcefully intervene in the domestic affairs of any East European Communist nation should it be deemed that threats to socialism were at large. The Brezhnev Doctrine was used as justification for the Soviet suppression of the **Prague Spring** in 1968. Mao opposed the Brezhnev Doctrine for a number of reasons: Mao did not want the USSR to set a precedent for intervening in the domestic affairs of other Communist countries. This could be used against the PRC, especially when the Cultural Revolution, a movement that contained virulent anti-Soviet tendencies, was in full flow. If the reforms of Czechoslovakian leader Alexander Dubček were a threat to the Soviet interpretation of socialism, then Mao's initiatives would surely fall into the same category. Further opposition to the USSR was expressed by Zhou Enlai, who equated the USSR with fascist politics. The Brezhnev Doctrine presented a potential threat to Mao's position of power within the PRC.

SOURCE 10

A Chinese political caricature of Nikita Khrushchev and Liu Shaoqi as 'revisionists'. The poster was circulated during the Cultural Revolution (1966–70). Liu Shaoqi had been Mao's designated successor but he was identified by Mao as the arch-revisionist of the CCP. He was purged during the Cultural Revolution and died in prison in 1969. One of Mao's intentions in starting the Cultural Revolution was to root out revisionism from within the CCP. It also targeted foreign influence. By combining the spectres of revisionism and foreign influence, and associating domestic opposition with Khrushchev, the CCP created a potent source of propaganda.

EXTRACT

From E. McGuire, *China, the Fun House Mirror: Soviet reactions to the Chinese Cultural Revolution, 1966–1969* (2001).

Most shocking was the outright murder of Soviet sympathizers by Red Guards. Li Pao-hua, the Anhwei First Party Secretary whose obituary was so affectionately written by his Soviet colleague, had been killed by Red Guards, after being tortured and dragged through the streets of Beijing wearing a dunce cap. The obituarist claimed that Li Pao-hua was known for his warm feelings to the USSR and had been on the board of the Sino-Soviet Friendship Society 'until his very last days'. Professor Ovcharenko reported that among those killed at a Beijing middle school he visited was a Russian language teacher, who was burned alive.

(...)

Chinese tourists inside the Soviet Union did not always behave according to expectation either, daring to bring the war of rhetoric to the symbolic heart of Soviet socialism. In an incident that made the paper for days afterward, Chinese tourists visiting the Lenin mausoleum on January 25, 1967 began rudely to violate the established and commonly known rules for visiting the V.I. Lenin mausoleum. They jumped over a barrier and began chanting Mao quotes, holding up their little red books. Soviet citizens in line 'waited patiently' and guards asked the Chinese to move on, but the Chinese just kept singing and even demanded that Soviet onlookers join them. Then one Chinese tourist allegedly hit a Soviet woman, and the rest began attacking other onlookers. This lasted a few minutes, until, according to *Izvestiia*, Soviet tourists 'locked arms, formed a human chain, and forced the Chinese group several metres away from the Mausoleum...'

ACTIVITY
KNOWLEDGE CHECK

The Cultural Revolution

1 With reference to Source 11, why did Mao use the Soviet Union to discredit his opponents in the CCP?

2 Using Extract 4, detail the ways in which the Cultural Revolution destroyed the remnants of the Sino-Soviet relationship.

3 How did the Brezhnev Doctrine scare Mao with regard to the Cultural Revolution?

A Level Exam-Style Question Section B

'In the years 1958–69, the Great Leap Forward was the most significant event in heightening Sino-Soviet tensions.'

To what extent do you agree with this view? (20 marks)

Tip

You must cover the whole time period specified. In your plan, clearly identify the ways in which the Great Leap Forward increased tension, then select three or four other events and measure their effect against that of the Great Leap. It is crucial to reach a sustained judgement as to whether the Great Leap Forward or another event was the most significant.

WHAT WAS THE SIGNIFICANCE OF MILITARY CONFRONTATION BETWEEN THE SOVIET UNION AND CHINA IN 1969?

As Sino-Soviet relations continued to deteriorate, the likeliest place where hostilities would spill over into conflict was the western border in Xinjiang, where tension had existed since the early part of the decade (see page 141) and the north-eastern border at the Amur and Ussuri rivers. The borders were contentious and dated back to the unequal treaties. China wanted its land back and the USSR was denounced as being no better than the tsars of old.

China had first raised the issue with Khrushchev in 1963, but little progress was made. Already by 1961, the USSR had 12 divisions and 200 aeroplanes manning the border; but by 1968 this had increased to 25 divisions, 1,200 aeroplanes and 120 medium-range missiles. Such a military presence on its border was one of the reasons why Mao reined in the Cultural Revolution when it threatened to target the PLA. He realised the possibility of conflict and needed the PLA to defend him from the Soviet threat.

From 1964 to 1969, there were a reported 4,189 incidents along the Sino-Soviet border. The Brezhnev Doctrine increased the chance of Soviet military intervention in the PRC should these incidents continue. The fanatically charged atmosphere of the Cultural Revolution emboldened China's resistance to Soviet revisionism and neither side backed down. Skirmishes broke out with increased regularity and ferocity.

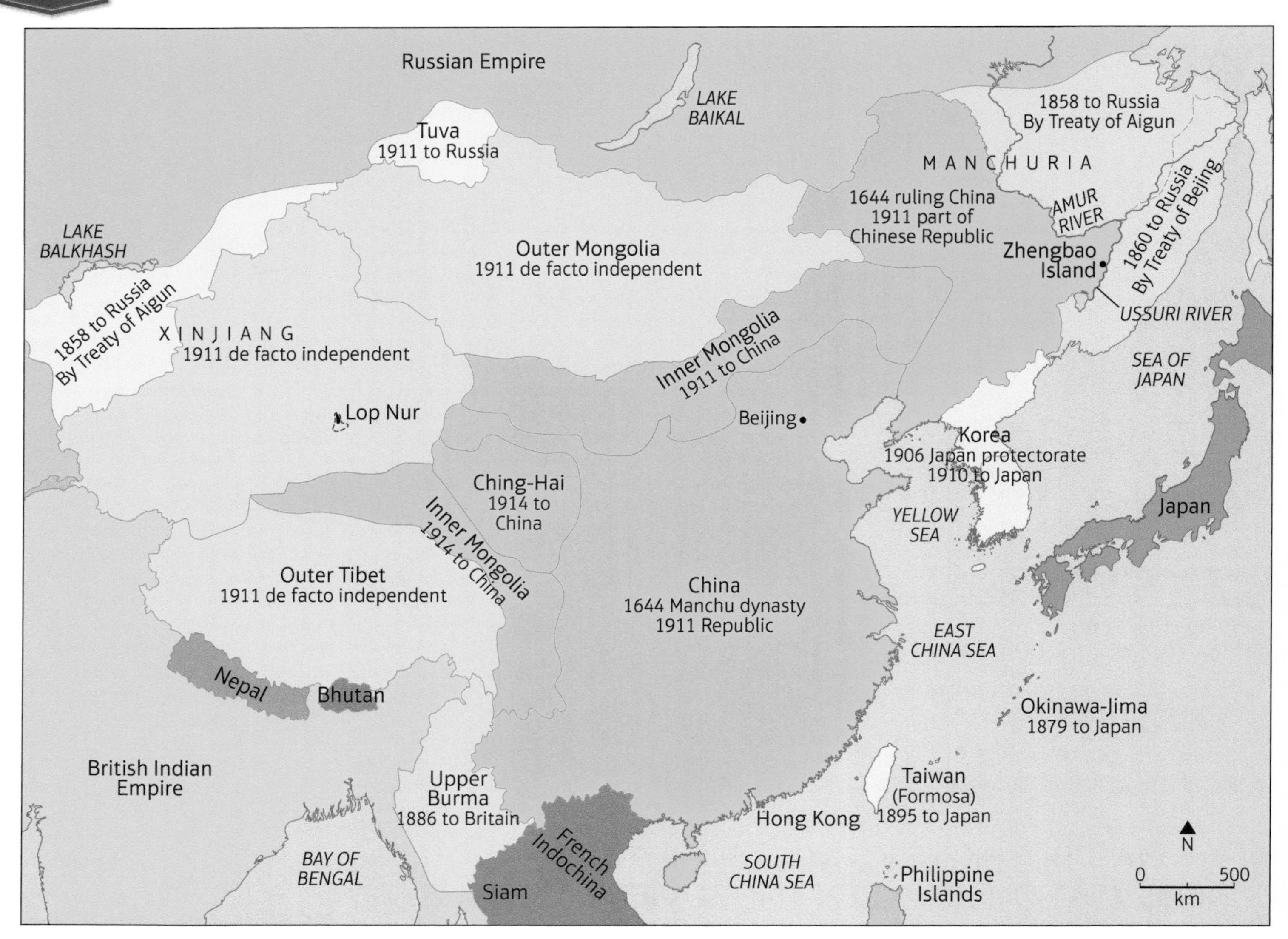

Figure 6.2 The border between the USSR and the PRC. China had long feared the USSR might try to break Xinjiang from the rest of the Chinese mainland and incorporate it into the USSR. Military conflict grew the most heated in the west, where China sought a renegotiation of the border decided by the Treaty of Aigun in 1858. If war was to break out, the CCP wanted it to happen in the east because the USSR would not be able to stretch its resources that far, whereas it would be easier to concentrate its efforts in Xinjiang.

SOURCE 11

From Lin Biao's speech to the Ninth Party Congress of the CCP, April 1969. Lin Biao had succeeded Peng Dehuai as Defence Secretary in 1959 and was appointed Mao's successor during the Cultural Revolution. Lin was an ultra-Maoist who had co-edited *The Little Red Book*.

Since Brezhnev came to power, the Soviet revisionist renegade clique has been practising social fascism more frantically than ever. In order to justify its aggression and plunder, the Soviet revisionist renegade clique trumpets the so-called theory of 'international dictatorship' and the theory of 'socialist community'. What does all this stuff mean? It means they will exercise 'international dictatorship' over you – dictatorship over the people of other countries, in order to form the 'socialist community' ruled by the new Tsars.

Fighting broke out in March 1969 on Zhenbao Island in the Ussuri River, part of the border between Russia and China. A Chinese ambush soon after led to the deaths of 60 Russians. Mao wished to teach the USSR a bitter lesson to stop future provocations on the border, and was keen to mobilise the Chinese public behind him. However, he was careful not to escalate the situation as he was aware that China could not match the USSR militarily. Some senior Russians urged nuclear attacks on China, specifically targeting industrial centres as well as the Lop Nur nuclear test site in Xinjiang. Brezhnev settled for ordering a large-scale missile attack in which approximately 800 Chinese were killed. Border clashes simmered and China and the USSR teetered on the edge of nuclear war. Mao feared a Brezhnev Doctrine-inspired invasion and ordered the construction of vast underground military shelters in major cities in China's interior. Both countries directed their nuclear weapons at each other. The Third World War loomed on the horizon.

EXTRACT

From J. Chang and J. Halliday, *Mao: The Unknown Story* (2005). Jung Chang had been a Red Guard at the beginning of the Cultural Revolution. However, she was appalled by the violence used by Red Guards and left the movement, going on to work as a 'barefoot doctor' in rural areas removed from the anarchy suffered in the major cities. Her parents were purged and persecuted as 'revisionists' during the Cultural Revolution. After Mao's death, Jung became an English language student and in 1978 emigrated to Britain to continue her studies. Here she is describing the military confrontation between the PRC and the USSR in 1969. (See also Extract 1 on page 133.)

Mao had presented the Cultural Revolution as a move to rid China of Soviet-style 'revisionists'. So, when he was gearing up to declare victory and inaugurate his post-Purge regime at the 9th Congress in April 1969, he looked for a symbol of triumph over the Soviet Union. He set his mind on a small, controlled, armed engagement with Russia, a border clash.

There had been many clashes along the 7,000-kilometre Sino-Soviet border. For the site of his battle, Mao chose a small uninhabited island called Zhenbao (Damansky in Russian), in the Ussuri River on the northeast border. This was a clever choice, as Russia's claim to the island was far from established.

On 2 March, using a specially trained and equipped elite unit, the Chinese laid an ambush that left 32 Russians dead and between 50 and 100 Chinese wounded or killed. The Russians brought up heavy artillery and tanks, and on the night of 14–15 March a much bigger encounter ensued, in which the Russians fired missiles 20 kilometres into China. About 60 Russians and at least 800 Chinese were killed. One CIA photo expert said that the Chinese side of the Ussuri was 'so pockmarked by Soviet artillery that it looked like a "moonscape"'. The Russians were obviously serious.

The fierceness of the retaliation took Mao aback, and he became worried that the Russians might invade, which he described to his inner circle as a possibility...

Mao had no effective defence against Soviet tanks, if they chose to target Peking [Beijing]. He had always banked on the size of China and its population as insurance against anyone wanting to invade. But ever since Malinovsky had sounded his close colleagues out about getting rid of him in late 1964, the idea of a quick Soviet thrust at his capital in co-ordination with his opponents had preyed on Mao's mind.

Eventually, a more diplomatic approach prevailed: USSR Prime Minister Kosygin met with the Chinese Premier, Zhou Enlai. The Chinese demanded talks to redress the border, the mutual withdrawal of troops from disputed areas, to avoid confrontation and, in the interim, to maintain the border status quo. An agreement was reached and the prospect of nuclear war dissipated. However, tension continued and Mao remained convinced of a Soviet invasion. The two nations had interpreted the outcome of the Kosygin-Enlai meeting differently. The USSR denied there was any border dispute and only agreed to withdraw troops from areas of conflict. It refused to leave the disputed areas, in which thousands of its citizens had resettled, without military protection. That said, military confrontation ceased and, although tense, bilateral relations began to normalise. In 1970, ambassadors were reinstated, Sino-Soviet trade expanded and transport links between the two nations were restored.

The closeness of full-blown war between the USSR and the PRC was a profound event in Chinese history. However, even when war looked imminent, the PRC had not backtracked and peace negotiations between the two nations had been between two equals. It proved to Mao how far China had come in a short time. China's development of nuclear weapons combined with Mao's aggressive rhetoric about nuclear war had transformed China into a formidable world power and had dissuaded the USSR from following the Brezhnev Doctrine and invading China. The CCP believed a redrawing of the Sino-Soviet border would have been an act of fraternity on behalf of the USSR. The USSR's refusal to amend the unequal agreements signed by Russia and China in the 19th century was proof to China that Soviet friendship was not genuine and that the USSR had only ever helped China to benefit itself. Military hostilities between the two had alerted the world that the Sino-Soviet alliance was no more and that they were more likely to declare war on each other than pose a nuclear threat to the Western world. The USA, as ever open to any developments that might give it an advantage in the Cold War, began to think of renewing relations with China in order to isolate the USSR.

Military confrontation with the Soviet Union in 1969 was the culmination of a period of hostility that stretched back to 1958. The border conflict led to a realignment of China's world view. The immediacy of a Soviet invasion made Mao re-evaluate the respective threats posed by the USA and the USSR. Mao concluded that China was as ideologically opposed to revisionist Russia as it was to the capitalist USA, and that the USSR, not the USA, had its armed forces on China's border ready to attack. The unprecedented war scare from August 1969 pushed Mao to go beyond ideological restrictions and dogma. Revisionist Russia, following the interventionist Brezhnev Doctrine, had superseded the USA as the most prominent threat to China's security. At this time, Mao also reconsidered his support for revolutionary parties in the developing world who had depended on China in the past but offered no meaningful support now. He said China needed to reduce foreign aid and focus on strengthening itself. This helped facilitate a renewal of diplomatic relations between the People's Republic and the USA on the basis of a shared desire to limit the influence of the Soviet Union. Mao hoped the USA would help China to develop its military capacity which would, in turn, draw Soviet attention away from the USA. It was a relationship of convenience that would contribute to a change in China's international outlook over the decades to follow.

ACTIVITY
KNOWLEDGE CHECK

The Sino-Soviet border dispute, 1969

1 How does Source 12 suggest the Soviet presence on the Chinese border was such a threat to Chinese sovereignty?

2 How useful is Source 12 to a historian assessing the USSR's responsibility for the 1969 border conflict?

3 How close did the USSR and PRC come to war in 1969?

4 Was the fact that the confrontation did not escalate to war due more to the actions of the USSR or the PRC? Explain your answer with reference to Extract 5 as well as your own knowledge of the period.

The Sino-Soviet split, 1958–69: conclusion

Mao's ideological radicalisation from the mid-1950s clashed with Khrushchev's peaceful coexistence. Mao saw nuclear weapons as the means to achieve world revolution; Khrushchev saw them as a deterrent that would prevent such a war. Khrushchev thought Mao a dangerous fanatic; Mao thought Khrushchev a coward and traitor. The USSR rejected Mao's Great Leap Forward out of hand. Collectivisation and the communes were ridiculed as backward and unworkable. In contrast, Mao viewed Khrushchev's desire to increase Soviet living standards as capitalist. The split developed into a schism as the Great Leap ran its course, and then the Cultural Revolution emerged, spitting anti-Soviet rhetoric. The Brezhnev Doctrine was interpreted as a threat to Chinese sovereignty. All this tension and distrust culminated in the border conflicts of 1969.

Nationalism certainly played a part. Mao resented China's exploitation at the hands of tsarist Russia, and his defensive response to Khrushchev's suggestion of military co-operation in 1958 demonstrated suspicion of Soviet intentions. Mao's desire to transform the People's Republic into a nuclear superpower was consistent with his belief that China would never again be subjugated to the humiliation of the previous hundred years. In line with this, Mao sought to increase the PRC's relevance on the world stage and present himself as the leader of the third world.

Mao's disdain for Khrushchev, whom he saw as an upstart, made matters worse. When Khrushchev delivered his Secret Speech in 1956 and launched de-Stalinisation, Mao was furious. Khrushchev's criticism of the cult of personality could easily be applied to Mao, as could his denouncement of the use of terror. This, coupled with his support for peaceful coexistence, tested Sino-Soviet relations. Mao's treatment of Khrushchev in 1958 worsened relations. Mao was seeking to humiliate Khrushchev, and Khrushchev's patience wore thin. As insults flew, the split grew, but the clash would have been less significant without the ideological differences that underpinned it.

Ideological differences over economic development played a significant role in the deterioration of relations. Mao's rejection of bureaucracy and expertise was opposed to the USSR's scientific principles. The Great Leap Forward in 1958 marked a huge ideological rift between the USSR and China. Mao rejected peaceful coexistence as a revisionist betrayal of Communism. Khrushchev's offer of reconciliation to Tito's Yugoslavia was indicative of this deviance, as was his failure to fully support China's claims over Taiwan in 1958 and India in 1962, as well as his capitulation during the Cuban Missile Crisis. The closest the USSR and China came to war was at a time when the regimes were on an ideological collision course. Mao feared the USSR might use the Brezhnev Doctrine as justification to intervene in Chinese affairs and end the Cultural Revolution where anarchy was, in Soviet eyes, threatening socialism. If not for the ideological polarity, neither the nationalist resentment, fear for its sovereignty, nor the personality clash between Mao and Khrushchev would have caused a split on such a scale that war looked likely.

ACTIVITY
SUMMARY

Sino-Soviet relations

1 On an A3 sheet, plot a graph to show the changes in Sino-Soviet relations. On the *x*-axis, mark each year 1958–69. On the *y*-axis, measure the level of animosity between the PRC and the USSR. Document each key event of this period on your graph.

2 What trends do you notice from your graph?

3 Which events had the greatest effect on the Sino-Soviet relationship? Pick the three events where your graph deviates the most and write a full justification of your choice.

4 Group the events from your graph into themes such as 'ideological', 'personality clash' and 'national security'.

5 Rate each group out of ten, measuring the extent to which it caused the Sino-Soviet split. Write 2–3 sentences for each factor, explaining its overall significance.

WIDER READING

Chang. J and Halliday, J. *Mao: The Unknown Story*, Jonathan Cape (2005)

Floyd, D. *Mao Against Khrushchev: A Short History of the Sino-Soviet Conflict*, Frederick A. Praeger (1964)

Landesberger, S and Van der Heijden, M. *Chinese Posters*, Prestel (2009)

Li, Dr Z. *The Private Life of Chairman Mao: The Memoirs of Mao's Personal Physician*, Random House (1994)

Luthi, L. *The Sino-Soviet Split: Cold War in the Communist World*, Princeton University Press (2010)

Lynch, M. *Access to History: The People's Republic of China 1949–76*, Hodder Education (2012)

Pantsov, A. *Mao: The Real Story*, Simon and Schuster (2012)

Whiting, A. 'The Sino-Soviet split', in R. MacFarquhar and J. Fairbank *The Cambridge History of China, Volume 14: The People's Republic, Part 1: The Emergence of Revolutionary China, 1949–1965*, Cambridge University Press (1987)

Reconciliation with old enemies and the return of Hong Kong, 1978–97

KEY QUESTIONS

- What was the significance of China's growing importance in world organisations?
- What was the significance of China's closer co-operation with Japan and better relations with the USA?
- What was the significance of the peaceful return of Hong Kong in July 1997?

INTRODUCTION

The turning point in China's economic development was Mao's death in 1976, whereupon unconditional rejection of the West and an aggressive stance in international relations ceased to be the guiding principles of Chinese foreign policy. Seeds of a thaw in Sino-American relations had been sown during Mao's final years: in 1971, US National Security Adviser Henry Kissinger visited China for diplomatic talks, which led to President Richard Nixon signing the **Shanghai communiqué** during his visit to China in 1972. In 1971, a vote of UN member nations had transferred China's place in the Security Council from the Republic of China in Taiwan to the People's Republic of China.

The main reason for this rapprochement was a mutual mistrust of the USSR (see Chapter 6). China had come to view the USSR, and not the USA, as the main threat to its security. However, the **Watergate scandal** removed Nixon from office and his successor, Gerald Ford, lacked the strength to win over conservative opinion in the USA, which still supported Taiwan and opposed Communism. After Mao's death, a domestic power struggle took priority in Chinese politics. However, by 1978, Deng Xiaoping had supplanted Mao's chosen successor, Hua Guofeng. Deng's outlook was very different from Mao's (see Chapter 2), and is best summarised by a popular slogan of the 1980s: 'international isolation leads to economic backwardness, causing political and military humiliation by foreign powers.'

Deng's politics were characterised by pragmatism and by the principle that a cat's colour was immaterial as long as it caught mice. By this, Deng meant that a policy's value was in its efficiency and effectiveness, not in its revolutionary purity. In practice, this meant that under Deng, the PRC would fulfil the prophecy of the Self-Strengthening Movement (see Chapter 2): it would open its doors once more to the West. However, Deng's vision was more holistic than that of the 1860s. Whereas the Self-Strengthening Movement aimed to empower China to reassert its isolation, now the goal was international integration and a wholesale modernisation of China's economy.

KEY TERMS

Shanghai communiqué
A diplomatic document in 1972 that expressed the hope for renewed Sino-US friendship, commercial, cultural and educational exchanges and a reconsideration of the Taiwan question. It was symbolic in China for establishing relations with capitalist powers for the first time in the history of the PRC.

Watergate scandal
A major US political scandal between 1972 and 1974, when the administration of President Richard Nixon was found guilty of abusing its power by bugging the offices of political opponents with concealed listening devices.

1978 – PRC establishes full diplomatic relations with Japan
PRC signs trade agreement with European Economic Community

1979 – China establishes full diplomatic relations with the USA
Deng Xiaoping becomes first CCP official to visit USA
Soviet Union invades Afghanistan

1980 – PRC joins World Bank
PRC joins International Monetary Fund

1981 – China opposes re-election of US-sponsored Kurt Waldheim as UN Secretary-General

1984 – World Bank project at Lubuge Hydroelectric Plant begins
China and UK sign Joint Declaration to agree handover of Hong Kong

1978 | 1979 | 1980 | 1981 | 1984

WHAT WAS THE SIGNIFICANCE OF CHINA'S GROWING IMPORTANCE IN WORLD ORGANISATIONS?

The United Nations Security Council

Securing membership of the UN Security Council had long been Mao's objective for two reasons.

- It would mean international recognition of the PRC as the sole legitimate government of China.
- It would allow China to participate in global politics on an equal footing to the USA, the USSR, Britain and France.

China's diplomatic presence in such powerful company, as the only non-Western, non-white, developing Asian country, satisfied its wish to establish a new global hierarchy. China indulged in ideological attacks, and its membership until the late 1970s was marked by abstentions and non-participation as methods of disassociation. China disliked UN peacekeeping missions, which it saw as a pretext for US ambitions to further its international influence and power. However, as China began to seek improved foreign relations, it abstained rather than exercised the right of veto that it enjoyed as a permanent member of the Security Council.

Deng's desire to open China to capitalist nations led to a marked shift in its attitude to, and conduct within, the UN. The PRC desisted from ideological polemics in the hope of developing trade and diplomatic links with the USA and the West. Co-operation with capitalist nations was essential to modernise China's domestic economy by acquiring advanced technology and training. China's rate of non-participation in UN votes fell from 32.3 percent in the 1970s to 6.2 percent in the 1980s. China also dropped its opposition to peacekeeping missions and began participating in subsidiary bodies. Deng said in 1982 that amicable relations with major states and institutions like the UN and the International Monetary Fund (IMF, see page 156) were to be prioritised over ideological struggle.

Deng had concluded that peace and development were the two dominant themes of the modern world. He believed them inseparable: peace cannot exist without development, and development cannot happen without peace. However, this did not mean that China acquiesced to the UN. It was more that their mutual interests coincided, and when they did not, China did not hesitate to stand up to the USA.

An example of this was in 1981, when it blocked the reappointment of US-sponsored Kurt Waldheim as UN Secretary-General in favour of a Tanzanian candidate. This was partly due to China's nominal leadership of the non-aligned Third World and partly a response to a hardening of the US stance on Taiwan. This illustrated a two-way relationship with the world's most powerful capitalist superpower that contrasted starkly with China's submission to Western nations from the 1860s to 1949.

Another significant difference was that China now played an active role in international politics. This cemented China's central position in international diplomacy and differed from the 19th century, when China had had no influence over the Western powers. An example of this came in 1980, when

1989 – Tiananmen Square protest
Fall of Berlin Wall

1991 – Collapse of Soviet Union

US Congress votes in favour of extending Most Favoured Nation status to China

1992 – Emperor Hirohito becomes first Japanese Emperor to visit China

1997 – Deng Xiaoping dies
Jiang Zemin visits USA

Hong Kong returns to Chinese rule

1989 1990 1991 1992 1997

China supported UN Resolution 462 to call for an emergency session of the UN General Assembly to discuss the USSR's invasion of Afghanistan. This also served China's interests, as it wished to humiliate the Soviet Union and further isolate it internationally.

The 1970s were an apprenticeship for the PRC, during which it familiarised itself with the workings of international institutions. By the 1980s, China had grown sufficiently confident to secure its priorities of improved relations with the West, leadership of the Third World and criticism of the USSR.

Two events altered China's participation in the UN in the 1990s. One was the consequences of the Tiananmen Square protests of 1989 and the other was the collapse of the Soviet Union in 1991. The CCP's crackdown on the protest at Tiananmen Square jeopardised China's relations with the West. International media reported in detail as the PLA brutally put down the pro-democracy protesters, and were unanimous in condemning the PRC for an abuse of human rights. Protests spread to the streets in many countries, but China's status internationally did not change. There was no diplomatic isolation and no economic sanctions. Significantly, China's importance as an international trade partner protected its standing and it settled its domestic issues without Western interference. Indeed, in 1990 as the UN prepared to enter the Gulf War, China was able to absolve itself of any lasting damage to its reputation in exchange for supporting the UN's mandate for intervention. A few days after China's support for military intervention in Iraq, the World Bank released a loan of US$114.3 million to support rural industries in China. Western powers no longer exploited and humiliated China.

ACTIVITY
KNOWLEDGE CHECK

China joining the UN Security Council

1 Write a speech for Deng to deliver to an international audience, in which you explain why China had dropped support for world revolution in favour of peace and development.

2 How would China's stance over the USSR's invasion of Afghanistan have reassured those in China who were concerned about its participation in international organisations?

3 Using two different coloured pens, draw a mind map identifying arguments in favour of and opposing China's membership of the UN Security Council.

4 Which do you consider the single biggest advantage and disadvantage of China joining the UN Security Council? Justify your answer fully.

5 Do you think the Chinese public would have supported or opposed China's membership of the UN Security Council? In the style of a newspaper front page, write an article justifying your view.

EXTEND YOUR KNOWLEDGE

Tiananmen Square protest

In April 1989, a protest took place at Tiananmen Square, Beijing, by students demanding democracy, freedom and the rule of law. Over the course of a few days, thousands of students poured into the city. Other major cities also erupted as criticism of the CCP intensified.

Frequent clashes occurred between the police and the protesters. The CCP hierarchy accused the protest of being anti-Communist, foreign inspired and keen to weaken China. The student protesters hoped that the modernisations applied to the economy would lead to similar political liberalisations, but this was precisely what the CCP leadership opposed.

By May, more than a million demonstrators had participated in protests in Tiananmen Square, as workers and other citizens joined the movement. In early June, Deng decided to send in the PLA to disperse the crowds in Tiananmen Square. Within days, the PLA had forcibly ended the protests. Casualties spiralled into the thousands and the international community was unanimous in its condemnation of the CCP.

SOURCE

The man standing in front of the PLA tanks was nicknamed 'Tank Man'. His identity was unknown and what happened to him after the police removed him remains unknown to this day. Western newspapers published the photo extensively and it is the most famous photograph associated with the People's Republic of China.

The collapse of the Soviet Union changed the global geopolitical landscape; the Cold War ended with China positioned at the centre of the new international order and as the only major Communist power.

UN peacekeeping operations changed significantly in the 1990s, with China supporting humanitarian interventions in Rwanda, Somalia and Haiti while abstaining from, rather than vetoing, economic sanctions to countries including Bosnia, Sudan and Kosovo. China did not want to endanger its trade relations by obstructing the UN's efforts in areas where it held no strategic interest. China also recognised that it did not have the economic or military might to deter the USA, and that its interests were best served by continued alliance and economic development under US auspices.

China's involvement in the UN signalled a new chapter in foreign relations. China's first period of prolonged contact with the West had been characterised by exploitation and humiliation: a belittled and enfeebled China at the whim of dominant foreigners. The China that re-emerged on the international scene in the late 1970s gained from international co-operation. Deng used participation in the UN to foster improved international relations, which held the key to economic modernisation. China had resumed its position among the family of countries.

ACTIVITY
KNOWLEDGE CHECK

Tiananmen Square protest and the collapse of the Soviet Union

1 Why might pro-democracy campaigners have been enthusiastic for political reform throughout the 1980s?

2 Why did the CCP crack down on the protest?

3 Assess the significance of the Tiananmen Square protest and the international reaction to it.

4 Why do you think Source 1 resonated so strongly with the Western world?

5 How do you think the CCP leadership would have reacted to Source 1?

6 Was the collapse of the USSR a good or bad thing for China? Make two lists supporting each perspective, then write an extended paragraph summarising your judgement.

The International Monetary Fund and the World Bank

China's decision to join the IMF and the World Bank followed a trend of the PRC rejecting its previous autarchic economic policy and fully opening trade and diplomatic relations with the rest of the world. Throughout the 1970s, China had established foreign trade links, and by 1978 it invited foreign investment, decided to use foreign currencies and enter foreign markets, and increased scientific collaboration with the outside world. China reorientated itself as Deng pressed on with the Four Modernisations (see page 60), and the next logical step was to liberalise the economy and join the IMF and the World Bank, both of which were UN affiliate institutions. The benefits were obvious: China would be able to pursue relations with foreign powers and would be eligible for low-interest loans, a departure from the extortionate loans offered to the Qings in their period of decline.

The IMF supported Deng's efforts in 1981 to rebalance the economy and achieve stability by making standby loans available. Due to continued contact and co-operation with the IMF, China learned how international economic systems operated. Deng was economically progressive (though not politically, as proved by the Tiananmen Square protests) and abided by the same rules as other countries. There was no exploitation; it was in the IMF's interests to support China's economic modernisation and development. Under IMF supervision, foreign investment poured into China, China invested abroad and competed for foreign contracts. The IMF encouraged reform in the following ways:

- a push for decentralisation in China: decision-making was no longer the exclusive preserve of the state
- less direct government involvement
- acceptance of free market values such as controlling money supply and interest rates
- changing the taxation system and extending foreign trade and loans.

Deng was determined to alter China's economic landscape permanently, and there followed a pronounced about-turn in the PRC's economic programme. Acknowledging that it was incapable of achieving Deng's vision alone, China opened itself to Western economics, and foreign investment came with training and education. Marxist economics rejects foreign trade as exploitative, but following exposure to free-market ideas, Chinese economists grew to support fiscal relaxation. In 1986, they increased interest rates and devalued the currency on the advice of the IMF. IMF membership also made economic policy more transparent, with the sharing of sensitive data benefitting economic development, a significant departure from the secrecy of the Maoist era.

The World Bank had a far more pronounced effect on China than the IMF, as its involvement was broader and reached all areas of the economy: social and regional development, environmental protection as well as macroeconomic reforms. In 1980, a World Bank delegation to China agreed five development loans, starting with a US$200 million education loan to improve university facilities for science and engineering. Subsequently, the World Bank agreed a US$125 million loan to increase capacity for containerised freight in harbours at Shanghai, Tianjin and Guangzhou. Two agricultural loans were also forthcoming: US$60 million to improve drainage and irrigation in Shandong, Anhui and Henan, and US$75 million to develop agricultural education and research. The final loan was of US$70 million. This was to enable the China Investment Bank to loan foreign exchanges (loans in different currencies to be used in dealings with foreign countries, for instance for the acquisition of industrial equipment) to small and medium light-industrial businesses while furnishing assistance in the use of foreign technology. At the same time, the World Bank agreed to fund Chinese industrialisation indirectly by arranging loans to the China Investment Bank. From 1980 to 1997, the World Bank issued 192 loans to China, totalling US$30 billion. Loans grew in regularity and scope after the success of the Lubuge Hydroelectric Project in 1984.

EXTEND YOUR KNOWLEDGE

The Lubuge Hydroelectric Project (1984)

The Chinese government chose this project to test the World Bank's modern project-management models. These included competitive bidding for procurement, the use of foreign supervision, and project appraisal techniques. Lubuge was the first Chinese project to introduce international competitive bidding for civil works, which the CCP had previously assigned unquestioningly to local construction forces. The Lubuge project was an outstanding success and, as such, a ringing endorsement of the World Bank. The methods used in the Lubuge project became good practice in China's vast construction industries.

In the spirit of its new approach, China consented to a World Bank report, a full and frank assessment of China's economy since the establishment of the People's Republic in 1949. While praising the provision of health care and education, and noting a mild redistribution of wealth as well as rapid economic and specifically industrial growth, the report criticised past errors. It concluded that the shortfalls of Maoist economics had slowed progress and there was insufficient emphasis on raising living standards. The publication of the report, in essence, enabled the World Bank to widen its remit to macro- rather than microeconomic considerations and to influence China's economic strategy.

World Bank investments contributed more to China than just money loaned. Concepts such as cost-benefit analysis and appraisal, competitive bidding, independent engineering supervision and environmental assessment became common. Another notable development due to World Bank involvement was the use of modern technologies in grain handling and power generation. Efficiency and sustainability became the bywords for the World Bank's effect on China's economy.

In 1981, the first of the agreed loans, the US$200 million education loan, went ahead. It focused on science, computer science and engineering departments at leading Chinese higher-education institutions. The aim was clear: to raise the standard and volume of Chinese graduates. The funding was directed at purchasing books and equipment to improve laboratories and testing centres, as well as developing and equipping computer centres. A profound effect of this loan was China's flexibility in the face of the World Bank's demand that 20 percent of all loans be ring-fenced for training purposes. China had hoped to spend the entire US$200 million on equipment. However, just as China permitted the World Bank access to its economy, co-operation slowed down. China pulled back from previous commitments. Of the proposed loans, only the US$60 million agricultural loan (providing irrigation and drainage facilities as well as agricultural support services for large areas of farmland) materialised immediately. This was as China sought to rebalance its economy by getting on top of spiralling inflation and government deficits. This proved to be only a short-term measure – supported by the IMF – and by 1982 China had resumed activities with the World Bank and the projects went ahead.

World Bank loans increased steadily thereafter. The World Bank also shifted perceptions of state-run industries and succeeded in disconnecting business and the state. The provision of social security, such as pensions and benefits, transferred from state-run businesses to the state itself. However, the CCP state apparatus could not organise this system – education, health care, housing and a guaranteed income – without first developing an efficient taxation system to fund it. Tax income received by the government would cover the losses of business profits which had previously gone to the state but which would now remain with the business itself. One explanation of the growing relationship and increased level of World Bank loans was that the bank asserted its independence from world governments. An example of this was a World Bank mission to China weeks after the eruption of violence at Tiananmen Square in 1989, to discuss how the impetus behind economic modernisation could be sustained at a time of domestic political discord.

By the early 1990s, China had become the World Bank's largest borrower and one of the largest recipients of technical assistance. In the 1990s, the emphasis of the Bank's operations for China spread to rural development, energy and environmental measures, health and education, poverty reduction, institutional development and transportation projects. Over time, ventures were increasingly located inland from the initial coastal sites. Only a few localities did not benefit directly from the World Bank's investment and expertise. In the period leading up to 1997, the World Bank's influence was evident as the CCP embarked on a programme of reform to create a **socialist market economy**. China defined the goals and the methods of its economic transformation:

- to concentrate on fiscal reform
- to modernise the function of state-owned enterprises and to privatise all but the largest companies
- to establish a universal foreign exchange rate
- to enable banking reform with the creation of three state-owned banks to subsidise and support state-directed programmes.

KEY TERM

Socialist market economy
An economic ideology where the state sector is dominant but there is influence from the open market. Unlike Mao, Deng recognised the need for capitalist tendencies to strengthen China's economy.

ACTIVITY
KNOWLEDGE CHECK

China and the International Monetary Fund
How did China benefit from membership of the International Monetary Fund?

EXTRACT

From *China and the World Bank: How a Partnership Was Built* (2006), by economist and China scholar Pieter Bottelier.

Not only did China accept the need for up-front economic and sector studies, it actively participated in them. The country had been closed to the outside world since the early 1950s and was essentially a black box for the World Bank in 1980. Only a handful of China's political leaders and senior civil servants had had international exposure and few understood western economics. The Bank was seen as a valuable source of technical advice, international experience and information on how other countries had succeeded or failed in their development efforts. The Bank was cast in the role of a guide. Since it was perceived as an independent, politically neutral organization, it was able to serve as a kind of 'air-lock' between China and the western world during the initial stages of reform. Both sides took the relationship seriously and carefully prepared for it. Getting to know China's economy, its problems and development options was very much a joint exercise in the beginning.

The Chinese sent a mission around the world to study the experience of other developing member countries with the World Bank, following which the State Council (China's cabinet) assigned responsibility for dealing with the Bank to the Ministry of Finance. MOF quickly built an administrative infrastructure within the ministry and across government agencies to manage the relationship. The State Planning Commission also played a key role in the relationship, particularly in defining project priorities. This ensured that the Bank's program became an integral part of China's development plan. Initially, the Ministry of Foreign Affairs also received Bank missions, but its involvement in the program remained small and was soon terminated. Few, if any member countries, equipped themselves so purposefully and so effectively at all levels for dealing with the World Bank as China did.

(...)

The Bank's program in China became very large indeed in the 1990s. To manage the program, the government established project units all over China, at the central, provincial, municipal and county-level. The number of Chinese staff on government payrolls involved in managing the Bank's program was estimated at 10,000 when the program was at its peak in the second half of the 1990s. During those years, there were rarely fewer than 100 World Bank staff/consultants in the field in China at any point in time to help prepare or supervise projects, or to undertake studies. The number of Bank-supported projects under implementation simultaneously - employing hundreds of thousands - was about 125.

The IMF and World Bank's impact cannot be underestimated. They facilitated an opening of the Chinese economy in two key ways: opening China to foreign investment as well as increasing transparency through the publication of key reports. The two institutions mentored China and taught it how to manage its socialist economy within a global framework. The World Bank's visit in 1989 signalled that political unrest at home would not derail China's economic modernisation and liberalisation.

Membership of, and participation with, the IMF and World Bank were central to Deng's vision of strengthening China. Like any good student, China absorbed much, learning about institutional organisation, the importance of training and efficiency, and the merits of private ownership and foreign trade – the World Bank and the IMF changed the face of China's economy permanently.

A Level Exam-Style Question Section A

Study Source 2 before you answer this question.

Assess the value of the source in measuring the impact of the PRC's membership of the World Bank on the development and modernisation of economic policy and the political liberalisation of the Communist regime, 1978–97.

Explain your answer, using the source, the information given about its origin and your own knowledge about the historical context. (20 marks)

Tip

Be mindful of the date of the publication. How does this limit measuring the World Bank's effect on China in this period? You will need to include your own knowledge of the World Bank's other activities as well as factors from throughout this chapter influencing the political nature of the CCP 1978–97.

SOURCE 2

From a World Bank report on a proposed loan to China for a University Development Project, 1981. The report documented China's economic progress from 1949 and although generally sympathetic to the PRC's accomplishments, it suggested that economic development in isolation from the world had shut China off from modern ideas that would optimise its efficiency and effectiveness.

Since 1977, there has been intense discussion within China concerning both the ends and the means of economic development. Though partly the result of political change, the debate has been fuelled by some important underlying economic considerations. Future growth will inevitably depend mainly on improving the efficiency of resource use, rather than on (as in the past) massive mobilisation of resources and fundamental institutional change. The benefits of technological innovation as a stimulus to improvisation have been overtaken by its costs in terms of backwardness and bottlenecks. And the remarkable progress made in industrialisation and in meeting basic needs has not been matched by - and has created a demand for - a commensurately rapid rise in general living standards.

Although its precise form and direction are still the subject of conflicting opinions and pressures, there is a general consensus in China on the need for change. This has found expression in the past two or three years in many policy innovations. ... But the state economy is inefficient both in converting inputs (especially capital and energy) into output and in matching supply with demand. Both problems have been aggravated in China by the virtual absence of medium-term planning since 1958, by technical weaknesses in annual planning and project appraisal, by the difficulty of achieving an appropriate balance of responsibilities between central and local government, and by prolonged inattention to such economic instruments as prices and loans - all of which have been partly the result of political turmoil. The commune economy, though fundamentally an efficient system, has been periodically handicapped by ill-considered instructions from above and by dilution of production team autonomy in production and income distribution decisions.

These shortcomings have prompted a set of reforms aimed at providing lower-level units with more freedom of manoeuvre, stronger incentives to seek efficiency and serve the needs of consumers.

ACTIVITY
KNOWLEDGE CHECK

China and the World Bank

1. What was the significance of the first set of World Bank loans to China?
2. Using Extract 1 to guide your thinking, say why China was able to make better use of World Bank involvement than most newly joined member states.
3. Make a list of all the benefits China received from co-operation with the World Bank. Rank each of these out of 10, with 10 being the most significant. Which factor was the most important? Justify your view fully.

Increasing diplomatic ties throughout the world

Consistent with its membership of the UN, IMF and the World Bank, China sought co-operation and trade with all countries, based on coexistence and a firm opposition to domination from the USA or USSR. China increasingly assumed the role of an influential responsible country. In order to achieve this substantial change in international perception, it was essential for China to strengthen its diplomatic ties throughout the world. Attempts to improve relations with Japan and the USA are discussed below, but China also sought improved relations with the rest of the world, notably the EEC (now the EU) and its Asiatic neighbours, as well as the developing countries of the Third World.

The PRC secured diplomatic relations with the EEC in 1975. China supported the EEC as economically it simplified trade, and politically it was a bulwark against any westward extension of Soviet influence. In 1978, the PRC signed an agreement with the EEC. It concerned itself with trade and economic co-operation, particularly the textile trade. This alliance was continued and extended in 1985 by a new agreement.

The EEC member nations, like the rest of the world, were appalled by the Tiananmen incident of 1989 and imposed an arms embargo that lasted beyond 1997. However, this did not have a knock-on effect on trade and from a figure of US$14.3 billion, bilateral trade between the EEC (by now the EU) and China had trebled to US$45.6 billion by 1995. In the years that followed, the EU became China's largest trade partner and China was the EU's second-largest partner after the USA. Relations with Europe were significant in continuing to move the PRC along the path of international integration, and China had gained a powerful trade partner.

Despite China's trade commitment with the EU, relations with neighbouring South-East Asian nations as well as the USA and Japan were of more strategic importance. Firstly, the proximity of China to South-East Asia made them ideal trade partners. In addition, South-East Asia boasted a large number of ethnic Chinese, making cultural and trade assimilation achievable. Closer Chinese collaboration in the zone of South-East Asia was also a means by which it could once more become the dominant regional power. In the days of imperial China, most of these countries had paid tribute to China. Now, as diplomatic relations were re-established, a new regional order emerged, which China hoped would closely mirror the former hierarchy. As a first step in an improvement in regional relationships, China softened its stance on worldwide revolution. Since 1949, China's call for socialist revolution scared the non-Communist governments of South-East Asia. While China still nominally supported revolution, it would only inspire other nations and would not offer any material assistance in support of any such risings. This action went some way to normalise relations.

China had two secondary aims in South-East Asia. By supporting the creation of the Zone of Peace, Freedom and Neutrality (ZOPFRAN), China hoped to boost its own economic ties to South-East Asia while simultaneously reducing the involvement of the USSR and the USA. In addition, China hoped to block the Soviet Union's ambitions of asserting influence in the region.

After the end of the Vietnam War in 1975, China felt that Vietnam had betrayed years of direct support by seeking closer relations with the USSR. China viewed Soviet influence as an obstacle to its own regional objectives. Hostilities quickly boiled over into war when Vietnam invaded the PRC-sponsored Cambodia in 1979. A short but bloody conflict followed. The USSR did not involve itself in the war, but stubborn Vietnamese resistance illustrated the outdated nature of China's military capacity. Compelled to withdraw, the PRC continued to fight Vietnam indirectly by supporting UN economic sanctions. Sino-Soviet relations improved in the 1980s after the USSR withdrew its support for Vietnam. The loss of Soviet assistance left Vietnam no choice but to seek improved relations with China.

The resolution of the Vietnam issue improved China's relations with Thailand, whose proximity to Vietnam had made it fearful of Chinese aggression. The settlement of the Vietnam-Cambodia issue chimed with Deng's belief that peace was inextricably linked to development. China restored diplomatic relations and trade with Malaysia, the Philippines, Singapore, Thailand, Burma and Indonesia. The relationship with Singapore was particularly indicative of the changing nature of China's politics. In Maoist times, Singapore was vilified ferociously for the crimes of capitalism, class oppression and friendship with the USA. However, under Deng, Singapore was rehabilitated and, moreover, served as an economic model for international integration. In the 1990s, China developed economic ties with South-East Asia, and Chinese emigrant entrepreneurs invested vast sums in the mother country.

EXTRACT 2

From M. Stuart-Fox, *A Short History of China and South-East Asia: Tribute, Trade and Influence* (2003)

For China, resolution of the Cambodia problem and normalisation of relations with Vietnam restored a relationship that Vietnamese arrogance and ingratitude had temporarily disrupted. For Vietnam, events going back to the founding of the PRC confirmed that even a radical change of ideology had not altered China's historic determination to dominate South-East Asia. For a brief period of less than a century, Chinese weakness and Western imperialism had combined to alter the regional balance of power. Then the Soviet Union had taken advantage of America's withdrawal of Vietnam. By the 1990s, however, European imperialism and Soviet communism had both departed. The European age in Asia was at an end.

ACTIVITY
KNOWLEDGE CHECK

China and South-East Asia

1 Extract 2 attests to the importance of China reasserting its dominance in South-East Asia. Why was this significant?

2 Why had the Chinese perception of Singapore changed from one of vilification during Maoist times to one of admiration under the leadership of Deng Xiaoping?

Mao had categorised the USA and the USSR as the First World, with their industrialised allies constituting the Second. The Third World was the non-aligned developing world, and China hoped these countries would gravitate to China and follow its leadership. Since 1949, China had been prominent in financing and advising revolutionary movements, but under Deng it dropped this priority. China toned down the role it had assumed in its fledgling years on the UN Security Council of promoting Third World interests and a radical redistribution of wealth. Instead, throughout the 1980s and 1990s, China urged African compliance with existing global economic frameworks. Bilateral trade increased steadily during the 1980s, but the limited strength of these enterprises prevented further Chinese investments. Between 1979 and 1990, China speculated only US$51 million in Africa, averaging US$500,000 investment per project. By the time Chinese entrepreneurship had matured in the 1990s, the investment environment in Africa had normalised and Chinese investment expanded rapidly.

SOURCE

From Deng Xiaoping, 'Seize the opportunity to develop the economy' in *Selected Works of Deng Xiaoping, Vol. III* (1990). Deng was the most senior and respected official in the CCP. By this time, he was the paramount leader of the CCP. While this was not an official position, it afforded him the power to control key policy decisions. This is an excerpt from a speech given to the Central Committee of the PRC.

There are many unpredictable factors affecting the international situation, and the contradictions are becoming increasingly evident. The current situation is more complex and chaotic than in the past, when the two hegemonist powers were contending for world domination. No one knows how to clear up the mess. Some developing countries would like China to become leader of the Third World. But we absolutely cannot do that and this is one of our basic state policies. We can't afford to do it and besides, we aren't strong enough. There is nothing to be gained by playing that role; we would only lose most of our initiative.

China will always side with the Third World countries, but we shall never seek hegemony over them or serve as their leader. Nevertheless, we cannot simply do nothing in international affairs. We have to make our contribution. In what respect? I think we should help promote the establishment of a new international political and economic order. We do not fear anyone, but we should not give offence to anyone either. We should act in accordance with the Five Principles of Peaceful Coexistence and never deviate from them....

We must understand theoretically that the difference between capitalism and socialism is not a market economy as opposed to a planned economy. Socialism has regulation by market forces, and capitalism has control through planning. Do you think capitalism has absolute freedom without any control? The most-favoured-nation status is also a form of control. You must not think that if we have some market economy we shall be taking the capitalist road. That's simply not true. Both a planned economy and a market economy are necessary. If we did not have a market economy, we would have no access to information from other countries and would have to reconcile ourselves to lagging behind.

A Level Exam-Style Question Section A

Study Source 3 before you answer this question.

Assess the value of the source in evaluating the change in direction of China's foreign and economic policy under Deng Xiaoping and the Chinese population's readiness to embrace his reforms.

Explain your answer, using the source, the information given about its origin and your own knowledge about the historical context. (20 marks)

Tip

The source informs the reader about Deng's view of relations with the Third World. You will need to analyse why Deng came to these decisions, as well as the factors not mentioned in the source that influenced Deng's thinking.

WHAT WAS THE SIGNIFICANCE OF CHINA'S CLOSER CO-OPERATION WITH JAPAN AND BETTER RELATIONS WITH THE USA?

The significance of closer co-operation with Japan

The relationship between China and Japan from 1860 to 1997 was tumultuous. As an article of faith in Confucian thought, China considered Japan a peripheral nation, a satellite of China, an upstart with great power aspirations and a desire to supplant China as the pre-eminent Asian power. Sino-Japanese relations reached their nadir in the 1930s (see Chapter 5) when Japan conquered and occupied vast regions of mainland China. From the 1970s, as China flung open the doors to foreign investment, it was hoped that relations between the two dominant oriental powers would take the form of those during the 1910s and 1920s, when China looked to its progressive neighbour for inspiration in achieving its own economic development. In 1972, as the PRC was establishing relations with the USA, China followed a similar route with Japan. It signed a communiqué in that year in which Japan recognised the PRC diplomatically, accepted China's claims over Taiwan and combined to forcefully oppose the concept of super-power hegemony in South-East Asia.

Treaties, trade and diplomatic visits

China built more substantial diplomatic relations and trade agreements with Japan on the foundations laid by the bilateral communiqué of 1972. Negotiations began in 1975, and in 1978 Tokyo and Beijing announced the signing of the Treaty of Peace and Friendship Between the People's Republic of China and Japan. As the title implied, it was to develop lasting peace and friendship on a basis of peaceful coexistence. In a nod to their shared history, the agreement stipulated that any Sino-Japanese dispute would be settled without resorting to the use, or threat, of force. The PRC also agreed not to renew the pointedly anti-Japanese Sino-Soviet alliance of 1950. In addition, it promoted a furthering of economic and cultural co-operation and collaboration. China and Japan each assured the other that they had no designs on establishing regional dominance. This satisfied China in nullifying the Japanese threat that had loomed ever since Japan overtook China in terms of modernisation during the 1870s. Japan's proximity offered an immediately accessible source of technology and expertise for China. Unlike the unequal treaties of the 19th century, this accord was mutually beneficial. Significantly, it also signalled to Japan that the more radical period of the Chinese revolution had passed and that if trade was encouraged, Japan would soon enjoy not only the import of crude oil but also access to the potentially colossal Chinese market for its consumer goods. The then prime minister of Japan, Takeo Fukada, opined that the bridge built between China and Japan by the Sino-Japanese Peace and Friendship Treaty was made of steel.

Bilateral trade between Japan and China had been growing steadily since the 1972 communiqué, with China exporting raw materials such as oil and coal in return for Japan's high-end technology, industrial plants and construction machinery, as well as low-interest loans. However, as a result of assimilation into world markets and finance, China had learned that it would not be able to sustain energy exports as domestic improvements and modernisations would consume energy to the extent that China itself would end up importing. By the 1980s, China had moved from exporting raw materials to exporting manufactured goods such as textiles, clothing and other labour-intensive products.

Japan also supported China's entry to the World Bank and IMF, and was the first country to offer bilateral loans with four major assistance packages amounting to US$13 billion, geared primarily at revitalising China's steel industry. As the 1980s progressed, domestic reforms to the Chinese economy reassured Japanese investors, namely that the CCP guaranteed Japanese firms compensation should their firms be nationalised, and that they were to be treated equally to Chinese state-owned enterprises.

By the dawn of the 1990s, there was a trade imbalance in bilateral trade in favour of Japan, which prompted some commentators within China to believe that this was reminiscent of the dark days of the 1920s and 1930s, when Japan viewed China as an opportunity to enrich itself at China's expense, in essence a commercial invasion. However, further liberalisation in China enabled heavier Japanese foreign direct investment (FDI). From the relatively low figure of US$2 billion by 1989, Japanese FDI had grown to US$10 billion by the mid-1990s. One notable Japanese investment was the Baoshan steel complex in Shanghai, funding for which was greatly accelerated upon Deng's victory in the power struggle with Mao's final successor, Hua Guofeng. By 1993, China had overtaken Germany, Taiwan and South Korea to be Japan's second-largest trade partner after the USA.

Due to China and Japan's unique historical relationship, marked as it was by the Japanese imperialism of the 1930s, frequent diplomatic visits between the two governments have been necessary. Indeed, Deng Xiaoping ratified the 1978 agreement during a visit to Japan, the first Chinese premier to visit Japan in an official capacity. In 1982, Premier Zhao Ziyang, on a visit to Tokyo, declared the three principles for continued relations: peace and friendship, equality and mutual benefit. In 1983, the General Secretary of the CCP, Hu Yaobang, added a fourth principle: mutual trust. A 1984 Japanese state visit to China announced the second loan programme amounting to US$4.3 billion annually for the years 1984–89. A subsequent visit in 1986 announced a third significant loan, details of which were announced during a high-level diplomatic visit in 1988. Loans under this agreement amounted to US$7.5 billion a year.

These high-level diplomatic missions aimed to preserve prosperous economic relations and international stability. A notable function of these trips was to communicate the Japanese political elite's non-confrontational attitude to the CCP in the face of growing Japanese public opposition to China, especially in the wake of the brutal crackdown on the 1989 Tiananmen Square protests. While denouncing the CCP's reaction, Japan was at pains to avoid any international re-isolation of China and limited the extent of economic sanctions. In a way, this was a realisation of the progressive school of thought in China at the turn of the 19th century that China and Japan must assert their interests collectively to retain their independence and identity in the face of Western economic growth.

Deng Xiaoping displayed his gratitude for Japanese support in the wake of the 1989 protest, claiming it reflected the genuine friendship between the two nations. Japan solidified this friendship in 1992 when, in a follow-up to Jiang Zemin's visit to commemorate the 20th anniversary of the signing of the joint communiqué, Emperor Hirohito became the first Japanese emperor to visit China.

Diplomatic trips intensified in their regularity, showing the endurance of the Chinese-Japanese friendship. During the period 1978–97, Sino-Japanese relations reached a new level. They had progressed from the 19th century, when China viewed Japan as inferior, and the 1920s and 1930s, when Japan invaded and occupied China to exploit its natural resources, to a time when relations became reciprocal.

EXTRACT 3

From C. Rose, *Interpreting History in Sino-Japanese Relations* (2005).

The factors of mutual complementarity of the Chinese and Japanese economies, the geographical proximity of the two countries and their cultural affinity were cited by both sides as providing the potential for a rapid and vast expansion of bilateral trade. China perceived Japan as a 'convenient and near source of plant imports, advanced technology, and credits on favourable terms, which would facilitate the speedier realisation of China's Four Modernisations'. Japan, for its part, was keen to develop economic ties with China 'in order to diversify its export markets and its sources of raw materials as well as reduce the degree of economic dependence upon the United States'.

SOURCE

From Jiang Zemin, *Speech to the Committee on Non-Governmental Organizations*, 1992. Jiang was the General Secretary of the Chinese Communist Party. Due to their close and at times strained historical relationship with Japan, Chinese politicians often made pronouncements extolling the virtues of Sino-Japanese friendship. High-level visits between senior representatives of both nations were common. Jiang himself made several diplomatic visits to Japan.

China and Japan are friendly neighbours separated only by a strip of water, and the people of the two countries have forged a profound friendship through their exchanges for more than two thousand years... Culturally our two countries have a lot in common that makes it easier for us to communicate with each other and help increase our mutual understanding and trust.

ACTIVITY
KNOWLEDGE CHECK

China and Japan

1 Create a thought shower identifying reasons why China sought improved relations and trade with Japan.

2 Create a four-column table and categorise the factors identified in your thought shower under the following headings: political, historical, economic and cultural.

3 What similarities and differences are there between Extract 3 and Source 4 in explaining the resumption of Sino-Japanese relations and trade?

4 How did Sino-Japanese relations differ in the period 1978–97 from the period 1860–1941? Why do you think relations were friendlier between 1978 and 1997?

EXTEND YOUR KNOWLEDGE

Chinese and Japanese history textbooks

Unsurprisingly, the most controversial aspect of recent Sino-Japanese relations has been the legacy of the Second Sino-Japanese War. China has consistently pressed for further apologies and claimed that Japan has been insincere and half-hearted in expressing its remorse for this period. In 1982, disagreement erupted in the unlikely sphere of history textbooks. Revisionist Japanese accounts questioned the narrative of events universally accepted by China and the West. They put forward the view that Japan was liberating itself from imperialism and that it was not a campaign of aggression. In line with this, Japanese revisionists have questioned the authenticity of events such as the Nanjing Massacre (see page 122). A Japanese textbook written in 1986 significantly downplayed Japanese atrocities and suggested that Chinese casualties were far fewer than had been previously accepted. Emperor Hirohito formally apologised to Chinese victims of the period on his state visit in 1992, and senior Japanese politicians have since echoed this apology. Although the Chinese and Western interpretation is now generally acknowledged, Japanese nationalists continue to view events such as Nanjing as a great myth that China propounded to secure greater trade concessions from Japan.

The significance of improved relations with the USA

It was a rapprochement in Sino-American relations that exemplified Deng's vision of China. Ever since the Korean War, Mao had been convinced that the USA was planning a nuclear attack to annihilate the People's Republic. The USA was China's enemy, and despite Mao's bravado in labelling the US a 'paper tiger', he saw it as the main threat to Chinese security. The deterioration in Sino-Soviet relations (see Chapter 6) was pivotal in adjusting this Sino-American mistrust. In addition, Deng believed that the USA, even more than Japan, was central to achieving China's modernisation and economic renaissance on the international stage. It was inconceivable that China could reintegrate into the world economic community without the blessing of the USA, the world's foremost capitalist and industrialised nation. If the USA established relations with China, it was likely that the rest of the developed world would follow suit. The PRC was no longer an international outcast that saw nuclear war as a means of waging class conflict. Under Deng's leadership, the PRC became a member of the world community on an equal footing and, most importantly from a US viewpoint, it was prepared to play by the established norms and rules of international diplomacy.

EXTEND YOUR KNOWLEDGE

Korean War (1950–53)

This conflict occurred when China sent its armed forces to combat US troops who had landed to defend South Korea from the attack by North Korea. The war ended with Korea splitting into a US-supported capitalist South and a Soviet- and Chinese-backed Communist North.

Full diplomatic relations, 1979

Full diplomatic relations with the USA demonstrated the extent to which Deng distanced himself from the Maoist regime that had preceded him. From advocating the principles of worldwide revolution under Mao, Deng called for unity against the Soviet Union. He also put far less emphasis on the global redistribution of resources and wealth. Steps towards normalisation continued through 1978, peaking with the visit of US National Security Adviser Zbigniew Brzezinski. At the end of that year, the USA and the PRC announced that they had reached an agreement. Full diplomatic relations would be effective from 1 January 1979.

The main sticking point in negotiations was Taiwan, which the USA had long supported. This alliance had grown from US disaffection with the CCP's victory in the Chinese Civil War, a view that the Korean War reinforced. The defence of Taiwan became a key pillar of the US foreign policy of containing Communism. A defence treaty signed in 1954 between the USA and Taiwan confirmed this friendship. When President Nixon travelled to China to meet Mao in 1972, he simultaneously sent the fiercely anti-Communist Governor of California, Ronald Reagan, to the Taiwanese capital, Taipei, to reassure Jiang Jieshi of continued US support.

The Sino-Soviet split caused a shift in world politics. It was now politically opportune for the USA to forge a friendship with China in order to stand collectively against the USSR. The strategic advantage offered by association with the PRC outweighed the ideological reasons for remaining allied with Taiwan. Full relations were reached in 1979 and included the exchange of ambassadors and the establishment of embassies. Most significantly, the USA abrogated the 1954 Mutual Defense Treaty with Taiwan and arranged to withdraw remaining US military personnel. The USA recognised the People's Republic as the sole legitimate Chinese state and that Taiwan was a part of China. However, the PRC agreed not to enforce its will militarily. Despite the severing of official diplomatic relations with Taiwan, the USA maintained unofficial links in the realms of diplomacy, culture and commerce. It pledged not to abandon Taiwan to Chinese aggression, and US arms sales to Taiwan persisted.

ACTIVITY
KNOWLEDGE CHECK

China and the USA

1 Why was Taiwan such a contentious issue in Sino-American relations?

2 How did China and the USA modify their respective stances on Taiwan?

3 In what ways does Extract 4 argue the USA was vital to China? Consider both short- and long-term reasons.

EXTRACT

From I. Hsü, *The Rise of Modern China* (1995).

On December 15, 1978, a sombre President Carter made a hastily arranged television appearance to announce that the United States had agreed to establish full diplomatic relations... Then, with obvious exhilaration, he announced that Deputy Premier Deng would visit the United States in January 1979.

The majority of Americans, while regretting 'dumping' the Nationalist government on Taiwan, found it hard to oppose the simple mathematics of the possibility of relations with 900 million people on mainland China compared with the 17 million on Taiwan.

(...)

Obviously, the initiative for breaking the Taiwan impasse came from China with Deng as the chief mover. Normalisation would give him the success that had eluded Mao and Zhou, facilitate his visit to the United States, increase trade, and make available to the Chinese American science, technology, capital and credit. In this light, Taiwan paled into relative insignificance. In any case, China was well aware it lacked the naval capacity to launch an attack on the island and was clearly too absorbed in the Four Modernisations to want a costly, nasty, and prolonged war over Taiwan. Accepting the status quo was expedient because it gave China an American recognition of its title to Taiwan, though not immediate possession of it.

Peking [Beijing] accepted the new view that China's relations with the United States were more important than Taiwan in the present world setting. The Soviet-Vietnamese treaty of November 1978 with its overtures of military alliance might have prodded the Chinese to seek a closer tie with the United States. Ironically, China's growing preoccupation with its two erstwhile allies may have prompted its rapprochement with its former enemies in the West. It is even possible that China was already contemplating a military confrontation with Vietnam over the worsening situation in Cambodia and that it was counting on a friendly United States to deter Soviet involvement. At any rate, the Soviet press blasted away at China's motives in seeking American and Western connections.

Deng's visit to the USA, 1979, and Jiang Zemin's visit, 1997

Whereas Mao eschewed foreign travel, Deng embraced it. Nothing could be more symbolic of the change of direction in Chinese economics and international politics than their most revered political leader travelling to the home of capitalism, and accordingly Deng arrived in January 1979 for a nine-day visit to the USA. He was the first high-ranking CCP official to travel to the USA in 30 years. On the first day of the visit, President Jimmy Carter and Deng met at the White House. Carter declared the opening of windows that animosity had shut for a generation, and talks went on for four hours. Deng made implicit warnings cautioning the USA not to trust the Soviet Union, which struck a chord with the conservative US political elite. Deng wowed the US public. He performed the role of goodwill ambassador, charming senators and representatives with a reasoned non-violent approach to Taiwan. While not denying that China was poor and backward, Deng ensured that bilateral relations would be on equal terms, in stark contrast with foreign power relations of the later Qing period. Deng signed trade contracts with the USA and also reached agreements on cultural as well as scientific and technological exchanges. Deng declared the visit a triumph. On returning to China, he informed colleagues within the **Politburo** he could not sleep for picturing the PRC emulating the grandeur of the USA's consumerist economy. If Deng had opened China to the prospect of foreign trade and investment, his voyage of discovery across the USA had given China a model to follow and an ally to help him modernise the PRC. Deng freed the PRC from the economic and cultural straitjacket it had worn since 1949.

KEY TERM

Politburo
The highest-ranking CCP officials who debated and decided Chinese policy.

SOURCE 5

Deng Xiaoping photographed with the Harlem Globetrotters basketball team in 1979. During the trip, Deng pressed China's interests with President Carter, his Democrat government and other influential senators. However, Deng was also careful to appear open to US culture. Another notable visit during the trip saw Deng don a cowboy hat at a rodeo in Texas. Interestingly, basketball is now one of the most popular sports in China, and several Chinese basketball players have played in the National Basketball Association.

SOURCE 6

From Deng Xiaoping in an interview in Hong Kong, 1981. It was published in *Ming Pao*, a Hong Kong Chinese-language newspaper. The people of Hong Kong kept abreast of political developments in China, not least because the British colony was due to return to Chinese rule in 1997.

The United States thinks that China is seeking its favour. In fact, China is not seeking any country's favour... China hopes that Sino-American relations will further develop rather than retrogress. However, this should not be one-sided... It is nothing serious even if the United States causes a retrogression in Sino-American relations. If worst comes to worst and the relations retrogress to those prior to 1972, China will not collapse... The Chinese people... will never bow and scrape for help.

Jiang Zemin's visit to the USA in 1997 was significant for different reasons. It came at a time when there was tension in Sino-American relations. Human-rights protests against the Chinese government, particularly in support of Tibetan independence, had been growing in intensity since the Tiananmen protests of 1989, and the USA suspected China of helping to develop the nuclear programmes of **rogue nations**. Conservative circles in the USA feared that China was supplanting the USSR as the USA's greatest rival. For its part, China resented the USA's moral condemnation of its handling of domestic affairs and that economic and arms sanctions from 1989 remained in place. It retorted that the USA was in no position to tell China who it could and could not supply arms to, given that the USA continued to sell arms to Taiwan. Congress had granted Li Denghui, the Taiwanese president, admission to the USA to give a speech at Cornell University. Outraged by this, the PLA fired missiles near Taiwan and conducted amphibious practice landings. PLA troops were mobilised in Fujian province across the strait from Taiwan, intimating invasion. However, this show of force only strengthened Li's candidature for the presidency in 1996 (Taiwan's first democratic election) and provoked the USA to send ships into the Taiwan Strait. China protested, but in the face of the US military it could do little but back down. Jiang was criticised for his handling of the affair. This was the context of Jiang Zemin's visit to the USA, through which he hoped to allay fears about his leadership as well as to consolidate and extend Sino-American relations.

KEY TERM

Rogue nation
A country deemed to pose a threat to world peace. It typically has an authoritarian regime that restricts human rights, criticises the USA, sponsors terrorism, and seeks to develop weapons of mass destruction. The USA considered Iran, Iraq, Cuba and North Korea as rogue nations in the period 1978–97.

The 1997 visit saw Jiang harangued by pro-democracy demonstrators. He defended the CCP, arguing there was no alternative but to suppress the Tiananmen protest to uphold national stability. This did nothing to lessen US distrust. President Bill Clinton maintained that intolerance of political dissent weakened China as a nation and stymied its political development. However, the Clinton administration achieved its goal of nullifying the PRC as an international threat. Through the PRC's role on the UN Security Council (pages 153–154), Chinese and US interests became increasingly linked, and Clinton was prepared to turn a blind eye to the PRC's human-rights record, facing the reality that he could not influence the PRC on internal matters. It became apparent that China was far more flexible in negotiations on matters such as trade and nuclear non-proliferation where the CCP's legitimacy and sovereignty were not in question.

Away from questions on internal affairs, Jiang made a more favourable impression. As a former engineer, he marvelled at the high-end technology at IBM's headquarters in New York and the AT&T operations centre in New Jersey. The US-China Business Council and the China Chamber of Commerce in the USA hosted dinners in his honour. Jiang visited Wall Street and enjoyed ringing the bell to signal the beginning of trade. While the PRC was unyielding on human-rights issues, Jiang assured the USA of continued support on the global stage. US business interests were certainly satisfied that whatever infringements of human rights might occur, foreign trade would not be jeopardised.

Jiang restored his reputation at home for not bowing before the USA's moral condemnation. He also proved himself an adept diplomatic operator in foreign affairs. This boosted his prestige after the misjudged heavy-handed approach he had adopted on Taiwan.

A Level Exam-Style Question Section B

To what extent would it be accurate to claim that the diplomatic visits of Deng Xiaoping and Jiang Zemin to the USA were most beneficial to China in terms of propaganda? (20 marks)

Tip

You need to evaluate the purposes of both these visits fully. You should consider the dates of these visits. Why were these significant?

ACTIVITY
KNOWLEDGE CHECK

Deng and Jiang's visits to the USA

1 Why were photos such as Source 5 important in improving Sino-American relations?

2 What do you think the purpose of Source 6 was? How accurate do you consider this portrayal of Deng's ideas is?

3 Was Jiang Zemin's or Deng Xiaoping's visit to the USA the most significant? How did you reach this judgement?

Growing trade

The nature of the Sino-American relationship had shifted significantly since full diplomatic relations had been set in place in 1979. At that time, the Cold War roared and the world stood on the brink of nuclear war. Mistrust ruled supreme. However, since the collapse of the Soviet Union and its eastern European socialist satellites from 1989 to 1991, the geopolitical scene had changed. The threat of war dissipated and the era of the two great superpowers was at an end. This changed the strategic requirements of the Sino-American axis: no longer did either side require the other to counter-balance the interests and influence of the Soviet Union. Trade lay at the heart of the relationship, and China still viewed the USA as the means of achieving its own economic acceleration.

EXTEND YOUR KNOWLEDGE

The collapse of the Soviet Union (1991)

The collapse of the Soviet Union was hugely complex but can be broadly attributed to three issues. Firstly, non-ethnic Russians, who had been assimilated into the Soviet Union, comprised over 50 percent of the USSR's population but never fully supported Soviet nationalist sentiments. Similarly, Communist ideology was accepted but never became entrenched in the hearts of its subjects. However, government through fear and repression succeeded in keeping these considerations quiet. Most significant to the Soviet Union's collapse was systematic economic decline. Soviet state planning failed to meet the needs of the state, and the economy became stagnant by the mid-1980s. The nuclear arms race and space exploration projects proved hugely costly but offered no material benefit in the short term.

As the Soviet leadership attempted to introduce economic reforms, political opposition emerged from the Soviet satellite states. Similar opposition brought down the Communist governments of Eastern Europe, and the USSR was unable to silence the ever-growing criticism of its totalitarian regime. In 1991, the USSR collapsed and broke up into 15 independent nations. This signalled the end of the Cold War era that had existed since the end of the Second World War in 1945.

EXTRACT 5

From O. Arne Westad, *Restless Empire: China and the World Since 1750* (2013).

The main reason why the CCP chose the market was that from the position of the early 1990s there seemed to be no other way out. Modernity was capitalist. The USSR had - very unexpectedly for the Chinese - collapsed, as had the socialist states in Eastern Europe. The United States led the way toward an increasingly integrated capitalist world economy, and those who opted out of it would fall behind... If the race to modernise could be better run with Nike trainers, then the Chinese Communists would put them on (especially if the shoes themselves were made in China).

ACTIVITY
KNOWLEDGE CHECK

Seeking a more open approach

In what ways does Extract 5 suggest that the collapse of the USSR affected China's economic policies?

Upon the establishment of full diplomatic relations in 1979, US exports to China consisted of steel and iron, cereals, raw textile fibres, machinery, fertilisers, vegetable oils and fats. In return, China exported feathers, cotton fabrics and fireworks. This level of trade reflected continued US restrictions on the export of military technology and equipment. In 1991, Congress extended the trade agreement permitting China the status of Most Favored Nation. This exempted Chinese exports to the USA from the high tariff rates stipulated back in 1930, a measure that had long been used to distinguish friend from foe among US trading partners.

In the 1980s, China's US imports diversified to include grain (US$699 million in 1988), chemicals and industrial raw materials (US$596 million), fertiliser (US$379 million), instruments and communications and transportation equipment (US$905 million) and wood products. As the decade went on, China imported finished manufactures and technologically advanced products. Among US imports from China, textiles and clothing accounted for more than 40 percent of the total value. From 1978 to 1985, bilateral Sino-American trade had increased from about US$1 billion to over US$7 billion a year. The prospect of finally accessing the vast Chinese market hooked US companies manufacturing consumer goods. US companies entered China, and early prominent investors included Heinz, R.J. Reynolds Tobacco, Coca-Cola, American Express, American Motors, General Foods, Gillette and Eastman Kodak. By 1985, Coke-bottling plants operated in Beijing, Guangzhou, Xiamen and Zhuhai. Also in 1985, the Great Wall Sheraton Hotel in Beijing became the first internationally managed concern in China to accept American Express. Kentucky Fried Chicken became the symbol of the US presence in China.

Deng saw US relations as imperative in helping China to achieve military parity, and he wanted to access US weapons technology in the fields of aviation and missiles. Initially, China imported trucks, recovery vehicles, helicopters, and training and communications equipment in addition to airborne cameras. However, in 1980 the USA loosened restrictions on weapons transfer by reassigning China's categorisation as an ally. This was a dramatic improvement as since 1949 the USA had recognised China on the same footing as a **Warsaw Treaty** country and since the mid-1970s, as Sino-American relations improved, as a new trading partner. The USA hoped this alliance would divert much of the Soviet Union's attention from the USA to the PRC. This strategic advantage during the Cold War was too tempting for the USA to resist. China did not partake in large-scale arms buying for immediate use. Deng's strategy was to use US support to deter armed conflict with the USSR, which like Mao he saw as inevitable. Accordingly, imports consisted of high-technology items such as computers and communications equipment for future integration into Chinese systems, rather than prioritising standard equipment that China lacked but which was soon to become obsolete in the face of more advanced weaponry in the 1990s. Deng recognised that the PRC was yet to awake fully from the slumber of the Cultural Revolution. During this period, chaos and anarchy had led to the closure of universities, scientific literature was unavailable and the CCP sent technology experts to the country to do menial farm labour to prove their revolutionary virtue. Deng knew that the absorption and successful implementation of Western technology would not be immediate and US co-operation was indispensable in achieving China's long-term modernisation.

Sino-American relations and trade cooled in 1989 as the USA, perhaps more than any other nation, protested against the CCP's ruthless suppression of the Tiananmen protests. The USA imposed partial trade and arms embargoes. However, President George H. Bush followed a soft policy on China that his successor, Bill Clinton, attempted to harden. Clinton proposed that the continued conferral of Most Favoured Nation should be conditional on improved human rights, free emigration, cessation of the export of goods manufactured by prison inmates, the release of political and religious prisoners, and efforts to preserve Tibetan identity. However, Clinton relented as US business and industrial interests flourished in the environment of increased Sino-American trade. Therefore, China continued to be a Most Favoured Nation while retaining its position on internal affairs.

Growing trade with the USA has been pivotal in shaping China's path. The USA, the home of capitalism, has been the blueprint for the PRC to emulate. Jiang's wonder during his visit to the USA in 1997 mirrored the emotions Deng had felt in 1979. The bright lights and digital-age technology – both civilian and military – had seduced China. The USA assimilated China into the international community through bilateral trade and membership of the World Bank and IMF, while China played the role of aspiring and enthusiastic participant and became an ally rather than a new threat in the post-Cold War era. That the PRC managed to achieve this while maintaining an iron grip over its internal affairs bears testament to Deng's recognition that for the Western world, at least in government circles, trade and international security are more important than putting pressure on China to conform to Western views on issues such as human rights. In the period 1978–97, China asserted itself far more capably and effectively than the self-strengtheners of the late Qing period had done.

KEY TERM

Warsaw Treaty
A Cold War agreement (1955–91) of friendship, co-operation and mutual assistance signed between Albania, Bulgaria, Czechoslovakia, East Germany, Hungary, Poland, Romania and the Soviet Union. All signatories pledged to come to each other's military aid should the need arise.

A Level Exam-Style Question Section B

'Out of all the bilateral relations China established, that with Japan was the most significant.' To what extent do you agree with this assessment of Chinese foreign relations, 1978–97? (20 marks)

Tip

You should not just list the terms of the various agreements in this period but consider their significance. You should also analyse the value of relations with Japan and measure these against links with the USA, Europe, South-East Asia and the Third World.

ACTIVITY
KNOWLEDGE CHECK

The advantages for China of relations with the USA

Put the following nine explanations for China seeking improved relations with the USA in order of importance. Write two to three sentences justifying your top three selections.

Access to high-end technology, to attract US firms to invest, to gain support for its membership of international organisations, propaganda value, the collapse of the USSR (1991), to secure support for 'One China, Two Systems', to isolate the USSR (1978–91), to improve its military capacity, and for China to assert itself on the world stage.

WHAT WAS THE SIGNIFICANCE OF THE PEACEFUL RETURN OF HONG KONG IN JULY 1997?

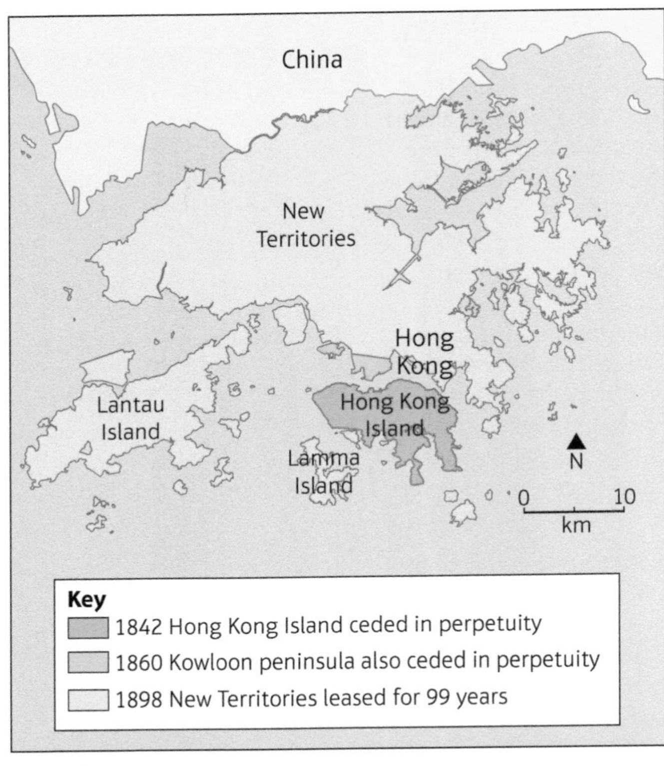

Figure 7.1 Hong Kong and China, and the years when China ceded different parts of Hong Kong to British rule. Although China had ceded the island of Hong Kong and the Kowloon peninsula to Britain in perpetuity, the colony would be impractical and unsustainable without the New Territories, which were due to return to Chinese control in 1997.

The importance of the peaceful return of Hong Kong in July 1997

The period 1860–1997 began with Britain forcibly opening China to trade. This heralded a century of humiliation and weakness that continued until the proclamation of the People's Republic in 1949. At the same time, Hong Kong, under British rule, had blossomed from a sleepy Chinese shipping port contemptuously dismissed by the British Foreign Secretary Lord Palmerston in 1842 as a barren rock, into an economic powerhouse and model of capitalist grandeur. Therefore, the presence of British rule and influence had remained present.

Even as Britain declined as a superpower after the Second World War, China continued to view it as a rival. During the Great Leap Forward (see Chapter 2), Mao identified Britain as the country to overtake in terms of steel production.

The 99-year lease China had granted Britain on the extension of Hong Kong (see page 94) was due to expire in 1997. It is fitting that the period 1860–1997 should end with China going full circle by reclaiming Hong Kong.

By 1997, China was the country on the ascent, whose economy boasted double-digit growth rates year on year in contrast to a Britain that still struggled to find its post-Empire identity. The transfer of Hong Kong back to Chinese rule was emblematic of how far China had come and how flexible it was prepared to be in order to develop its socialist economy. China wished to assume rule of Hong Kong at the expiration of Britain's lease for two reasons. Firstly, Hong Kong's economic prowess would significantly boost China, and secondly it allowed China the opportunity to remove the last physical memory of 19th-century Western imperialism.

The return of Hong Kong is significant in closing one chapter of China's history and opening another. After it rejoined the People's Republic in 1997, China left the running of Hong Kong largely unaltered. As the historian Westad suggests, Hong Kong was the hen that laid golden eggs, and China would not ignore benefits to its economy offered by Hong Kong's model of success. Hong Kong was an industrial and trade conduit that connected the PRC to the world. China applied the 'One Country, Two Systems' idea to Hong Kong. By allowing Hong Kong to retain its capitalist practices, the PRC also succeeded in portraying itself internationally as tolerant, a long-time goal of the Communist government. Whatever system Hong Kong followed, it was now part of China.

EXTEND YOUR KNOWLEDGE

'One China, Two Systems'
This idea, developed by Deng Xiaoping, was that China should resume rule over Hong Kong but that Hong Kong would retain its own capitalist economic and political systems, while the rest of the PRC followed the socialist model. The CCP hoped the idea could also be applied to Taiwan.

Negotiations and terms

As a prelude to negotiations, the British ambassador visited the mainland in 1979, ostensibly to improve trade. With Hong Kong and China on friendly terms, negotiations began in 1982. Victory in the Falklands War in 1982 had buoyed the British prime minister, Margaret Thatcher, who was typically uncompromising. She suggested to Deng that Hong Kong should remain a British colony beyond 1997. Deng rejected the proposal and frankly told the British delegation that, if it so desired, China could invade and conquer Hong Kong in an afternoon and there was nothing Britain could do about it. Thatcher ironically mirrored the fall of Britain since imperial times when she tripped and fell outside the Great Hall of the People after negotiations in 1984. Another British proposal was that China would re-assume control but Britain would remain in charge of the day-to-day running of Hong Kong. Deng also dismissed this as unacceptable. Continued belligerence by both parties meant that negotiations dragged on until 1984, when China finally got its way.

EXTEND YOUR KNOWLEDGE

Anglo-Chinese differences regarding the return of Hong Kong to the PRC

The government of Margaret Thatcher had hoped to retain control of Hong Kong after 1997. Even after Deng had shattered this hope, Britain attempted to protect its interests by introducing democratic reforms.

In 1992, Margaret Thatcher's successor as prime minister, John Major, adopted a sterner approach to the return of Hong Kong and appointed Chris Patten governor of Hong Kong. To the despair of the CCP, Patten pushed on with electoral reform to the extent that Li Peng, the head of the CCP's Hong Kong office, labelled him a sinner of a thousand years. None of Patten's reforms survived China's takeover of power in 1997.

The PRC and Britain had agreed a Basic Law for Hong Kong that has safeguarded Hong Kong's economic and political systems. While Britain believed it was protecting the people of Hong Kong, China never intended to export socialism as practised on the Chinese mainland and designated Hong Kong a Special Administrative Region.

In 1984, Britain and the PRC signed a Joint Agreement in which Britain accepted China's claims to Hong Kong and arranged for its return to China. The Joint Agreement specified that sovereignty of the entire colony would be transferred to the PRC on 1 July 1997. (The leasing of the island of Hong Kong in 1842 and the Kowloon peninsula in 1860 had been in perpetuity, but without the other enlargements leased for a century in 1898, its future was impractical.) Britain would run Hong Kong until this time. China agreed to allow Hong Kong to govern itself autonomously and to turn it into a Special Administrative Region (SAR). Beijing would nominate a chief executive to replace the British governor. Most reassuring for the people of Hong Kong was a guarantee to preserve the capitalist order and the Western legal system, along with rights and freedoms for at least 50 years from 1997.

Nevertheless, in 1989 the suppression of the Tiananmen Square protest made Hong Kong fear what might lie in store. Pro-democracy protests on an unprecedented scale broke out in the colony, and Britain undertook to introduce democratic reforms before returning Hong Kong to China. The PRC accused Britain of hypocrisy, saying that having governed Hong Kong for 150 years in the absence of democracy, it was now attempting to stir up trouble for China. Nevertheless, Britain persisted and Governor Patten pressed on with reforms to the Legislative Council to permit the people of Hong Kong to elect more representatives. This action angered the PRC and unnerved Hong Kong businessmen who were keen not to antagonise the mainland. Even British diplomats recommended that Patten should delay reform until the lease expired. A British diplomat at the time likened efforts to democratise Hong Kong to selling a house and then starting to redecorate it from top to bottom in a colour that the new owner does not like. For its part, China made clear that after 1997 it would disregard any British reforms.

EXTRACT

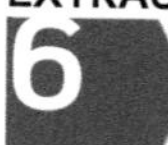

From J. Farndon, *China Rises: How China's Astonishing Growth Will Change the World* (2007).

The whole build-up to the handover had been fraught. The process dated back to 1984, when British Prime Minister Margaret Thatcher had signed the agreement with the Chinese to hand Hong Kong back to China when the British lease expired in 1997. The British, of course, signed the agreement without bothering to consult the people of Hong Kong, but following Deng Xiaoping's 'one country, two systems' formula, it guaranteed Hong Kong's essential economic and political structure, including independent courts and free speech, under a Chinese law called the Basic Law.

ACTIVITY
KNOWLEDGE CHECK

The return of Hong Kong to Chinese rule

1 According to Extract 6, why was Hong Kong's return to CCP rule alarming to the people of Hong Kong?

2 Were there reasons other than those in Extract 6 why the citizens of Hong Kong would have opposed returning to Chinese rule? Can you think of any benefits for Hong Kong?

British executives were captivated, just as their 19th-century forebears had been, by the allure of the open Chinese market. A 1995 British government delegation to China secured US$1.6 billion in orders and the promise of billions more to follow, on condition that Britain toned down its democratic overtures in Hong Kong. Patten continued his initiatives, much to the chagrin of China, and elections to the Legislative Council in 1995 gave more power to the people of Hong Kong. By that time, however, the PRC had passed a Basic Law that entrenched all of the 1984 Joint Agreement guarantees, and this proved far more enduring than Patten's reforms, which China reversed on the transfer of sovereignty in 1997, just as it had promised to do.

At midnight on 30 June 1997, China officially reclaimed sovereignty over Hong Kong. Jiang Zemin beamed as the flag of the People's Republic replaced that of the UK, and the PLA moved in and occupied the Hong Kong barracks. Tung Chee-haw, a former shipping tycoon, became Hong Kong's CCP-sponsored chief executive. Beyond this, nothing much changed, except that schools taught children in Chinese rather than English. The PRC still wanted to unite with Taiwan under Communist rule and hoped that Hong Kong would prove the applicability of the 'One China, Two Systems' model. Hong Kong has flourished since returning to Chinese sovereignty, and the fears of the British and the residents of Hong Kong have proved largely unfounded. The PRC has abided by the Basic Law and Hong Kong continues to chart a capitalist course. The British left Hong Kong and so China finally governed itself. Although Taiwan has remained outside the PRC's control, it is a Chinese republic, not governed by the West. All of China was now under Chinese rule.

EXTRACT 7

From J. Fenby, *The Penguin History of Modern China: The Fall and Rise of a Great Power 1850 to the Present* (2013).

The handover had been inevitable since Deng's initial meeting with the colonial government in 1979. The Paramount Leader [Deng] had been intent on reclaiming this example of China's pre-Communist weakness on the expiry of the land leases in the New Territories in 1997. In 1984, the Joint Declaration between Britain and China sealed the agreement, followed by the Basic Law for the territory drawn up in 1990. The deal was straightforward. Britain was not going to try to hold on, and negotiated what it considered the best accord available in keeping with Deng's formulation that the handover would result in 'one country, two systems'.

Hong Kong would remain as it had been materially and socially for fifty years, and the PRC would be able to prevent any developments, such as democracy, that might be seen to threaten its own one-party rule. There was a promise of elections, but what these would consist of was left vague... as a senior official was reported to have put it, 'the Chinese have nothing against elections; they just rather like to know the result before voting takes place'. As the chief mainland negotiator, Lu Ping, acknowledged subsequently, Beijing focused on keeping the colony's Chinese tycoons happy, reassuring them that they would not lose anything from the handover.

ACTIVITY
KNOWLEDGE CHECK

The significance of Hong Kong

1. In what ways does Extract 7 show the significance of Hong Kong's return to Chinese rule?
2. Do you think Hong Kong played a more significant role in addressing China's past or its future? Explain your answer fully.

A Level Exam-Style Question Section B

To what extent do you agree with the view that the return of Hong Kong in 1997 was the most significant development in Chinese politics in the years 1978–97? (20 marks)

Tip

Reread this chapter to identify all of the developments in this period. Remember that you need to evaluate each of these to determine which was the most strategically important.

EXTRACT 8

J. Farndon, *China Rises: How China's Astonishing Growth Will Change the World* (2007).

The lone student standing in front of a tank in Beijing's Tiananmen Square in June 1989 is firmly etched in the consciousness of the western world as one of the defining images of the twentieth century, and the massacre of hundreds of student protestors in the square by the Chinese army remains an ineradicable blot on the history of the People's Republic.

EXTRACT 9

From J. Fenby, *Tiger Head, Snake Tails: China Today, How It Got There and Why It Has To Change* (2012).

The students who staged a six-week occupation of China's central space broadened out their criticism to blame the Party for the shortcomings that had developed during the 1980s. Corruption was a main cause for complaint but there was a general alienation from the system which brought the CCP's legitimacy as the true representative of the nation into severe question...

The regime's inability to control events was symbolised by the way in which the demonstration derailed one of Deng's main diplomatic strokes, the visit of Mikhail Gorbachev as the result of a rapprochement with the Soviet Union. The Soviet leader had to be smuggled into his meeting with the Chinese by the back door of the Great Hall of the People because the front was blocked by the protestors.

Foreign television crews which had gone to Beijing to cover the visit sent out dramatic reports – 'What a time, what a place, what a story,' the US network star, Dan Rather, told CBS viewers. 'It's the people's square all right. More than a million Chinese demanding democracy and freedom, and proclaiming the new revolution.'

EXTRACT 10 From J. Keay, *China: A History* (2008).

The students had taken their cue from the May Fourth protests of 1919 and the Qingming Incident of 1976. But the leadership was more mindful of 1966 and the start of the Cultural Revolution. Then, too, radical youth had descended on the capital en masse, denounced the Party and its leadership, elected its own leaders and challenged the whole power structure. A repeat of the chaos that had ensued then would now derail the modernisation process, discredit the Party, endanger the government, and plunge the country back into chaos....

In the 1960s the Western world had lost no sleep over the excesses of the Cultural Revolution; China was a global irrelevance; such things were to be expected of Marxist-Leninist fundamentalists in the Third World. But in the 1990s, with China a major trading partner and emerging world power, the televised defiance and the ruthless repression of a popular movement for democratic rights could hardly be ignored. The USA responded with economic sanctions and a suspension of weapon sales and high-level contracts; a few other Western countries followed suit; and Hong Kong, counting down the days till its 1997 handover, witnessed such large demonstrations of sympathy that its last British governor was emboldened to introduce some belated democracy of his own. But as Beijing had calculated, most of this was window-dressing. No nation broke off diplomatic relations, no multinational corporation withdrew, and there was no renegotiation of Hong Kong's future. For the world too, it was business as usual. Within a matter of months normal relations with the USA resumed, as did the rate of inward investment; in fact in 1991–93 it rose by a staggering 500 per cent.

THINKING HISTORICALLY Evidence (6b)

The strength of argument

1 Read Extract 8.

   a) What is weak about this claim?

   b) What could be added to it to make it stronger?

2 Read Extract 9.

   a) Is this an argument? If yes, what makes it one?

   b) How might this argument be strengthened?

3 Read Extract 10.

   a) How has the writer expanded their explanation to make their claim stronger?

   b) Can you explain why this is the strongest claim of the three sources?

4 What elements make a historian's claims strong?

Conclusion

The proponents of the Self-Strengthening Movement, 1860–95, did not live long enough to see their vision achieved. However, Deng Xiaoping succeeded in fulfilling their prophecy by opening China to foreign commerce without exploitation. The improvements achieved in this period were significant both symbolically and materially. China gained permanent membership of the UN Security Council, and of the World Bank and IMF (both UN auxiliary institutions), cementing its place in the global order. This was indicative of a change in China's priorities. Under Mao, China had sought to change the world by promoting worldwide revolution, but under Deng, it sought to forge a new identity as a prosperous economic power. To achieve this, Deng recognised that China needed to join, not overthrow, the existing order. Funding, support and guidance from the World Bank and IMF changed the strategic vision of the PRC. China realised that in order to join the rest of the world it needed to learn their secrets. Finally, China rid itself of the Maoist maxim 'better red than expert' and decisively shifted to what Mao had called the capitalist road. Deng's pragmatism contrasted with Mao's dogma. Deng's flexibility in adopting capitalist measures as well as allowing two economic systems to exist within one China proved to be the guiding principles behind China's remarkable economic renaissance.

The short-term requirements of the Chinese economy demanded a re-evaluation of China's diplomatic relations with the outside world. Until the rise of Deng, China had remained isolated, apart from links to the Eastern European bloc and the African revolutionary movements. While useful as propaganda, China's role in Africa did not assist its economic modernisation. Deng was certain that China's economic salvation lay in forming links with the West and abandoning revolutionary rhetoric. Accordingly, China established full diplomatic relations first with Japan and then the USA. Not only did this draw a line under historical enmity, namely Japan's invasion and occupation of the Chinese mainland in 1931–45 and US involvement in the Korean and Vietnam wars, it also gave China access to what it valued most: advanced technology, training, bilateral trade and loans. It provided the international framework from which Deng would bring about China's economic modernisation.

China's emergence from the era of humiliation culminated in the handover of Hong Kong. Although Britain attempted to manipulate negotiations to its own advantage, China secured the return of Hong Kong on its own terms. Deng's proposal of 'One China, Two Systems' demonstrated a pragmatic flexibility in contrast to the ideological dogma that had existed since 1949. Hong Kong was an economic model to emulate and enhance, not one to replace with the rigid socialist model of the mainland. Accordingly, China assigned Hong Kong as a Special Administrative Region in 1997. Since then, China has stood with the West to uphold the world order in the face of new challenges.

SOURCE 7 A cartoon by Chappatte, 1979. It shows Deng Xiaoping wearing a Western suit and holding a mobile phone and a briefcase. In the background skyscrapers tower over a pagoda, and contrast with the flag of the PRC in the foreground.

ACTIVITY
SUMMARY

Reconciliation with old enemies and the return of Hong Kong, 1978–97

1 Why and in what ways did Deng Xiaoping's economic leadership of the PRC differ from that of Mao?

2 How did China's membership of the IMF and the World Bank differ from China's dealings with foreign powers between 1860 and 1978?

3 How did Sino-American and Sino-Japanese relations change from 1978 to 1997? Draw two graphs showing how relations improved and declined in this period.

4 In what ways did the 1984 Joint Declaration indicate a new direction in Chinese politics and economics?

5 How useful to the historian is Source 7 in analysing Deng Xiaoping's economic policy?

WIDER READING

Fenby, J. *The Penguin History of Modern China: The Fall and Rise of a Great Power 1850 to the Present* (second edition), Penguin Books (2013)

Hsü, I. *The Rise of Modern China* (fifth edition), Oxford University Press (1995)

Jacobsen, H.K. and Oksenberg, M. *China's participation in the IMF, the World Bank, and GATT - Toward a Global Economic Order*, University of Michigan Press (1990)

Pollack, J. 'The Opening of America', in R. MacFarquhar and J. King Fairbank (eds) *The Cambridge History of China, Volume 15: The People's Republic, Part 2: Revolutions within the Chinese Revolution, 1966–1982*, Cambridge University Press (1991)

Stuart-Fox, M. *A Short History of China and Southeast Asia: Tribute, Trade and Influence*, Allen & Unwin (2003)

Preparing for your A Level Paper 3 exam

Advance planning

Draw up a timetable for your revision and try to keep to it. Spend longer on topics that you have found difficult, and revise them several times. Aim to be confident about all aspects of your Paper 3 work, because this will ensure that you have a choice of questions in Sections B and C.

Paper 3 overview

Paper 3	Time: 2 hours 15 minutes	
Section A	Answer 1 compulsory question for the option studied, assessing source analysis and evaluation skills.	20 marks
Section B	Answer 1 question from a choice of 2 on an aspect in depth for the option studied.	20 marks
Section C	Answer 1 question from a choice of 2 on an aspect in breadth for the option studied.	20 marks
	Total marks =	60 marks

Section A questions

There is no choice of question in Section A. You will be referred to a source of about 350 words, printed in a Sources Booklet. The source will be a primary source or one that is contemporary to the period you have studied, and will relate to one of the key topics in the Aspect of Depth. You will be expected to analyse and evaluate the source in its historical context. The question will ask you to assess the value of the source for revealing something specific about the period, and will expect you to explain your answer, using the source, the information given about its origin and your own knowledge about the historical context.

Section B questions

You will have a choice of one from two questions in Section B. They will aim to assess your understanding of one or more of the key topics in the Aspect of Depth you have studied. Questions may relate to a single, momentous year, but will normally cover longer periods. You will be required to write an essay evaluating an aspect of the period. You may be asked about change and continuity, similarity and difference, consequences, significance or causation, or you may be given a quotation and asked to explain how far you agree with it. All questions will require you to reach a substantiated judgement.

Section C questions

You will have a choice of one from two questions in Section C. Questions will relate to the themes of the Aspects of Breadth you have studied, and will aim to assess your understanding of change over time. They will cover a period of not less than 100 years, and will relate either to the factors that brought about change, or the extent of change over the period, or patterns of change as demonstrated by turning points.

Use of time

- Do not write solidly for 45 minutes on each question. For Section B and C answers you should spend a few minutes working out what the question is asking you to do, and drawing up a plan of your answer. This is especially important for Section C answers, which cover an extended period of time.
- For Section A it is essential that you have a clear understanding of the content of the source and its historical context. Pay particular attention to the provenance: was the author in a position to know what he or she was writing about? Read it carefully and underline important points. You might decide to spend up to ten minutes reading the source and drawing up your plan, and 35 minutes writing your answer.

Preparing for your A Level exams

Paper 3: A Level sample answer with comments

Section A

These questions require you to analyse and evaluate the source with respect to its historical context.

For these questions remember to:

- look at the evidence given in the source and consider how the source could be used in differing ways to provide historical understanding
- use your knowledge of the historical context to discuss any limitations the source may have
- use your historical understanding to evaluate the source, considering how much weight you would give to its argument
- come to a judgement on the overall value of the source in respect to the question.

Study Source 1 in Chapter 6 (page 134) before you answer this question.

Assess the value of the source for revealing the reasons behind the Sino-Soviet split and Mao's objectives during the Taiwan Crisis of 1958.

Explain your answer, using the source, the information given about its origin and your own knowledge about the historical context. (20 marks)

Average student answer

The source is from a book written by Dr. Li Zhisui about the Taiwan crisis in 1958. As Li had been Mao's personal doctor, this is a useful primary source, although as it was published in the USA it is likely to be unsympathetic to Communism and, therefore, of limited use. Relations between the PRC and Russia had got worse during the 1950s and this deteriorated further when Russia failed to support China's attack of Taiwan. Mao's actions at this time caused the Sino-Soviet split. However, China was unable to bring Taiwan under Communist rule as Mao had hoped.

This is a weak opening paragraph because it fails to explicitly and accurately address the enquiries within the question. The reasons behind the split are not specified, although Mao is said to be at fault. The comment about Mao's hope of bringing Taiwan under Communist rule is inaccurate and directly at odds with the source. The claim about the nature of the source is a low-level assertion and also contradictory.

Li Zhisui argues that all Mao wanted to achieve was to make his government look strong and show the world leaders 'that he could not be controlled' and that he did this by bombarding Quemoy and Matsu. Mao also wished to invade Taiwan and take it over. It also shows that during the crisis Mao knew there was a risk of the USA dropping a nuclear bomb on China and that Mao 'would not have minded if it had'. This was because Mao wished to start a nuclear war as his goal was to eliminate capitalism and make the world Communist.

The points show a general understanding of the evidence in the source. The paragraph has some focus on Mao's intentions during the crisis but the knowledge used to substantiate this is too brief, the idea of Mao wishing to take over Taiwan particularly requires development. This paragraph could be improved by reference to the source's attributions to ascertain its value to the historian.

As the conflict grew more heated and Mao flexed his muscles, it became clear he was not going to secure Khrushchev's support. The USSR was a nuclear superpower but one that favoured peace over war. Mao wanted nuclear war and because of this Sino-Soviet relations deteriorated. China resented what Mao saw as the USSR looking down its nose at China. He thought this was just like how China had been treated during the 19th century. Therefore, it is clear that the Sino-Soviet split happened because Russia would not support Mao's aggressive stance. This is because Khrushchev put forward the idea of 'peaceful co-existence', which meant that he was happy for both capitalism and communism to operate at the same time. Mao's doctor lived through the events explained in the source, therefore the source is very useful to the historian.

There is some relevant knowledge demonstrated of the roots of the Sino-Soviet split but this lacks detail. There is too much informal expression in this paragraph, such as 'Mao flexed his muscles' and 'looking down its nose'. The response would benefit from detailed references to the source – without this, it will not secure high marks. The comment about the source's usefulness is an unsupported assertion.

However, the source is not of much use to the historian as Li Zhisui moved to the USA, a capitalist country. This means that he would not say positive things about Mao and the PRC. The source is also of limited purpose because it says that retaking Taiwan 'was never Mao's intention' because uniting China under communist rule was exactly his desire. He supported the idea of 'one China, two systems'. As the source says, Mao did not want Taiwan 'to slip away'. The account was written in 1994, long after the crisis, which brings the source's credibility into doubt. If the source was from a CCP Politburo member, it would be far more useful to the historian.

Although there is an attempt to show that the source's attribution limits its use, this is not developed. The point in the last sentence is a supposition that is not necessarily true. There are attempts to include information not referenced in the source but this is done in a confused manner as the idea of Mao wishing to assimilate Taiwan into the PRC is not fully developed, and the 'one China, two systems' formula was advocated by Deng Xiaoping in the 1980s, not by Mao at the time of the Taiwan Crisis.

Another limitation of the source is that it does not fully explore the reasons behind the Sino-Soviet split. It does not consider that Khrushchev and Mao disliked each other and the impact this had on relations between their two countries. The source would also be more reliable and helpful if it mentioned that Khrushchev thought the establishment of the People's Communes was a foolish idea and he did not like China forming an alliance with Albania.

There is a valid point being made in this paragraph, that the source does not fully evaluate other factors behind the emerging split between the USA and USSR. However, it only lists some factors and fails to sufficiently analyse their effect on Sino-Soviet relations. In addition to this, there is no source referencing or consideration of attribution at all in this paragraph. All main body paragraphs should integrate source referencing, own knowledge and attributions.

Overall, the source is of little value for revealing the nature of the split and Mao's objectives during the 1958 crisis. It shows that Mao was ambitious and wanted to make China look strong. He wanted to bring Taiwan under his rule. The split is shown by Mao opposing 'Khrushchev in his new quest for peace'. It also shows that Mao did not want to be controlled by anyone. Li Zhisui was Mao's doctor and his book was published in 1994 so his memories are unlikely to be accurate. He also moved to the USA so is probably lying to make China look bad.

The points about reliability are weak and based on assumptions. There is a judgement about the source but this is not substantiated. Understanding of both enquiries is shown throughout the response but the evidence used is either misunderstood or insufficiently evaluated. Successful responses will reference the source clearly and support this with detailed evidence and considered analysis of the source's attribution.

Verdict

This is an average answer because:

- it shows a basic understanding of the source material and identifies some key points, which could be explained and illustrated more clearly
- it shows some knowledge of context, but this could be developed
- it has some evaluation of the source material, but this tends towards assertion and would benefit from specific development
- there is some overall judgement, but it needs more development to make it substantial.

Use the feedback on this essay to rewrite it, making as many improvements as you can.

Paper 3: A Level sample answer with comments

Section A

These questions require you to analyse and evaluate the source with respect to its historical context.

For these questions remember to:

- look at the evidence given in the source and consider how the source could be used in differing ways to provide historical understanding
- use your knowledge of the historical context to discuss any limitations the source may have
- use your historical understanding to evaluate the source, considering how much weight you would give to its argument
- come to a judgement on the overall value of the source in respect to the question.

Study Source 1 in Chapter 6 (page 134) before you answer this question.

Assess the value of the source for revealing the reasons behind the Sino-Soviet split and Mao's objectives during the Taiwan Crisis of 1958.

Explain your answer, using the source, the information given about its origin and your own knowledge about the historical context. (20 marks)

Strong student answer

'The Private Life of Chairman Mao' is the memoir of Mao's physician, Dr Li Zhisui. Its value is slightly limited as the purpose of memoirs is to sell copies and because of this, as well as the book not being written until 1994, Li's testimony may be exaggerated and his emigration to the USA may be evidence of ideological opposition to communism. It neither addresses all the factors behind the Sino-Soviet split, such as the strained personal relationship between Khrushchev and Mao and the profound ideological differences between the two leaders, nor does it mention Mao using the crisis to pressure the USSR into increasing its support of China's nuclear programme. However, these shortcomings are outweighed by Li's personal insights into Mao's behaviour. Overall, the source is valuable in revealing the nature of the Sino-Soviet split and Mao's objectives during the Taiwan Crisis of 1958. Li correctly identifies firstly that during the Taiwan Crisis, Mao's objective was to obstruct Khrushchev's idea of 'peaceful co-existence' and secondly that Mao's maverick and belligerent attitude to 'peaceful co-existence' was the root cause of the Sino-Soviet split.

> This is a strong introduction because it outlines the factors to be discussed in the main body as well as the historical context. It shows good understanding of the source and reaches a judgement. It is sensible to use the wording of the question to ensure the response remains on topic.

The source does have some limitations in that several factors behind the split are not explored. This is in part because Li's purpose in publishing his memoirs was to portray his relationship with Mao rather than to provide a detailed analysis of the Sino-Soviet split. Li does state that Mao wanted to 'undermine Khrushchev in his new quest for peace' but does not fully convey Mao's distaste of the Soviet leader. Mao labelled Khrushchev a revisionist and resented what he interpreted as Khrushchev's chauvinistic attitude in issuing demands of the PRC earlier in 1958. The rift between the PRC and the USSR worsened as ideological differences came to the fore, with Khrushchev criticising Mao's Great Leap Forward as impracticable and erroneous. Therefore, it is fair to say the source does not give full coverage to the reasons behind the Sino-Soviet split.

> A focused opening that provides some important context, illustrated with specific evidence that is not covered in the source material. The awareness of the personal and ideological animosity between Khrushchev and Mao is particularly strong. The paragraph also contains valid observations about the source's attribution in order to evaluate the source's utility in revealing the reasons behind the Sino-Soviet split.

Linked to this, the source's usefulness is limited by an incomplete analysis of Mao's objectives during the Taiwan Crisis. As the source was published in the USA and is still banned in the PRC, it is fair to assume it has a perspective that is unflattering to the memory of Chairman Mao. For this reason, it portrays Mao exclusively as a maverick adventurer whose bravado was designed to 'keep Khrushchev and Eisenhower dancing, scurrying this way and that'. However, Mao's intentions were somewhat more nuanced as he wished to use the crisis to pressure the USSR into accelerating its assistance to the PRC's development of nuclear weapons. Mao hoped that by provoking the USA into threatening nuclear war, the USSR would furnish the PRC with nuclear weapons so as to protect itself from imperialist attack. Therefore, the source only gives an artificial impression of Mao's objectives during the Taiwan Crisis.

This paragraph uses the source's attribution as well as accurate own knowledge to establish Mao's objectives during the Taiwan Crisis beyond what is included in the source. It clearly answers the question at hand.

The source is useful as it depicts Mao's maverick behaviour as jeopardising the Sino-Soviet alliance. Mao wished to pose a 'challenge to Khrushchev's bid to reduce tensions between the Soviet Union and the United States'. Mao supported the idea of permanent revolution and opposed 'peaceful co-existence', Khrushchev's 'new quest for peace'. Mao felt that Khrushchev was betraying Communist principles by contemplating nuclear non-proliferation. Mao's desire to bring about nuclear conflict dissuaded Khrushchev from further assisting China's nuclear programme. Mao saw nuclear weapons as the means to achieve nuclear conflict, whereas Khrushchev saw them as a deterrent to avoid the very conflict Mao so cherished. This was one of the main contributing factors to the Sino-Soviet split. The source is useful as Li enjoyed direct daily access to Mao and was a trusted confidante meaning that his account is likely to be accurate in rendering Mao's political outlook.

Central to Mao's thinking during the Taiwan Crisis was his wish to prove he 'could not be controlled'. Li correctly identifies Mao's overarching objective was not one of conquest – 'to retake Taiwan [...] was never Mao's intention' – but rather to secure the PRC's independence in the face of the demands issued earlier in 1958 by the USSR for joint Sino-Soviet naval Pacific operations, under Soviet direction. Mao believed the USSR was displaying great power chauvinism towards China and he wanted to demonstrate 'China's importance in the triangular relationship among China, the Soviet Union, and the United States'. Key to achieving this was for China to obtain nuclear weapons, and to this end Mao was prepared to risk 'the United States... drop an atom bomb on Fujian province, and Mao would not have minded if it had'. Mao thought that China's immense population would allow it to withstand a nuclear attack while convincing the USSR to speed up its assistance of China's nuclear programme. As the source was published after Mao's death, it is free from the culture of fear that silenced Chinese opposition to Mao within the Chairman's lifetime. For these reasons, the source is of considerable use in identifying Mao's true objectives during the crisis.

These paragraphs reference the source extensively to explain the reasons behind the Sino-Soviet split. The inferences from the source are supported by detailed knowledge of the political context. There is an obvious recognition of the timescale of the Sino-Soviet split as only own knowledge relating to 1958 is deployed. The paragraphs successfully convey a line of argument regarding the source's utility. They similarly evaluate Mao's objectives during the Taiwan Crisis. A clear and analytical understanding of the crisis is clearly communicated and particularly impressive is the knowledge demonstrated of the Soviet Union's demands of 1958 and their effect on Mao's subsequent decision-making.

Overall, the source is of considerable use in revealing the reasons behind the Sino-Soviet split and Mao's objectives during the Taiwan Crisis of 1958. While the accuracy of Li's recollections can be questioned as it was published in the USA, which may lead to it having an anti-PRC slant, and published in 1994 long after the events recounted occurred, this is outweighed by Li's unique input regarding Mao's thought process at this time. As it was published after Mao's death, Li was free to accurately describe the events of 1958 without fear of retribution. The source does not evaluate every reason behind the split, nor does it give more than a surface analysis of Mao's objectives during the 1958 crisis but this is because the source is an extract form Li's memoirs rather than a book dedicated to the Sino-Soviet split and the Taiwan Crisis. The source is very useful as it correctly portrays Mao's maverick handling of diplomacy, his outright opposition to 'peaceful co-existence' and his reckless attitude towards nuclear war as being central to the Sino-Soviet split and Mao's objectives during the Taiwan Crisis.

A balanced conclusion that fully answers the set question. It summarises the points argued in the main body clearly and reaches a sustained judgement as to the validity of the source.

Verdict

This is a strong response because:

- it identifies and illustrates the key points in the source
- it deploys some effective own knowledge to develop these points and provide context
- it reaches a clear and substantial conclusion.

Paper 3: A Level sample answer with comments

Section B

These questions require you to show your understanding of the period in depth. They will ask you about a quite specific period and require you to make a substantiated judgement about a specific aspect you have studied.

For these questions remember to:

- organise your essay and communicate it in a manner that is clear and comprehensible
- use historical knowledge to analyse and evaluate the key aspect of the question
- make a balanced argument that weighs up differing opinions
- make a substantiated overall judgement on the question.

To what extent did the Qing Empire become stronger during the 1860s? (20 marks)

Average student answer

In 1860, the Tianjin Treaty ended the Second Opium War. China was unable to stand up against Britain and France and their superior armies and navies. China was a society based in Confucianism and did not like foreigners and capitalism. There are many factors that suggest the Empire became weaker in the 1860s, but others argue it became stronger. After the treaty many Christian missionaries came to China. After existing in isolation from the West for centuries, China lost power and foreigners took control.

This is a weak opening paragraph because it concentrates on the background of the Second Opium War rather than its consequences. Although it loosely implies that there is a debate surrounding the 1860s and whether China grew stronger or weaker through the decade, it fails to clearly introduce the factors that will be discussed in the essay. It would also be improved if there was a justified line of argument in answer to the set question.

Due to its defeat in the war, China realised that it was weak. It had been beaten by Britain and France and decided it had to modernise its army and to use Western weapons like rifles and cannon. In the West, there had been the industrial revolution and they now fought wars in a more modern way that outclassed China. China had thought it was superior to the West, and after it won a minor victory it refused to surrender. This made the British and French angry and they continued to fight and eventually won easily. Therefore, the Emperor thought China had to change. He introduced ideas to reform its economy. People were sent to the USA and other countries to research how they ran their countries and how to bring those changes to China. Factories were set up in Shanghai and China traded with Britain. China also tried to follow in the footsteps of Japan who had been humiliated by foreign countries but had rejected its tradition and adopted capitalism to make itself stronger. Therefore, losing to Britain in the war was a good thing for China in the long run.

This paragraph is too vague. It includes information about China before the 1860s which is not directly relevant to the question. It does allude to some relevant factors, but there are too many points being made with insufficient detail. The link to the question at the end of the paragraph is weak as it relates to the Second Opium War rather than the 1860s as the question specifies.

Another thing that helped the Empire in this time was the Zongli Yamen. This was a foreign office that was set up and helped China to work with other countries. In addition to this, foreign-language schools were established and they helped by translating Western books into Chinese and also training Chinese people to speak English and French. A big part of China's problems was that it did not know anything about the West, so these two things helped. If the Empire could speak English and work with foreigners, it would help it to grow stronger. This was in contrast to earlier when Chinese emperors had said there was nothing that China could learn from Western countries and thought China was stronger and culturally superior to Britain. In the 1860s, therefore, China became stronger by working closely with Western countries and would not be defeated again.

This paragraph identifies a couple of notable achievements but is unable to develop these to satisfactorily show how they strengthened the Qing Empire. Like the previous paragraph, it drifts into discussing pre-1860 China, which is irrelevant, and the last sentence is inaccurate: despite these modernisations, China went on to suffer several other humiliating losses over the coming decades.

The changes that happened in the 1860s were caused by defeat and because of this they showed how weak China was. Foreign powers were able to govern themselves in areas they took over. This meant that the Qing Empire was weak and had no control over its own territory. In these areas, foreigners and Chinese citizens who committed crimes went to courts that followed Western laws. This was humiliating as Asian countries used to look up to China as their leader, but now China could not even control what was going on in its own country.

Although this is a relevant paragraph, it is too brief to gain significant credit and does not use enough specific evidence. It would benefit from using and explaining relevant terminology such as 'extraterritoriality' and 'tributary status'. The first sentence is also weak. It suggests that any change caused by defeat weakened the Qing Empire despite stating in a previous argument that the reforms Japan introduced following its own humiliations in the 1850s actually helped it to strengthen itself. The best essays follow a consistent line of argument.

China was a country that followed Buddhism and Confucianism, with some areas that were Muslim. However, during the 1860s Christian missionaries were allowed to travel around China and spread Christianity. Christianity argued that China was a backward country and that the people were barbarians. Churches were built and Christian propaganda spread through the Empire. This showed that the Emperor had lost power and that Christians were now dominant in the country. Millions of Chinese people converted and wanted China to adopt Western ways. Therefore, the Qing Empire was becoming more and more Christian.

This is a weak paragraph as it over-estimates the effect Christian missionaries had in the 1860s. There are several inaccurate statements here. With more appropriate knowledge and examples, this could become a strong point.

In conclusion, the 1860s weakened China completely. Christians spread a message that was hostile to the Qing Empire and China had become weak. Foreign powers now ruled most of China, whereas before 1860 it was the opposite and China was the most powerful country in the world.

This conclusion is focused solely on the weakening effects of the 1860s and does not summarise any factors that strengthened the Qing Empire. It also makes generalised, sweeping statements that are inaccurate and, in the case of the final sentence, not relevant to the set question.

Verdict

This is an average response because:

- it does not sustain focus on the specific question
- it deploys some accurate knowledge, but this is not used to best advantage
- it makes a judgement, but it lacks the illustration and explanation to be substantial.

Use the feedback on this essay to rewrite it, making as many improvements as you can.

Paper 3: A Level sample answer with comments

Section B

These questions require you to show your understanding of the period in depth. They will ask you about a quite specific period and require you to make a substantiated judgement about a specific aspect you have studied.

For these questions remember to:

- organise your essay and communicate it in a manner that is clear and comprehensible
- use historical knowledge to analyse and evaluate the key aspect of the question
- make a balanced argument that weighs up differing opinions
- make a substantiated overall judgement on the question.

To what extent did the Qing Empire become stronger during the 1860s? (20 marks)

Strong student answer

The terms of the Treaty of Tianjin, 1860, weakened the Qing Empire, with Christian missionaries being given the freedom to travel and proselytise throughout the Empire. They presented ideas that directly challenged central tenets of Confucianism, such as the secondary role of women. The treaty also opened up China to foreign powers in the form of extraterritoriality. Treaty ports such as Nanjing and Tianjin came under the control of foreign powers and this served to weaken China and shook its citizens' faith in the Qing and their mandate to rule. However, on the other hand, during the 1860s progressive elements in China, such as the Self-Strengthening Movement, pursued a policy of modernisation. Following the example of Japan, China introduced reforms to overhaul its outdated army, economy and political processes. It was hoped that these changes such as the introduction of foreign-language schools and the Zongli Yamen would prevent China from further humiliations and see it develop in a similar way to Western powers. Overall, the Qing Empire was strengthened during the 1860s because it emerged from its international isolation and gave China the chance to strengthen itself to meet the challenge of the Western imperial powers.

This is a focused introduction providing context that is illustrated with specific detail. The factors that are going to be discussed are also introduced, as is a judgement in answer to the question.

The immediate focus of the Self-Strengthening Movement was the military, whose weaknesses had been exposed by Britain and France during the Second Opium War. It was hoped that through modernising its military along the lines of Western powers, the Qing Empire would be able to resist Britain and the other imperial nations from further exploiting China. The Jiangnan arsenal was established in Shanghai in 1865 and succeeded in manufacturing Western-style ships, guns and cannon. A similar arsenal in Nanjing promptly followed. Other significant developments in the 1860s were the Tianjin Machine Factory and the Fuzhou Navy Yard. In addition to this, the most promising Chinese students were sent to further their learning in the West. These reforms bore fruit in the 1860s, when the revitalised Qing army was able to subdue both the Taiping and Nian rebellions which threatened to overthrow the Qing Empire. Therefore, it can be concluded that the 1860s was a decade of militarisation that woke China from a slumber caused by isolation and empowered its military to protect the Qing Empire from internal threats to its existence.

This is a strong and clearly structured paragraph. It presents a clear point that is developed with examples and analysis and evaluation. The point of the Self-Strengthening Movement is then linked clearly to the question by explicitly demonstrating how it strengthened the Qing Empire in the 1860s.

Another factor that indicates the Qing Empire was strengthened during the 1860s is the creation of the Zongli Yamen and the opening of foreign-language schools. These were both significant in showing a change of attitude in Chinese politics. China's humiliating opening to the West as a result of the Tianjin Treaty had been brought about by an almost total Chinese ignorance of Western society. Therefore, these reforms were an attempt for China to learn Western ways as a method of self-strengthening. The establishment of the Zongli Yamen showed that the Qing Empire recognised that dealings with foreign powers would now be an ever-present part of Chinese politics. The Zongli Yamen translated works on international law which enabled them to secure a significant diplomatic victory over Prussia, which had illegally captured three Danish ships in Chinese waters. The Zongli Yamen was able to secure Prussian compensation for this breach of international law. Such a victory would have been previously inconceivable. Indeed, the Zongli Yamen stood in stark contrast to the diplomatic blundering exhibited by Chinese negotiators during the Second Opium War. Similar to this were the foreign-language schools that opened in China during the 1860s. First in Beijing and later in Shanghai and Guangzhou, the foreign-language schools helped to familiarise Chinese elites with Western learning. Central to the schools was obviously the teaching of European languages, but also maths and science. Although only on a limited scale, both the Zongli Yamen and the foreign-language schools strengthened the Qing Empire by familiarising China with Western education and diplomacy, both of which allowed China to further its self-strengthening.

This is another high-level paragraph that convincingly puts forward the view that the Qing Empire grew stronger through the 1860s. Both examples – the Zongli Yamen and the foreign-language schools – are used as evidence to support the stated line of argument.

The effects of the Tianjin Treaty weakened the Qing Empire during the 1860s. The most significant part of this agreement was extraterritoriality. This concept was that areas of China came under direct foreign control, meaning that they were not governed by the Qing or subject to their laws. Under the treaty nine foreign ports such as Nanjing and Tianjin were opened to foreign control. This evidently weakened the Qing Empire because it no longer ruled all the land within its borders. However, the strengthening of China's military as well as its diplomatic and educational processes offset extraterritoriality and allowed it to be limited to the treaty ports. The Qing Empire remained in power and foreign powers, Britain foremost amongst them, supported the Qing Empire to protect the gains it had secured through the Tianjin Treaty. Therefore, although extraterritoriality weakened China, it was a controlled loss and did not threaten the continued rule of the Qing.

The weakening effects of the 1860s are clearly illustrated but measured against the strengths to support the overall judgement.

Another important factor in identifying the extent to which China was weakened during the 1860s was the presence of Christian missionaries in China. The Tianjin Treaty gave missionaries the freedom to roam the Empire and preach Christianity. Missionaries directly challenged key features of Confucianism and the Qing Empire such as the subjugation of women in the form of concubinage and foot-binding. A Chinese convert to Christianity, Hong Xiuguan, led the Taiping rebellion which attempted to overthrow the Qing Empire. Although this was a substantial challenge to the Qing, the effect of the missionaries was limited. The number of Chinese converts was minimal and most Chinese opposed the missionaries and their preaching. Due to this opposition, missionary influence did not stretch beyond the treaty ports. Missionaries were associated with the foreigners who had defeated China in the Second Opium War and, as such, were largely met with hostility. What is more, some of the work missionaries did in the realm of educational provision helped the Qing by providing it with capable administrators. Missionaries also undertook work in curing those afflicted by opium addiction. Therefore, the weakening effects of missionaries paled in comparison to factors that strengthened the Qing Empire. For instance although the Taiping rebellion was Christian inspired, it was put down by a military that was modernised and strengthened during the 1860s.

This factor is explained in full and compared to other factors. It continues to present a consistent line of argument.

In conclusion, it can be said that the factors arguing that the Qing Empire was strengthened during the 1860s were of greater significance. Although extraterritoriality and missionaries weakened the Qing by presenting a clear challenge to the long-established status quo, the modernisation of the Chinese military and its diplomatic and educational processes served to prolong the Qing Empire. During the Second Opium War, it appeared possible that the Qing Empire might disintegrate and that China might be partitioned. However, the reforms it introduced propped the regime up, familiarised it with Western ways and thinking, and breathed new life into the Qing dynasty.

This is a good conclusion that weighs up the factors in the main body before reaching a substantiated conclusion.

Verdict

This is a strong response because:

- it identifies a range of key factors and links them into an argument
- it deploys some sound factual knowledge to illustrate and develop the points being made
- it examines both sides of the argument and argues a judgement.

Paper 3: A Level sample answer with comments

Section C

These questions require you to show your understanding of a subject over a considerable period of time. They will ask you to assess a long-term historical topic and its development over a period of at least 100 years, and they require you to make a substantiated judgement in relation to the question.

For these questions remember to:

- organise your essay and communicate it in a manner that is clear and comprehensible
- use historical knowledge to analyse and evaluate the key aspect of the question covering the entire period
- make a balanced argument that weighs up differing opinions
- make a substantiated overall judgement on the question.

How far would you agree that the key factor behind industrialisation in the years 1860–1997 was provided by central government? (20 marks)

Average student answer

From 1860 to 1997, the government intervened in the Chinese economy several times in order to bring about industrialisation, and by 1997 China had become an industrial superpower. The first major period of government intervention was during the Self-Strengthening Movement from the 1870s to the 1890s.

Accurate but descriptive. The response is correct in what it is asserting but no argument is established here, so this introduction sets a narrative tone for the essay, not a discursive one.

The Self-Strengthening Movement was created by Li Honzhang, a senior Chinese mandarin. Li believed that China could only develop if Western-style economic practices and industry were introduced. The Qing government did not want to introduce Western-style political changes along with these industrial ideas, so there were limits to the scope of the Self-Strengthening Movement. Following the Chinese Revolution of 1911, the Beiyang and the Kuomintang governments attempted to industrialise China. Sun Yat-sen's railway plan resulted in an increase in rail tracks being laid and later Jiang Jieshi built roads in order to defeat the communists.

The question does not focus on political developments in China, so exploring the lack of political change as a result of the Self-Strengthening Movement is unnecessary. Instead it would have been better to examine self-strengthening in greater depth and explore in what ways China industrialised during this period.

Both of these developments are examples of industrialisation led by the government, which shows that government intervention was a key factor in industrialisation in China before 1949. After 1949, when the Communist Party took over, Mao was dedicated to industrialising China and he travelled to the USSR to ask for Stalin's help. This shows that there were other factors in China's development other than the Chinese government itself, and foreign powers like the USSR helped China to develop by supplying expertise and aid. In the 1950s, China followed Soviet plans, but this resulted in disaster during the second Five Year Plan, which actually caused the Chinese economy to shrink and 40 million people to die of famine.

This is a good point, that China's government alone was not the sole power in the development of the country. However, this point requires further development, detail and explanation. How effective was Soviet help in developing China? What drawbacks were there?

It is also important to mention in the previous section that European powers, Japan and America all had a significant role to play in the industrialisation of China.

This was an example of China's government acting to undermine economic development. Mao wanted to rapidly industrialise China in order to build up the country's military power, which led him to industrialise Western China in a project known as the 'Third Front'. However, the most successful industrialisation of the Communist era came under Deng Xiaoping. Deng's market reforms led to the growth of Special Economic Zones in China and the development of state-owned and private capitalist enterprises. This demonstrates that by 1997 state power was the most significant factor in the industrialisation of China.

This reads more like a paragraph in the middle of an essay than a conclusion. The points here are basically correct but they require development or run the risk of being simple generalisations. A conclusion should draw conclusions from the entire period, based on all the evidence and ideas that have been examined. This paragraph just focuses on aspects of Mao Zedong and Deng Xiaoping's economic policies.

Verdict

This is an average answer because:

- it does not directly address the question but drifts off into historical narrative
- it is vague and imprecise with some key dates but little development of each key point
- the conclusion is under-developed and does not fully address the question
- there is no clear line of argument anywhere in the essay.

Use the feedback on this essay to rewrite it, making as many improvements as you can.

Paper 3: A Level sample answer with comments

Section C

These questions require you to show your understanding of a subject over a considerable period of time. They will ask you to assess a long-term historical topic and its development over a period of at least 100 years, and they require you to make a substantiated judgement in relation to the question.

For these questions remember to:

- organise your essay and communicate it in a manner that is clear and comprehensible
- use historical knowledge to analyse and evaluate the key aspect of the question covering the entire period
- make a balanced argument that weighs up differing opinions
- make a substantiated overall judgement on the question.

How far would you agree that the key factor behind industrialisation in the years 1860–1997 was provided by central government? (20 marks)

Strong student answer

By 1997, China had been dramatically transformed into an industrial superpower after a century in which the country struggled to modernise. Successive regimes in China each had a significant role to play in developing Chinese industry, but the extent to which central government played the most significant part in this process is contested. Private enterprise, local governments and foreign powers also played a significant role in China's development.

The introduction contains a clear line of argument, explaining what the answer will be examining. The line of argument is placed within a wider context and a brief overview of the period is given.

During the self-strengthening era, both China's government, foreign powers and individual Chinese entrepreneurs played a significant role in developing Chinese industry. China's railways and steamship services were developed by European powers, which were able to exert influence over the Chinese government in order to extend control over Chinese territory and trade. China's Qing government was divided over the question of industrial modernisation, with some Qing administrators like Li Hongzhang arguing that industrialisation was important, but others, along with Dowager Empress Cixi, sabotaged economic reform. New industrial enterprises such as coal mines, railways and factories were often set up as private businesses. They were owned by government officials who believed in the philosophy of self-strengthening but who also enriched themselves. Therefore, the achievements of the self-strengthening era were the result of a complex mix of government initiatives, foreign intervention and private business. Central government's role was not insignificant but must be seen in context with other, competing factors.

This paragraph ends with an evaluation that supports the original statement in the introduction. It shows that during the self-strengthening era, the idea that the state decided everything in Chinese industrialisation is too simplistic. Instead, a more nuanced and complex picture emerges.

Following the 1911 revolution, the development of civil war and warlordism in China meant that foreign powers were reluctant to invest in Chinese industry and infrastructure. Central government was one of the few forces within China capable of pursuing industrialisation, but it had fundamentally different objectives to the Qing-era Self-Strengthening Movement. In the Beiyang government, Sun Yat-sen was concerned with using railways to hold the former Chinese empire together. This meant that while railways were gradually built throughout the 1920s, industrialisation was limited in other areas and investment overall in China was low.

When Jiang Jieshi became leader of China, central government's industrialisation was guided by a need to defeat the Communists and therefore was focused on road building and the creation of a telegraph system for military purposes. After 1949, Mao eliminated foreign intervention in the economy, with the exception of China's new relationship with the USSR, and by the mid-1950s all private enterprise had been nationalised. Therefore, between the 1950s and the late 1970s, the state was the only power in China able to influence industrial development.

Following Mao's death in 1976 and the reforms of Deng Xiaoping from 1978 onwards, the state still dictated the pace and scope of industrial development. However, the creation of Special Enterprise Zones and the opening up of China to foreign investment created conditions similar to those of the self-strengthening era. By the end of the 20th century, China's economy was still led by central government, but the economic philosophy that governed the country had changed and free enterprise was allowed.

This paragraph takes the preceding evidence and offers an interpretation as to what it means. By demonstrating that foreign influence from Europe, Japan and America ended in 1949 and that all private industry was nationalised, it becomes clear how powerful the state became in the development of Chinese industry.

In conclusion, these changes demonstrate that under the Qing and nationalist governments the state had an important, but not sole, responsibility in bringing about industrialisation. However, after 1949 the power of the state and its involvement in the economy dramatically expanded, even though communist economic ideas were largely abandoned after Mao's death.

A clear conclusion that examines all factors discussed in the response and comes to a substantive judgement.

Verdict

This is a strong answer because:

- it starts with a clear line of argument and it rejects the simplistic idea about the state set out in the question
- each paragraph presents evidence to support the line of argument
- there is a continual focus on evaluating the role of the state
- the conclusion fully addresses the question.

Index

Acknowledgements

The authors and publisher would like to thank the following individuals and organisations for permission to reproduce photographs and text in this book.

(Key: b-bottom; c-centre; l-left; r-right; t-top)

akg-images Ltd: 106; **Alamy:** AF Fotografie 80, Alain Le Garsmeur China Archive 49r, colaimages 139, Interfoto 27, 146, Interfoto 27, 146, Lordprice Collection 13, Mary Evans Picture Library 111r, National Geographic Image Collection 6, Nik Wheeler 49l, Stocktrek Images, Inc. 124, World History Archive 33, 59, 115, Zoonar GmbH 41; **Bridgeman Art Library Ltd:** Pictures from History/ Bridgeman Images 92; Getty Images: Bettmann 155, 165, Fotosearch 135r, Photo 12 111l, VCG 8; **Globe Cartoon:** Chappatte in The New York Times 172; **International Institute of Social History, Netherlands/IISH:** Zhao Yannian and Qian Daxin/Pub- Donghua renmin meishu chubanshe 1953/ Private Collection 142b; **Magnum Photos Ltd:** Henri Cartier-Bresson 23; **Mary Evans Picture Library:** 67; **Solo Syndication/Associated Newspapers Ltd:** 113; **Stefan R Landsberger Collection/http://chineseposters.net:** Institute of Social History 142t, International Institute of Social History (Amsterdam) 126; © **The Trustees of The British Museum. All rights reserved:** Lu Shaofei 135l; **TopFoto:** 68

Cover image: Bridgeman Art Library Ltd: Pictures From History

All other images © Pearson Education

Figures
Figure 1.2 from Kwang-Ching Lui, Steamship Enterprise in 19th-century China, *The Journal of Asian Studies*, Vol. 18, Issue 4, pp.435–455 (1959), reproduced with permission.

Text
Extract 1 p.14 from *Treaty Ports in Modern China Law, Land and Power*, Routledge (Bickers, R. and Jackson, I. 2016) p.8, © 2016 Routledge; Extract 2 p15 from *Coal Mining and China's Economy and Society 1895–1937* (T. Wright, 1986) © Cambridge University Press 1984, with permission from Cambridge University Press; Extract 3 p.18 from *The Penguin History of Modern China*, Penguin (J. Fenby, 2010) p.115 (2nd revised edition published 2013); Extract 4 p.18 from *China: How the Empire Fell*, Routledge (J.W. Esherick and C.X. George Wei, 2013) p.94 © 2014 Joseph W. Esherick and C.X. George Wei; Extract 5 p.22 from *The Penguin History of Modern China*, Penguin (J. Fenby, 2010) (2nd revised edition published 2013); Extract 6 p.35 from *Mao: The Unknown Story*, Penguin (J. Chang and J. Halliday, 2005) p.465, Used by permission of Random House, an imprint and division of Penguin Random House LLC. All rights reserved. Any third party use of this material, outside of this publication, is prohibited. Interested parties must apply directly to Penguin Random House LLC for permission; Extract 7 p.35 from *Mao's China and After: A History of the People's Republic*, 1st ed., Free Press (M. Meisner, 1977) p.113, Copyright © 1977, 1986 by The Free Press, A Division of Macmillan, Inc. Copyright © Maurice Meisner. Reprinted by permission of Simon & Schuster, Inc. All rights reserved.; Extract 1 p.41 from *The Penguin History of Modern China*, Penguin (J. Fenby, 2010) p.66 (2nd revised edition published 2013); Extract 2 p.46 from © F. Dikotter, 2013, *The Tragedy of Liberation: A History of the Chinese Revolution 1945–1957* 1st ed., Bloomsbury Publishing Plc; Extract 3 p.54 from *Mao's Last Revolution*, Cambridge, Mass., by Roderick MacFarquhar and Michael Schoenhals, The Belknap Press of Harvard University Press, Copyright © 2006 by the President and Fellows of Harvard College; Extract 4 p.58 and Extract 2 p.133 from © F. Dikotter (2010), *Mao's Great Famine: The History of China's Most Devastating Catastrophe, 1958–62*, 1st ed., Bloomsbury Publishing Plc; Extract 5 p.61 from *The Penguin History of Modern China*, Penguin (J. Fenby, 2011) (2nd revised edition published 2013); Extract 6 p.61 from *The Search for Modern China*, W. W. Norton and Company (J. Spence, 1999) Copyright © 1990 by Jonathan D. Spence; Extract 7 p.61 from *Mao's Crusade: Politics and Policy Implementation in China's Great Leap Forward* Oxford University Press (A. Chan, 2001) © Alfred L. Chan 2001. By permission of Oxford University Press, USA; Extract 2 p.70 from *The Great Chinese Revolution: 1800–1985*, 1st ed., Harper & Row (J. King Fairbank, 1986) Copyright © 1986, 1987 by John King Fairbank. Reprinted by permission of HarperCollins Publishers; Extract 3 p.74 from *The Last Stand of Chinese Conservatism: The T'ung-Chih Restoration, 1862–1874*, by Mary Clabaugh Wright. Copyright © 1957 by the Board of Trustees of the Leland Stanford Jr. University, renewed 1985. All rights reserved. Used by

permission of the publisher, Stanford University Press, sup.org; Source 3 p.72 from *Sources of Chinese Tradition, Vol. 2: From 1600 Through the Twentieth Century*, 2nd ed., by William Theodore de Bary and Richard Lufano (eds) Copyright © 2000 Columbia University Press. Reprinted with permission of the publisher; Extract 4 p.74 from *China: A New History, Enlarged Edition*, by John King Fairbank and Merle Goldman, Cambridge, Mass.; The Belknap Press of Harvard University Press Copyright © 1992, 1998 by the President and Fellows of Harvard College; Extract 5 p.83 from *Discovering History in China: American Historical Writing on the Recent Chinese Past* by Paul Cohen Copyright © 1984 Columbia University Press. Reprinted with permission of Columbia University Press; Source 5 p.78 from *The Cambridge History of China Volume 10: Late Ch'ing 1800–1911, Part 1*, Cambridge University Press (T. Kuo and K. Liu, 1978) p.526 © Cambridge University Press, 1978, with permission from Cambridge University Press; Source 6 p.78 from *Changing China: Readings in the History of China from the Opium Wars to the Present*, by Gentzler, J. Mason Reproduced with permission of Holt, Rinehart & Winston, Incorporated in the format Republish in a book via Copyright Clearance Center; quote bottom of p.90 and Extract 5 p.120 from *China's Wars: Rousing the Dragon, 1894–1949*, Osprey (P. Jowett, 2013) with permission from the author; Extract 1 p.89, Extract 1 p.111, Extract 4 p.118, Extract 5 p.166 from *Restless Empire: China and the World Since 1750*, 1st ed., Vintage (O. Arne Westad, 2013) Copyright © Odd Arne Westad. Used by permission of Random House, an imprint and division of Penguin Random House LLC. All rights reserved. Any third party use of this material, outside of this publication, is prohibited. Interested parties must apply directly to Penguin Random House LLC for permission; Extract 2 p.90, Extract 6 p.120 from *The Modern History of China*, Weidenfeld & Nicolson (H. McAleavy, 1968), with the permission of Orion Publishing Group Ltd and also reproduced with permission of International Thomson Publishing in the format Republish in a book via Copyright Clearance; Extract 3 p.94, Extract 5 p.103 from *Modernization and Revolution in China*, by J. Grasso, J. Corrin and M.G. Kort (1997). Reproduced with permission of M.E. Sharpe Incorporated in the format Book via Copyright Clearance Center; Extract 4 p.95, Extract 10 p.171 from *China: A History*, 1st ed., Harper Press (J. Keay, 2008), Reprinted by permission of HarperCollins Publishers Ltd. © 2008 John Keay; Extract 6 p.103 from *A History of China*, M. Rossabi. © 2014 Morris Rossabi. Reproduced with permission of John Wiley & Sons, Inc.; Extract 2 p.114, Extract 7 p.121, Extract 8 p.122 from *Generalissimo: Chiang Kai-Shek and the China He Lost*, Simon & Schuster (J. Fenby, 2005), with permission from David Higham Associates; Extract 3 p.114 from © F.S. Northedge, 1986, *The League of Nations: Its Life and Times 1920–1946*, Leicester University Press. Used by permission of Bloomsbury Publishing Plc; Source 6 p.117 from *The Reluctant Combatant: Japan and the Second Sino-Japanese War*, by Minoru, Kitamura; Si-Yun, Lin Reproduced with permission of UPA in the format Republish in a book via Copyright Clearance Center; Source 7 p.119 from *Red Star Over China*, 1st ed., Random House, Inc. (E. Snow, 1938) Copyright © 1938, 1944 by Random House, Inc., Excerpts from *Red Star Over China* by Edgar Snow, copyright © 1938, 1944 by Random House, Inc, © 1961 by John K. Fairbank, © 1968 by Edgar Snow. Used by permission of Grove/Atlantic, Inc. Any third party use of this material, outside of this publication, is prohibited; Source 8 p.123 from a letter written by Ernest H. Forster to Tokuyasu Fukuda, 1937, The Forster Family; Extract 1 p.133 from *Mao: The Unknown Story*, Penguin (J. Chang and J. Halliday, 2005), Used by permission of Random House, an imprint and division of Penguin Random House LLC. All rights reserved. Any third party use of this material, outside of this publication, is prohibited. Interested parties must apply directly to Penguin Random House LLC for permission; Source 1 p.134 from *The Private Life of Chairman Mao* by Dr Zhi-Ssui Li, copyright © 1995 by Dr Zhi-Sui Li Used by permission of Random House, an imprint and division of Penguin Random House LLC. All rights reserved. Any third party use of this material, outside of this publication, is prohibited. Interested parties must apply directly to Penguin Random House LLC for permission; Extract 3 p.135 from The Boxer Rebellion, Alpha History, http://alphahistory.com/chineserevolution/boxer-rebellion/ G. Kucha and J. Llewellyn, The Boxer Rebellion, Alpha History, accessed 18 January 2017, http://alphahistory.com/chineserevolution/boxer-rebellion/; Extract 4 p.147 from *China, the Fun House Mirror: Soviet Reactions to the Chinese Cultural Revolution, 1966–1969* Berkeley Program in Soviet and Post-Soviet Studies Working Paper Series (E. McGuire, 2001) http://escholarship.org/uc/item/0fs1526m, with permission from Elizabeth McGuire; Source 5 p.138 from Between Beijing and Moscow: Ten Newly Available Chinese Documents, 1956–1958, translated and annotated by Zhang Shu Guang and Chen Jian, *Cold War International History Project, Bulletin, The Cold War in Asia*, Issues 6–7, p.153 (J.G. Hershberg, ed., 1996), Woodrow Wilson International Center for Scholars; Extract 5 p.149 from *Mao: The Unknown Story*, Penguin (J. Chang and J. Halliday, 2005), Used by permission of Random House, an imprint and division of Penguin Random House LLC. All rights reserved. Any third party use of this material, outside of this publication, is prohibited. Interested parties must apply directly to Penguin Random House LLC for permission; Extract 1 p.157 from *Working Paper No.277, China and the World Bank: How a Partnership Was Built*, Stanford Center for International Development (P. Bottelier, 2006), with permission from Pieter Bottelier; Source 2 p.158 from *A World Bank Country Study: China: Socialist Economic Development* World Bank (1980), © 2017 The World Bank Group, All Rights Reserved.; Extract 2 p.159 from *A Short History of China and South-East Asia: Tribute, Trade and Influence*, Allen & Unwin (M. Stuart-Fox, 2003) Copyright © Martin Stuart-Fox 2003, reproduced with permission of Allen & Unwin Pty Ltd; Extract 3 p.162 from *Interpreting History in Sino-Japanese Relations: A Case Study in Political Decision Making*, Routledge (C. Rose, 2005) © 1998 Caroline Rose. Taylor and Francis e-library 2005; Extract 4 p.164 from *The Rise of Modern China*, Oxford University Press, Inc. (I.C.Y. Hsu, 1995) Copyright © 1970, 1975, 1983, 1990, 1995 by Oxford University Press, Inc. *The Rise of Modern China* by Immanuel C. Y. Hsu (1995). By permission of Oxford University Press, USA; Extract 6 p.169, Extract 8 p.170 from *China Rises: How China's Astonishing Growth Will Change the World*, Virgin Publishing (J. Farndon, 2007); Source 6 p.165 from *The Cambridge History of China, Volume 15: The People's Republic, Part 2: Revolutions Within the Chinese Revolution, 1966–1982*, Cambridge University Press (R. MacFarquhar and J.K. Fairbank, 1991) p.463 © Cambridge University Press 1991; Extract 7 p.170 from *The Penguin History of Modern China*, 2nd, revised ed., Penguin (J. Fenby, 2013); Extract 9 p,170 from *Tiger Head, Snake Tails: China Today, How It Got There and Why It Has To Change* (J. Fenby, 2012) Copyright © 2012 by Jonathan Fenby, with permission from David Higham Associates.